THE CORNISH MINER

By the same author
   Cornwall and its people
   a composite work including:
   Cornish Seafarers, 1932
   Cornwall and The Cornish 1933,
   Cornish Homes and Customs, 1934

THE CORNISH MINER

An Account of his Life
Above and Underground from
Early Times

A. K. HAMILTON JENKIN
M.A., B.LITT., F.S.A.

DAVID & CHARLES REPRINTS

0 7153 5486 8

First published 1927
Second edition 1948
Third edition 1962
This new impression published 1972
© 1972 A. K. Hamilton Jenkin

Reproduced and printed in Great Britain by Clarke Doble & Brendon Limited Plymouth for David & Charles (Publishers) Limited South Devon House Newton Abbot Devon

INTRODUCTION TO THE FOURTH EDITION

THE publication of *The Cornish Miner* in 1927 established the position of A. K. Hamilton Jenkin as the historian of the industry. Coming of a family which has been closely concerned with that industry for more than 200 years, Mr Jenkin can truly be said to have the Cornishman's love of mining 'in the blood'. His knowledge of the subject has been gained, and added to throughout the years, not merely by intensive research in books and documents, and conversations with the older generation of miners but through personal experience of conditions underground. His early reminiscences go back to the days of working by candle-light, of hand drilling and ladder climbing, of bal maidens 'spalling' the ore at surface and old style mine managers in frock coats and top-hats riding to work on horseback.

Of all his books on Cornwall, *The Cornish Miner* must surely be regarded as his classic and has circulated in far corners of the world where many Cornishmen will have read it with nostalgic memories of home. It is most appropriate, therefore, that this work should now be re-issued at a time when the industry in Cornwall is showing every indication of a strong and soundly based revival. At long last it seems to have been realised at Westminster and in Whitehall that the mineral wealth of Britain, and of Cornwall in particular, is still potentially important to the economy of the Nation. As a member of the Cornish Mining Development Association Mr Jenkin is one of those who has helped to bring about that realisation.

In his case we also owe him a great debt of gratitude for the researches embodied in his companion volume *Mines and Miners of Cornwall* in which he has described some eight hundred of the lesser-known mining adventures of the county, many of them recorded therein for the first time. Of no less importance are the documents, reports and plans preserved in his personal collection.

These he has made freely available to all those who have been carrying out investigations in Cornwall, leading in no small measure to the present revival of the industry.

JOHN H. TROUNSON
Chairman, Cornish Mining Development Association

REDRUTH, 1972

PREFACE

It has been said that the test of every real book is that it should have had at least one enthralled reader—and this, at any rate, the present volume can claim. Whether I have been able to pass over the footlights any of my own enthusiasm for the subject I have here treated remains to be seen, but for myself I do not regret the hours of labour which have passed uncounted in making the attempt.

Cornish mining is an industry which has changed so rapidly in character and outward appearance during the last two decades that it is possible, even for one born within the century, to indulge now in reminiscence of many things passed away and forgotten—a privilege for the most part only for those of advancing years. Having been "reared," as they say in Cornwall and America, in the heart of the mining areas, I got my first insight into the realms of underground romance as a child, when, wandering in the red-stained, granite-hilled country-side surrounding my home, I first made friends with the enginemen in their "Cornish Castles" or gazed outside in silent awe at the huge iron "bobs" of the pumping-engines as they lifted and bowed themselves like labouring giants above the shafts.

Not easily forgotten either are the moments when the wheels on the poppet-head high above started to move and the lithe-limbed bob of the old "fire-whim" which faced the pumping-engine raced upwards and down, faster and faster, as the rope came in on the drum and drew the "gig" to day; or how, peering down into the darkness and steam, dim lights began to show, to be followed a moment after by the arrival at surface of a dripping iron box and the pale faces of men with candles guttering in their battered hats. How often I pondered to myself concerning the world they had just left and thought, with "awful joy," of their work below! Faint with appreciation, I have approached the doors of the granite-built "drys" and listened to the light-hearted chaff of the men, as they recounted, for my benefit, of the dangers of their work.

Nor were the miners my only friends. Certain kindly old gentlemen in rusty frock-coats and tall hats (still at that date the regular insignia of a Cornish Mine Captain), to whom I had become a familiar object, were good enough to show me on more than one occasion round the "floors," where the tin stuff was being "cobbed" by the "bal maidens" in long sheds adjoining the stamps. Though frequently waxing eloquent above my head, I learnt not a little from these instructors of the processes of stamping, burning, buddling, framing, tozing, packing, etc., to which tin ore is subjected after being "brought to grass," and came to understand why our Cornish streams run red to the sea and how the smelting-works got their beautiful ingots of silvery tin which filled the trucks on the old-fashioned mineral railways around the mines.

It was not until later years that I started to turn my early enthusiasms to account, but the candle once lighted was never put out, and from being an admirer only I became a student of the subject, past and present. If, as time has gone on, I have been able to take any share in helping to revive public interest in the fine old industry which in later years has passed through so severe a depression, or to put on record the endurance and heroism of the miners who have lived in, worked, or emigrated from these areas, I feel it but a scant return for what they and the industry have given to me in the way of heartfelt sympathies and a student's joy.

St. Ives,
    Cornwall, 1927.

CONTENTS

	PAGE
INTRODUCTION TO THIRD EDITION	7
PREFACE	9
LIST OF COMMON ABBREVIATIONS USED IN NOTES	17
INTRODUCTION	19

Mines and Miners of Yesterday and To-day. Work in a Modern Tin-mine. The Romance of Mining.

CHAPTER

I. THE TINNERS UNDER THE STANNARIES 27
The Tin Trade in the Old World—Growth of the Stannaries—Early Uses of Tin—Bounding—Coinage—Streamers and Miners—Early Tin-works.

II. STREAMERS AND BLOWERS 48
Elizabethan Tinners—Alluvial Streaming—Streamers and Smugglers—Feast Days and Superstitions—Forgotten Trades, Blowers and Mule-Pack Men—The Contraband Tin Trade.

III. ABOVE AND UNDERGROUND, 1500-1800 83
The First Underground Mining—Seventeenth-Century Methods—Beginnings of Copper-mining—Introduction of Gunpowder—Prospecting by Adits—Water-Wheel Pumps—The Coming of Steam—Boulton and Watt in Cornwall—Underground Work in the Eighteenth Century—Old-style Tin-dressing—The Use of Water Power—Methods of Tin Smelting—Privateers and Tin Ships—Copper Smelting in Cornwall.

CHAPTER	PAGE
IV. VARYING FORTUNES OF THE MINERS, 1500–1800	122

Economic Features—Classes of Tinners—"Sweating" the Elizabethan Miner—Prosperity under the Commonwealth—Starvation Times—Feasts, Fights and other Recreations—Early Adventurers and Capitalists—Leasing of Mine Setts—Payment of Men, by Tribute and Tutwork—The Tinner in Health and Sickness—How a Tinner Lived—Wrecking Propensities—Corn Riots—Stannary Companies—The Worst Depression Known—Pewter Going Out of Fashion—Intervention of the East India Company—Trevithick versus Boulton and Watt.

V. MINERS AND ADVENTURERS DURING THE GREAT REVIVAL	171

The Increase of Mines and Miners—A Changing Country-side—Roads, Railways, Foundries, Smelting Works—Development of the Cornish Pumping Engine—Other Mechanical Improvements—Mines' Great Profits—The "London" Adventurer—Jovial Count Dinners—Peace in Industry—Absence of Strikes.

VI. THE MINER AT WORK, 1800–1870	203

A Scene in the Mining Districts—Tributers' "Bal" Bills—Strange Happenings Underground—Poor Air—Dangers from Blasting—Rough Conditions—Ladder Climbing—Boys Underground—"Tributers'" Tricks—Copper and Tin Sampling—The Dressing of Ores—Women and Children on the Mines—A Hardy Race.

VII. THE MINER AT HOME, 1800–1870	246

Coming to Surface—Night Walks—A Miner's Home—A Miner's Wife—A Miner's Food—Building a Cottage—Fondness of Children—Overcrowding—Ill-Health — High Death-rate — "Bal" Club Abuses — Mine Doctors—A Miner's Characteristics—Pride of Workmanship—Fisherman and Farmer—Desire for

CONTENTS

CHAPTER		PAGE
	Education—Dame Schools and Sunday Schools—Local Preachers—Billy Bray—No Politicians—Love of Justice—Holidays—Wrestling and Hurling—Tea-fights and Finery—Haunters of the Mine—Dying Customs.	
VIII.	FIFTY YEARS OF CHANGE IN THE MINES	302
	Figures and Statistics—Decline of Copper-mining—Temporary Slump in Tin—Precipitate Abandonment of Mines—Introduction of New Methods—Machinery Displaces Men — Disappearance of the Cost-Book Company—Discovery of Tin below Copper—The "Electric" Boom of 1906—Cornish Mining Holds Its Own—The War Period—The Subsequent Slump—A Healthy Revival—Tin Prospects for the Future.	
IX.	THE EXODUS OF THE 'SEVENTIES AND THE MINER OF TO-DAY	321
	The Breaking-up of Old Traditions—Again a Changing Country-side—Early Pioneers in Cuba and Mexico—Across the Rockies—Cornish Miners at Sea—Hardships of Travel—Amusing Stories—The Great Trek to the Rand—Cornish Colonies in England—Conditions Improving at Home—An Alarming Increase of Mortality—Decay of Tributing—Need of Prospectors—The Ideal of Theory and Practice.	
INDEX		345

ILLUSTRATIONS

FACING PAGE

A CORNISH MINER		64
AS USED BY THE OLD TINNERS	{ GRINDING-MILL AND POUNDING-STONES FOR TIN ORE	65
	GRANITE MOULD FOR CASTING INGOTS OF TIN IN A BLOWING-HOUSE	65
FREE SETTING TRIBUTERS OF TO-DAY	{ AN IMPROVISED VENTILATING COWL	65
	STREAMER USING SQUARE BUDDLE, TREVAUNANCE, 1924	65
HOISTING	{ WITH A HORSE-WHIM (OLD STYLE)	80
	BY COMPRESSED AIR FROM A WINZE (NEW STYLE)	80
A MINING LANDSCAPE. OLD CORNISH STAMPS AND DRESSING FLOORS, DOLCOATH		81
DRILLING HOLES FOR BLASTING	{ MACHINE DRILLING (NEW STYLE)	96
	HAND DRILLING A "BACK" HOLE (OLD STYLE)	96
ST. IVES CONSOLS MINE (*circa* 1870), SHOWING CHILD LABOURERS		97
BOTALLACK MINE IN 1863		112
COMING TO SURFACE	{ RIDING IN A "GIG" (NEWER STYLE)	113
	MAN-ENGINE IN UNDERLAY SHAFT (OLDER STYLE)	113

WHY seeke wee in corners for pettie commodities, when as the onely mynerall of Cornish Tynne openeth so large a field to the Countries benefit ?—this is in working so pliant, for sight so faire, and in use so necessarie, as thereby the Inhabitants gaine wealth, the Marchants trafficke, and the whole Realme a reputation : and with such plentie thereof hath God stuffed the bowels of this little Angle, that it overfloweth England, watereth Christendome, and is derived to a greater part of the world besides. In travailing abroad, in tarrying at home, in eating and drinking, in doing ought of pleasure and necessitie, Tynne, either in his owne shape, or transformed into other fashions, is always requisite, always readie for our service : but I shall rather disgrace, than endeere it by mine overweake commendation, and sooner tire myselfe, then drawe the fountaine of his praises drie.

RICHARD CAREW, *Survey of Cornwall*, 1602.

MAMMON. This night I'll change
All that is metal in my house to gold :
And early in the morning, will I send
To all the plumbers and the pewterers,
And buy their tin and lead up ; and to Lothbury
For all the copper.
SURLY. What, and turn that too ?
MAMMON. Yes, and I'll purchase Devonshire and Cornwall,
And make them perfect Indies !

BEN JONSON, *The Alchemist*, Act II, Sc. I.

LIST OF COMMON ABBREVIATIONS USED IN NOTES

(Other Authorities are given in full as they occur)

Boulton & Watt MSS. =	Collection at the Royal Cornwall Polytechnic Society, Falmouth.
Add. MSS. =	Additional MSS. in British Museum.
Harl. MSS. =	Harleian MSS. in British Museum.
Cal. S.P. Dom. =	Calendar of State Papers, Domestic.
Cal. Treas. Pap. =	Calendar of Treasury Papers.
Chyandour =	Chyandour Estate Office, Penzance.
Hist. MSS. Comm. =	Reports of Historical MSS. Commission.
Philosoph. Trans. =	Transactions of Philosophical Society, 1668 and 1671.
Parl. Pap. 1842 =	Parliamentary Papers (1842) XVI, Report of Children's Employment Commission.
Parl. Pap. 1864 =	Parliamentary Papers (1864), Report of Commission to Inquire into All Mines of Great Britain, Not Coal.
R.C.P. =	Reports of Royal Cornwall Polytechnic Society.
R.G.S.C. =	Transactions of the Royal Geological Society of Cornwall.
R.I.C. =	Reports or Journals of the Royal Institution of Cornwall.
Stat. Soc. =	Transactions of the Royal Statistical Society.
Vict. Hist. of Cornwall =	Victoria County History Series.
Bottrell =	William Bottrell, *Tales and Hearthside Stories of West Cornwall*.
Carew =	Richard Carew, *Survey of Cornwall* (1602). References are to the edition of 1769, unless otherwise stated.
Cunnack =	Richard Cunnack, MS. Notes on Cornish Mines.
Lewis =	G. Randall Lewis, *The Stannaries*.

Pryce .. .. = William Pryce, *Mineralogia Cornubiensis* (1778).

Tonkin .. .. = Notes to the 1811 edition of R. Carew's *Survey of Cornwall*. Also Tonkin MSS. in the County Museum, Truro.

Tinners' Grievance .. = Aggravii Venetiani (1697).

Maton .. .. = W. G. Maton, *Observations of the Western Counties* (1794-6).

Spargo .. .. = Thos. Spargo, *Mines of Devon and Cornwall* (1865, etc.).

Worth .. .. = R. N. Worth, Historical Notes Concerning Progress of Mining Skill in Devon and Cornwall. R.C.P.S. (1872).

INTRODUCTION

To the visiting stranger few ideas are more depressing than that of a mining town. The very words as they are spoken conjure up visions of tall head-gears looming through the smoke and rows of dreary houses beneath the thick pall of a Black Country sky.

So when the shoals of summer visitors begin their annual influx to the Cornish coast, where they are awaited no less eagerly than were the pilchards of old, those who go to the extreme west speed up their cars as they pass through the mining areas and drive on, trusting for better things beyond.

After leaving Plymouth and the wooded shores of the dividing Tamar, the route passes onwards through quiet villages and insignificant towns where never a thought beyond seedtime and harvest seems to have stirred the minds of a purely agricultural population. Thus, if he looks neither to the right hand nor to the left, a traveller may reach almost to Truro before there is borne upon him the recollection that he is passing through one of the oldest mining camps of the world, an El Dorado of incalculable price, and the home from whence thousands of mining pioneers have gone out to every distant corner of the world.

Between Truro and Camborne the scenery changes rapidly. Ascending from the village of Chacewater, the road winds upward on to a desolate tract of country exposed along the skyline to every wind of heaven and sloping away on the north side to the Bristol Channel and to the south towards the estuary of the Fal. This is the land of abandoned mines, or, as a Cornishman would say, "knack't bals," where tall, gaunt engine-houses with smokeless stacks point like fingers to the sky. Away to the left hand of the road, by the little town of St. Day, are situated once-famous groups of tin and copper mines. There is Creegbrawse and, adjoining it, Poldise, both of which were at work and of ancient standing before the earliest discovery of America. Beyond them again are the United and the Consolidated Mines, situated on a desolate moor of which one square mile alone was considered the richest piece of ground in the Old World. Here millions of pounds' worth of metallic ores have been raised, forests of timber have been used to support the ground, and rivers of water have been brought to surface by the aid of fleets laden with coal. Near and far and all around where the mineral lodes extend, red piles of stone and sand and tall engine-houses by walled-in shafts mark the course of the miners' labour underground. This is the great copper district whose riches were for the most part worked out by the 'sixties or 'seventies of the last century, but which has still to be mined for the deeper tin zone which is now recognized as underlying the copper.

In the mining towns of this district on a Saturday night an observing eye may note from what scattered regions of the earth the men have returned. There, to all appearance, is the Yankee, very pleased with his gold-filled teeth and check patterned overcoat—here the returned miner in soft slouch hat from the mining camps of South America. Amongst another group the talk is all of the Rand, whose dust-filled gold-mines have sent more money home to Cornwall than any other camp in the world, though none has given more cause for dread to mining families, whose best and strongest have perished there. Home for a while in their native town, where the naphtha lights glare out on a Saturday night and the standings are filled with " Tom trot " and " clidgy " as of old, men who have lately mingled with far-distant peoples rub shoulders with those who have hardly ever left the confines of their parish. Yet in this age-long occupation of the Cornish people the same interests and associations bind them together, as they did their fathers who worked in the old mines which extend beneath the very houses and streets to-day.

That Cornish mining is not a thing of the past very soon becomes apparent to those who look about them after leaving Redruth. Here the streams in the valleys run a bright red and are turbid with the sands carried down from the roaring mine-stamps (ore-crushing machines) on the hill-sides higher up. Throughout their whole length these streams provide a living to many families who are engaged in extracting the particles of

INTRODUCTION

tin which they contain. All along the course of the river, and in some places down to the very verge of the sea itself, little red-stained wheels turn brushes of heath or griglan, buddles and round frames slowly circulate and wooden contrivances fill up with water, topple over with a swish, and busily right themselves again. Nobody seems to attend to all these curious "engines," which work on unconcernedly amidst the surrounding growths of furze as if trained by long tradition to know their own business.

From the road, however, between Redruth and Camborne sights very different appear, betokening the modern activities of an up-to-date industry. On this side and on that tall head-gears are outlined against the sky, surmounted by wheels which whirl in contrary motion as the skips pass upwards and down from the shaft-bottom three thousand feet or more beneath. To-day, behind the head-gears, the powerful winding-engines which give motion to these wheels puff out their clouds of steam in steady rhythm as they fulfil the perfected design of the great Camborne engineer who first experimented with them in this district more than a hundred years ago. And now to these are added electric power stations, foundries, mineral railways, and all the other features of the New Age, on whose threshold only Trevithick stood, as he planned and invented with prophetic judgment.

Still overtopping all, however, even to-day, are the massive Cornish pumping-engines, whose beams, protruding above the shafts, alternately rise skywards and slowly sink again as they force up the water from the subterranean world beneath. Standing by one of these engines and watching the pump rods slowly rise and fall in the black abyss of the shaft, many people have realized for the first time what the call of mining means—a call not a whit less strong for those who know it than that of the sea itself. What a ship is in the docks, so are these surface features in the mines: both link the everyday world of labour with one where man meets the elements face to face. The sailor's life is, perhaps, the more dramatic. His deeds of pluck, as his ordinary routine work, are performed beneath the open sky, whilst the miner's work-place, eighteen hundred feet and more beneath a waking or a sleeping world, is known to few, and illuminated only by a guttering candle in the fastness of enclosing rock.

A miner's life is thus spent between two worlds. For a period of seven or eight hours out of every twenty-four his occupation carries him away from the ordinary haunts of men—out of sight and out of hearing—into the dark underworlds of industry which lie beneath the red-stained mining areas. To enter that world, so utterly unknown to most people, wherein the miner year in and year out pursues his unseen labour, a visitor must don the uniform of the place. This consists of a thick flannel shirt, trousers and coat of red-stained tattered canvas, heavy boots, and on the head a skullcap surmounted by a specially hardened felt hat. To this last a candle is attached with a lump of sticky clay. Thus equipped and with spare candles slung from a button of his coat, the miner stands round the steaming shaft, waiting for the coming of the " gig " or cage " to grass." Presently a bell rings in the engine-room, the black steel rope in the shaft begins to move rapidly upward, and in a few minutes with a creak and a rattle the gig draws up to the surface. In appearance this " vehicle " resembles an oblong iron box divided into two stories and hung on end from the aforementioned rope. Wheels attached to the side enable it to run swiftly over a wooden track prepared for it in the shaft. Like everything else, this, too, is red-stained, and dripping wet with the water which in many places spouts like a shower-bath from the rocks below. Out from the gig squeeze three, four, or even six ragged-looking men, whose pale faces contrast strongly with the red hue of their clothing. Into the place which they have vacated others immediately get, again the bell rings, the gig lifts off its catches and a moment afterwards, with breathless speed, drops downward into darkness. At certain places in the shaft the speed lessens for a moment as the gig passes by the entrance to some level, where a glimpse may be got of men sitting with their candles waiting their turn to ride to surface. A shouted remark, perhaps, passes between these and one of the men riding in the shaft, and then the gig, as if suddenly endued with new life, plunges downward again with increasing swiftness between the dripping walls of granite. At last the speed slackens finally, glimpses of lights may be seen below, and

INTRODUCTION 23

the air grows perceptibly hotter as the gig, with a series of jerks, slows down to a standstill.

On first stepping out into this new world the visitor looks around with some bewilderment. Candles stuck here and there to the rocky walls throw light on a novel scene. Out from the dark level, which forms at this point the entrance to the mine, little iron trucks are being pushed towards the shaft by men whose bodies, stripped to the waist, look glistening white in the darkness. Each man carries his own light in these gloomy passage-ways, attaching his candle to either his miner's hat or the "tram" itself. Stumbling along on the rough, wet track behind a miner, who picks his way unhesitatingly through the divergent tunnels and over abysses which drop into deeper workings below, the visitor at length reaches the lode itself. Here in some dim cavern the lights of the miners shine out twenty, thirty, or one hundred feet above his head, as, with swinging hammers or the aid of roaring machine-drills, they break the mineral ores piecemeal from the lode. The rock thrown down from the inaccessible places where the men are working extends like a glacier of stone to the foot of the level. Here the trammers are loading the little trucks which have already been seen on their way towards the shaft, picking up rocks, heavy with sparkling tin, with an ease which is as much knack as strength. The air in these large open spaces near the lode is warm and damp, tasting of the acrid smoke of dynamite, released after blasting. This, however, represents only one small section of a great mine. Above and below, men are working in the same way, attacking the mineral vein at a higher or lower level. Connecting these levels are many small internal shafts or "winzes," through which it is necessary to squeeze with considerable agility in order to descend the ladders to where the miners are working. To reach the lodes cross-cuts have in many places to be driven through unpayable country, and these, from being much smaller, are frequently hot and very dry, so that, even with the compressed air from the drills, the work is hard and the lightest clothing is felt as an encumbrance. Two or three hours' wanderings through such cross-cuts, levels, raises, winzes, and stopes will suffice to satiate most visitors with the wonders of life and labour underground. Bidding, therefore, good-bye and good fortune to the civil and kindly group of men in whose company these few hours of his life have passed, the visitor will return to the shaft, and, getting into the gig, ride upwards with a sense of tired relief. As daylight once more dawns above him and the sunlit air from sea and downs sweeps over and past with glorious exhilaration, the contrast with the miners' world, where even light and air are luxuries, can only then be fully realized.

Though perhaps, once bitten twice shy, the traveller may never again descend into those gloomy labyrinths, the surface of the mining regions will ever hereafter hold a new meaning for him. The great heaps of stone, no longer ugly disfigurements only, will tell of inky shafts and far-reaching levels beneath his feet. The beams of the pumping-engines rising and falling with their measured beat will speak of toiling miners hundreds of feet below, whilst the old engine-houses, in their veteran dignity, recount of generations now past, of levels, cross-cuts, and shafts which no longer see the flickering candle and where the water-springs have regained once more their old ascendancy.

The shafts of Cornwall, could they be all numbered, would prove as the sands of the sea, whilst the underground tunnels alone extend into thousands of miles. Through these dim passage-ways have come and gone to their labour generations of hard-working men, from the early miner of Elizabethan times, with his little iron pick and wooden shovel, to the men of to-day, whose high explosives and thundering rock-drills wake the echoes beneath our feet. What manner of men were they in those early times, the ordinary men, the working miners whose names are all forgotten, but whose work can still be traced by moor and cliff and hill-side in this ancient Duchy? Or, again, what of the men of later date, in the first six decades of the nineteenth century, when Cornwall was mistress of the mining world and her exports of copper and tin reached out to the far ends of the earth? How, amidst all this prosperity, did the miner fare? How did he live, eat, drink, and amuse both mind and body when released from the darkness and his dangers compassed round?

To answer such questions and, where possible, show the

development which took place from one century to another in the miner's work and life will be the object of this book, and when, as the reader draws to an end, he surveys what has gone before and glances onward to the future, he will, I believe, agree that it is a tale fit, as Sir Philip Sidney would say, "to hold children from play and old men from the chimney-corner."

THE CORNISH MINER

CHAPTER I

THE TINNERS UNDER THE STANNARIES

I

"Cornish tin," it has well been said, "is the one famous product of ancient Britain." (1) For tin, that pure metal which, as Henry Belasye quaintly put it, "is so excellent in Cornewell that it's only not sylver," was as much sought after by the ancients for their weapons and ornaments of bronze as we of a later day desire it for our motor-cars and tin-plating.

The literary reputation of the commerce in this metal in the ancient world was immense but, at the same time, shadowy; for it is clear that the dwellers by the Mediterranean knew but little of the dim Western sources from whence their supplies of tin were drawn. It is true that Strabo's account, said to be partially based on Poseidonius, is filled with picturesque detail. According to him, the tin country consisted of ten islands, one of which was uninhabited, the others occupied by people who wore long black garments, were girded, and carried staffs and looked like the Furies in the theatre. They bartered their tin and lead for pottery, skins, salt, and metal implements. Originally only the Phœnicians from Cadiz traded with them, and they kept their route a secret. On one occasion, when a Roman ship followed a Phœnician trading vessel, the captain of the latter ran his ship on a shoal to compass the destruction of his pursuers. In the end, however, the Romans found their way to the islands. Thus —Strabo. From further statements, however, it is evident that he himself was not much clearer than the others where the far-famed islands lay, and his account cannot therefore be taken too literally. Uncertain indeed as regards detail, the sum total of the literary evidence still remains, nor is the archæological evidence much more helpful in throwing light on the early history of this industry. A few objects have from time to time been discovered by tin stream workers in the silt of Cornish rivers, but the account of their provenance is generally too vague to teach us much. Cornwall, too, has been turned over and over during the Middle Ages and in modern times by tin-miners, and remains of Roman or earlier periods may easily have made their way into recent debris. (2) Blocks of tin likewise preserved in museums and pronounced by older authorities as " certainly Roman " are now stated by their descendants, with equal certainty, to be mediaeval, if not of later date, so that the reader is apt to find in the multitude of his counsellors much confusion. Tin slag, however, has, in certain instances, been found in connection with really ancient, and not merely mediaeval, furnaces. In the course of excavations at the famous 300–200 B.C. hill castle of Chun, near St. Just, there was discovered, in the year 1925, a series of small smelting-pits, in one of which lay a lump of metallic slag which an assay proved to be tin. That we are thus perfectly safe in assuming an antiquity of over two thousand years for this Cornish industry there is no doubt, but as far as any details go we are still almost entirely in the dark.

As a natural result the early period, that is, from the beginnings down to the Norman Conquest, has long been the debating ground of theorists. In spite, however, of all that has been written on the Cassiterides and Ictis, on the extent of the Roman administration of the tin-works, or of the later Saxon invasion, all three remain the most complicated of problems still. What evidence there is has been very ably marshalled in the Romano-British section of the *Victoria History of Cornwall*, and from it this much may be said to emerge :—

1. That there was, in all probability, a very ancient commerce of tin between some point of South Western Britain and the Mediterranean.

2. That the Romans exercised considerable influence over the Cornish tin trade, especially during the third century A.D.

3. And that after their withdrawal the Saxons probably penetrated the eastern parts of the county, where they were not without an eye to the advantages of the alluvial stream-tin.

The last we hear of Cornish tin in antiquity is about A.D. 600, when, in the life of John the Almsgiver, it is related that an Alexandrian seaman sailed to Britain with corn, relieved a famine, and returned with a cargo of tin, which was miraculously changed into silver on the way. So far, then, as literary evidence goes, the history of the Cornish tin trade in antiquity may be said to begin with the romance of the Cassiterides in Herodotus and to end with the legend of John the Almoner in the *Acta Sanctorum*.

It is only fair, however, to say that as the learned have had their theories, so the simple have evolved romances to fill in the gaps where history itself is wanting. Among the latter the coming of the Phœnicians is still in full possession at this very day. Old workings in Elizabethan times were referred to by the tinners as "attal Sarsen" or "Jews' offcasts." Smelting-places of mediaeval times or earlier are still called "Jews' houses," Jew, Saracen, and Phœnician being equally confused in identity as well as date in popular imagination. According to one story, the brass-work of Solomon's Temple was made from Cornish tin, whilst in another St. Paul himself is said to have preached to Cornish tinners and to have actually bought tin from Creegbrawse Mine near St. Day. Yet another tradition states that tin-smelting was only first discovered by St. Piran, the Cornish miners' patron saint, which reduces the industry to the status of a painfully modern affair ; whilst the belief, on the other hand, that Joseph of Arimathæa was a tin-worker, redounds to the credit of the industry, and should certainly find mention here. In these simple tales we see the same process at work as among the more learned—the desire to see back farther and farther into the early annals of this once world-famed industry, of whose dim antiquity, at any rate, there can be no question and no denial.

It is not until the middle of the twelfth century A.D. that the documentary history of the Cornish tin industry can be said to begin : and even then it consists of little more than lists of figures gathered from the early Pipe Rolls, showing the relative output of tin from the two counties of Cornwall and Devon. Of the men who were actually engaged in the tin-works of this period we know practically nothing.

In 1194 Richard Cœur de Lion embarked from Portsmouth for the French War, leaving the administration of England in the hands of Hubert, Archbishop of Canterbury. To gain money for his master, Hubert, in 1197, turned his attention to the tin-works of Cornwall and dispatched thither one William de Wrotham as "Custos" or Warden of the Stannaries. William de Wrotham managed things well, both for the King's revenue and the regulation of the tin trade, drawing up, with the assistance of juries of tinners, a code of strict but useful laws for the regulation of the traffic in tin and the testing of the weights used for official measurement.(3)

The earliest Charter of the Stannaries which is known dates from the year 1201. In it were confirmed the already ancient privileges of the tinners "of digging tin, and turfs for smelting it, at all times, freely and peaceably and without hindrance from any man, everywhere in moors and in the fees of bishops, abbots, and counts, . . . and of buying faggots to smelt the tin without waste of forest, and of diverting streams for their works, just as by ancient usage they have been wont to do."

Throughout the thirteenth, fourteenth, and fifteenth centuries the tin trade appears to have been, on the whole, progressive, although subject to very considerable fluctuations. In the fourteenth century great quantities of tin were used in the making of brass cannons; and in 1337 the production of tin in Cornwall reached the highest figure on record up to that time. The effect of the Black Death on the stannaries, however, was so disastrous that by 1350 the production of tin had fallen to a third of what it was in 1337. (4) Though the production rose again before the end of the century, it was not for long, and throughout the whole of the fifteenth century, for reasons not clearly understood, the output of tin was fluctuating and often very small.

The chief use for tin at this time was for making church bells and, in Constantinople and the East, for plating the insides of copper utensils. The demand, however, for the metal had not yet reached any very great proportions owing to the fact that pewter was still, for the most part, regarded as a luxury for the rich only. (5) Nevertheless, by the fourteenth century other trade routes had been opened across Europe, and Cornish tin, in addition to going through France to Marseilles, was finding its way via Bruges overland to Venice. (6)

In the meantime, in Cornwall, the tin-works were growing in size and in importance, and the position and rights of the tinners were becoming consolidated. One of the developments out of the Charter of 1201, which had placed jurisdiction over the tinner in the hands of a warden, had been the division of the mining districts into several provinces or "stannaries." "The local limits of each of the four Cornish stannaries have never been accurately defined, for they seem to have spread vaguely outward from the aggregation of tin-works in certain situations favourable to them. Five tracts of stanniferous wastrel, with their adjacent vales, supplied the ancient stream works of Cornwall. The moor between Launceston and Bodmin, in which the Fowey River has its source, gave its name to the northern stannary of Foweymore; Hensborough Beacon, with the tin grounds of Roche, Luxullian, and St. Austell formed that of Blackmore. A smaller district on the north coast extending inland to Truro constituted the stannary of Tywarnhail, whilst the stannary or united stannaries of Penwith and Kerrier included two great tracts of waste, Kerrier lying to the north of Helston, and Penwith between Lelant and the Land's End." (7) Within these stannaries the tinner lived subject to stannary law, much as a soldier is subject to military law. Of the four stannaries, Blackmore seems to have been the most ancient, and to it appertained several privileges not found in the others. The "moor" itself was divided into eight tithings—Trethevy, Boswith, Treverbin, Pridis, Trenance Austle, Tremedris, Tregarrack, and Miliack, and to each tithing-man or representative it was granted to summon any tinner of Blackmore without writ. (8) The Tinners' Charter also is said by old chroniclers to have been originally granted to the stannary of Blackmore alone, and was appointed to be kept "in the Tower of Luxulian in a Coffer with eight Locks and eight Keys whereof every of the said Tythings ought to have a key." (9)

Amongst all the privileges of the tinners, that of being able to enter ground and therein search and dig for tin, which was known as "bounding," was probably the oldest and certainly the most important. (10) This, together with the appointment of a warden with sole jurisdiction over them, freed the tinners from the exactions which the manorial lord exercised over the ordinary serf, and probably gave to the tinners from early times that hardy independence of character for which they have always been noted. In the matter of bounding the Devon tinners were originally the most highly privileged, being permitted to enter any man's land, enclosed or unenclosed, and therein dig for tin without licence, tribute, or satisfaction. In Cornwall, on the other hand, the tinner was prohibited from entering into several or enclosed land until the owner's leave had first been obtained, (11) and after this, if mineral was discovered, it lay in the latter's power either to work it himself, set it out to farm, or leave it unwrought. (12) In wastrel or unenclosed land the Cornish tinners, like those of Devon, could enter freely and search for tin, though here again not without certain acknowledgment of the owner's right in the form of "toll tin" or lord's "dish." This, in earlier times, generally consisted of a fifteenth part, "saving in such places where a special custom hath limited another manner of toll." "When a mine (or stream work) is found in any such place," continues Carew, "the first discoverer aymeth how farre it is likely to extend, and then at the foure corners of his limited proportion, diggeth up three turfes, and the like (if he list) on the sides, which they term Bounding, and within that compasse, every other man is restrained from searching." By this system the poorest man might become a partner in a work and, in a sense, be his own master. In order to assist them in working their bounds the tinners were allowed to drive adits through other men's works, as well as to divert streams. No person, however, we read, "shall under any pretence whatsoever spoil or divert any Pot-waters running to any Man's house for dressing of Meat or for the service of his Family, nor divert any Water from any Antient Mill." Such matters as these, however, giving rise to variance of opinion, it was added that "all force in matter of tin and going armed to tin works or washes is punishable by our customs." (13)

Bounding, however, like many other privileged customs, was very complicated in its latter-day working and frequently led to law suits in the Stannary Courts. Though restrained from entering into several without special leave, the Cornish tinner was privileged to regard as wastrel "all inclosed lands that have been antiently bounded and assured for Wastrel by payment of Toll tin before that the hedges were made upon the same." In a like manner the "Prince's several and enclosed Ancient Assessionable Duchy Mannors" were also deemed to come under the title of Wastrel. (14) Bounds, being legally in the nature of Chattels Real, could be devised by will, in a way similar to other property, subject to their being renewed according to custom. (15) In bounded land, the bounder and not the mineral lord had the exclusive right of granting setts or licences to work, and as a consequence the terms were settled between himself and the adventurers alone. In some places the "dish" paid by the mine (which was commonly 1/6th in the eighteenth century, but had dropped to 1/15th again by 1830–40) was divided equally between the bounders and the mineral lords, but in St. Agnes the bounders generally claimed 7/13ths and the lord 6/13ths. (16) The difficulties of reconciling not only the mineral lords but the multitudes of bounders, each with their petty rights, became, in later times, a serious bar to the opening up of large mines in Cornwall. Cases have been known where a shareholder in a mine has bought from some ancient bounder a piece of ground containing perhaps the main engine-shaft, and has subsequently drawn a considerable royalty therefrom at the expense of his fellow-adventurers. Every square yard of wastrel in the mining districts was formerly plotted out into bounds, each bound having its own peculiar name. Such were "Clear Diamond," "Little Dagger," "Down Dribble," "North Goodluck," "Goodmorrow Neighbour," "Little Between," "St. Gracious," "Wheal Jose," alias "Cloam Dish," "Higher Recover the Fault," "Merry-between," "Great St. Mark," "Polticca," "Pitspry," "Pitpaddy," "Park Buggens," and literally many hundreds of others. The actual form and shape of the bounds added still further complications to the system. The original bounds seem to have had four corners only, but, in later times, the Stannary Law mentions side-bounds also. "By this it should seem that side-bounds were not understood only as cut in enclosures to assert the right there, but extended out o the line from corner to corner." (17) Frequently, as appears from old maps, the bounds possessed by different owners overlapped by two or even three. The fractional parts of the tin "farm" which the bounders thus claimed were complicated in the extreme, and not infrequently it was discovered that in the passage of time the parts had increased to considerably more than the whole! Thus in 1776 the parts of ownership in Perran Great St. George tin bound amounted to so much more than the whole that it was stated that "the matter hath for these many years past occasioned divers disputes and squabbles by some claimers taking the whole of their dues at one time, some another, others claiming a part having the same time no dues left for them." ... It is accordingly resolved to bring the matter before the Vicewarden of the Stannaries." Two years later the parts claimed by five bounders in a neighbouring set

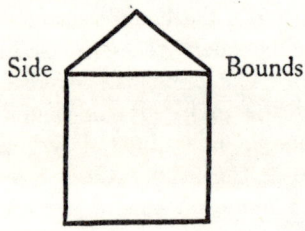

(Great Carnmeal, St. Agnes) amounted to no less than $\frac{4}{3}\frac{5}{6}$. "I believe there was never a worse noise to an account before," wrote an agent in 1792, after attending a meeting at one of these mines. (18)

By the time that Pryce wrote in 1778, bounding in many cases consisted simply in the landowner's agent, known as the Toller, Renewer, or Bounder, visiting his bounds once a year (generally on the Feast of St. John, St. Peter, or St. Paul), where, after cutting the turfs in the prescribed manner, "he retired to some house of entertainment there to take dinner or other refreshment in commemoration of the annual renewing day." (19) For some time, therefore, before bounding lapsed altogether (in the early part of the nineteenth century), the system had ceased to fulfil its original purpose. Practically no new bounds were being taken out for the simple reason that nearly all wastrel land was already held by the descendants of ancient bounders, who, though often possessed of no interest in mining themselves, kept up their claim on the chance that a mine might one day be started which would either pay them "farm" or buy them out.

Next to "bounding," probably the most important privilege of the tinners in early times was that of having their disputes (matters connected with life, limb, and land excepted) tried in their own Stannary Courts. These were generally held in each district once in three weeks, although certain customary courts were kept on the morrow after certain fairs, "for the benefit of such as do attend the fair and the court." (20) If one of the parties only was a tinner and the other an outsider, the matter was still tried in the Stannary Court. The charge ordinarily read on the opening of one of these courts was a peculiar one: "Good men yee shall understand that wee are assembled here this day for a Good and Godly purpose that is to minister justice as much as to say that I with you and you with me may endeavour with all our Powers to put down vice and extoll vertue all which to be brief is comprehended in this word justice. . . . Now if the Pagans as Cicero with the learned Romans with divers others having no hope of salvation had such reverence unto Justice . . . so needs must we the more earnestly," etc. (21) Whether, in spite of this solemn preamble, the justice of a Stannary Court "savoured more of affection than reason" (as Carew delicately put it) it is not for us to say, but there can be no doubt that the right to hold such a court was a factor of great importance in establishing the independence of the working tinner. The chief abuse which found its way into stannary matters was due to the interference of unscrupulous lawyers, who not only stirred up strife and disputes to their own benefit, but protracted the suits to such lengths that in the end the tinner was frequently unable to pay his debts, and both he and his work would fall utterly into the lawyer's grasp. "Whereas the Tinner's privilege (as I am informed)," wrote a seventeenth-century writer, " is to have their proceedings at Law upon payment of a penny only, and to appear in person and to speak and act for themselves that their causes may be the sooner ended." (22) Rarely, however, do such conditions of pastoral simplicity and directness flourish under the ægis of law, so that stannary jurisdiction was in most cases quite beyond the comprehension of the ordinary tinners, who were dependent on others for their interpretation of it. Thus we learn that Mr. Udy West, of Redruth, about 1710, was called the "Father of the Tinners," for the simple reason of his being so well versed in these matters. (23)

In close connection with the Stannary Courts was the Stannary Gaol at Lostwithiel, whose reputation, if a trifle less unsavoury (in every sense of the word) than that of Lidford, (24) was still sinister enough. The allowance to the stannary gaoler, in taking prisoners to Lostwithiel, was at the rate of 2d. a mile, after which expense a fairly prolonged stay at the gaol seems to have been expected of most prisoners. Certain prisoners at mainprize, however, were not kept in strict confinement, but were allowed liberty of the whole borough of Lostwithiel, "to extend so far as the houses of the inhabitants shall reach and no farther." (25)

In addition to the holding of courts, the tinners were by Royal Charter granted the privilege of having a Convocation or Parliament of their own for the regulation of stannary affairs. Of the actual value of the "Cornish" or Stannary Parliaments to the working tinner opinions differ. The Convocation, it is true, had powers granted it to reverse even the decisions of the King or Council of State itself, in cases where such proved prejudicial to the tin trade, but it is doubtful if any but the opinions of the great mine-owners were ever consulted on such questions. Indeed, the writer of an account of a Cornish Parliament held in 1750 stated that "during the time of an election, gentlemen think it worth while to come down into the County who are never seen in it at any other time and to neglect their business and the pursuit of their affairs for three months together, without having or pretending to have the least knowledge of tin or stannary matters." (26) The four-and-twenty Stannators who made up the Cornish Tinners' Parliament were elected according to ancient constitution by the Mayor and Council of Launceston, Lostwithiel, Truro, and Helston, representing respectively the stannaries of Blackmore, Foweymore, Tywarnhail, and Penwith and Kerrier. In its ordering the Stannary Parliament seems to have differed little from that of the House of Commons. It met, however, at irregular intervals,

THE TINNERS UNDER THE STANNARIES 37

perhaps in all not more than nine or ten times, the last being in 1752. (27)

A privilege much more particularly affecting the lives of the working tinners was that of exemption from ordinary taxation. This included not only freedom from tolls and dues at fairs, ports, and markets, but also relief from ordinary levies such as that of tithes and the fifteenth. (28) When levies were made at all, as they sometimes were through special interposition of the Lord Warden, it generally amounted to an appeal to the tinners rather than a command. Thus, in the year of the Armada, the Mayor of Exeter wrote "beseeching" the Devon stannaries "to contribute towards the charge of setting out ships in a warlike manner for the Queen's service." (29) In 1597 the Queen herself addressed a letter to Sir Walter Raleigh as Lord Warden of the Stannaries, in which she suggested that as the Company of Tinners had refused to give contribution, as the rest of the shire had done, towards the expenses of the late voyage to Cadiz, he should try what he could do by authority and persuasion "to endeavour to draw some reasonable portion from them, as their means will allow." (30)

Lastly, in order that the tinners should not be too frequently called off from work which was rightly regarded as of national importance, they were declared exempt from any military summons save that of their Lord Warden only. In any case, the difficulty of collecting the tinners, scattered throughout their lonely working places, must have made it almost impossible to summon them at a short notice. Their knowledge of trenching, however, made them valuable in works of defence. Parties of tinners were employed in the strengthening of Plymouth Citadel in 1597, (31) and mention will also be found of tinners being sent overseas as "pioneers" in the Dutch and Irish wars.

The privileges of their class being, in early times, at any rate, very considerable, the question naturally arose who was and who was not a tinner. The answer is not clear. In its widest application the term included not only miners and streamers but smelters, carriers, charcoalers, carpenters, smiths, tin merchants, and even the owners of tin bounds. For ordinary purposes, however, the tinners were generally understood to be those who were actually engaged in the getting or preparing of tin for the market.

That the privileges and exemptions enumerated above were granted to the tinner at a price is very apparent to anyone who studies the administration of the tin trade. To each of the stannaries was appointed from earliest times a coinage town, whither all tin smelted in the district had to be carried, and a tax amounting to 4s. a cwt. paid before it could be sold. (32) In ancient days Liskeard and Lostwithiel served as the coinage towns for the two eastern stannaries, Truro and Helston for the western. In course of time, however, as the output of tin gradually fell off in the east whilst steadily increasing in the west parts of Cornwall, Penzance was added as a fifth coinage town. (33) To one of these towns all tin raised within the stannaries had to be brought, and here twice (or, latterly, four times) in the year the Royal officers attended. At noon on the first day of the coinage a great company of people assembled in the coinage hall, the controller and receiver, with the stamping hammer and weights, the weigher and assay master, porters, country chapmen, merchants from London, pewterers, factors, and a sprinkling of Italian and Flemish traders. At the hall they would be met by the tinners themselves, whose tin had been dispatched many days before on pack-horses or mules from all the surrounding country. When order had been made, an open space was roped off in front of the company, the King's beam was brought out, and the weights were solemnly unsealed and handed to the weigher. The assay master then made ready his hammer and chisels, and the steward, controller, and receiver took their seats facing the beam. When all was in readiness, the porters brought out the blocks one at a time and placed them upon the scales. The weight of each was shouted out by the "peaser" or weigher, and was taken down by three officials. The blocks, on leaving the scales, were taken in hand by the assay master, who chiselled a small piece from a corner of each and rapidly assayed it to make sure the metal was of proper quality. (34) If satisfactory the controller, with a blow of the hammer, struck upon the block the Duchy Arms, which in England, at any rate, was a guarantee both of its purity and of its having paid the coinage.

The duration of the coinage varied from two to twelve days, according to the amount of tin waiting to be coined. On the morning of the last day the crier was sent out through the streets to make proclamation to the tinners of the intended adjournment. (35) The numbers of people assembled at these times must have made brisk trade for the shop-people and inn-keepers, and coinage conferred a considerable importance on the towns in which it was held. In later times Truro had the largest of all coinages. "A stranger," wrote Maton about 1793, "will be much struck at his entrance into this town, to see the blocks of tin that lie in heaps about the street. Every block worth 10 or 12 guineas, weighing 320 pounds—a load too great for a thief to carry off unseen." (36) Ten years later Polwhele wrote, "To its various merchandise Truro must ascribe its recent architectural improvements, where, as in ancient Tyre, the tin glitters in its streets and all its merchants are princes." (37) Though in later times the coinage was held, when necessary, four times a year, the Midsummer Coinage was generally the largest and accounts for the fact that this was the foremost among the festive days in the tinners' calendar.

As will be seen, the gravest objection to coinage lay in the fact that the tinner, unless he was a mere spalliar or day-labourer working for hire, could only sell his produce, at the most, four times in the year, and in the meanwhile generally had to borrow ready money in order to exist. The lender was usually the tin merchant himself, whose rate of interest was commonly excessive. It was with a view to preventing the poor tinner thus being squeezed out of existence by the merchants that the Government from time to time attempted to make the buying of tin a State monopoly. To effect this, officers were sent down twice in the year, at the Midsummer and Michaelmas Coinages, with orders to buy up all tin for the Crown "at a reasonable and fixed rate," hoping by these means to cut out the London and Cornish tin merchants. The scheme, as a whole, met with but indifferent success, although it was introduced at occasional intervals, whenever the tinners' lot became more than usually oppressive. The fact that the tin was paid for on these occasions in hard cash meant that considerable sums in bullion had frequently to be carried down from London through the wild and roadless West Country, with dangers on every hand from loss in transport over creeks and rivers and from lawless plunderers by the way. Among the papers relating to pre-emption is an interesting note concerning the " charges of Sir Richard Smith for his journey into Cornwall in February 1606, for the buying of Tynne to his Majestie." These charges included the " hire of twentie and six horses to carry Thirteene thousand poundes from London to Trewrowe . . . as well as meat for the said horses for tenn daies. Also the wages, diett, horsehire and horsemeat for sixteene men to guard the said Treasure with pistolls and petronells at 6s. a peece for twenty daies going into Cornewall and retourning from thence." (38) The weak point in the system of pre-emption was the difficulty of fixing the price to be paid for the tin, with a view both to allowing the tinners a reasonable margin of profit and to meet the fluctuation of market prices. Cromwell alone really solved the difficulty by abolishing the coinages altogether, and during the ten years of the Commonwealth an unbounded prosperity reigned in the mining areas. With the return of the Monarchy and the reintroduction of coinage, the same difficulties began again. (39)

Long before coinage was finally abolished in the year 1838, the whole system had become a burdensome anachronism. All the privileges and immunities which the tax had formerly secured for the tinners had long since been rendered valueless by change of time and circumstances, while to the producers the delay in business which the coinage entailed had year by year become more intolerable. " If a demand should suddenly arise," wrote the author of a pamphlet in 1833, "and an unforeseen opportunity offer (as has frequently happened), the buyer may be ready on one side and the seller have his commodity on the other, but, through the intervention of this vexatious process, the transaction cannot be completed till the season shall have come round when the futile ceremony of coining may be performed." (40) Nor was delay the only objection to coinage. The machinery of collection had in the course of centuries become so elaborate that the perquisites actually amounted to 1s. 3d. a cwt. over and above the regular tax of 4s. Thus there were fees to cutters, fees to poisers, fees to pilers, fees to scales-

THE TINNERS UNDER THE STANNARIES 41

men, fees for the use of the beam, drink money, gift money, house money, and dinners to the officers of coinage. (41) "The necessity for reform," wrote Mr. Lewis, "was scarcely denied by anyone, and finally, in 1838, the whole system was quietly swept away in favour of a small excise duty levied at the smelting-house." (42)

II

Up to this point use has been made of the term "tin trade" rather than "mining," and "tinner" rather than "miner," in order to avoid the confusion which exists between the early alluvial stream works and underground mining proper. The idea that mining has been carried on in Cornwall "from the coming of the Phœnicians" to the present day is, of course, a complete fallacy, although a very common one. The early tin-works in Cornwall consisted only in laying bare the deposits of detrital ore which were found along the banks of rivers and in the low grounds and moors amongst the granite hills. Everything goes to prove this. In none of the early charters is any hint given of underground operations, while, on the other hand, the frequent mention of "moors" and "streams" shows clearly enough the alluvial nature of the tinners' workings.

Though instances of underground mining existed in very ancient times, (43) Pryce was almost certainly right in thinking them to have been of small extent before the middle of the fifteenth century. (44) Beare, whose account of the stannary of Blackmore was written about 1586, describes only streaming. Carew, in 1602, speaks of streaming and mining, but from the primitive nature of the tinners' tools, consisting of wooden shovels tipped with iron, picks, and wooden bowls, it is clear that the works were still largely in the soft alluvial stage. Indeed, the rich values of the tin found in those "stream" deposits made it unnecessary for the early tinners to seek any farther for their supplies. It was not until the partial exhaustion of the alluvial deposits had begun that the tinners began to look about them for the parent vein or mineral lodes.

A parallel to all this may be found in Nigeria, the Malay

States, or any other young tin-mining country to-day, the only material difference being that the Cornish tinners, not having the assistance of huge mechanical dredgers, turned over the moors by hand, working in little parties with "pick and showl" and diverting the streams from miles around to assist them in their washing operations. The output in their case was accordingly small and the exhaustion of the Cornish tin alluvials was proportionately delayed.

Throughout the streaming period speculation had always been rife amongst the more intelligent tinners as to how the tin had originally found its way into the moors, and for this "Noyes fflood" was generally held responsible. The theory was a useful one, whether true or not, for when the tinner started searching for the lode he had a picture in his mind of a fan-shaped deposit of stones extending downwards and outwards from some point on the hill-side whence the flood had torn them. By following these up from the low grounds at the foot of the hills he discovered, as it were, the handle of the fan, or, in other words, the outcropping of the lode itself. The tracking of the tin stones was performed according to the now lost art of "shodeing," that is, by sinking small pits around the base of the hills and observing the lie of the stones and the direction from which they must have come. Gradually these converging pits would trace the flow of the tin stones to a single line, by following which up the outcrop of the parent lode was almost always found. "When the tinners meet with a loose single stone of tin ore," wrote Pryce, "either in a valley, or in plowing, or in hedging, though at a hundred fathoms distance from the vein it came from, those who are accustomed to this work will not fail to find it out." These veins, or "lodes," as they are always called in the West Country, soon became the chief object of the tinner's attention, and with the first following of them underground, mining in its modern sense had begun, and the streamer had become the first Cornish miner.

The privileges and responsibilities already described as attaching to the stannary system of course affected both streamers and miners equally, for though the nature of their work became, as time went on, increasingly different, both were in the fullest sense of the word "tinners."

Throughout the sixteenth century the Cornish tin works probably consisted more of alluvial workings than of mining proper, and it was not until the seventeenth century, and still more in the eighteenth century, that the latter came to the fore and "streaming" to a certain extent declined. In addition to shodeing there were, of course, many other ways of finding lodes. " Mines have been discovered," wrote Pryce in 1778, "in the sea cliffs, among broken craggy rocks, or by the washing of the tides or floods ; likewise by irruptions and torrents of water issuing out of hills and mountains, and sometimes by the wearing of highroads." A feature regarded by the tinners from earliest times as the favourable indication of mineral was the appearance of the *ignis fatuus*, Will-o'-the-Wisp, or Jack-o'-Lanthorn, which, fifty years ago, were known by the streamers of the Porkellis Moors as " tin lanterns." (45) As might be expected, amongst a whole population concentrated in thought upon the eager search for metals, dreaming geniuses were to be found in almost every mining parish, whose visionary fancies are still commemorated in the name Wheal Dream. The use of the divining-rod and the science of " dowsing " does not appear to have been known in Cornwall before the eighteenth century, and was not therefore among the methods employed by the ancient lode searchers.

Once discovered, the usual way of working the lodes in early times was either by sinking pits upon them, by driving tunnels along their course from the outcrop, or else by exposing them in open trenches known as " coffins " or " goffens." The latter were sometimes fifty or sixty feet in depth and were carried for great distances along the " back." (46) " The largest I have heard of," wrote Carne in 1822, " was at the Sealhole Mine in St. Agnes : it extended nearly half a mile in length, but a considerable part of it has been filled up." Many were still visible a hundred years ago in Wendron, St. Agnes, Madern, Gwinear, and St. Just, where, as in the last-named parish, the word " coffin " is prefixed to the names of several of the lodes— " Coffin Carrarack," " Coffin Garrow," (47) etc.—referring, it is supposed, to the nature of the open workings once existing along their backs. Amongst more modern mines a good example of this kind of work can yet be seen on the Great Perran Iron

Lode. Situated in the borders of a desolate sand country, these mines had for a considerable period remained unworked and the dark chasms had become the haunt of owls, who might frequently be seen fluttering about them, till on some sudden surprise they dropped away into the silent darkness beneath. Side by side with this form of open or daylight workings went, no doubt, much of the early cliff mining, where rich lodes, exposed by the sea or weathering, must soon have attracted the attention of the miner. In some places like the Droskyn Lode at Perranporth, tall graceful arches have been left by the removal of the mineral ground; in others, especially near St. Agnes, the cliffs resemble the section of a rabbit warren, being crossed and recrossed with a labyrinth of little tunnels.

It is clear that the methods adopted in the first mining varied in different places according to the nature of the shallow deposits. In the parish of St. Just, for instance, the floors of tin at shallow depths were doubtless worked at an earlier period than the lodes. Of these "floors," the Bunny at Botallack Mine is the best known. The highest floor here was so shallow as to be level with the surface, and tradition reports it to have been discovered by some of the tinstone having been kicked up by horses going over it. To this succeeded a floor of country from one to three feet thick; then followed a second floor of tin, under which was another floor of country; and in this manner no less than seven floors of tin succeeded each other, the thickness of each being from six to twelve feet. Some of them were full forty feet in diameter, but in general they were not so large. In another part of Botallack there were no less than ten floors of tin. In the tenement of Trewellard likewise were several tin floors wrought near the surface, the deepest, in 1821, being only seven fathoms below it. (48) From the fact that some of these rich deposits were certainly worked at an early period, it appears that the parish of St. Just may be at least as likely as half a dozen other places to have formed the far-famed Cassiterides of the ancients!

The transition from open workings to underground was based on a natural necessity, but it was slow. For centuries all three forms of mining, stream works, cliff workings and shaft mining, went on together side by side. To-day almost every valley and moor, from the Tamar to the Land's End, shows traces of the streamers' presence, not a cliff or headland where there is mineral but the miner has driven in his shallow workings; whilst every hill-side and waste in the mining districts is pitted with shafts and shallow workings. The earliest of these, concerning which we have no record, are all classed together indiscriminately as "old men's workings," and to those who have an eye for such things they seem as milestones in the long course of the industry's progression. From the practical point of view, however, the production of the old men's workings was small indeed and confined to the shallowest levels, so that Cornwall, in spite of its age-long fame as a tin-producing country and the many large mining operations which have been carried out in it during the last hundred years, is still believed by many of the most eminent geologists to contain more tin within its boundaries than has ever yet been removed by all its miners.

NOTES.

1. *Vict. Hist. of Cornwall*, Romano-British Section, 15.
2. *Vict. Hist. of Cornwall*, Romano-British Section.
3. W. C. Borlase, *Sketch of Tin Trade*, 32.
4. Lewis, 39–40.
5. W. C. Borlase, *Sketch of Tin Trade*, 30.
6. Lewis, 58–9.
7. Lewis, 89.
8. *Laws of the Stannaries* (1754), 79.
9. Brit. Mus. Add. MS. 6713, fol. 2.
10. Lewis, 158.
11. To this rule there appear to have been exceptions, Stephen Trevanion, parson of Ladock, complaining in 31st of Edward III that "tin miners have come and mined and dug within the sanctuary of the said church, to the great damage of the said parson, and destruction of the trees and turbary."—Cf. De La Beche, *Geology of Cornwall*, etc., 627.
12. Carew.
13. *Laws of the Stannaries*, 51.
14. *Laws of the Stannaries*, 95.
15. *Laws of the Stannaries*, 62. These were sometimes bequeathed to the Church as an act of piety. Camborne parish possessed a number of tin bounds in the seventeenth century.—Cf. Overseers' Accounts, MS.
16. "Farm" tin = portion payable to the bounder. "Toll" tin = part payable to the lord of the soil out of the bounded land. "Lords'"

dues = money payable where no bounds exist. Cf. F. Hill, *Inquiry into Tin Bounds*, N.D., Morrab Lib., Penzance.

17. *Laws of the Stannaries* (edit. 1808), 61. Bounds, it may be noted, are always spoken of in the plural, i.e. as " a Tin Bounds " or " Pair of Bounds." " Park of bounds " is also frequently used, and probably contained several pairs of bounds. Tin bounds in Devonshire in the eighteenth century were defined by the following limits : " Head Weare, first side Bound north or west. The second, the third, the first side Bound east or south. The second, the third, the Water Leet, the Tail Bound." Cf. Plymouth Inst. 1890-4, 110-12.

18. Papers in Chyandour Office.

19. *Mineralogia Cornubiensis*, 140. The " Bounders' Arms " might be seen as an inn sign in more than one Cornish village within recent years.

20. *Laws of the Stannaries*, 46.

21. B.M. Add. MS. 6713, fol. 152*b*.

22. Tinners' Grievance, 1697.

23. Tonkin. Notes on Carew. Survey of Cornwall.

24. To save confusion in the Devon stannary gaol it was reported by Hals, on I know not what authority (beyond that of the proverbial reputation of " Lidford law "), that prisoners were hanged first and tried afterwards. If found innocent a priest was appointed to pray for their souls. Cf. Add. MS. 29, 762, fols. 57-8.

25. *Laws of the Stannaries*, 34, etc.

26. Proceedings of the Convocation of the Stannaries, by a Cornishman, 1751.

27. Cf. Lewis, 127-30.

28. Lewis, 158, etc.

29. Cal. S.P. Dom. Eliz., 1581-90, 503.

30. Cal. S.P. Dom. Eliz., 1595-7, 372.

31. Cal. S.P. Dom. Eliz., 1595-7, 373.

32. Cf. Carew.

33. This was in 1663. In 1704 little or no tin was received for coinage at Liskeard, whilst at Lostwithiel some 300 or 400 blocks only were coined each quarter, as compared with 2,000 blocks at Truro, 700 at Helston, and 500 at Penzance (MS. in private possession). By 1778, according to Pryce, more tin was coined at Penzance at each quarter than at Liskeard, Lostwithiel, and Helston in a whole year. When coinage was finally discontinued in 1837, the towns were Calstock and St. Austell for the east, and Truro, Helston, Hayle, and Penzance for the west.

34. Lewis, 151.

35. *Laws of the Stannaries*, 121.

36. Maton, 171.

37. *Hist. of Cornwall*, vii, 12.

38. B.M. Add. MS. 5755, fol. 250.

39. Lewis, 220.

40. The Tin Duties, 1833.

THE TINNERS UNDER THE STANNARIES

41. The Tin Duties, 1833.
42. *The Stannaries*, 156.
43. Cf. infra, chap. on Underground Men.
44. Cf. Pryce, *Mineralogia Cornubiensis*, 141.
45. In the Icelandic Grettis-Saga the hero Grettir's courage is displayed in the rifling of the barrow of Karr the Old. Perceiving the appearance of a flame above the tumulus, he knows it to be a sign of hidden treasure.
46. It is stated by Hunt and several other writers that the old men were in the habit of planting " scaws," i.e. elder-trees, to mark the course of lodes, the mouths of adits, etc. This I have heard more than once confirmed by oral tradition as well as having personally observed its truth. On the opening up of an old wet mine called Wheal Freedom in the estate of Craskin, near Helston, about 1855, an enormous " skaw " tree was observed growing over the shaft, which many of the adventurers regarded as a good indication of riches being left by the old workers. Some of the more timid, however, pointed out a thorn-tree just opposite, which they claimed was the old men's sign that the work was poor. This was a conundrum, till suddenly one of the adventurers exclaimed : " Don't you see they had got a good thing, but on account of the water 'twas hard to come by."—R. Cunnack MS.
47. Better known than these is Coffin Crista, one of the lodes of the famous Botallack Mine. This, however, according to Henwood, was spelt Corpus Christi on old plans.
48. R.G.S.C., ii, 326-1.

CHAPTER II

STREAMERS AND BLOWERS

I

"THE tinners of Cornwall," wrote a traveller in 1810, "may be divided into two classes, the streamers and miners. They are men who are occupied in two distinct departments of the same general branch, but whose habits, manners, customs, genius and understanding bear little or no resemblance to each other." (1)

Everyone who knows Cornwall to-day might be expected to know something of the Cornish miner, his work, his dress, and his general characteristics. The streamer, on the other hand, is a far more elusive person, almost akin to the "Jacky Lantern" of the moors in which he worked. Here and there he may be found just mentioned in the older books on Cornwall, but, compared with the miner, he has led for the last hundred years but a shadowy existence, seemingly only half on the borders of reality, a ghost from the industry's past. In the first part of this chapter, devoted more particularly to streamers, (2) is brought together for the first time information gathered from many sources, books, and MSS., and conversations with old people who had themselves been streamers, as were their fathers before them.

In popular conception the Cornish tinners, from Elizabethan times onward, seem to have been regarded as a rough, hardy, and lawless crew, dwelling more or less without the pale of civilization, in the confines of "West Barbary." "Her Majesty and you," explained a writer to Lord Burghley in 1586, "have placed Sir Walter Raleigh as Lord Warden of the Stannaries, but amongst so rough and mutinous a multitude, 10,000 or 12,000, the most strong men of England. It were meet their governor were one whom the most part well accounted of, using some familiarity and abiding amongst them." (3) Poor and unlearned as the tinners were, dwelling in the midst of the wild moors where they were cut off even from the rest of the population of Cornwall, few people at that time would have followed the latter part of the writer's advice, and it is certain that "proud" Raleigh never did. Yet those whose business necessitated their living amongst the tinners give a much more pleasing account of their character.

"About 36 years past," said a writer in 1586, "my fortune was to be present at a wash of a Tynne work in Castle Park by Lostwithiall, where there was a certain gentleman present whom I could name, gatheringe out from the heap of tynn certain glorious cornes affirmed them to be pure gold which the tynners permitted him very gently, as they will gentilly suffer any man to doe most chiefly if any of liberalitie will be shown amongst them, but the value of one 2d. to drink, then shall you have them very diligently go to their Buddles themselves and seek out amongst their cornes of tynne which they call Rux, the finest and most radiant cornes and present them to you." (4)

The usual manner of setting a mine or stream of alluvial tin on work in Elizabethan times was as follows :—

"When the ground intiseth with probabilitie of profit, the discoverer doth commonly associate himselfe with some more partners, because the charge amounteth mostly verie high for any one man's purse, except lined beyond ordinarie, and if the worke doth faile, many shoulders will more easily support the burden. These partners consist either of such Tinners as worke to their owne behoofe, or of such adventurers as put in hired labourers. If the worke carrie some importance, and require the travaile of many hands, they elect one of their company, whom they terme their Captaine." (5) "Then," continues another writer, "make they a Goad or rodd (6) pard (6) four square, being in length or shortness according to the number of workers in this Goad. Every one of these fellow workers shall have his place skotched out to him which they call that man's park" (? Cornish "field"). To this working place it was the captain's duty to see that each man applied himself diligently. To the "park" every man paid so much a day, which was termed "spale," and each tinner brought his own tools, the cost of them being taken into consideration when pay-day came. If a man fell sick in bed, his spale, we are told, "was reduced during the time of his illness."

If, on the other hand, he was sick but able to come to the work and just sit by on the "burrough," he paid nothing at all.

"The like cherishing," says the same writer, "they use among them that if one of their work fellows, altho the simplest of them all, fall sick at his work, this fellow shall be cherished amongst them and the best bottle of drink shall be sought for him, yea *aqua vitæ* itself or any good preservation that they can come by shall speedy be sent to comfort this sick man, and in conclusion they appoint men diligently to bring him home to his house, if he is not able to go himself, with no less care than if he had been their father, brother, or natural Child." (7)

"The most part of the workers of the black tyn and spaliars, however, are very poor men," wrote Beare, in his account of the stannary of Blackmore, in 1586, "as no doubt that occupation can never make them rich. And chiefly such tyn workers as have no bargains but only trust to their wages, although they have never so rich a tynworke, they have no profit of their tyn if they be hired men, saving only their wages, for their masters have their tyn. Now, if they should chance to be farmers (8) themselves and their work fall bad, then run they most chiefly in their master's debt. The farmer knoweth not how his work will doe until time hath proved it and must needs live in hope all the year which for the most part deceiveth him. Concerning the wages of the tynner working his dole, on the other hand, the common wages is but £3 a year. Yet must the worker find himself meat and drink, which is little above 2d. a day. This poor man, happily, hath a wife and four or five small children to care for, which all depend upon his getting—whereas all his wages is not able to buy himself bread. Then, to pass over the poor man's house, rent, cloathing for his poore wife and children besides divers other charges daily growing upon them—O, God, how can this poore man prosper? Yet this much I confess. Of the wealthiest tynners which happily worke together in one tyn worke with the poor man, they are very charitable and merciful towards their poore fellow-workers. For at dinner time, when they sit down together beside their tynwork, in a little lodge made up with turfes covered with straw, and made about with handsome benches to sit upon— then every tynner bringeth forth out of his scrip or tyn **bagges,**

STREAMERS AND BLOWERS 51

his victuals, his bread, his bottle of drink, as the rich tynners will lack none of them—then is their charitie so great that if one, two, three or else more poore men sit amongst them, having neither bread, drink or other repast, there is not one amongst all the rest but will distribute at the largest sort with their poor workfellows that have nothing. So that in the end this poor man having nothing to relieve him at the worke, shall in fine be better furnished of bread, cheese, butter, beefe, pork and bacon than all the richest sorte." (9)

Thus at least two classes of tinners were employed in the sixteenth-century stream works—the working adventurer, and the hired labourer or spalliar put in by the non-working adventurer. The spalliar, as has already been described, was the poorest class of tinner, receiving a fixed wage in money without any chance of gain from the fluctuations of value in the stream of tin. The working adventurer and the non-working adventurer, on the other hand, received their shares, not in money, but in kind. The periodical sharing up of the tin stones or "braws," as they were called, provided the tinners with various opportunities for merry pranks, concerning which a sixteenth-century writer may be quoted in his own words :—

"When a Gentleman or a husbandman having rights working among them happly sendeth a servant of his house to save his hired Tynn, himself for the day being occupied about other business, after time that it falleth late toward the eventide, then consent they together for dividing of their Tynn stones which they call brawes. . . . Then gather they together as many heaps of stones as they be workers in the Tynn work, appointing this Gent's servant to chose out his Master's part of the brawes, because his master is a gentleman and they would in no wise absent or seem to defraud him of his right. The poor man meaning good diligent service toward his Master choosing the greatest heap of all the other (which are nothing else but great black stones without any tynn, good for no purpose), and to please his Master the better one knave or other giveth him of their part of the stones, saying that they are very good Tynn braws, which the poor man taketh very thankfully and home straight to his Master goeth he, heavily loaden with stones, with his skripp, bosom and breeches all stuff up with black stones.

He when he cometh home to his Master braggeth to him of his good success of his braws, forthwith presenting them. The Gentleman knowing the merry use of the Tynners, prayseth very much his servant diligence and commendeth him for a profitable servant." (10)

The arrival of a new hand at a tin-work was also the signal for the playing off of a number of "merry devices," more especially if he appeared an ignorant or simple fellow. One of these was to send him on an errand to the next work, to borrow a " Cord to meet their work with," or else maybe a barrow. On his arrival at that work they would send him on to the next, and so on all the day, the poor man in the meantime at a loss to know what it is all about. "Some, however," says the writer, "pretend to be more simple than they are, and go merely and lie and loyter under a tree, returning at night pretending to great weariness." (11)

Yet another "merry device" used and known amongst the tinners of the whole stannary of Blackmore was this: "When occasion of talke is ministred of Owls, foxes, hares, Catts or Ratts, then it behoveth them to beware chiefly, for then must you speake in Tynners' language and in no other language than Tynners have decreed. The Owle must be called a *braced farcer*, the fox a *long Tayle*, the hare a *long ear*, the Catt a *Rooker*, and the Ratt a *peep*. (12) The tynners often introduce these words of a set purpose that they may bring you to name some one of these. Yea, sometime the cunningest of them, forgetting their terms or thinking of no such matter, may be deceived into not naming a fox a Long tail, or Catt a Rooker, etc. This fellow in misusing his terms is guilty of a very heinous offence, but in no danger of death or pillory, but is finable or rated by decree of all the Tinners of Blackmore which is to pay for a gallon of ale, for this drink shall speedily be fetched at the ale house and as merrily drank amongst them." (13)

Charitable as the tinners were towards one another and courteous to visitors to their works, they yet possessed a keen eye for the monopoly of their industry, and were very jealous of interlopers. The same writer states that "if any Britton, Frenchman, stranger, alien, etc., search, digg or mine for tin," all the tin they raised was to be forfeited and themselves committed to Launceston Gaol. (14) It is true that in 1620 a petition of the Stannators speaks of certain working tinners "in number and degree the least and meanest part of us," as being "for the most part foreigners and hired to work in our Tinworks for day wages," (15) but it is quite probable that many even of these were "furriners" only in the Cornish sense of the word, and hailed from no farther off than some neighbouring county, or, at most, from Ireland.

During the fifteenth century, however, considerable numbers of German miners were finding their way into England, where, on account of their superior knowledge of ore extraction and metallurgy, their presence was encouraged by English mine-owners. (16) By the sixteenth century, at any rate, several of these men had come to Cornwall. About the year 1580, Sir Francis Godolphin, one of the greatest of the early Cornish mine-owners, had over a German mineral man, by name Burchard Cranyce, or Craneigh, to assist him at his works near Godolphin. He it was who, in all probability, supervised the erection of the first stamps in Cornwall, which are traditionally said to have been set up by a member of the Godolphin family. (17)

In 1584 another German, Ulricke Frose, was in charge of mining operations and copper smelting at Peran Sands. Here he seems to have actually introduced German miners, much to the disgust of one of the adventurers, who complained of the high wages paid to Dutch (*sic*) miners "when Cornish men may serve so well at less charges." "English miners," he writes, "are as skilful as any in Europe," and to prove it he proposes a competition with the German labourers at the works at Treworthye. Knowing what the Cornishmen felt about the introduction of foreigners into their mines, the uproar likely to have resulted from such a "competition" may well be imagined. The upshot was that Ulricke, after writing pathetically that his sight was failing him through care and want of sleep, was shortly afterwards removed to the smelting-house at Neath, "as more suited to his quietness."

German workmen, indeed, were not destined always to bear away the palm in respect of skill in mining and metallurgical operations, and the Cornish were already to the forefront in these matters. In 1607–8 a King's Warrant to the Warden of the Duchy of Cornwall says that, "in our sylver mine lately discovered in our Realme of Scotland, We think fitt to use the service of some of the Myners of our Duchie of Cornwall whoe are held to be the best experienced and most exercised in such workes of all other our People. We therefore command you to order to our Deputie Warden to levie within our said Duchie Twentie Myners of the ablest bodies and best experienced in such workes and to send them forthwith into Scotland, assuringe them that they shall have there good usage and good paye. . . . And further our pleasure is that you cause to be levied (over and above the aforesaid Twentie Myners) the number of XIII personnes more to be ymploied in that our Service, viz., Captaine Tymberers, Twoe. Smythes for hard worke, Twoe. Ruffbudlers, Twoe. For a leavell budle, One. Boylers, Twoe. For the Canves, Twoe. For the Colerake, Twoe." (18)

The clearest account of streaming, as indeed of all other forms of mining during the eighteenth century period, is that given by Pryce :—

"When a streaming Tinner," he writes, "observes a place favourable in situation, he takes a lease, commonly called a set, of the landowner or lord of the fee, and agrees to pay him a certain part in Black Tin, that is tin ore made clean from all waste and ready for smelting. The consideration is generally 1/6th, 1/7th, 1/8th or 1/9th, as can be settled between them, or instead thereof the streamer contracts to employ so many men and boys, and to pay the landowner for liberty from 20s. to 30s. a year for each man, and proportionately for each boy. He then sinks a hatch (or shaft) three, five or seven fathoms deep on to the rocky 'shelf' or clay bed on which the Tin gravel lies stratified in the bottom of the valleys." (19)

In the course of one of the workings of the famous stream of alluvial tin at Pentuan in 1852, the head of one of these old shafts or hatches was discovered about ten feet below the then level of the valley. It was filled with the sand of which the superimposed ten feet was composed, and its depth to the tin shelf on the rock below was about fifteen feet. The square framework of the shaft was made of oak, blackened throughout by age and having the ends regularly morticed, though the tenons were very small compared to those now made. The interstices

STREAMERS AND BLOWERS

of this framework were formed of oak twigs similarly blackened and regularly interlaced. At the bottom of this shaft was found an arrow-head, together with a small chisel about eight inches long, both apparently made of an extremely hard alloy. (20)

The stratum of stream tin found on the shelf varied from one to ten feet in thickness, and in breadth from one fathom to almost the width of the valley. In actual size the tinstones varied from a walnut to the finest sand, the latter constituting the principal part of the tin stuff, which was intermixed with stones, gravel, and clay, just as it was torn from the adjacent hills. After sinking the shaft on to this gravel-bed, the tinner tried a sample of tin on his shovel, in order to judge whether the place was worth working or not. Some places were poor, others very rich. The latter were called by the tinners in their native Cornish, " Beuheyle," or in English, " Living Stream." Having decided to work the ground, the streamer then " goes down to the lowest or deepest part of the valley and digs an open trench, called a 'level,' taking the utmost care to lose no levels in bringing it home to his place of working." This level served to carry off all water and waste from the workings. The streamer then proceeded to remove the overburden, viz. the loose earth, rubble, and stone which covered the tin, " so far and so large as he can manage with conveniency to his employment." If, in the progress of his work, he was hindered by water, he " teemed " (or laded) it out with a scoop, or else discharged it by a hand pump. If these simple devices proved insufficient, he generally erected a rag and chain pump, or, better still, if a rivulet of water was to be rented cheaply, a water-wheel with balance-bobs. This latter invention, which was similar to those employed in small mines, served effectually to keep the water to a certain depth, and was extensively employed by streamers from early times. (21)

About the year 1812 a party of streamers, at work on what they supposed to be a piece of untouched ground in Drift Moor, near Penzance, found, six feet below the surface, an ancient water-engine (i.e. rag and chain pumps) made almost completely out of wood. The wheel was twelve feet in diameter, the different parts being fastened together by wood pins. The pump appeared to have been made from one piece of timber sawn in two lengthwise and each part scooped out, so that when united they formed a tube of seven inches in diameter. The small buckets connected to the chain were also of wood. The only iron in the whole machine consisted of the milliards of the wheel, two bends on the axle, and the chain of the pump. (22) For what cause it was abandoned thus beneath the surface of the moors, whether on account of some overwhelming flood or other disaster, remains one of the many mysteries connected with mining.

Whilst such engines as these were being erected for keeping the workings clear of water, the men continued digging up the tin and washing it by casting each shovelful into a "tye," or an inclined plane of boards over which a cascade of water ran. Here the tin was turned over and over again with a shovel, till, the water having "flitted away" the lighter waste, the heavier ore only remained, consisting of more than half tin. The rubbish from the tail of the tye, being allowed to flow into the rivers, was carried down in some cases as far as the sea, causing much damage to otherwise arable ground in the valleys, as well as silting up creeks which were formerly accessible to shipping. Though laws were made at various times from the reign of Henry VIII onwards to restrain tinners from allowing silt to flow into rivers, they seem to have had little effect, and the present state of the Hayle River, in which the tide formerly flowed above St. Erth Bridge, or the Par Estuary, where it used to reach to St. Blazey Bridge, bears witness to the damage done by streamers and latter-day miners.

The first operation of cleansing the stream tin took place in the bottom of the level, where, as has been said, a stream of water flowed. After this the different grades of ore, carefully picked and separated, were raised to the surface of the moors, where they underwent a second cleansing in a small tye called a "gounce." The finest tin of all was lastly treated by passing it through sieves of wire or horsehair, the latter being known as a "dilluer" and requiring considerable skill in its manipulation. After two such washings the richer tin was ready straightway for the blowing-house. The poorer grade ore, on the other hand, had generally to be crushed, like mine tin, in order to separate it from the waste with which it was associated. (23)

In early times this operation of crushing was performed by a crazing mill, consisting of an upper and a nether grinding-stone. On the back of the upper stone of one of these mills found on Dartmoor were four holes, at equal distances from each other and from the central " eye " hole. Into these holes prongs were evidently fitted which carried two bars, so that the stone could be revolved by either horse or man power. The tin stuff inserted through the central " eye " was ground to sand between the revolving upper and the stationary nether stone, and passed out at the sides.

This primitive type of mill, corresponding to the Roman hand-mill, doubtless sufficed for most stream tin. (24) The larger nodules, however, were probably broken down by hand on the rocks containing circular cavities which are found in many of the Cornish streaming districts and in nearly all the Dartmoor blowing-houses. The size of these cavities or depressions varies considerably; nine inches by nine and five inches deep might perhaps be taken as an average. In every case they are polished quite smooth, a result evidently obtained by attrition.

"There is very little doubt," writes Mr. Burnard of the Dartmoor stones, " that these cavities are ancient mortars used by the 'old men' for pounding up the larger nodules of stream tin or else for breaking up the slag, so as to get at the prills or globules of tin contained in the same after the first smelting. They are not moulds ; for they are too numerous and their interiors are too smooth to have been the receptacles of molten metal. They cannot have been the bottom stones of primitive stamps, for if formed in the process of stamping they would have partaken more of the shape of a stamp-head, which certainly has never been round and pointed. They cannot have been formed by revolving crazing-mill spindles—their shape and number on a single stone forbids this. The traditionary idea among the moormen is that they were used for *beating up the tin*, (25) and this is also confirmed by a like belief amongst the Cornish tinners." The pestle used with these mortars was probably a heavy rounded stone or " bully," though iron may have been used.

It is clear, however, that from comparatively early times water-power was employed for crushing down the poorer grade ore, insomuch that the townsmen of Plymouth complained in 1600 that the course of their water was being diverted contrary to statute by the number of "clash-mylls" set up on the river flowing from Roburghe Downs. (26)

The best account of streaming after Pryce's time is to be found in Hitchens and Drew's *History of Cornwall* (1824), where the working of a stream with a shallower overburden is thus described :—

"A set having been taken up according to the rules prescribed by stannary law, a stream of water is conducted on the surface to the spot where the tinner intends to begin his operations. At the same time a level is also brought home to the spot from below, as deep as the ground will permit and the workings require, in order to carry off the sand and water. The ground is then opened at the extremity nearest the sea or the discharge of the water ; from which place the streamers proceed towards the hill. On the ground thus laid open, a stream of water is turned in from the surface, which, running over an almost perpendicular descent, washes off the lighter parts of such ground as has been previously broken by picks, carrying them through the under-level called the 'tye,' and leaving behind the sandy ore, and such stones as are too heavy to be thus removed. In this stream the men, provided with boots for the purpose, continue to stand, keeping the sand and gravel at the bottom in motion. From it they select the larger rubbish, throwing it on one side, picking from their shovels such shode as appears. The precipice over which the water runs is called the 'breast' ; the rubbish thrown away, 'stent' ; the sand, including tin, 'gard' ; the walls on each side of the tye, 'stiling' ; and the more worthless parts which are driven away by the stream, 'tailings.' The gard, the shode, and occasional pebbles of pure tin ore that are found, being carefully selected from the 'stent' and 'tailings,' undergo a separation. The pebbles, if pure, are reserved for smelting ; the shode, when the stones are large, is broken by 'sledges' until reduced to a convenient size for the stamps. The gard, on the other hand, though also prepared for the same stamps, is first put through another process. Being taken from the tye and laid on its banks, it is collected together and carried to a small floor, where an oblong pit is made resembling a grave,

STREAMERS AND BLOWERS

but not more than two or three feet deep and known as the 'gounce.' Above it is placed, on an inclined plane, a frame of iron bars called a 'ruddle,' bearing some resemblance to a gridiron. At the head of this a stream of water is continually running, into which the gard is thrown with a shovel. The gard, being carried to the ruddle by the water, undergoes a separation, the more stony parts being thrown off by the bars, while the finer, in which the tin is chiefly lodged, are carried by the water through the ruddle and from thence into the gounce below. In this gounce the gard is wholly confined, but as its bed lies on an inclined plane, the heavier and richer parts stay near its head, while the more inferior parts are carried towards its extremity. When the gounce is full, these parts are taken out and deposited in distinct heaps, from whence they are taken to stamps with the shode." (27)

Streaming, as will thus be seen, was in most cases a fairly simple undertaking requiring the outlay only of comparatively small sums of capital. The most famous, however, and perhaps the richest of all Cornish alluvial streams, namely, that of Carnon, situated on a branch of the Falmouth River, was worked in the early decades of the last century under conditions of such extraordinary difficulty as might well tax the powers of the best modern engineering equipment of to-day.

Carnon stream, as Henwood first saw it about the year 1816, consisted of "a machine in a desert of red sand, heaped into vast piles and bollows. The only herbage visible was a few tufts of the sea daisy, whilst here and there in the trenches might be seen the tinners working knee-deep in water and a few squalid half-clad boys wheeling the tin ore to the stream-head in barrows." (28) As time went on the tin-bearing ground was found to extend more and more towards the flow of the river, and it became necessary to build a dam to keep back the tide. At length this ground, too, became exhausted and a series of shafts had to be sunk, with the aid of coffer-dams, in the mud one hundred and twenty yards from the shore, whence they were drained by engines with flat rods carried out on piers. The workers were now forced to support the whole roof of the mine, a difficult task indeed, it being composed of loose friable material with the added weight of many thousands of tons of water above it. The depth of the stream at neap tides was never less than six feet, whilst at the spring tides it varied from ten to sixteen feet, and even more at the equinoxes. "I have seen," wrote Henwood, "a vessel of 200 tons burthen directly over the mine when the miners must have been at work about fifty or sixty feet below her keel." The levels were supported with wooden planks and pillars from seven to eleven inches thick. The main levels were four by six feet, the side levels slightly less in size. When worked out, the ground was allowed to fall in, the increase of water from this cause being never sufficient to retard the course of the work. At length the river became so broad that the shafts could no longer be reached with flat rods, since the vibration was so great that the power of the engine was diminished by more than one-half when applied to the pumps in the shaft. At the point where the tin ground continued richest, the river expands and is nearly a mile wide and twelve or sixteen feet deep. Here the adventurers actually were obliged to construct an island, a feat of engineering which with infinite pains, labour, skill, perseverance and cost was at length effected, though not before the tide, driven by gales of wind, had on two or three occasions washed away in a single night the labour of months. At last, however, an island some thirty or forty yards in diameter was formed by countless boatloads of sand obtained from the river-bed nearby. The question now was how to sink a shaft in a parcel of loose sand so recently put together. To effect this a cylinder was made twelve feet in diameter, of wrought-iron plates, riveted together. This was forced into the sand and buried by placing a platform on top of the cylinder and weighting it with stones. Another series of plates was then built on to the buried cylinder and sunk in a like manner. Sometimes the enormous weight of a hundred tons was required to accomplish this. The shaft having been made, piles had to be driven into the sand on which to erect the two steam-engines. This extraordinary mine at length reached the producing stage and was worked for some years, the tin gravel yielding as plentifully as ever and going richer all the time under the middle of the river. It was not until the 'fifties of the last century that the Carnon alluvial stream was considered to be fully worked out. (29)

STREAMERS AND BLOWERS

Such an undertaking as this, however, was by no means usual in alluvial streaming, which in later as in earlier times was much more frequently carried on by a few families on their own in the rough moorlands, or financed on a small scale by one or two small local adventurers. The accounts which old people still living give of such streaming sixty years ago show how conservative this branch of the industry remained and how little changed in its methods from those employed in ancient times.

The streaming "sets" were generally taken for a year at a time, from May to May, by a "pare" or company consisting of two men and four boys, (30) as often as not all members of a single family. The system then pursued was to put up a small water-wheel eight to twelve feet in diameter to drain the pits or "hatches." The soil from top to bottom was next turned over and roughly washed over a grate, a turf being placed beneath to catch the finest grains of tin. The gravel was afterwards stripped and the "head" searched for the prills of tin, which were picked out by hand from among the worthless "kegs." Large rough stones placed in the bottom kept the drainage good as the workings advanced, the waste being constantly thrown backwards. The tin was in black grains, generally much waterworn. In the Porkellis Moors, where these accounts were mainly gathered, it was formerly a curious sight to see each of the little piles of selected tin gravel left by the streamers planted with sprigs of furze or prickly thorn, to prevent them being swallowed by the geese, of which great numbers pastured in the moors. Throughout the length and breadth of the Porkellis Valley it was rare to meet with a piece of ground which had not been turned over at least once by the countless generations of streamers who had worked there. Yet in spite of this it was said that sixty or seventy years ago, even with the low price of tin then ruling, a steady man with moderate industry rarely failed to make a living for himself and his family on the moors, although the actual amount of stuff thus raised by hand labour and washed in the rudest manner was small. (31)

The streamers, however, were frugal and saving. It was related that one man, out of a wage of two guineas a month, contrived to save £100, and many families still living in the neighbourhood have by their industry and economy raised themselves to positions of independence. Seventy or eighty years ago twenty "pares" or more of men were at work in the Porkellis Moors, a company for the most part agreeing amicably enough. Thus in wet weather, or if any work lay more than ordinarily deep, so as to render the small pumps inadequate, all would come together to assist in the work of baling out the water. Then, at the end of the week, resort would be made to some neighbouring inn or "kiddlywink," where homely bread and butter was qualified with a little liquor which had probably never known the custom officers' inspection. (32) Only in the drought of summer was the harmony of the stream works sometimes broken, for, as a sixteenth-century tinner noted, "A stream work being without water is even as a windmill without wind." There were at one time two parties in these moors known as Mamalukes and Pirates, between whom feelings ran particularly high. At such times each would with their shovels be cutting down and building up the watercourses to spite the other—until the season changed, when both used to fall to work once more in peace and harmony. (33) It was a fine thing then, so those who can remember say, to see the streamers at dinner-time repairing to their moor-houses, and as their songs arose to hear that now silent valley "ringing with praise to the God of Heaven."

Many of the streamers of older times, a hundred years and more ago, found smuggling a profitable side-line to their trade, and the wild moors wherein their stream works lay a most effective hiding-place for secreting their goods after a successful run :—

"No riding officer would like to venture among the stream leats and bogs in Trewe Moors," an old West-Country tinner told Mr. Bottrell, in the course of one of those rambling conversations which throw so much light on the secluded life of West Cornwall in the past. "Scores of ankers (barrels) of Brandy were often kept among the burrows till the innkeepers, gentry, and other regular customers wanted them. Now and then there was a bit of a shindy with the streamers, excisemen, and riding officer for mere sham, and the smugglers would leave an anker or two, now and then, to be taken in places where they never kept their stock. This served for a decoy, and the Government crew knew well enow that that was their share and they had better not look for any more."

In some cases the streamers built quite large moor-houses, and when the men lived far from their work, or there was much liquor to be guarded, frequently remained for a week at a time, only going home to visit their families on Sundays and to procure a fresh lot of provisions. Moor-houses of this sort might be more than thirty feet long and twelve feet wide, provided with a broad, deep chimney in one end and a wood corner that would hold a cartload of turfs, and furze enough to do the cooking for a week. Between the fireplace and the end wall of the house was contrived a place to be entered from the wood corner, large enough for storing away a score of ankers or more, besides other goods which required to be kept dry. When the wood corner was full no person could see that the chimney-end wall was double. A low doorway, no more than four feet high, was made in the middle of one side wall. There was room enough and to spare on the left side of the entrance to pile up more tin than they ever washed out in six months; so they had no occasion to take their stuff to the smelting-house when the price was low. On the chimney side of the door, some planks fastened to stakes driven into the floor kept together, quite tidy like, a few burns (bundles) of heath, rushes, ferns, or straw, which served for the men to stretch themselves on when they remained overnight. There were frequently no windows but the port-holes all round, which were wanted to have a shot at the wildfowl that came over the moors in large flocks in the winter.

"Well," said Uncle Jan, "those old moor-houses were comfortable places enough, with the tin piled up in one end, a blazing turf fire in the other, and plenty of good liquor. We lived there like fighting-cocks. When we wished to have a few rabbits for a pie, we had only to go out with a dog and half a dozen nets to set in the gaps round a barley arish and come back in an hour or two with as many rabbits as were wanted for a week."

Many of the hardy old gentlemen from the town and about, who often came over the moors hunting in the winter, would thus stop and pass a jolly night with the streamers, and would while away the time with stories and age-long traditions of the Cornish people concerning the appearance of the knackers and piskies and the crocks of buried gold beneath the carns, till morning broke." (34)

The streamer, like the modern china-clay worker, was generally a man of fine build and splendid health, engendered by open-air work and the action of piggal (beat-axe) and visgey (pick) in expanding his muscles. (35) It was the streamer rather than the miner (who, although wiry, is generally slight) who won for Cornishmen that reputation for wide shoulders which is said to have made a Cornish regiment take more room on the parade ground than any other.

The streamer of sixty years ago, in his working dress consisting of a striped blanketing shirt, with jacket and trousers of the same, and huge knee-boots (broogs) plaited with iron, was a strange and picturesque figure. "A party of them returning from their work sounded like the shambling gait of a troop of horses," said a writer in 1810. (36)

In the streets of Penzance on a feast day or Saturday afternoon, the more prosperous "high country" tinner could always be recognized in his blue smock-frock, corduroy trousers, ruddy with tin stuff, and high-poled Sunday hat. (37) Living in remote and desolate places, their conversation and ideas were largely confined to their own class, and amongst them beliefs in omens and spirit influences presiding over every action remained late. "The burning of a candle, the colour of a flame, the emission of sparks from the half-extinguished embers, were all ominous and portended some future event. The chattering of magpies, the croaking of ravens, the howling of dogs, were all portentous of disaster. Of magpies it was said :—

> One is sorrow, two is mirth
> Three is a wedding, and four is death.

But if the hearer spat towards these birds while uttering these notes of destiny, the spell was broken and the charm dissolved. If you showed money to the new moon you were certain to have some gift before the moon disappeared, in proportion to the value of the coin you showed. If the palm of your hand itched, you would have something given you very soon, but of uncertain value. Similarly the white specks which appeared under your thumb-nail were of the same indication, but similar

A CORNISH MINER

GRANITE MOULD FOR CASTING INGOTS OF TIN IN A BLOWING-HOUSE. (See p. 70)

GRINDING-MILL AND POUNDING-STONES FOR TIN ORE. (See p. 57)

AS USED BY THE OLD TINNERS

STREAMER USING SQUARE BUDDLE, TREVAUNANCE, 1924 (See p. 339)

AN IMPROVISED VENTILATING COWL.

FREE-SETTING TRIBUTERS OF TO-DAY

specks under the nails of the fingers were considered portentous of disasters, and both gifts and disasters were sure to take place when the ominous specks grew out sufficiently to be cut off. Such beliefs as these, although especially noted amongst tinners by the above-quoted writer in 1810, were not at that time confined to any one section of the people. The character of the tinner, however, for reasons already indicated, probably changed more slowly than the rest of the population.

At home by his fireside of piled-up turfs, Couch found him in 1866 no less interesting a being than of old, and this not only on account of the peculiar manner of his life, unchanged from ancient times, but "for the stores of wild tradition with which he will entertain you if long acquaintance has entitled you to his confidence." (38) As late as 1866 the streamers of East Cornwall were still in the habit of keeping several feasts and holidays seemingly peculiar to themselves, or else so long neglected by the rest of the population as to have been forgotten. Writing of the ancient stannary of Blackmore, Couch says : "The first red-letter day in the tinners' calendar is Paul's Pitcher-day, or the eve of Paul's Tide (January 24th). It is marked by a very curious custom, not only among tin streamers, but also in the mixed mining and agricultural town and neighbourhood of Bodmin, and among the seafaring population of Padstow. On the day before the Feast of St. Paul, a water-pitcher is set up at a convenient distance, and pelted with stones until entirely demolished. The men then leave work and adjourn unto a neighbouring alehouse, where a new pitcher, bought to replace the old one, is successively filled and emptied, and the evening is given up to merriment and misrule."

On inquiry amongst the tinners, Couch found this generally upheld as an ancient festival intended to celebrate the day when tin was first turned into metal—in fact, the discovery of smelting. It was, too, the occasion of a revel, in which, as an old streamer observed, there was an open rebellion against the water-drinking system enforced upon them whilst at work. At Bodmin the boys were accustomed, on Paul's Eve, to slink along the streets and hurl a pitcher, commonly stolen and filled with unsavoury contents, into any house where the door had been incautiously left open, a custom borrowed from Shrovetide.

The next feast observed by the streamers of Blackmore was "Friday in Lide," (39) or the First Friday in March. "I have heard this archaism," wrote Couch, "only among tinners, where it exists in such sayings as ' Ducks won't lay till they've a drink'd lide water.' Friday in Lide was marked by the serio-comic custom of sending a young lad on the highest ' bound ' or hillock of the work, and allowing him to sleep there as long as he could ; the length of his siesta being the measure of the afternoon nap for the tinners throughout the ensuing twelve months. The weather, as may well be imagined, was not usually conducive to a prolonged sleep at this period of the year, especially in the high moorlands of the Bodmin district." It was still, however, the custom in East Cornwall eighty years ago for husbandmen to sleep in the middle of the day during certain portions of the year. Perhaps it still is !

Midsummer Day, which was much celebrated at this time by the miners of West Cornwall, was observed by the East Cornwall streamers only by the elevation of a bush or tall pole on the highest eminence of their "work." Another tinners' feast, however, more especially kept up in the stannary of Blackmore, was "Picrous Day," or the Second Thursday before Christmas, which was celebrated by a supper and much merry-making. To this festivity the owner of the tin stream contributed at the rate of 1s. per man. The tradition amongst the tinners was that this feast was intended to commemorate the discovery of tin by a man named " Picrous " and had nothing to do, as Couch once thought, with the pasties and pies consumed at it. Who, or what, this " Picrous " was is difficult to say. The feast, however, falls on the same day as " Chewidden," (40) on which, according to the western men's tradition, tin was first smelted. It may be noted, too, that Friday in Lide very nearly corresponds with St. Piran's Day (March 5th), which, during the second half of the eighteenth century, was still observed by western miners as a general holiday, money being allowed in all the considerable mines for the men to make merry. It is nevertheless curious that the Blackmore streamers, amongst whom the remembrance of ancient feasts seemed to have survived longest, knew nothing, in 1866, of either St. Piran's Day or Chewidden ; whilst amongst the streamers of West Cornwall the only day especially observed in latter years was Midsummer. (41) On this day a pole surmounted by a bush of sycamore would be erected on the highest bank of the work, and when night came on great bundles of furze, fifty or more in number, were ignited and might be seen blazing away in all parts of the moors.

Though all such celebrations as these are now disused and streaming itself has long been moribund, it is hardly yet quite dead. Within recent times it is said that in some of the out-of-the-way moors amongst the granite hills of mid-Cornwall one or two men might be found at work on a patch of tin alluvial, and here, labouring in much the same way as their forefathers worked in the days before London was a town, they formed the living link between the present and an immemorially ancient past.

II

In the bringing of tin to its "white" or metallic state almost as many subsidiary trades were employed in the days of streaming as there are to-day.

After being washed and prepared for smelting in some place adjoining the work, stream tin, like that from the mines, was placed in little canvas bags on horseback (42) and carried often miles across country to the nearest blowing-house. In early times dogs are said to have been employed for this purpose on Dartmoor, being lighter of foot in crossing the quags and morasses in winter. (43) The introduction of mules for carrying probably dates in Cornwall from the seventeenth century. Cornishmen of Elizabethan times were still apt to regard them as monsters, and "some were so wise as to knocke on the head or give away the issue of this race as uncouth mongrels." (44) On the backs of either horses or "moyles" almost the whole merchandise of the county continued to be carried till late in the eighteenth century :—

"I have heard my mother relate," wrote Dr. Davy, "that when she was a girl (about 1760) there was only one cart in Penzance, and that if a cart occasionally appeared in the streets, it attracted universal attention. Pack-horses then were in general use for conveying merchandise, and the prevailing manner of travelling was on horseback." (45)

The carrying connected with the mines alone kept a host of men and animals in employ, and in the less busy seasons farmers could always find work by hiring out their horses to the mines. At the Port of Hayle, in 1758, there were "usually above five hundred, oftentimes a thousand, horses at work in carrying coal." (46) In the year 1750, however, the treasures of tin being raised from Polberro Mine in St. Agnes proved so great that sufficient horses could not be found in the whole neighbourhood to carry it to Calenick melting-house. "Ploughs" (47) were accordingly used here for the first time in carrying tin, "a very unusual sight," wrote Borlase, "though doubtless a more effectual draught where the ways will admit of wheels." (48) Though horses and "moyles" continued to be employed in vast numbers down to the earlier decades of the last century, the use of "ploughs" became more general, and in the latter years of the eighteenth century they are frequently mentioned in the mine cost-books as being used for the removal of pumps and other heavy materials.

By 1841 the use of mules was said to be almost entirely suspended, although a few were still kept by an individual in the St. Just district and might be seen wending their way through the lanes to Penzance, laden with copper ore. (49) Old people living recently in Morvah parish could remember the laden "moyles" carrying tin from the Garden Mine down to Portherras Stamps, (50) and others in Penzance recalled the strings of these animals tethered outside Chyandour Office whilst their drivers went to dinner. (51)

The very earliest form of smelting was probably carried on close to the tin-works themselves. Here small pits or furnaces were dug and a fire kindled. Upon this the richest of the stream tin was thrown, and the metal afterwards gathered from among the ashes and sand. (52) Out of this early process developed the "Jews' houses," which were apparently built in the shape of inverted cones, of hard clay, about three feet broad at the top and three feet deep. A blast of air conveyed by a common bellows to the lower part of the furnace served to create an intense heat, and the molten tin was

STREAMERS AND BLOWERS 69

discharged from a small opening at the foot. The possibility of thus directing the flow of the metal probably made way for the "astragalus" blocks mentioned by Diodorus Siculus, a shape which may have corresponded to the curious specimen now preserved in the Truro Museum. (53)

The blowing-house, as distinct from the more ancient "Jew's house," seems to have been in general use by the middle of the fourteenth century, and had evidently not changed much in appearance when Carew and Beare described it in Elizabethan times. It was a rude structure, probably built of rock and turf and covered with a thatched roof. In this the lighter particles of tin used to accumulate as the sparks flew upward, until in the course of time it became worth the owner's while to burn it down once, perhaps, in seven or eight years. "A strange practise (certes)," writes Carew, "for thrift's sake to set our house on fire, yet this casualtie may be worth the owner some ten pound by the yeere or better, if his Mil have store of sutors."

These blowing-houses were either owned by the blower himself or more frequently rented from the owner of the land on whose ground they stood. Thus in the year 1659 "Chitroose" blowing-house, in the parish of Illogan, was let by John Bassett, of Tehidy, to John Mill, blower, at a yearly rent of 26s. 8d. "in good and lawful money of England," to be paid at the four great feasts of the Church and "two fatt Capons yearly at the feast of the Birth of our Lord and at Easter," or in lieu 16d. for each capon, the said lessee yielding also to the Bassetts "five days' work yearly in the summer," or 4d. for each day, as well as "20s. for heriot or farleife for and upon the deaths of the said people," the whole to be paid through George Treweeke, who was the county supervisor of blowing-houses at that time. (54) Within the blowing-houses the tin was laid out on charcoal, stratum super stratum, in a moorstone furnace which was composed of massive blocks of stone clamped together with iron in order to withstand the united forces of fire and air and called, on account of its strength, "the Castle." The charcoal, having been ignited, was fanned to an intense heat by two large bellows, eight feet long and two and a half wide, worked by a waterwheel outside.

As the process of smelting proceeded, the furnace was fed at short intervals with three or four shovels of ore and two or three half-shovels of charcoal, no flux of any kind being employed. The amount of charcoal thus consumed amounted to 24 sixty-gallon packs to 8 twelve hundredweight of tin in a "tide" of twelve hours. The powerful current of air generated by the bellows was such as to force the tin out, as it became smelted, through a small hole at the bottom of the furnace, where it fell into a large moorstone trough called the "float." From this it was ladled into an iron boiler, about three feet in diameter, with a small fire under it to keep the metal sufficiently liquid. Two or three large pieces of charcoal which had been soaked in water were then laid upon the tin and plunged to the bottom by means of an iron instrument. A violent ebullition was immediately excited and a little slag, which previously had been mixed with the metal, rose to the surface and was skimmed off. A minute or two afterwards the metal was tried by taking up a ladlefull and pouring it again into the mass, when, if it appeared quite bright like silver and of a uniform consistence, the purification was complete. (55) Nothing more was afterwards required than to cool the tin to a proper degree and ladle it into lesser moulds known respectively as slabs, blocks, or pieces of tin, in which form it was sold in every market in Europe. Good Cornish stream tin would thus afford from 65 to 75 per cent. of the very purest "grain" tin, the latter being always preferred above mine tin both on account of its greater natural purity and from its being smelted in this way at a charcoal fire. When Pryce wrote in 1778, grain tin fetched 10s. or 12s. per hundredweight more than mine tin in the open market.

It was formerly the practice of each tinner, on desiring to have his ore smelted, to pay the owner of the blowing-house 20s. for every "tide" or twelve hours, in return for which the blower was obliged to deliver to the tinner, at the ensuing coinage, one hundred gross weight of white tin for every three feet, or one hundred and eighty pounds of stream tin blown. This was equal to fourteen pounds of metal for twenty of mineral, clear of all expense. More recently, however, stream tin was blown and sold by sample, just as mine tin is smelted to-day. (56)

The blowers themselves were a class of men highly skilled in their profession. "I have heard the blowers of tyn report,"

STREAMERS AND BLOWERS

wrote Beare in 1586, "that there is great consideracon to be had in the blowing-house in making their hearth, when they set their blowing-house at work, for a blower that is expert in his occupacon as soon as he cometh into a blowing-house being set to work if he do but once hear the billows blowing will discern what falt there is in the hearth." (57) The blower's was a hard and laborious occupation as well as being a skilled one, and even Carew (to whom it was doubtless a common sight) wondered that "the blowers extreame and increasing labour, sweltring heate, danger of skalding their bodies, burning the houses, casting away the worke, and lastly their ugly countenances, tanned with smoke and besmeared with sweate, could induce any man to undertake such pains and perill."

To the average man employed in a tin-smelting works in Cornwall to-day the occupation of a "blower" would be as unknown as that of a Spitzbergen collier, so entirely has this method of smelting become a part and parcel of the past. The existence only of the word "blowing-house" (Cornish, "chy whetha," and possibly "foage") as a place-name serves to remind the curious of this once important "mystery."

Down to the end of the seventeenth century, however, all tin, whether from mine or stream, had to be blown, and altogether some thirty blowing-houses were at work up and down the county. Owing, however, to the increasing scarcity of wood, attempts had been made from quite early times to smelt tin and other metals with pit coal. None of these gained any marked success, and it was not until the year 1702 that the first reverberatory furnace in Cornwall was erected at Newham by a German called Moult. (58) From this time onwards mine tin came to be generally smelted in this way. Stream tin, however, being of a larger grain and superior grade, continued to be blown on charcoal, and, as already stated, fetched a higher price. When Pryce wrote in 1778 both methods of smelting were in general use, the largest blowing-house being at that time at St. Austell. The old blowing-house here probably came to an end in 1777, but a new one was immediately erected on its site. (59) By 1808 it seems probable that the St. Austell new blowing-house was the only one at work, since tin was being brought to it not only from all the neighbouring streams, but from places so far distant as Plympton St. Mary, Sheepstor, Dartmoor, and Callington in the east, and Wendron and Illogan in the west.

Very picturesque were the names given to many of the streams which appear in the old blowing-house ledgers : " Piskey Meadow," " Poor Man's Work," " Gover and Gothers," " Turn About," " Cost is Lost," " Sweep-all," " Travellers' Delight," " Jew's House," " Best-to-agree," " Plain Dealing," " Luck and Fortune," " Happy Recovery," " Peace and Good Will," " Britons Merry," " Come by Chance," " Bold Adventure," " Landra Stennack," " Stennack Filly," " Stennack Ladder," " Stenna Gwin," " Tye Welkin," " Lower Gun Deep," " Biscuppa Skence," to mention but a few. (60)

With the revival in prices which took place in the early nineteenth century, the production of stream tin began to increase again, and in 1811 Polwhele states that " a new blowing-house was erected at Penzance," probably on the site of a more ancient one at Lower Quarter, in Ludgvan parish. (61) Blowing-houses continued in use as long as stream tin was produced in any quantity, and it was not until about seventy years ago that the last blowing-house, at St. Austell, finally came to an end.

At a time when the blowing-houses were working full blast, each consuming more than a thousand packs a quarter, and charcoal at 1s. 6d. a pack, (62) the trade in this sort of fuel was a considerable one. Closely connected with the blowers, therefore, were the colliers and coal carriers, whose business it was to prepare charcoal for the smelting. " For," said a sixteenth-century writer, " no man can make his Tynn white (63) without the use of Coale, and therefore are they to be numbered amongst the number of Tynners, for the occupation of the one cannot well stand without the other." (64)

The gradual deforestation of Cornwall necessitated even in early times considerable journeys to reach timber suitable for charcoaling. In the sixteenth century order was made within the stannary of Blackmore that " if there be not Wood coale nor more cole sufficient within the Stannary to blow the Tynn of the said Stannary, the Tynners may send their servants to Dartmouth Forrest, and thereto make cole in any place where they list, paying for such Turf cutting and pasture as the Tynners or any other persons occupying the said Forrest have paid for the same." (65) On these long journeys, "peradventure thirty or forty miles," between the blowing-houses and the coppice woods the collier claimed the privilege of pasturage, "craving for his horses in the carrying of his coal free pasturing from the owners of the commons or waste grounds which he passed by on his way." (66)

Arrived on the slopes of Dartmoor, parties of colliers must often have remained encamped for weeks, being doubtless joined by others of their kind from the Devon stannaries. There is no actual description of the colliers at their work, but Carew speaks of their felling the timber, piling and framing it to be burned, and afterwards "fetching the same, when it is coaled, through farre, foule and cumbersone ways to the blowing-house." Doubtless they resembled in almost every respect the charcoalers who may be met with in the forests of France and Italy to-day. Judged from their manner of living, the colliers are likely to have been a rough lot, and it was, no doubt, with a sense of relief that the few inhabitants of the district watched the last of the long train of horses turning westward, back over Tamar, to the Cornish moors from whence they came.

The charcoal, like everything else in the sixteenth century, was carried in horse packs, each one measuring $2\frac{1}{4}$ yards in length by three-quarters in breadth and containing about three bushels. For testing the packs "the ancient tin masters would always have at their blowing-houses a lawful hogshead with one end struck out," and into this each pack had to be tipped and measured before it was accepted. (67)

In addition to the supply of wood coal from Dartmoor, large quantities were imported by sea from the New Forest. In a petition of 1695 certain mariners of the Isle of Wight stated that they and others had been employed "almost time out of mind in the carrying of charcole by sea from the New Forrest into Cornwall for the use of the Refyners of Tynn." Judged by their own statements it would appear indeed that the greater part of the supply was then derived from this source, the petitioners adding that owing to certain exactions "by the Mayor of Southton," not only were they being hindered in their trade, but "the tinners, consisting of many thousand souls, were injured and almost undone." (68)

The last step in getting tin ready for the market was the coinage. During the weeks immediately preceding these all-important occasions in the tinners' year, quantities of smelted tin would be waiting in every blowing-house throughout the stannaries for transport to the nearest coinage town. Each block of tin, in addition to bearing its own house-mark showing where it had been smelted, was marked according to its quality with the letters, H, S, P, or R, denoting the four grades, Hard Tin, Sinder Tin, Pillian Tin, and Relistian Tin, respectively. (69) The days before a big coinage would see the mule tracks for miles around filled with strings of animals and their drivers wending their way towards the town. Once arrived there the confusion and vexatious delays may be imagined. The housing of men and animals alone must have entailed considerable expense. This, however, was not all, for, in addition to the tax of 4s. a cwt., which had to be paid on the tin coined, numbers of petty officers and officials had to be satisfied before the business could be finished. The following account of tips expended by one smelter at the Midsummer Coinage, 1705, will give an idea of the abuses which even at that date had crept into the system.

	£	s.	d.
(70) Given to Mr. Heyden for Pendue	1	0	0
,, the Barrowmen		2	6
,, ,, Shouldermen		1	6
,, ,, Cuttars		1	6
,, ,, Poyzer Men		2	0
,, ,, Numarator			6
,, ,, Treasurer's Toller		1	0
,, ,, Doorkeeper			6
Spent with the Coinage Officers at Newham		12	0

Only when all these affairs were settled and every tax, lawful and unlawful, had been paid was permission at last granted to the owners to carry away their tin, back, perhaps, by the very way it had come, to the port of shipment.

Much of the tin thus sold was absorbed by the London pewterers, whose reputation was world-wide. From early

STREAMERS AND BLOWERS

times, however, a good deal found its way across Europe, and from thence to the East : "Concerning the marts and marketts of Cornish tin," a sixteenth-century writer noted, " Lyons in Ffraunce is one of the best unto which wee repaire, where much may be learned concerneing tynn and where there will be repaire of Barbarians, Egiptians and sundrie other nations that gladly will buy the same. Also in Africa, Asia and Armenia for the most part they use this metall, for the varnishing of the inside of their lattyn, Brasse and copper vessels. And it is known that there is an English house of the sellers of this commodity in Babilon and their price there is 4s. a pound of the same." 71

To escape the burdensome tax and vexatious delays of coinage, the smuggling of tin was regularly practised from early times. De Wrotham calls attention to it in his letter of 1198, and it was certainly continued throughout the Middle Ages. By the reign of James I it had reached such a pitch that it was stated that " certaine wandering petie Chapmen or Tinkers, haunting much about the Tinne workes doe make it an usual Trade to buy blacke tinne by the Bowle, and white Tinne uncoyned by the pound weight, or other small quantitie, and so doe carrie the same from the worke houses to certain private places of receipt, till having gotten by this unlawful meanes some stores they vent and spend the said Black Tinne before it bee blowen, and sell the said white Tinne before it be coyned, by sea or by land, where they find best Chapmen." (72) Smuggling of this sort was not confined to any one class ; merchants, sailors, blowers, and miners equally doing their share of it. In the private cellars of many Cornish seaport towns, especially at Fowey, Truro, and Penryn, " kettles " were set up, where, under pretence of melting into bars tin duly coined in the block, uncoined tin was prepared. In 1696 a Truro merchant was accused of having two tons of such tin in his possession. (73) After it had been smelted it was run off into wooden moulds and in the form of small portable pieces known as " pocket tin," was sold to seafaring men and wandering pewterers. Often too, smuggled tin was rushed by night on board ships which frequented the coast between Fowey and Mevagissey, " under colour of coming to buy Cornish slate and stone." (74)

As the following letter shows, a good deal of this tin found its way to the "east parts," where there was a ready sale for it.

From the Lords of Council to Sir Thomas Rowe, English ambassador at Constantinople :—

"Whereas complaint hath been made to the Prince his highness, by the farmers of the pre-emption of tin, that both His Majesty suffereth great loss in his customs, and that they are very much hindered by the secret exportation of tin in slabs, moulds, and bars; whereof a great part is (as we are informed) brought to the ports of Constantinople, Aleppo, and Smyrna; although we have taken the best course we can here for the remedying of this abuse; yet we . . . pray you take special care, that when any ships shall arrive in those ports, you cause diligent search to be made for such tin brought without the licence of the farmers, and if any shall be found, to seize the same, satisfying the mariners for it, in some reasonable way, but not so as that they may be encouraged to use the like fraud afterwards.

"WHITEHALL,
"*June* 26, 1624." (75)

In later times, when Holland had become the chief centre in Europe for the distribution of Eastern tin, smuggled tin from Cornwall found its way there also. By the end of the eighteenth century almost every Dutch tin founder was said to be provided with a stamp of the Duchy Arms, and whatsoever his tin might be, by inscribing it "block tin" he made it pass for English. (76)

The wholesale defrauding of the revenues made it imperative to attempt some means of putting a stop to this contraband trade. A long code of stannary law was accordingly formulated in the seventeenth century, regulating movements of the tin and the persons through whose hands it passed. Thus no tin might be moved from the blowing- or smelting-house to any place except the regular coinage towns, neither might it be carried by night nor by any route but the shortest. The owners of blowing-houses were required to register at the Stannary Court, and their blowers had to be sworn against the embezzlement of tin within their charge. Each house had likewise to enter its "hot mark or sign of tin" in the book of blowing-house marks kept anciently in the Exchequer at Lostwithiel, and latterly in the Stannary Court. (77) Twice in each year the owners of blowing-houses were to certify the quantity of tin blown for the Midsummer and Michaelmas Coinages. The following is a typical certificate:—

"A particular of the Peices slabbs and Spoonefulls of tynn Blown att the Blowinge howse of St. Nyott from Midsommer 1644 to Midsummer 1645, the Marke of the house being a fflower de Luce; John Dale gen. and Walter Hodge Owners, Walter Hodge and John Dale Blowers.

			waight
Midsomer: 1644.	Mr. John Bere	7 slabbs	600
	Jacob Moone and Hugh Wills	17 slabbs	1,300
	Jacob More Nicholas Thomas Harris	12 slabbs	1,000
	Richard Bennett	1 slabb	80
	Richard Hunt	1 slabb	120
	Wm. Marshall	1 slabb	50
Christmas: 1644.	Mr. Bere	2 slabbs	200
	Nich. Couch	3 slabbs	300
	Hugh Wills	3 slabbs	280
	Thomas Harris	1 slabb	100
	George Jeffry	2 slabbs	160
Our Lady Day: 1644.	Mr. Bere	4 slabbs	360
	Hugh Wills	6 slabbs	600
	Nich. Couch	3 slabbs	300
	Phillipp Harris	2 slabbs	150
Midsomer: 1645.	Mr. Bere	4 slabbs	360
	Hugh Wills	6 slabbs	600
	Nich. Couch	3 slabbs	300
	Phillipp Harris	2 slabbs	150
	George Jeffry	2 slabbs	120

"This is the totall summe of all the Blowing as neere as wee cann remember." (78)

The authorities, however, must soon have realized that regulations such as these were useless without someone to enforce them, and accordingly, during the latter years of the seventeenth century, an appointment was made of a supervisor of blowing-houses. The onerous duties attached to this office soon made the appointment of three assistants necessary, and even then their task was by no means an enviable one. Each man was responsible for some seven or eight blowing-houses, in addition to which he was expected to keep an eye on all suspicious-looking craft frequenting the creeks along the coast. Naturally these officials were not at all popular amongst the tinners, who, as they constantly complained, hindered them by all possible means in their work, and on the slightest pretext haled them before the Stannary Courts for punishment. (79) Under these circumstances the supervisors, in course of time, seem to have decided to adopt the line of least resistance. "Of all offices belonging to the Tin," wrote Pryce in 1778, "this, though instituted on very good principles, is now the least regarded. If the supervisors, who now receive each of them eighty pounds per annum for doing nothing, were obliged to visit these houses twice a week, their trouble would not be great, and their diligence might answer the end, and make their places serviceable to their country." (80)

They, however, probably felt that they had learnt a lesson, and that the safest and easiest course lay in non-interference. Indeed, four officials, however zealous in the cause of duty, could have done very little among a population of born smugglers, and it was probably not until the final abolition of coinage in 1838 that tin smuggling ceased altogether.

NOTES.

1. *The Tradesman*, v, 249.
2. Streamers that is, in the old sense of *alluvial tin stream workers*.
3. Cal. S. P. Dom. Eliz., July 7, 1586.
4. Harl. MS. 6380, fol. 53. This MS. contains a valuable account of the stannary of Blackmore, written by a tinner called Beare, about 1586.
5. Carew. The term "Captain" was probably introduced by German

STREAMERS AND BLOWERS

miners during the fifteenth century. In Germany the mining captains had a regular uniform in which they paraded to church on Sunday. Cf. L. Simonin, *Underground Life*, 459.

6. Goad = a land measure. It represents nine feet, and two goads square is called a yard of ground.—E. Cornwall Glossary, N.E.D. Pard = past partic. of " pare." Pare = to slice off the turf covering the ground. —N.E.D. Rodd = rod = square pole or perch.—N.E.D.

7. Add MS. 6713, fol. 25.

8. That is, one who " farms " or rents the produce of a stream work from the mineral owner.

9. Add. MS. 6380. Quoted in *West Briton*, June 22, 1838.

10. Add. MS. 6713, fol. 27.

11. Add. MS. 6713, fol. 26*b*–27.

12. It is interesting, but at the same time quite natural, to find that such " taboos " as these, which have long been noticed amongst fishermen and huntsmen in all countries, should have existed among the Cornish tinners also. Yet the miner is, after all, but a huntsman after metals, with all the huntsman's innate desire to propitiate, or at least avoid provoking, the genius of good fortune. The term " braced farcer " for an owl I am unable to explain. " Rooker " presumably means here a " cunning thief." " Peep " was an old term for " squeak."

13. Add. MS. 6713, fol. 27*b*.

14. Quoted by R. N. Worth, R.C.P.S. (1872), 114.

15. Cf. Pearce, *Laws of the Stannaries* (1725).

16. Lewis, 18. W. Harrison, in his *Description of Britaine, 1586*, Bk. III, xviii, 117, says, however: " Copper is lately not found, but restored again to light. However, as strangers have most commonly the governance of our mines, so they (the landowners) make small gaine of this in the North parts of England." As a counterblast to this we have the tradition that the tin-mines of Bohemia were first discovered by a Cornishman !

17. Worth, R.C.P.S. (1872), 97. Cranyce, Krunz, or whatever his right name was, seems to have been a man of great experience, and Cornish mining undoubtedly received much benefit from his teaching. Before coming to Godolphin he had erected a blowing- or refining-house of his own at " Larian," or Lerryn, at the cost of £300, a great sum for those days.—Cf. L. E. Salzman, *English Industries of the Middle Ages*. Cf. also Norden, *Map of Hundred of West*, printed in 1728.

18. Rec. General's Accounts, Roll No. 275.

19. *Mineralogia Cornubiensis*, 132.

20. *Penzance Antiq. Soc.* (1852), 88–90.

21. Pryce, 133.

22. R.G.S.C., iv, 50–1.

23. Pryce, 134.

24. *Plymouth Instit.* (1887–90), 108.

25. *Plymouth Instit.* (1887–90), 227.

26. Letter of Raleigh to Cecil.—Cf. E. Edwards, *Life of Raleigh*, ii, 211.

27. Hitchens and Drew, *History of Cornwall*, 603–4.

28. Carnon Stream, in its earlier days, was noted for the small particles of gold which were discovered in the alluvial silt. For the preservation of these " prills " the tinners usually carried a quill with one end cut off and fitted with a plug of wood, and into this small receptacle the bits of precious metal were carefully dropped. The finding of these was considered a perquisite of the tinner, and was of sufficiently frequent occurrence to warrant the men being paid at a lower rate than in parts where the gold did not exist. In the silt, too, were found traces of older workers, among these being wooden shovels, such as are now preserved in Truro Museum, and a pick formed from the antler of a stag.

29. George Henwood, *On Tin Streams*, 1854.

30. Per Mr. Jeffrey, of Wendron Carnkie.

31. Richard Cunnack MS., lent by the kindness of his nephew, Mr. F. H. Cunnack, of Helston.

32. Per Mr. R. Rapson, of Boderluggan, MS.

33. Per Mr. R. Rapson, MS.

34. Bottrell, *Traditions of West Cornwall*, i, 170–1.

35. Bottrell, ii, 78.

36. *Tradesman Magazine*, v.

37. Bottrell, ii, 207.

38. *R.I.C. Journal*, vi, 131, 1866.

39. March. A. S. Hlȳda.

40. " Chewidden " or " Jew-whidden " is for Cornish " Dê-Yew-Widn "—" White Thursday."

41. The 1st of May, being the beginning of the streamers' year, was also celebrated to a certain extent in recent times by drinking and jollification. Per Mr. Jeffrey, of Wendron, Carn Kie.

42. Philosophical Trans., 1671.

43. Bray, *Tamar and Tavy*, ii, 376. Agricola shows them to have been similarly used in Germany in the sixteenth century.

44. Carew.

45. *Life of Sir Humphry Davy*, i, 8.

46. Borlase, *Nat. Hist. Cornwall*, 45.

47. Plough = West Country word for a " wheeled cart."

48. Borlase, *Nat. Hist. Cornwall*, 188.

49. R.C.P.S. (1841), 94.

50. Per Mr. Gendall, of New Mill.

51. Per Mr. Richard Bolitho. Perhaps the very last of the race of Cornish muleteers was an old man who died at Trink within comparatively recent years. In his younger days he is said to have kept a string of 200 mules. He went by the name of Neddie Bennets.

52. During excavations of the famous 300–200 B.C. hill Castle of Chun, near St. Just, there was discovered, in 1925, a series of small furnaces, in

HOISTING

WITH A HORSE-WHIM (OLD STYLE). (See p. 88)

BY COMPRESSED AIR FROM A WINZE (ABOUT 1890)

A MINING LANDSCAPE. OLD CORNISH STAMPS AND DRESSING FLOORS, DOLCOATH. (See p. 187.)

[Photo Gibson, Penzance

one of which a lump of tin slag, answering exactly to this description, was found. The discovery proves that tin has been streamed in Cornwall for two thousand years, at any rate, and in all probability much longer.

53. Cf. Lewis, 16–17.
54. Tehidy Minerals Office.
55. W. Phillips, *Mineralogy* (1826), 223.
56. Pryce, 136.
57. Harl. MS,. 6380, 56*b*.
58. Pryce, 282.
59. Among the chief expenses in the blowing-house accounts are for the inspection and buying of various woods and coppices in the district for charcoaling. After each of these "vewings" of the woods the "colliers" were given "1s. to drink." The blowers likewise were often "given to drink," probably in more senses than one, theirs being a thirsty occupation. They were paid at St. Austell in 1771, by the "tide" or twelve hours, at 2s. 6d. per tide, "boarding themselves." Most of the other items of expense explain themselves. "Paid oil for bellows, 1s. 6d. Paid for soap, 1s. 10½d. Paid for Cloth for Coal Packs and for making 'em and Mending others, £1 9s. 4d. Paid for Hogs' Lard, Paid the Proprietor of the Hors Tarter for Covering the Mare, 9s. Paid for cutting, bringing home, and saving the hay. Paid Turnpikes and gave Tinners 3s. 3d." One entry, however, which is constantly recurring is hard to explain. It is "for building the house" once, twice, or even seven times in a quarter. Was "the house" a part of the furnace, like "the Castle"? Cf. St. Austell Old Blowing-House, Book of Charges begun January 3, 1771. Now in Chyandour Office, Penzance.
60. St. Austell Blowing-House Books.
61. *Hist. of Cornwall*, Bk. III, chap. iv, 136.
62. St. Austell Blowing-House Cost (1771).
63. I.e. smelt it. "Black tin" is the prepared and concentrated ore, containing approximately 70 per cent. metal when sold to the smelters. "White tin" is the name for the metallic tin obtained after smelting.
64. "Moor coal," that is, peat, was also extensively used for blowing the richer stream tin, but where greater heat was needed charcoal had to be employed.—Philosophical Transactions, 1671.
65. Add. MS. 6713, fol. 140*b*.
66. Add. MS. 6713, fol. 16*b*.
67. Add. MS. 6713, fol 149.
68. S. P. Dom. Will. and Mary, 14, fol. 1.
69. Add. MS. 6713, fol. 18*b*.
70. See an article on these account books by Major Henderson, *R.I.C. Journal*, 1913.
71. S. P. Dom. Eliz., 243, fol. 334.
72. S. P. Dom. Jas. I, vol. 187, 47.

73. Cal. Treas. Pap., 1557–1696, 524.
74. S. P. Dom. Jas. I, vol. 187, 47.
75. See R.G.S.C., iv, 81.
76. W. G. Maton, *Western Counties*, i, 171.
77. Cal. Treas. Pap., ii, May 15, 1686.
78. Bodleian Library, Clarendon MS., 1901, fol. 186.
79. Lewis, 155.
80. *Mineralogia Cornubiensis*, 285.

CHAPTER III

ABOVE AND UNDERGROUND, 1500-1800

It is generally asserted that underground mining in the West Country dates from the middle of the fifteenth century, (1) a statement which, applied only to tin-mining, appears to be true enough.

Records of the earliest underground working, however, are to be found not in connection with tin, but with the groups of royal argentiferous lead-mines at Beer Alston, Beer Ferris, and Birland, on the Cornish borders and Combe Martin on the north coast of Devon. Owing to the fact that large sums of capital were doubtless more readily available for such mines than for privately-owned enterprises, many important mining developments are to be found here at considerably earlier periods than in any of the other districts of the west. The mention of adits occurs in one of these royal mines in 1308, (2) but greater interest still attaches to an account of mining operations at " Byrlande " in 1303. The writer, whose name is not known, addresses his letter to the Lord Treasurer thus : " Because I know well that you are desirous to hear and know good news of the state of the King's mine in my care, I let you know, sirs, that we are drawing ore from day to day in great abundance, and that it increases so much from one day to another, God be thanked, that it will soon by multiplication overcome all the workmen of the country even if there were far more than ever there were. For it will yield, by evidence that we see, more ore this present summer and the winter following than it has ever done in the two best years since it was first found . . . for whereas we could do nothing before this time in the winter by reason of the abundance of water, except it was by drawing off the water by leather buckets, which was done at very great expense, now we shall be able, thanks to God, to do as much and win as much in Winter as in Summer, because the water will have its full course out of the mines through the adits (*par my les anidodz*) down as far as the deepest part of the mine, without our drawing off any of the water in the manner aforesaid. Some, Sirs, have been in despair before this time of this work, but now comfort themselves . . . because they did not see how the matter would be."

The mine itself, it appears from later statements, employed more than two hundred workmen, the smelting and refining being done with timber obtained from the royal wood of " Calistok " (? Calstock), half a league distant. (3)

Seeing that even at this date the skill of the miners was such as to enable them to take advantage of the deep valleys and to pierce the hill-sides with adits, it is not surprising to find that a hundred and eighty years later mining had reached a high degree of organization and efficiency in this district.

The next most important account of mining after the one mentioned above is an account roll of Beer Ferris Mine for the years 1480-1. The working force here, at this time, included miners, pumpmen, carpenters, smiths, chandlers, sawyers, washers, roasters, refiners, charcoal-burners, and carters —in fact, nearly all the representatives of the workmen employed by a modern mine. The workings were partly drained with windlass and buckets, as in earlier times, but the addition of a small suction pump worked with a waterwheel marked a more recent development. The silver lead ore raised from the mine was broken by hand and then taken to a furnace to extract the metalliferous parts, and afterwards to a refining-house to extract the silver. Ten men were employed at the fining-house, and forty-seven charcoal-burners were kept busy in supplying them with fuel. The number of miners is stated on one roll to have been seventy-nine, although the number kept in regular employment was probably less than this. (4)

Very little is to be learnt of the social side of the miner's life at this period, although his status seems to have been fairly good, and his wages, 4d. a day, compared favourably with that of other skilled workmen of the time.

The next best piece of evidence on the development of underground mining is found in a series of letters describing work on the copper lodes of the Perranporth district in the year 1584. Mining operations here were in charge of the German miner,

Ulrick Frosse, whose troubles and anxieties with his Cornish workmen have already been described. On July 22, 1584, he wrote to one of the adventurers : " Mr. Carnsewe was here to see our workes and mine at Perin Sand and went down with me into the bottom of the worke and so up alongst the new audiet we made which is at this present about fifty fathoms long under all the old works. Great springs of water we light on still in going up which will put us to great charge in the end, I fear me. We have yet above seventeen or twenty fathom to the deep shaft where the most ore was left by report, to which we think to come about the latter end of August, with God's help." . . . (5)

It is Carew who supplies the earliest picture of the Cornish miner at his work, as, indeed, of almost every other branch of life in Elizabethan Cornwall. The mines in his day (1585–1600) had in some cases already reached the remarkable depth of fifty fathoms (300 feet). Into these places the miners were "let down and taken up in a stirrup by two men who wind the rope," (6) either because ladders were not yet known in Cornwall or the workings were too small to allow of them being fixed. Most of the mining seems to have been in the " goffen " stage, that is, excavations along the back of the lode, standing open to the day. If, however, the lode lay slope-wise, as was common, the tinners were accustomed to dig down to a certain depth and then pass forward underground " so farre as the ayre will yield them breathing which as it beginneth to faile, they sinke a shaft down thither from the top, to admit a renewing vent." (7)

No system of artificial ventilation seems to have been known at this date in Cornwall, although in Germany bellows and cowls fixed at surface were in use for ventilating mines during the sixteenth century. (8) By 1668, however, the Mendip miners had discovered the art of bringing down air, at least twenty fathoms underground, through pipes of elm " exactly closed," (9) and the same system had probably by that date been introduced into Cornwall. At any rate, Cornish tinners had come to realize the value of a stream of water for conveying air, an anonymous writer noting in 1671 that " if we have water we never want sufficient air for respiration." (10)

Of the appearance of the Cornish miner at this date we have, unfortunately, no record ; but the description of the Mendip miners, who worked " in frocks and waistcoats," using " tallow candles, fourteen or fifteen to the pound, each of which lasts three hours," (11) gives us some clue to what things may have looked like underground in Cornwall.

In their passage underground the early miners were frequently hindered by the loose earth, hard rocks, and great streams of water which they met with. In spite of propping with " frames of timber," wrote Carew, the loose ground " now and then falling down, either presseth the poore workmen to death or stoppeth them from returning." (12) The old Mining Law givers of Mendip struck the true note of danger in the opening words of their proclamation when they wrote : " If any man whatsoever he be, intends to *venture his life* to be a workman in the said occupation of a miner . . ." and they were but making provision for what only too frequently happened when they enacted that, " if any man by any means of this doubtful and dangerous occupation, doth by misfortune take his death by the falling of the earth upon him, by drawing or stifling or otherwise, as in times past may have been : the workmen of this occupation are bound to fetch the body or bodies out of the earth and to bring him or them to surface to a Christian burial at their own proper costs and charges, although he be threescore fathom under the earth. . . ." (13)

When the rock was hard and the danger consequently less, the extremity of the miner's toil increased in like proportion. The only tools of the Elizabethan tinner consisted of a " pick-axe of yron about sixteene inches long, sharpned at the one end to pecke, and flat-headed at the other to drive certaine little yron wedges," wherewith they cleft the rocks. " They have also," wrote Carew, " a broad shovell, the utter part of yron, the middle of Timber, into which the staffe is slopewise fastened." (14) One hundred years later the tools used by a Cornish miner were still much the same, consisting of a " beele or Cornish tubber (a small double-pointed pick of 8 or 10 lb. weight) which might last half a year in a hard country, but required pointing every fortnight at least, a sledge from ten to twenty pounds weight, new ordered once a quarter, and gadds or wedges of two pounds weight, foursquare and well-steeled at the point, which required sharpening every two or three days." (15) With such primitive means at his command the tinner contrived to do remarkably good work, and places may be seen to-day where the ancient miners have driven for long distances through firm rock solely with the aid of picks and gads and strenuous toil. "Yet sometimes," wrote Carew, when the rock grew unusually hard, the tinners were "so tied by the teeth, as a good workman shall hardly be able to hew three foote in the space of so many weekes."

The regulation size of a drift or level in 1670 was seven feet high and "three foot over," allowing room for two shovelmen and three beelemen to work at a time. Many of the workings, however, especially the adits, were "scarce half so large," and, as in the "Conquer" set of branches at Wheal Fortune (Breage), the ancient levels were "so extremely narrow that it would seem scarcely possible for a man to get through them." (16) Further instance of the same sort may be seen to-day in the "old men's" cross-cuts at Great Work Mine, which in many places are not more than four feet high and only two feet four inches across in the widest part. They were, as it seems, purposely driven egg-shaped so as to allow room for the hands in rolling barrows up the steep and irregular inclines from the lode to the shaft. The walls present no appearance of ever having been drilled or blasted and are smooth and polished from the generations of miners who, bent and doubled, half pushed and half dragged their laden barrows through them. In many of the old adits even smaller conditions than these prevailed, and in places where it is manifestly impossible for a barrow to have gone, the old men must either have carried out the dirt in sacks or dragged it behind them in "trays" with a rope. Where the ground has been opened to a greater width to extract the lode, "stonen stemples," consisting of blocks of granite moorstone, were commonly fixed in the roof, and with such skill and exactitude was this done that, seen above one's head to-day, they appear as even and level as railway sleepers. (17)

"Meantime," wrote Carew, "while the miners thus play the Moldwarps, unsavourie Damps doe here and there distemper their heads, though not with so much daunger in consequence as annoyance for the present." This constitutes what is, I believe, the sole reference to the health of the Cornish miner, prior to the middle of the eighteenth century. Though Carew did not appear to think the miners' occupation so very prejudicial to health, he admitted that in most places their toil was "so extreame as they cannot endure it above foure houres in a day, but are succeeded by spels; the residue of the time, they weare out at Coytes, Kayles, or like idle exercises."

The chief exercise of ingenuity required by the miner in his work has always been in getting rid of the water. The sixteenth and seventeenth centuries were essentially the wet periods throughout all the mines in England, and the Calendars of State Papers contain constant references to inventions for draining mines, nearly all of them by Germans. "In Cornwall," wrote Carew, "they pray in aide of sundry devices, as Addits, Pumps and Wheeles driven by a streame, and interchangeably filling and emptying two Buckets with many such like: all which notwithstanding, the springs do so incroche upon these inventions as in sundrie places they are driven to keepe men, and somewhere horses also at worke both day and night without ceasing, and in some all this will not serve the turne. For supplying such hard services, they have alwaies fresh men at hand." "In the driving of adits alone," wrote Carew, "if you see how aptly they (the tinners) cast the ground for conveying the water, by compassings and turnings to shunne such hils and vallies, as let them by their too much height or lownesse, you would wonder how so great skill could couch in so base a Cabbin, as their (otherwise) thicke clouded braines."

As the mines grew deeper, however, and shafts were sunk below the natural drainage outlet, mechanical power had again to be employed to raise the water to adit level. This either took the form of the windlass and bucket, as before, or else the rag and chain pump. A development out of the windlass and bucket method was the horse whim, in which the rope from the shaft passed round the barrel of a huge upright drum called the "cage," which was turned by a team of horses. This was, in all probability, an invention of the seventeenth century, when the deepening of the mines and the serious encroachment of the water called for every device of which the mechanical wit of that day was capable. (18)

A system of waterwheels and bobs for working short tiers

of pumps was, as already stated, in use much earlier, and no particular change is known to have taken place in these during the seventeenth century, except in their increasing number and efficiency. By the end of the seventeenth century, small wheels of twelve or fifteen feet diameter were still reckoned the best machinery for draining mines; and if one or two were insufficient, a series were often applied to that purpose, all worked by the same stream of water. "I have heard," wrote Pryce, "of seven in one Mine, worked over each other." Side by side with these were used the rag and chain pumps, generally worked by human labour. The rag and chain pump consisted of an endless chain broadened out at intervals by leathern bindings, to fit snugly into a wooden pipe from twelve to twenty feet in length. It was worked by a handle on a flywheel at the surface and, catching up as it did a series of short columns of water, served very well to drain shallow workings. In deeper mines a series of these pumps were necessary, and a four-inch pump drawing twenty feet employed from twenty to twenty-four men working five or six at a time in six-hour spells. (19)

In spite of all such devices, the water difficulty continued to harass the miner; whilst the low price of tin obtaining at the end of the seventeenth century ill rewarded him for his increasing charges.

"I went a mile farthur on to the hills" (near St. Austell), wrote a lady traveller in 1695, "where there were at least twenty mines, all in sight, which employ a great many people at work almost night and day, including the Lord's Day, which they are forced to to prevent their mines being over-flowed with water.

"More than a thousand men and boys are taken up with them; few mines but had twenty men and boys attending, either in the mine carrying the ore to the little bucket which conveys it up, or else others are draining the water or looking to the engines that are draining it. The ore is drawn by a windlass, two men keep turning, bringing up one and letting down another. They have great labour and expense to drain the mines with mills that horses turn, and now they have mills or water engines that are turned by the water, which is conveyed on frames of timber and trunks, which falls down on the wheels as an overshot mill. They do five times more good than the mills they used to turn with horses, but, then, they are much more chargeable. I saw not a windmill all over Cornwall or Devon, though they have wind and hills enough, but it may be it is too bleak for them."

From this scene of bustling activity she passed on again "six miles good away" towards Redruth, seeing a "100 mines, some of which were at work, others that were lost by the waters overwhelming them." (20) In spite, however, of present discouragement, the miners and adventurers held on then as they have done since, time and again.

"Instances too many they have in Cornwall and Devon," said a writer in 1636, "that a return to a work forsaken cannot be made without great cost. If it be a water-work the charge of drawing the water out will be very great, and both wet and dry works, by the fallings of the ground, will be very chargeable to rid and repair." (21)

The opening years of the eighteenth century saw a greater development of mining activity than had ever been known before in Cornwall.

"Large numbers of the inhabitants," wrote Borlase in 1758 "have their attention so much engrossed by tin and copper that agriculture and all other employments are neglected in the greedy quest of metals." (22) Twenty years later, Pryce wrote of tin as that "darling metal which, among the working Tinners, holds her Empire in the heart." (23) The spirit of mining adventure which was in the air affected all classes equally. "If a mine," wrote Pryce, "when she is first discovered, throws up a large profit to the adventurers and fails soon after to their loss and detriment, they nevertheless pursue their object under the most unpromising circumstances, with unremitting ardour, patience, industry and resolution scarcely parallel in any other unfortunate undertaking under the sun. Every little stone of ore brings along with it new hopes, and fresh vigour. It fans the glimmering flame of adventure, which had been kindled before by the fire of a certain Provincial Spirit, that seems to animate the natives of Cornwall, and to deserve that success which they cannot always command." (24) It was none the less a fact, as Pryce adds, "that the rapid increase of the produce of our Tin Mines for the last thirty years is scarcely credible: it is, however, a fact that we have coined three thousand six hundred tons of Block Tin in one year, which is double the quantity coined annually sixty years ago." (25)

In respect of copper, the increase of production since the early years of the eighteenth century was perhaps even more extraordinary. Worked on a small scale, and very secretively, at the end of the sixteenth century, (26) copper in Cornwall seems to have been regarded as of little or no value during the hundred years which followed. It was not until the last decade of the seventeenth century that this metal again came into serious notice and some suspicion, at least, of its value began to be felt.

"I am informed that at Trevascus in Cornwall, where has been dug more than 1,000 tuns of oar, there is one spot known 32 foot broad, 8 foot deep and how long none can tell," stated a chronicler in 1697; (27) whilst another writer in 1699 added that the county of Cornwall was "better by many Thousands for the Copper yearly raised there." (28)

"One of the Eastern tryers whispered me that all the dizzo (29) was excellent copper and that he would give a £1,000 for what is in sight," wrote George Powell in 1696, in his baudy play, which he graced with the name of *The Cornish Comedy*.

This Eastern tryer may well have been one of those "Bristol gentlemen," possibly Mr. John Costar himself, who, visiting Cornwall in 1710, made it his business "to inspect the mines more narrowly" and to buy up the copper ore, of which he found some three thousand tons lying idle, at the "advanced price" of £6 or £7 per ton. (30) However selfish his motives, Mr. Costar justly earned his title of "the father of Cornish copper mining." By 1758 similar ore was selling at from £10 to £20 a ton, and copper-mining, from being a hole-in-the-corner industry, had risen to a position of even greater importance than tin-mining itself. In 1787 the total number employed in the copper-mines of Cornwall alone amounted to 7,000 persons, of which North Downs and the Consolidated Mines each employed more than a thousand. (31) This position copper-mining maintained down to the 'sixties of the last century, at which time Cornwall was supplying more than three-quarters of the world's annual consumption of copper, at a value of over £1,000,000 sterling.

Hand in hand with this rapid development of the industry, and indeed rendering it possible, came various improvements in mining methods. The old men had pursued their laborious way underground by boring holes, in much the same way as Cornish quarrymen used to cleave blocks of granite. Into holes bored to a shallow depth, by a bit terminating in a quadrangular point, were placed two semi-cylindrical rods of iron or steel, called "feathers," just of an equal length with the hole; and then a steel wedge of the same length was driven between the flat sides of the two feathers, which, if sufficient care had been taken to bore the hole obliquely, broke off the rock piecemeal. This wedge was called a "tearer." When the ground was more than usually hard, the miners had no other resource than to wear away the face of the rock in the same way as masons cut stone for building. (32) Side by side with this the still more ancient method of fire-setting was probably employed, whereby the rock was heated to a high temperature with burning furze faggots, and then had water thrown over it, which caused it to split. (33) This method, which was in use in the Mendip Mines in 1668, had many drawbacks, as, apart from its slowness, a change of wind at surface rendered the smoke a real menace to men at work in other parts of the mine.

The blasting of rocks by gunpowder seems to have been first introduced into England about 1670, when it was employed by Prince Rupert's German miners at the copper-mines of Ecton. From Staffordshire it spread into Somerset, and soon afterwards to Cornwall, where, according to tradition, it was first employed in the St. Agnes Mines. (34) It is very probable that its introduction to Cornwall may have been due to the German Becker, though, according to Breage parish register, "Thomas Epsley, of Chilcumpton parish, Sumersitsheere, was the man that brought that rare invention of shooting the rocks which came here in June, 1689. He died at the ball (bal) and was buried at Breague the 16th day of December in the year of our Lord Christ 1689." (35) In 1792 an old Zennor man stated that he remembered having heard from his father and other old men that blasting had been first introduced by Germans into the eastern part of the county ; and that it was brought to the west (i.e. Lelant, Zennor, and St. Ives) in their time by two eastern men called Bell and Case, and was used by them in "Trevigha bal," and that they affected to keep the mode of operations secret, till a man of Zennor, hiding himself upon a bolt, saw what they were about. This he thought must have happened "about ninety years ago" (i.e. about 1700). (36)

Down to the middle of the eighteenth century practically the same devices remained in use for draining the mines as hitherto, although everything was on a larger and more efficient scale. The driving of adits was carried on at this time to a hitherto unprecedented extent, and so completely was the mining country " bled " by these and other underground workings that in many places where formerly a shaft could not have been sunk fifteen fathoms without being overwhelmed with water, fifty fathoms might now be reached without meeting with a drop. (37)

In the year 1748 the "county adit," as it is sometimes called, was started by one of the Williams family near Bissoe Bridge, in Gwennap, and gradually extended to the western boundary of Poldice. (38) During the fifty years which followed, driving was intermittently continued till the adit eventually reached a length of thirty miles and drained no less than forty-six mines, the farthest of which was $5\frac{1}{2}$ miles from its mouth. (39) Being of benefit to so many mines, the divided payments for the cost of the upkeep of this adit were very complicated. In the cost-books of the St. Day Mines during the latter part of the eighteenth century are frequently to be found such entries as " 3/10 of £248 15s. 4d. being Poldice adit cost above the separation of the adits to end of January 1796 = £46 12s. 10d.," or again (worse still !) : "To 1/3rd of 7/8ths of £129 19s. 0d. being Creegbraws Adit Cost April 1796 = £37 6s. 4d." (40)

Adits driven for considerable distances across country were sometimes the means of discovering far more valuable lodes than the ones they were originally intended to drain. The mid-eighteenth century was a great period of lode discovery in Cornwall, and it is not an exaggeration to say that several mines, still working, owe their existence to the development of these years. The old men, in fact, had generally only worked such lodes as had "backs" plainly appearing on the surface. The driving of adits proved the country in a way which had never been done before, and great deposits of copper ore were discovered in localities which had hitherto been thought outside the mineralized zone. Amongst such was Pool Adit, or, as it became known in later times, Trevenson Mine, which proved enormously rich in copper about 1740, and was one of the chief mines in establishing the great wealth of the Basset family, who owned the whole of the shares. From 1747–60 Pool Adit gave to the Bassets a regular income of £10,000 or £11,000 a year, whilst the "Long Close" Adit Dish averaged another £4,000, a great income considering the then value of money. Encouraged by such discoveries as this, the driving of adits was often undertaken as mere seeking adventures, without being bound for any particular mine. (41) As Pryce said: "The expence of an adit is slow and small; therefore it is easily borne. Two or three hundred pounds an year is scarcely felt by eight or ten persons, than whom seldom fewer are concerned; and this too upon the chance of finding a vein, or veins, that may throw up an amazing profit presently after discovery."

The average size of these adits being only six feet high and two and a half over, (42) it was hardly possible for more than one man to work in the end at a time, and many years were often occupied in such an undertaking. "Some levels," wrote Pryce, "have taken thirty years to complete, and I have been concerned in one that took seventeen years to bring home to the mine." (43) Owing to low costs, however, such methods were then economically possible. Thus the charge of Penventon Adit for one year from August 1, 1767–September 9, 1768, amounted in all to £165 18s. 6d., during which time ten shafts were sunk at £3 per shaft and 326 fathoms were driven. The lowness of prices is further illustrated by the fact that the cost of "building of a Hutt near the Adit for the use of Thomas Clark sharpening tools and for keeping candles, pick hilts, etc.," was 3s. 6d., whilst "Tom Davye (long), for his trouble inspecting the Adit, and Simon Davye with him," was rewarded with 5s. 7d. (44) Yet even in these days it was generally considered a sound axiom amongst adventurers that, in an adit, expense was not so much to be considered as speed in driving. Frequently, therefore, the old miners availed themselves of a soft or clay-filled "cross-course" to drive up their adit to the mine, and would follow its tortuous twistings for long distances rather than incur the great expense of driving direct through hard ground. Water, however, was frequently met with in these cross-courses and proved a serious inconvenience to the miners. "As to the Seal Hole Addit," wrote Mr. Bolitho's agent from St. Agnes, in 1778, "they have had many misfortunes, for by the water and the slimey ground the timber would not keep it abroad, for they have lost their addit end three times, so that the addit end is not nigher home than it was six months back. But now they are gone back about thirty fathoms in the addit to drive to the West of this Floocan, which I believe will take off the water." (45) In addition to such inconvenience as this, more timbering was required in soft ground, and new lodes were not so easily discovered in a cross-course as when driving through the "country" rock. All these matters were, of course, carefully weighed by the cautious adventurer. (45)

The actual work of bringing home the adit to a waterlogged mine was always a dangerous task in the days before long-distance bore-holes could be put out, and such hazardous undertakings were generally performed by picked miners at an advanced price. "Whenever they are apprehensive of coming towards the house of water, as the miners term it," wrote Pryce, "they bore a hole with an iron rod towards the water about a fathom or two or so many feet further than they have broke with the pick-axe. As they work on, they still keep the hole with the borrier before them that they may have timely notice of the bursting forth of the water, and so give it vent or passage. Yet notwithstanding all this care and prudence, they are often lost by the sudden eruption of the water. In some places, especially where a new Adit is brought home to an old mine, they have unexpectedly holed to the house of water before they thought themselves near it, and have instantly perished. Some have driven by the side of the house of water and have perished also by its unexpected eruption." (46)

Of such a kind was the disaster which occurred in one of the St. Just Mines some fifty years ago, which was thus described by an old miner of that parish : "I can mind the day the four men was drowned holing through into the house of water in

North Levant. 'Twas a Monday and I was working afternoon core out Spearn. They say the end they was driving had been bone-dry all along. When the men got down that day they stopped out at the beginning of the level to touch a pipe of bacca, and told the boy to go in and clear up the end 'gainst they started to work. Over a while the boy came out and said: 'We ain't far off the water now, Uncle Nick, for tes running through in the end.' 'Git away,' said the man, 'theest took fear, booy.' What happened after that they don't know, but 'tis supposed the men went in to work and the first blow they struck on the drill, the water burst through upon them. One man was found afterwards with the tram thrown on top of him yards back in the level, and one they never found for a week. The two other men, as I said, I seed myself broft into the carpenters' shop and laid out 'pon the binch." That was all the story, as the old miner told it, and it was all that can ever be known of that and many another drama of the underground life of Cornwall. No one remained to tell of the miners' last moments. Imagination only can picture the silent dripping end, the dim candle-light, the first blows of hammer on boryer, and then, without warning, the rush of cold air in the inky blackness, a heart-leap of struggle and fear, and a moment afterwards the bodies of men, tools, timberwork, and wagons caught up and swept onwards like straws in the terrific wall of water, filling the narrow level from floor to roof. (47)

Apart from such dangers as these, work in an adit end had many drawbacks, owing to damp, lack of room, and poor air. In places where driving was continued without intermission both day and night, the difficulty of ventilation and getting rid of powder-smoke was most pressing. Bellows for forcing in air had been employed in the sixteenth century (and probably much earlier) in the German mines and were introduced by the Tonkin family into Goonlaze Adit in 1696. There is no evidence, however, of their finding favour elsewhere in Cornwall. At any rate, the usual means of ventilating underground workings in the eighteenth century was simply by placing a close-fitting floor of boards, called a "sollar," on the bottom of the level from the shaft to the working end. By this means a current of air was maintained, blowing in through the space

DRILLING HOLES FOR BLASTING

MACHINE DRILLING (NEW STYLE). (See p. 335)

HAND DRILLING A "BACK" HOLE (OLD STYLE). (See p. 217)

[Photo Gibson, Penzance

ST. IVES CONSOLS MINE (CIRCA 1870), SHOWING CHILD LABOURERS. (See p. 233) beneath the sollar as far as the working face and then rising and passing out again along the roof of the level. In sinking shafts where it was impossible to obtain ventilation by such means, pipes were used to bring down a current of air from a funnel fixed at surface, which, like a ship's ventilator, could be turned to meet the wind whichever way it was blowing. (49)

Though the number of deep adits driven in the eighteenth century served to keep the mines drained to a far greater depth than was possible in Carew's day, the water difficulty was only delayed, not overcome. " With all the skill and adroitness of our Miners," wrote Pryce in 1778, " they cannot go any considerable depth below the Adit before they must have recourse to some contrivance for clearing the water from their workings." At this time the use of the rag and chain pump was not wholly discontinued, although it was falling into disfavour " on account of the great expence and the destruction of the men." In cases where it was employed, the pumps were placed upon stulls or sollars, the men working at them " naked, excepting their loose trousers, and suffering much in their health and strength from the violence of the labour, which is so great," wrote Pryce, who was a mine doctor, " that I have been witness to the loss of many lives by it." (50) " As an alternative to this, water was frequently drawn to adit in shallow mines by a windlass and small water-barrels ; but if the water exceeded a certain number of barrels in a core of six or eight hours, the adventurers generally gave over drawing by hand and erected a horse whym." The largest barrels drawn by the whim contained 120 gallons apiece and had to be drawn by four horses, at a rate of not less than two barrels a minute in order to make the expense worth while. This was only possible, of course, in perpendicular shafts. (51)

In deep mines where the hoisting of ore was done through long inclined shafts, fifty or sixty fathoms upon the underlie, the wear and tear on horses and tackle was tremendous, and the kibbal or bucket in which the stuff was " haled " rarely came half-full to grass. (52) In these shafts the ropes had to be renewed every two months, yet even so the danger of their breaking and the capstan swinging back as the heavy kibbal crashed through the shaft was a constant one. The usual cost of drawing water in wooden barrels was 2s. a hundred, whereas the lode stuff in iron kibbles cost 8s. a hundred. (53) Seeing that a single mine, such as Polgooth, was sometimes using no less than twenty-six shafts at once, (54) the number of horses formerly kept in employment by the mines was very great. No less than sixty were owned by Dolcoath in the early years of the last century, (55) and payments for oats and persons making hay frequently occur in the cost-books of the period. (56) The mines, however, in earlier times more often hired than kept their own horses, and it was a common thing for the low-paid captains to eke out their wages by lending a horse or two to the mine.

Probably the most effectual engine for mine drainage down to 1777 was still the old water-wheel and bobs, which, by Pryce's time, had reached a high degree of efficiency. The small wheels of twelve and fifteen feet diameter placed one above another had formerly done good service, but such "petit engines" had now nearly all been demolished and a single large wheel of thirty or forty feet diameter substituted in their stead. In Cook's Kitchen Mine a water-wheel forty-eight feet in diameter, working tiers of wooden pumps of nine inches bore, drew water from eighty fathoms under the adit, and Pryce was assured that if the stream of surface water had been sufficient to fill the buckets of the wheel, she would have drawn forty fathoms deeper with the same bore. (57) Several of these old wooden pumps have been found from time to time in the course of unwatering long-abandoned mines. Part of the working barrel and the wind bore of one found in Wheal Castle, St. Just, are preserved in the Penzance Antiquarian Society Museum. (58) Another was found more than thirty years ago in Wheal Reeth, near Godolphin Hill. The most interesting of all, however, on account of the illustration which accompanies it, is the description of one found about 1855 in an ancient mine called Wheal Freedom, near the estate of Craskin, in Wendron parish : " Soon after pumping was begun here a column of old wood pumps were found fixed in the shaft. These were of elm-trees and the bore eleven inches in diameter. The working piece valve and wind bore were very remarkable. With the view no doubt to keeping the valve moist there was a bend made in the wind bore arrangement, which the contracted valve way must have greatly

ABOVE AND UNDERGROUND

interfered with the operation of pumping. The rods and rod-bucket had been removed. Much surmise was excited as to the motive-power used for draining the shaft with these pumps, as there was insufficient water in the valley during the greater part of the year and too small a fall to work pumps of such a size. It was thought that the land, being covered with trees at one time, may have attracted more water than at present." (59)

The time, however, was coming when the Cornish mines were to be rendered independent of such power, and that " by that most useful, powerful, and noble machine the fire engine," of which Cornwall by 1778 had several that were the largest in the kingdom. Concerning the first introduction of steam into the county, speculation has long been rife. Savery's steam-pump of 1696 had, in 1705, been superseded by one of Newcomen's design. There is a vague tradition that the first of these new engines was worked at " Balcoath," near Porkellis, in Wendron, the steam being raised by turf fuel. This engine, it is said, was subsequently moved to Tregonebris, and then to Trevenen Mine, both ancient tin-works in the Wendron district. (60) According to other accounts steam was first used at Wheal Vor, in the parish of Breage, between 1710 and 1714. The pumps of the Newcomen engine on this mine are said to have been arranged in six lifts of ten fathoms each, a separate rod for each lift being hung from the engine-beam. In confirmation of this, about 1815 a subsequent reworking of Wheal Vor disclosed a " sollar " having six holes in it, corresponding to the reported number of rods for which they doubtless served as guides. (61) On another occasion a very similar discovery was made in an old shaft on Wheal Virgin, Gwennap. Here, according to a well-authenticated tradition, an engine was originally erected with a single bucket-rod attached to the nose or extreme point of the " bob." As the water increased in quantity and the mine went deeper, six more bucket-rods were added from time to time, three on each side of the bob, all lifting simultaneously. Many years afterwards, when the timber was being taken out of the shaft, an indubitable proof of the accuracy of this tradition was found in a sollar or flooring of timber having seven holes in it, through which the respective rods passed to their lifts of pumps. (62) Whether this belonged to the Boulton and Watt period or to an earlier Newcomen engine, as in Wheal Vor, cannot now be said. It is certain, however, that one of the earliest Newcomen engines at work in the county was that erected at Wheal Rose, in St. Agnes, some time about the year 1725, (63) though so "very chargeable" did it prove that the adventurers were fain to bring home an adit of a mile and a half in length to save the cost of continuing it. (64) The great quantities of coal consumed by these engines probably accounts for the fact that only one was at work in the whole county in 1742. (65) After this the advance must have been rapid, for about a dozen were at work in 1758, and (66) by 1778 more than sixty had been erected and half the older ones were rebuilt and enlarged. Extravagant and costly, however, these engines still continued to be. (67) As may be seen from illustrations in Borlase's *Natural History of Cornwall* and on some of the tokens or "Cornish pennies," the power was applied from the engine-beam to the shaft-rods by a chain which passed over a semicircular wheel which formed the nose of the "bob." The water was entirely raised by suction on the upstroke of the engine, and the multiplying of the tiers or lifts of pumps known, in descending order, as the "House Water," "Tye," "Rose," "Crown," "Lily," "Violet," and "Puppy" lifts (68) entailed the setting in motion of a huge dead-weight at every stroke of the engine. The boxes, too, and clacks (valves) of the Newcomen engines, being made of sewn leather, were constantly going amiss, this proving in some mines a misfortune of almost daily occurrence. On such occasions every man on the mine was bound under penalty of a fine to give his labour at the capstan, if required, and in other ways to assist whilst the clack or box was changing. (69) In larger mines the men usually received some compensation for this work, which frequently entailed an attendance far into the night under the most exposed conditions.

The first Boulton and Watt engine set to work in Cornwall was at Wheal Busy, or, as it was then called, the Chasewater Mine, in 1778. Three others were in course of erection during the same year at Ting Tang, Owen Vean, and Tregurtha Downs. (70)

The coming of Boulton and Watt to Cornwall instituted a new era in Cornish mining, and there is no doubt that they were

ABOVE AND UNDERGROUND

among the greatest benefactors the industry has ever known. Until they came, fifty to eighty fathoms below adit had been considered a fair depth for one of the old-type fire-engines to drain. Many mines, however, were prohibited from attaining even this depth on account of the enormous amount of fuel used by such engines. In 1779 the mines of Wheal Virgin, Wheal Maid, West Wheal Virgin, and Carharrack, lying contiguous to each other, were wrought by no less than seven of the old-type fire-engines, each mine being worked by a separate set of adventurers, and the expense of drawing the water from the whole divided in proportion to the produce of each. This arrangement, however, was found to be so costly that the mines ceased working in the latter part of the same year. In the year 1780 a new set of adventurers was formed to work these mines under the name of the Consolidated Mines. They were set to work in 1782 with five Boulton and Watt engines, and whereas the seven Newcomen engines formerly employed consumed in one year 6,362 weys of coal, the Boulton and Watt engines consumed only 2,030 weys in the same period, showing a saving of 4,332 weys, which, with coal at 50s. a wey, amounted to a saving of £10,830 in one year. (71) The Boulton and Watt engines, with their enormous increase of power and economy, did not take long in displacing the older Newcomen engine. Five years after their first introduction to Cornwall, twenty-one had been set up and only one Newcomen remained, which disappeared in 1790. (72) By the year 1798 there were no less than forty-five Boulton and Watt engines at work in the county. (73)

Great as had been the mechanical improvements for draining mines, the actual conditions under which the miners worked were hardly less primitive than they had been one hundred years earlier. "The Cornish mines," wrote Maton in 1794, "are descended into by means either of a bucket, a rope tied round one's thighs, or ladders. In some mines any one of these methods may be adopted. A person who should prefer either of the two first must often descend in the same shaft wherein the steam-engine works, and the noise arising from its movements, together with the appearance of the rod above one's head, causes the most uneasy sensations. The miners themselves invariably recommended to us the ladder shafts." Even these, however, were often only a roughly boarded-off section of the main shaft, through which the great iron kibbles or buckets rattled up and down with deafening noise, bumping from side to side with a jovial free-and-easy swing and always with the danger of throwing out a rock on to the miners climbing beneath.

From the following account of an actual descent of a mine made about 1784, it is clear that even a visit at this date involved considerable danger, whilst the conditions under which the miners worked, year in year out, were almost incredibly hard and laborious :—

"When you declare your intention of descending into a mine the Captain takes you into a room and equips you in a woollen shirt, trousers, nightcap (!), and jacket, as for stockings they are unnecessary, but they tie a pair of old shoes on the feet, and being accommodated, each person with a candle in his hand and half a pound suspended from his neck, is completely equipped and is conducted to the mouth of the mine. It requires a strong stomach and a large degree of curiosity to go through all this—for besides the fatigue and toil in the mine, the cloaths they give you are greasy and filthy to a degree, smell abominably and are often stocked with a republic of creepers. A miner went first to serve as a guide and to caution us against the danger which frequently arises from the broken staves in the different ladders, for the Captain told us that if we made a false step to one side or the other we should be ground to atoms in the steam-engine or dashed to pieces in the shaft. The descent resembles a large well with an immense machine, for the purpose of draining the water, in motion all the way down. We continued to descend ladders which were from four to five fathoms in length, and being soon wet through, weak from want of proper respiration and half-stifled with the fumes of sulphur, began to hesitate whether we should proceed or not. I had no idea of the difficulty and danger attending such an undertaking and only wonder that accidents are not more frequent among the miners, who run up and down these slippery places like lamp-lighters, singing and whistling all the way. At about eighty fathoms depth we came to a vein of copper-ore where some poor creatures were busied in the process of their miserable employment—with hardly room to move their bodies, in sulphurous air, wet to the skin and buried in the

ABOVE AND UNDERGROUND

solid rock these, our fellow-mortals, live and work for their daily bread, pecking out the hard ore by the glimmering of a small candle whose scattered rays will hardly penetrate the thick darkness of the place. Proceeding in our descent, we reached at length the bottom of the mine and stood 130 fathoms below the surface of the earth. In this mine is a vein of tin also, and a communication is dug from the Copper to the Tin. Through this we crawled upon our hands and knees and afterwards had to cross through a rapid stream whose waters rushed abundantly over us, as we crawled along in space just sufficient to admit us upon all fours. Working our way thus in a direction from north to south, we came at last to the shaft of the tin-mine. Here we saw two figures that hardly wore the appearance of human beings, *singing at their work*. We found it exceedingly difficult to pay them a visit, as we had to descend by a single rope down a chasm, never broader than a chimney, until we reached the Loade where the miners were employed.

" Having wandered until we were weary among these dismal caverns we began to ascend again. Before we reached the top I found myself so faint that I should not have been able to proceed had it not been for the water from the steam-engine, which, although very disagreeable in the beginning of our descent, we found very refreshing upon our return. It falls over every part of your body like a shower of rain, and when the heat of the mine combines with the fumes of sulphur to fatigue and oppress you is the only remedy which can be procured. It is impossible to describe the luxury one feels in breathing again the fresh air and washing with cold water after these subterranean exercises. The heat of a mine is excessive. The miners are quite naked when engaged at their work, and they told me that the change of climate and the revolutions of winter and summer were not to be perceived at their great depth." (74)

This account of the rough and ready conditions prevailing underground at this date is borne out by that of another traveller, who visited a mine near St. Ives about the year 1780.

"We had to descend," he writes, " by ladders perpendicularly mounted, which in many cases had some staves wanting. Having descended about thirty fathoms, we quitted the ladders and walked, or rather crawled, through an adit of some length, but before we had the power of reaching the end of it, we heard the vessel ascending, which is drawn up filled with water from the bottom of the mine and which emptied itself into the passage where we were. In short, before we could think of any methods of shelter (if there had been any possible) we found the water pouring in a torrent against us and wetting us nearly to our middle. It seems the people above did not know we were there and had resumed work after their dinner-hour. Our guide, to prevent a second wetting, flew up, as it were, over the ladders, and in a few minutes, by the cessation of the rumbling noise which the vessel caused in striking against the sides of the shaft, we found he had gained the top and succeeded in stopping the labourers.

" Proceeding on our way we soon descended to another landing-place on the verge of a dark, deep gulph, over which was placed a single plank only about a foot wide and fifteen long. With my candle in one hand and the side of the plank held fast by the other, I slowly ventured over on my knees. Onwards we went, climbing up and down, just as the Miners found it most easy for them to dig, till at last we arrived at the body of tin, which they were then working about seventy or eighty fathoms below the surface. . . .

" On our arrival at the top, I found myself in a manner wet through, in the dirtiest state imaginable, and in a most profuse perspiration."

The writer of this account was a stranger to Cornish miners and their kindly hospitable ways, yet his last remark is worth quoting, seeing how often the character of the eighteenth-century tinner has been maligned. " On leaving the mine," he wrote, " I met with an extraordinary instance of liberal disinterestedness in our very civil and obliging guide, for on offering him a douceur for his attention and trouble, he refused it, and intreated me not to think myself under any obligation to him." (75)

Side by side with the growth of deeper mining came a corresponding development in the dressing of tin and copper ores. In the sixteenth century, tin ore, after being brought above ground in the stone, was first broken in pieces with hammers, and then carried, either in waynes or on horses' backs, to a stamping-mill, " where three, and in some places six, great logges of timber, bound at the ends with iron and lifted up and downe by a wheele driven with water, doe break it smaller." "From the stamping mill," continues Carew, "it passeth to the crazing mill, which betweene two grinding stones, turned also with a water wheele, bruseth the same to a fine sand."

The most important development of Carew's time had been the introduction of the wet stamper, in which the small stones were covered with a trickle of water and kept beneath the stamp-heads till they were crushed to sand. This small stream, "after it hath forsaken the mill," was made to descend a series of stages, "upon each of which at every discent lyeth a greene turfe, three or foure foote square, and one foote thicke." On these was caught the sandy ore, and each one was subsequently tossed to and fro by the tinner under a stream of water, whereby the light waste was dispelled, whilst the heavier substance remained fast in the fibres of the turf. "After it is thus washed," continues Carew, "they put the remnant into a wooden dish, broad, flat, round, and having two handles at the sides, by which they softly shogge the same to and fro in the water between their legges, as they sit over it, until whatsoever of the earthie substance that was yet left be flitted away." (76) "Some of later times," he added, "with slighter invention and lighter labour, do cause certaine boyes to stir it up and downe with their feete, which worketh the same effect." (77)

The majority of employees on the mine dressing-floors, from the seventeenth century onwards, were boys from seven to eighteen years of age, who, says Borlase, "by being taken in so young, become healthy and hardy by using themselves to cold and to work with naked wet feet all day long, summer and winter alike, and learn early to contribute to their own maintenance." (78) Such was the opinion of the learned doctor, writing in his warm study. The bal boys' opinion of the matter was never asked and might have been differently expressed. That they were hardy enough as a race there is no doubt, and nearly a hundred years later the "lappior" or buddle boy might still be seen treading out the tin sands in much the same manner.

Many processes had been added to those of Carew's day, by the time the anonymous writer described Cornish mining in 1671. (79) Among these may be mentioned "sizing" the tin in hair sieves, "dilleughing" in canvas sieves, and working over the slimes on a "reck" or hand-frame. The latter device consisted of an inclined frame of boards six feet long by three and a half broad, suspended on two pivots at each end, like a cradle. Over it flowed a gentle stream of water which distributed the tin over its surface, the richest at the top, the poorer grades flowing on to the bottom. At frequent intervals, when the proper distribution had taken place, the person in charge, generally a woman, tipped up the frame sideways, and the different grades of tin fell into "covers" prepared for them below. Down to the end of the nineteenth century these hand-frames were to be found in almost every tin-stream.

By the latter half of the eighteenth century the number of separate processes and variations of each process had increased to such an extent that Pryce confessed himself unable to describe one-half of them without danger of prolixity and confusion. The underlying principle, however, in every one was the same—namely, that of gravitation, tin itself being heavier than most of the impurities found associated with it. Thus the design of all tin-streaming operations from earliest times to the present day has been to enable the flow of water, whether it be a stream or gauged to a tiny trickle, to concentrate and deposit the heavy tin sands, whilst "flitting away" the lighter particles of waste.

An important development in tin-dressing, in use from the seventeenth century onwards, was that of burning or calcining the sands after their first washing, in order to drive off the sulphur and arsenic which are frequently associated with tin ore. Arsenic to-day is a by-product of fluctuating but often considerable value to the Cornish mines, thanks to the activity of the boll-weevil in the American cotton-fields. In the eighteenth century, however, being practically valueless, the poisonous fumes, instead of being condensed in flues, were allowed to go off from the short stacks of the burning-houses, to the devastation of all tender herbs and vegetation in the neighbourhood. The fumes were especially fatal to bees, "many of which," wrote Borlase, "have been killed off by the burning-houses of late years." (80) The effect of the fumes on the men who attended the burning-houses was sometimes hardly less fatal, and in almost every case those who made it their sole and constant employment greatly impaired their health by it. (81) The fuel used for this

ABOVE AND UNDERGROUND 107

burning was sometimes pit coal, but more often "burns" of furze, (82) the cutting and preparing of which for the mines kept quite a number of men in work. The sulphurous nature of the fumes released from the "brood," however, generally made the process of calcining largely self-consuming, once the furnace had been raised to the proper temperature.

After stamping and burning the tin sands were again returned to the dressing-floors, where they underwent innumerable cleansing processes, buddling, dillewing, chimming, tozing, and packing.

Tin-dressing in the eighteenth century, as now, was a particular trade to itself, entirely different from that of the underground miner, and rarely changed for any other occupation about the mine. During earlier times, when almost every process in tin-dressing was performed by hand, a peculiar skill and judgment was required by the tinner, on whose art the final profit of all depended.

Few, if any, of the tin-mines in the eighteenth century had sufficient water-power on their own set to do all their stamping. (83) Wheal Sparnon, in Redruth, had six sets of stamps in 1765, four of which, at any rate, were rented, two belonging to Mrs. Eliz. Michell, one to Captain Richard Painter, and one to Pednandrea Adventurers. The rent for one of these stamps was 4s. a week, and the total cost of the six amounted to only £87 a year. (84) Such stamps as those which had constant work and water would employ one man and five boys; and one hundred sacks could be carried, stamped, and dressed in the space of a few days, at the average rate of about 4d. per sack, or one guinea and a half per hundred. (85) Even so, the comparatively small amount of which they were capable necessitated having great numbers of these stamps. In the parish of St. Agnes alone there were twenty-five different sets at work in the year 1790, (86) either owned by the mines, rented by them from private owners, or in the hands of working tin-dressers, who treated mine ore on tribute for a certain percentage of its value. The number of persons engaged thus in this one parish must have been close on a hundred and fifty.

The number of stamps, water-wheels, and other engines at work throughout the mining districts in eighteenth-century

Cornwall made every rivulet of value to those through whose land it flowed. Money paid for "leave of water" is thus a constantly recurring item of expense in the cost-books of these days. Fifty pounds a month (87) was not uncommonly charged to mine adventurers for diverting quite small streams, and when this was done by a landowner without any recompense to his grist-mills tenants—to work a mine on his own land from which he was also drawing large royalties as mineral lord—it is easy to see, as Pryce says, for whose benefit the mines of Cornwall were at that time worked.

The smallness of most Cornish "rivers" necessitated a very careful use of such water as there was. Tonkin, writing of St. Agnes in the late seventeenth and early years of the eighteenth century, says : "The water arising in Trevaunance, in conjunction with Breanick watercourse, drives twelve stamping-mills and a grist-mill, which have been set for £240 per annum. There was formerly in Trevaunance Coom a Blowing House with another grist-mill, but the water beginning to decay in his time, the Pell adit being then begun, my grandfather, Thomas Tonkin, removed them to Melonbrey, commonly called Lenobrey. The water cut off by the Pell adit, as above, was brought back again to the said Coom by a leat cut at very great expense through the cliff from the tail of the adit by my father, Hugh Tonkin, in 1696, and (now) runs over all the said stamping-mills and grist-mills except the upper one." (88)

Similar economy was practised at Dolcoath, where, many years later, two large water-wheels were in use for pumping. The famous plan of the mine printed by Pryce in 1778 shows that the water flowing over the first wheel at surface descended a short distance through the shaft, from whence it flowed back through a shallow level to work a second wheel. After turning this the water finally left the mine by the adit. Still more complicated were the arrangements at Trenethick Wood and Trevenen Mines, near Helston. In order to drain these mines the Cober River was diverted into Trevenen Mine, and thence into Trenethick, from whence it flowed out by the adit. From the tail of this adit the water was conveyed by a second adit (cut for the purpose) into the Cober Valley, in the hill-side above Lowertown. A water-wheel placed between the shallow and deep adits drained Trevenen Mine when it was originally worked. Trenethick Wood Mine was drained by a large hydraulic engine erected by Trevithick about 1800, and subsequently by a large water-wheel." (89)

Through the skill and resourcefulness of the old miners, mere rivulets were often conveyed many miles across the country to drive an engine and then returned as far back as possible to serve other mines and stamping-mills. Thus, in the Redruth district, the water from Trewirgie Downs Mine, together with that from Wheal Beauchamp, after being brought in by a leat through Wheal Sparnon, was allowed to fall through one of the Pednandrea shafts, thereby increasing the flow of water coming from the adit of this mine. From the tail of the Pednandrea adit, which empties near Plain-an-gwarry, the water was conveyed a distance of six miles, out through North Country, Wheal Peever, and Sinns Common, and so back to Scorrier. Here, the ground rising to a level of ten fathoms above the leat, the water was brought through a tunnel 700 fathoms in length, which, entering the hill between Wheal Rose and Wheal Hawke (and passing almost under Wheal Chance), came out again between Scorrier and Killifreth, and thus delivered the water to its final destination at Wheal Unity. (90)

Two other important leats are shown in Richard Thomas's map of the Camborne–Chasewater mining district in 1819, both bringing in water at different levels from Selligan (Carnkye) to the mines round the foot of Carn Brea. The upper one went only as far as Wheal Druid, where it worked a water-pressure engine which had been originally erected by Richard Trevithick. The lower one, after passing by, or through, the mines of Barncoose, Tregajorran, Wheal Fanny, Wheal Providence, and Tin Croft, joined with the water coming down the Entral Valley in supplying the great Cook's Kitchen Mine. (91)

Still later the value of a stream of water in a mining country was described by Carne, who wrote of St. Just in 1822 : " In the short distance between Bostraze and the sea the stream which passes through Nancherrow turns the wheels of no less than seventeen stamping-mills and three grist-mills." (92) The water for the engines of many of the mines which cling to the face of the cliffs in this district had frequently to be brought through leats cut in the most precipitous places. In not a few instances the launders, by which the water is conveyed across some 'zawn" or chasm, can still be seen, supported by chains slung from some overhanging rock above. In spite, however, of all the skill and adroitness shown by the miners of the eighteenth century in conveying water, many of the surface engines were forced to lie idle during the driest months of the year, between May and October. "You'l have a very small quantity of Farm (tin) at Michs. Coynage," wrote one agent to the mineral lord in September, 1783, "as there is no work Stamp'd from Wheal Clay, and no water for the Stampises." (93)

The early decades of the eighteenth century had seen great changes in the methods of smelting tin no less than in that of mining and preparing the ore. Down to the beginning of the eighteenth century, all tin ore, whether from the mine or alluvial stream, was brought to a metallic state in the blowing-houses, of which a description has already been given. Owing to the scarcity of wood fuel, however, attempts had been made from early times to try to smelt tin with pit coal. Amongst the first of the would-be inventors was Sir Bevil Grenville, whose experiments, conducted about 1640, came to nothing. (94) It was not until the year 1703, under a patent of Queen Anne, that a German chemist, Francis Moult, together with a Mr. Lydall, set up "iron furnaces" for smelting tin with fossil coal at Newham, near Truro. (95) Angarrack Smelting Works were started by the same firm in the following year (1704), and in 1711 their main business was transferred to Calenick, (96) which long continued to be one of the chief smelting-houses of Cornwall. The invention of the reverberatory furnace followed soon after this, and, though stream tin continued to be blown in the old fashion, the "melting-houses" soon absorbed most of the mine ores. To start with, however, the new method was regarded with great suspicion, and the first year or two must have been an anxious time for the two partners. Not only did they have the natural opposition of the blowing-house owners, but the officers of the coinage themselves "earnestly recommended" to the tinners to avoid "the new melting-house" and to continue "to make their Tinn fine in the Blowing-houses. You will find by the inclosed accompt," they wrote, in February 1704, "that there are a great many tared (i.e. below standard) pieces of tin this Coynage, particularly at Helston . . . . which we found increased by the great quantity of tinn sent thither after us from the new melting-house erected near Truro for melting the tinn with Sea Coale after a new projection, which we observed afforded a great deale of Foule tinn." In spite of opposition, however, "the new projection" had come to stay. On January 21, 1706, the officers wrote from Truro, "we coined in all at this place 2,372 Blocks, a vast quantity. The Melting house has thrown in an incredible quantity . . . we continued coyning till night put an end to our labours." Ten days later they wrote : " They brought vast quantities of tin to Helston from the eastern houses and the melting house at Truro—906 Blocks coined," and whilst at Penzance " we had account that the three Western Blowing Houses would send in but 400 pieces and about 100 pieces from a New Melting House erected by Mr. Lyall in these parts that Melts with Sea Coale, (97) we now fear the quantity will amount to 600 or 650 Blocks." By May of the same year, the coinage officers had altered their opinion of the new method, and they declared that " the Melting House Tinn passes the Essay Master with less Tare in proportion than the Tin generally does that is brought to be coyned from the Blowing Houses," although it still fetched a somewhat lower price. (98)

The account-books which are still in existence of the original smelting-works at Newham show that twenty men were employed at a wage of about 25s. a month ; " Mr. Heyden," the overseer, alone getting £3. The work of landing coals, clay, lime, brick, and sand from the River Fal was done almost entirely by barrow-women. In addition to their monthly wage, the smelting-house men got certain allowances, the chief of these being for drink on the occasions of the hot and exhausting labour of "kettleing the tin." " Drink money" seems almost always to have been allowed to the "tinners" also, as an encouragement to bring their tin to Newham. (99)

The tin run off from the first smelting was laden into moor-stone moulds, to form slabs or blocks of about $\frac{3}{4}$ cwt., and these were afterwards run down again in a gentle fire. From this melting the metal flowed off through an open tap-hole into a large basin called the "float." While this was doing the workmen stood by, and raising the tin arm high with iron ladles, allowed it to fall plashingly back into the pool of silvery liquid metal. (100) This method of deoxidization, which entailed hours of heavy sweltering labour, was, at a later date, superseded by the device which still obtains of allowing a large block of green apple-wood to fall suddenly from some height into the basin of molten tin. The effect is instantaneous and remarkable. In a moment the dim smoky atmosphere of the smelting-house is lighted by a fountain of molten metal which, springing up fifteen feet or more into the air, falls splashing back into the basin, where the tin now boils like quicksilver, with volcanic fury. The workmen, in their leather aprons, seem to regard the flying specks of tin with complete unconcern, whilst the sight of their pasties keeping warm for dinner round the edge of the boiling basin gives a truly Cornish atmosphere to the scene. As soon as the tin has reached a correct degree of refinement it is ladled into bevelled moulds, formerly of moorstone but now of brass, and each ingot stamped with the smelters' house-mark.

Down to 1838, the tin smelter was paid by a deduction of a certain share from the quantity of metallic tin which he promised to deliver to the owner at the ensuing coinage. These promissory notes, known as "tin bills," were negotiable, like bills of exchange, and were often bought and sold. In most cases the owner sold the bill to the smelter himself, who, from the mid-eighteenth century onwards, has virtually taken the place of the old tin merchant. (101)

The isolation of Cornwall from the coalfields of England probably accounts for the fact that no manufactory of tin-ware has ever been established in the Duchy. What is more surprising is that throughout the eighteenth century hardly any of the Cornish block or bar tin was exported direct from Cornwall to its consumers in Holland, Turkey, and America. (102) In the majority of cases it was shipped in small vessels to London, from whence it was frequently carried back again past the Cornish coast.

The earliest information that we have concerning the trade of the "tin ships" between Cornwall and London is derived from the series of letters written between 1703–17 by the

[*Photo Preston, Penzance*

BOTALLACK MINE IN 1863. (See p. 248)

RIDING IN A "GIG" (NEWER STYLE). (See p. 334)

MAN-ENGINE IN UNDERLAY SHAFT (OLDER STYLE). COMING TO SURFACE (See p. 183)

officers of the pre-emption, during a time in which the tin was being bought by the Crown to save the tinners from the usury of the middleman or merchant. The tin, we learn, was at this date shipped to London in small vessels of fifty or sixty tons burden, some ten or a dozen of which were kept in constant employment. The Lostwithiel tin, which was always much less in quantity than that annually coined at Truro and Helston, had to be transported down the River Fowey in lighters before being placed on board the sea-going vessels, the river even in these days being too much silted up by sand from the alluvial tin-streams to admit of vessels of any draught. The tin from Truro was mostly shipped at "Mopus," though some was carried to Falmouth, Helston tin was taken to Gweek, whilst the Penzance tin was shipped either locally or from the Mount. In time of peace the freightage of the tin to London was 20s. a ton. On the many occasions, however, in which England was engaged in war with France, there was added to the usual risks attending sea transport in small and often overloaded vessels the danger from enemy privateers, and the tin ships had in consequence to proceed to London under strict convoy. At such times, in order to save the men-of-war the additional journey of sailing round to the Mount's Bay, the Penzance tin was carried overland on horseback to Helston, and from thence shipped with the Helston tin from "Gweeg" (Gweek). Here the convoys called for it and, proceeding to Falmouth, picked up the vessels bearing the Truro tin. The little fleet then sailed together up Channel, hugging the coasts as far as Fowey, where signal was made for the Lostwithiel tin ships to join them.

In March 1704–5 fourteen vessels were waiting in Falmouth laden with tin to the value of at least £60,000, a great deal too much to be entrusted to the slender convoy of one man-of-war, as the officers of the pre-emption complained. Two years later we read of two tin ships being taken by three privateers from Dunkirk, owing to insufficient guarding. The chief danger arose from the small French *picqueeroones*, who frequently lay so close under the land as not to be discovered until it was too late. Even ships loading far up in the rivers were not considered out of danger of these. "The coasts being infested much with small French Privateers," wrote the officers in 1705, "we are apprehensive the ships at Helford do not lie quite out of reach of danger, though we gave the masters strict order to keep aboard and maintain strict watch to prevent any surprise by boats, if the enemy should make any such attempts." They recommended, however, that a man-of-war should be sent to keep guard at the mouth of the Helford River whilst the ships at Gweek were loading, the river itself having no fortification to defend it.

Owing to contrary winds and other causes of delay the time occupied in conveying the tin to London was often excessive. "None of the tin ships are returned, and the Coynage Halls here and at Helston are so full of old Tinn that we have no room for receiving the Tinn at this Coynage or indeed to work. . . ." (103) wrote the officers from Truro in January 1705. Such delays did not greatly affect the tinners at times when the traffic was in the hands of the Crown and loans of ready money were being guaranteed them at a reasonable rate of interest. When, however, as in 1744, England was again at war with France, and there was no pre-emption and no regular system of convoys for bringing the tin ships (104) to London, the working tinners began to suffer severely. Had it not been for the influence of Sir John St. Aubyn, who, at last, succeeded in convincing the Admiralty of the necessity of appointing such a convoy, they would doubtless have suffered even worse than they did. As it was, there were not wanting moneyed men who, by tempting the tinners with ready cash to sell their tin at low prices, hoarded the metal till safe transit could be obtained, and thus contrived to make fortunes at their expense. (105)

On account of the cost of bringing coal to Cornwall, copper ore, which requires much more fuel than tin for its reduction, was from early times mostly smelted in South Wales. From the mid-eighteenth century, therefore, the fleet of shipping which was employed in bringing coal to Cornwall for the engines on the mines (106) found a ready return freight in the shape of copper ore. In every little Cornish port the important mines of the district had their own bins or hutches, where the ore was deposited prior to its shipment. Many of these may still be seen on the quays at Truro, Trevaunance, Portreath, Hayle, and elsewhere.

Copper smelting, however, was not finally given over to the

ABOVE AND UNDERGROUND

South Wales buyers before several serious attempts had been made to do it in Cornwall—and failed. Of these probably the earliest were the works at Perranporth, which have already been described as conducted by Ulrick Frose in 1586. After these had been removed to Neath, nothing is heard of Cornish copper smelting till the eighteenth century, except for a note made by Celia Finnes in 1696, that "they do melt a little at St. Ives, but nothing that is considerable." (107) In the early years of the eighteenth century, however, an attempt to smelt copper was made at Polruddan, St. Austell. After this, Mr. John Pollard, of Redruth, and Mr. Thomas Worth, of St. Ives (the latter had probably been connected with the St. Ives smelter), made another trial—and failed. After these, Gideon Cosier, of Piran Zabuloe, erected a smelting-house at Phillack, but being taken off by a fever, the same was continued by Sir William Pendarves and Robert Corker, Esq. At their death the business again fell through. Then a small beginning was made at Lenobrey, in St. Agnes, where some copper was smelted with good results, but was given over shortly after for want of a stock to go on with. (108)

At last an attempt was made which was crowned with success. About the year 1754, one Sampson Swaine, supported by several Camborne gentlemen—Mr. Harry John, Rev. Wm. Trevenen, Mr. George John, and Mr. John Vivian, of Rosewarne—erected furnaces at Entral and Rosewarne Downs. (109) From here they shortly afterwards removed to the Phillack estuary, near Hayle, where their factories and furnaces, together with workmen's and managers' houses, formed the nucleus of the present-day suburb of Copperhouse. Maton, who visited the works about 1790, has left a rather terrible picture of the deleterious effects upon the men of this employment. "Nothing can be more shocking than the appearance which these workmen exhibit," he writes. "Some of the poor wretches who were lading the liquid metal from the furnaces to the moulds looked more like walking corpses than living beings." (110) Making allowance for the sallow complexions of the men being heightened by the glare of the fires, there was still much truth in Maton's description, for, as Hitchens and Drew stated some years later, an emaciated appearance was common amongst all the men, and many, with less robust constitutions, found early graves. (111) The Copperhouse Works, together with the copper-sheet rolling mills at Treloweth, continued in a fair way of prosperity down to the year 1806, when the works were sold up and copper smelting was finally removed to South Wales. (112)

NOTES.

1. Pryce, 141.
2. Lewis, 194 *n*.
3. Cf. P.R.O. Ancient Correspondence Book 48, No. 81. My best thanks are due to Mr. Clowes, of the Duchy of Cornwall Office, who first called my attention to this letter, parts of which are here translated from the Norman French.
4. Cf. Mr. Lewis's summary, 194–5.
5. Quoted in G. G. Francis, *Smelting of Copper in the Swansea District*.
6. Such primitive methods for raising and lowering the men were in use in the collieries down to the fifties of the last century, when clusters of men might be seen riding to surface in the stirrups of a rope, from pits a thousand feet deep.—*Coal and Coal Pits*.
7. Old workings exactly answering to this description may still be seen on the back of the Gool-pelles lode near St. Ives. These are known locally as the "Old Doman" (i.e. Old Woman).
8. Cf. illustrations to Agricola's *De re Metallica*.
9. Philosoph. Trans., 1668.
10. Philosoph. Trans., 1671. This almost sounds as if the bringing down of air by means of a jet of water might even then have been used, although there is no direct evidence of its introduction into Cornish mines till 130 years later.—Cf. Henwood, R.G.S.C., viii, 220.
11. Philosoph. Trans., 1668.
12. Carew.
13. Cf. R.G.S.C. (1846), 330, 338.
14. Examples of these early Cornish shovels may be seen in the County Museum at Truro.
15. Philosoph. Trans., 1671.
16. Cunnack MS.
17. In certain places underground the name or initials of some former worker may be seen cut in the walls of the drift or level. Mr. Cunnack mentions such a one, dated about 1760, in Wheal Fortune, Breage, where, as in Wheal Vor, curious old earthenware lamps or "chills" were also

discovered. I well remember myself, whilst walking through the third level of Geevor Mine towards Wheal Carne, seeing the glint of the candle bring into momentary relief the simple epitaph, " K. 1790 "—the last memorial of some long-forgotten miner.
18. Cf. Lewis, 10.
19. Lewis, 11.
20. *Through England on a Side-Saddle*, 1695.
21. Cal. S.P. Dom., 1635-6, 550.
22. *Nat. Hist.*, 85.
23. *Mineralogia Cornubiensis*, Intro. ix.
24. *Mineralogia Cornubiensis*, Intro. viii.
25. *Mineralogia Cornubiensis*, Intro. xi. (1778).
26. Cf. Carew.
27. John Houghton, *Collections for the Improvement of Trade*, ii, 187, ed. MDCCXXVII. Five copper companies were formed in England about this time : Dockwra, Hern, Derby, Welsh, and Cumberland. A lot of stock-jobbing was done and money spent, but little found in return.
28. Proposals concerning English and Welsh Mines and Minerals, 1699.
29. The core or best parts of the lode.
30. Borlase, *Nat. Hist.*, 205.
31. Boulton and Watt MSS. " Account of the State of the Principal Mines of Cornwall at the time of the Introduction of Mr. Watt's Engines."
32. R.G.S.C., iv, 85.
33. Tonkin's Notes to Carew's *Survey*, ed. 1811, 37.
34. R.G.S.C., iv, 71-94.
35. Copied from Breage parish register.
36. R.G.S.C., iv, 86.
37. Pryce, 142.
38. Henwood, R.I.C. (1869), 17.
39. R. Thomas, *Report on Survey of Mining District*, 1819.
40. Wheal Unity Cost-Book.
41. Pryce, 149.
42. Pryce, 148.
43. Pryce, 149.
44. Cost-Books. Other adits being driven in this area between 1740-70 were " Dolcoath Deep Adit," in the lands of eleven adventurers, who included Francis Basset and Sir John Molesworth, " New Dudnance Adit," " South Long Close Adit," and " New Penhellick Adit." Longclose Adit " Dish " alone (consisting of $\frac{1}{12}$) gave the Basset family as much as £5,766 in the year 1760, and in 1765 their dues from the mines of this district were close on £20,000.—Various MSS.
45. Letter at Chyandour.
46. Cf. R. Thomas's Report, 1819.

47. Pryce, 168.
48. A similar disaster, involving a much greater loss of life, occurred in Wheal Owles, St. Just, in 1893.
49. Pryce, 147. This device, known as a " cow," is still occasionally used in sinking small shafts and other workings in West Cornwall. The method of ventilating mines by allowing a stream of water to fall close to the end of an air-pipe is not mentioned by Pryce, and was perhaps not known in his day. It was in use, however, in Tincroft Mine in 1802, in Dolcoath in 1807, in Crenver and Wheal Abram in 1814, and in North Roskear in 1817.—R.G.S.C., viii, 220.
50. Pryce, 151.
51. Pryce, 150–1.
52. Pryce, 165.
53. Wheal Gorland Cost, 1794.
54. Maton, i, 155.
55. *Life of W. West*, 1.
56. Cf. Poldice Cost, 1808.
57. Pryce, 151.
58. For an explanation, cf. Penzance Nat. Hist. and Antiq. Soc. Report, 1891–2.
59. R. Cunnack MS.
60. R. Cunnack MS.
61. R. Cunnack MS.
62. W. Francis, *Gwennap*, 13.
63. It is said by Joseph Hornblower, the first member of that family to come to Cornwall.—Cf. Henwood, R.I.C. (1871), 43.
64. Tonkin MS., St. Agnes.
65. Worth, 22.
66. Borlase, *Nat. Hist.*, 174–5.
67. The coal consumed by the engine at Great Work mine for December 1760 was sixty-six weys odd, which, with coal at 45s. a wey, cost £150. Added to this the carriage from Hayle at 13s. 6d. a wey, which was divided amongst twenty carriers, gave a total cost of £295 for coal consumed in one winter month. In December 1762, however, the coal bill only amounted to £107. The cylinder of the Great Work engine had been brought from Ludgvan-Lees Mine in 1754.—Cf. Great Work Cost-Book, 1759–64.
68. W. Francis, *Gwennap*, 54–5.
69. Pryce, 189.
70. Pryce, 313.
71. Boulton and Watt MSS. "Account of Mines of Cornwall at the Time of Introduction of Mr. Watt's Engines." A wey or weigh = 3 tons, or 144 bushels.
72. Worth, R.C.P.S., 1872.
73. Boulton and Watt MSS.
74. "A Tour into Cornwall," by James Forbes, 1794. A MS. for-

ABOVE AND UNDERGROUND

merly in the possession of Mr. J. A. D. Bridger, Penzance, and viewed by his kind permission.

75. Swete MS., 1780. Also seen through kind permission of Mr. J. A. D. Bridger, Penzance.

76. This seems to closely correspond to "searging" with a hair-sieve, a process still used by the tin streamers near St. Austell.

77. *Survey of Cornwall*, 12 (1769). This latter is the earliest mention of what may have been either the Cornish square buddle or the slime "trunk," both of which were to be found in nearly all mines until late in the last century.

78. *Nat. Hist.*, 180.
79. Philosoph. Trans., 1671.
80. *Nat. Hist.*, 250.
81. *Nat. Hist.*, 134.
82. Cost-Books, 1760–1800.

83. Great Work Mine, in 1759–64, possessed two sets of stamps of its own, whose charge was regularly entered in the monthly cost of the mine. The treatment of its "leavings," however, kept six other, privately owned, stamps at work.—Cf. Cost-Book. In the valuation of Chacewater Mine in 1790, six sets of stamps are included.—Cf. Boulton and Watt MSS.

84. Wheal Sparnon Cost, 1766. The stamps were no longer merely great logs of wood as in Carew's day, but were provided with heads of iron, which had increased from 40 lb. in 1671 to 140 lb. weight in 1778. There is a tradition that during Sydney Godolphin's time (Queen Anne) convicts were sent into Cornwall, and that at " Tranno "(?), in Breage, a kind of treadmill operated by convict labour was used to drive a stamping-mill.—R. Cunnack MS.

85. Borlase, *Nat. Hist.*, 181.
86. Chyandour Papers. Poor Rate Assessment.
87. Maton, i, 152.
88 Tonkin's MS. at R.I.C. Library, Truro.
89. R. Cunnack MS. Notes.
90. Richard Thomas, Map of Camborne to Chasewater, 1819. Also Report.
91. Both these leats are crossed to-day by the rough road which leads from Carn Brea village to the Castle.
92. R.G.S.C., ii, 333.
93. Chyandour Papers.
94. Pryce, 282.
95. Pryce, 282.
96. R.I.C. Journal, xix, 1913.
97. I.e. at Angarrack. The increasing use of pit coal, so far from rendering Cornwall more wooded, caused a greater neglect of coppice woods than had been of old, and largely accounts for the bareness of West Cornwall to-day.—Carew, 1811. Tonkin's note, 70.
98. The above facts are derived from a MS., in private possession,

containing copies of the letters of the officers of the pre-emption in Cornwall, 1703-17, to Sydney Godolphin, Lord High Treasurer.

99. Books at Chyandour.
100. Pryce, 284.
101. Pryce, 291.
102. Pryce, 295.
103. Extracts from Letter Book of the officers of the pre-emption.
104. W. C. Borlase, *Sketch of Tin Trade*, 55. In ordinary times the tin ships provided a useful means for the Cornish people conveying parcels and goods to the metropolis. The boxes of Cornish minerals, which Dr. William Borlase was at such pains to provide for the Ashmolean Museum in Oxford, were nearly all dispatched to London in this way—by the "Turnpenny" tin ship.
105. In 1756 George Borlase, brother of the Doctor, wrote complaining that the town of Penzance was quite defenceless, being without arms, ammunition, or any ship of force, "so that an enemy privateer could strip the town and set fire to it afterwards without the least hazard, and as there is a great deal of tyn lying dead, their plunder upon that and other trade could not be less worth than £50,000."—Lanisly Letters, MS. copy.
106. In 1799 the quantity of coals annually consumed by the "Fire-Engines" in Cornwall was estimated at 60,000 tons, in carrying which, and returning with copper ore, 8,000 to 10,000 tons of shipping was constantly employed.—Report of Committee on Copper Mines, 1799. The coal was landed at various small ports, such as Newham, Daniell's Point, Pill, etc., on the Fal River, Marazion in Mount's Bay, Lelant, St. Ives, Portreath, Trevaunance, the Gannel, and Newquay on the north coast.—Old Cost Books. Hayle, however, was perhaps the chief port of the coal fleet, which greatly increased in size with the renewed activity in mining in the early decades of the nineteenth century. The following entries in the diary of an old St. Ives resident, Captain Tregarthen Short, are of interest in showing this:—

"*March* 5, 1833.—A large number of vessels sailed from this port and Hayle. The wind suddenly flew to the north, with a strong gale. Over twenty vessels put back—some to St. Ives, others went round the land.

"*March* 8, 1833.—Sailed the Welsh fleet, twenty-nine sail.

"*February* 11, 1834.—Wind N.N.W. Sailed the whole of the wind-bound vessels for their several destinations coastwise, also the *Amity* and *Mary* for the Mediterranean with fish. . . . Arrived and gone into Hayle a great many of the Welsh fleet; some of them have been up Channel for fourteen weeks."

107. *Through England on a Side-Saddle*.
108. Pryce, 277-8.
109. MS. Note by James Vivian in what is now my copy of Pryce's *Mineralogia Cornubiensis*.
110. Maton, i, 233.

111. *Hist. Cornwall*, i, 62.

112. A furnace for reducing copper ore by a blast which had been erected by Richard Trevithick at Dolcoath, after working for a number of years on the mine, was likewise abandoned about the same date.— Cf. *Life*, by F. Trevithick, ii, 10. A copper smelting works was also established for a short period at North Downs, near Redruth, from whence it was removed to Tregew, on a branch of Falmouth Harbour. Considerable numbers of small parcels of ore were at one time bought by this company.— Cf. Pryce, 280.

CHAPTER IV

VARYING FORTUNES OF THE MINERS—1500-1800

I

THAT "a tinner has nothing to lose" and that he is "never broke till his neck's broke" were proverbial sayings once very familiar to Cornishmen.

During the Middle Ages the Cornish tinners were, as a whole, far less protected by mining law than their fellow-workmen in Germany and those of other trades in England. Between the Mediaeval Guild and the Stannaries there was, as Mr. Lewis has shown, this difference, that "whilst the Guild afforded mutual protection and limitation of competition amongst its members, the whole essence of the Stannary was to encourage individual enterprise and competition." (1)

Stannary law and stannary privileges, owing their origin, as they clearly do, to a desire to increase the production of tin and the consequent revenues, may be ascribed to interested regal condescension rather than to any mutual combination on the part of the tinners. On the other hand, the system of coinage, by which the tinner was forced to pay for these privileges, must have weighed so heavily upon all as to make it extremely doubtful whether, if refusal of a kingly proffer had been possible, they would ever have been accepted.

As it was, the fact that tin might only be sold on two, or latterly four, occasions in the year threw the tinner from earliest times upon the tender mercies of the middleman or tin merchant, who advanced him small sums of ready money in return for a promise of delivery of tin at the next coinage, frequently of double or treble the value. Thus before the all-important occasion arrived, the poorer tinner's stock of tin was almost always overpledged.

Of the economic conditions of tinners and of their relations with these dealers practically nothing is known before the fourteenth century. De Wrotham, in 1198, just mentions that there were four classes of people in the stannaries—diggers, smelters, ore buyers, and tin dealers. It was not until 1304, when the merchant tin buyers in Cornwall petitioned the King that they might have the two feasts of All Saints and St. John the Baptist on which to pay the coinage duties, that it becomes clear that the tinners, in return for ready money, had already adopted the expedient of pledging their tin in advance to the merchants, who subsequently discharged the coinage duties for them. (2) Throughout the fifteenth century the same methods were pursued, and in 1455 we are told that "Italian merchants with ready money go about the country and, seeing the needs of the poor tinners, buy the tin cheap, as well as wool from the wool growers." (3) Further evidence on this subject has been collected by Mr. Lewis in his *History of the Stannaries*, but sufficient has been said to show the state of affairs under which the tinner laboured from early times.

With the increasing charges of working the tin in the sixteenth century, the grievances of the tinners became more acute. "To the enhanced cost, not only of food, clothing, and other necessities of life, but also of timber, rope, iron, candles, and mining requisites, daily becoming more and more important with the increasing depths of the works and the change from stream to lode mining, corresponded not, as one might expect, a threefold or fourfold rise in the price of tin, but an increase in price of only about one hundred per cent." (4) Every writer at this time makes the same complaint: "The usurer, money man, or merchant," it was stated about 1590, "buyeth of the poore tynners their tynn before the Coinage at £15 or £16 to the thousand weight, and sells it again to the pewterers of England for £28, or commonly £30, the thousand, making a hundred for a hundred in the year." (5) "The yearly value of the tin," says another writer in 1595-7, "is reckoned at £36,000, of which one-third is ordinarily borrowed beforehand of the merchant at 10, 8, or 7 per cent., to be repaid in tin. The poor tinners have lost £20 per 1,000 lbs. of tin paid by them instead of loans. The masters also make 15 per cent. gain on loans of money to the poor working tinners." (6)

The most vivid picture of all is given by Richard Carew, who wrote : "To these hungrie flies (the merchants) the poore labouring Tynner resorteth, desiring some money before the time of his pay at the deliverance (at the Coinage). The other puts him off at first, answering he hath none to spare ; in the end, when the poore man is driven through necessitie to renew his suite he fals to questioning, what hee will do with the money ? Saith the Tynner, 'I will buy bread and meate for myselfe and my household, and shoes, hosen, peticoates and such like stuffe for my wife and children.' Suddenly herein, this owner becomes a petie chapman : 'I will serve thee,' saith he. He delivers him so much ware as shall amount to fortie shillings, in which he cuts him halfe in halfe for the price of four nobles in money, for which the poore wretch is bound in Darbyes bonds, to deliver him two hundred Waight of Tynne at the next Coynage, which may then be worth five pound or foure at the verie least."

This example of usury so wantonly practised by the London merchants was followed (or rather exceeded) by the richer of the working tinners towards their brethren. "Whether it proceedeth from this hard dealing," concludes Carew, "or that the Tynners whole familie give themselves to a lazie kind of life, depending only on his uncertain gains, it hath been duly observed that the parishes where Tynne is wrought rest in a meaner plight of wealth than those which want this damageable commodite : and that as by abandoning this trade, they amend, so by reviving the same they decay againe, whereas husbandrie yeeldeth that certayne gaine in a mediocritie which Tynne workes rather promise, than performe in any large measure." (7)

It is, of course, a mere coincidence, although a curious one, that the last years of the sixteenth, seventeenth, eighteenth, and nineteenth centuries were all periods of great depression in Cornish mining.

As early as 1575 it was stated that "the tynn works do decaye, not onely for the contynuall workinge in the same whereby the worke is more deeper and therefore more chargeable to come by, but most chieflie for that the Tynners fyndinge smale comoditie thereby forsake the said worke and fale to Tyllage." (8) Twenty years later, Sir Fra. Godolphin, writing from the "Cornish Mynt," said : "In this time of great dearth of corn and other provisions, the tin mines also growing daily more chargeable to be wrought, by the greater depth, the greater quantity of timber required, the greater charge for drawing up water springs and the scarcity of wood, to beat down the price would either greatly discourage the tinners or cause them to fall into general discontent." (9) In 1597 the same writer stated that he believed " there were 10,000 idle loiterers in this small county." (10)

With prices fluctuating and conditions of life rapidly changing it is difficult to estimate how poor the Elizabethan tinner really was. In 1586, as has already been said, the wages, or rather dole or share, of a Blackmore streamer amounted to some £3 per year, out of which he had to keep himself, which cost about 2d. a day, and support his wife and family, to say nothing of payment for rent and clothes. (11) Such wages, one would imagine, could hardly have been sufficient to support human life. Carew, on the other hand, writing about the same time, or a few years later, states that the miners or " hirelings " received 8d. per day, or from £4 to £6 per year. The study of wages in Cornwall is a peculiarly deceptive one, since from earliest times the mining population has generally worked under a form of "tribute," that is, a share of the values produced by the mine or stream. This meant that a man might earn high wages one month and practically nothing the next, his livelihood depending on the uncertainties of nature's bounty. (12) This kind of working, though it was instrumental in producing first-rate miners, was apt to encourage in all but the steadiest men a reckless gambling spirit, and accounts for the fact that, as Carew said, the tin parishes were formerly " in a meaner plight of wealth " than those in which agriculture was the predominant industry.

When, however, it is stated that the tinners, towards the end of the sixteenth century, were turning from mining to husbandry, it ought not to be supposed that either streaming or mining stopped. In mining then, as now, an increase in the price of metal met with a corresponding mining activity ; new works were started or old ones revived, and more men were drawn in from other trades, attracted by hopes of high wages. As soon, however, as the boom subsided such mines closed down, and the men sought other employment. The real tinner or miner was, and is, differently created, being, like the poets, " born not made."

However poor his takings, so long as they suffice to keep body and soul together he will cling to the occupation which has for him the excitement and lure of a life adventure. In spite of statements, therefore, that the tinners were turning to tillage at the end of the sixteenth century, the output of tin from Devon and Cornwall, amounting to a yearly average of 1,100 thousand weight, remained almost unchanged between 1580 and 1596. (13)

During the last years of the sixteenth century, in order to relieve the tinners from their bondage to the tin merchants, a system of pre-emption was introduced. Loans were made to the tinners by the Crown on a large scale, at low rates of interest. Though excellent in its intention, pre-emption does not seem to have benefited the tinners very much; for whilst the prices of all commodities continued to rise, the price given for tin by the monopolists remained stationary. The Petition of the Tinners of Cornwall to the King in 1636 says that, "having been assembled to enquire concerning the causes of the decay of tinning and means to prevent the same, we can collect no other main reason but the daily increase of charge in our works, by reason of their deepness, whilst the price received is in no way advanced." (14)

The picture given by Westcote of the Devon tinners in 1630 corresponds to the same in Cornwall. Of day-labourers in tin-works, he writes: "Of these there are two sorts. One named Spalior or searcher for tin, than whom (as it seems to me) no labourer whatsoever undergoes greater hazard of peril and danger, nor in hard, coarse fare and diet doth equal him, bread the brownest, cheese the hardest, drink the thinnest; yea, commonly the dew of heaven: which he taketh either from his shovel or spade or in the hollow of his hand. (15) Miserable men! may some men say in regard to their labour and poverty; yet having a kind of content therein . . . and, these people though the most inferior are yet, notwithstanding, *liberi homines*, free-men of state and condition, no slaves." (16) Though their pay was slight, their holidays were numerous, the tinners' calendar, as Carew says, allowing them "more Holy-dayes, than are warranted by the Church, our lawes, or their owne profit." Their holy-day "exercises" consisted of "wrestling, hurling, football, leaping, dancing with music, especially in their festivals, to exhilarate their hearts, which made them fit for the wars or any other employment whatsoever, wherein hardiness, strength, or agility was required. But now," writes Westcote, "these exercises are by (Puritan) zeal discommended and discountenanced, yet no better nor so good used in their stead."

"To the regime of monopoly alternating with usury," wrote Mr. Lewis, "followed in the years 1650 to 1660 a policy on the part of the Commonwealth of complete *laissez-faire* as regards the stannaries, and certainly it must be admitted that in this respect, where Stuart nostrums had failed, Cromwellian non-interference was accompanied by a return in the Stannaries to a condition of abounding prosperity." (17) With the abolition of the coinage duty and of the pre-emption, there began a new era. "The price of tin rose. Multitudes of tradesmen left their callings for that of mining. Still the prices rose. Old abandoned works were filled again and new ones taken." And all this, says the chronicler, was owing to the tinners' freedom to sell at all times and at the best price. (18) The price of tin had actually risen from £3 to £6 per cwt., when, with the Restoration and consequent reaction, the Coinage rules were reimposed and coincidentally the wave of prosperity subsided, (19)

The years which followed were disastrous ones for the tinners of Cornwall. "To show the deplorable circumstance of the poor labouring Tinners," wrote the author of a pamphlet in 1697, "we will suppose (for demonstration sake) there are Eight Thousand Tinners yearly employed about the Tinning-Trade, although I am satisfied they much exceed that number." After deducting working expenses and coinage duties, "all that remains clear to be divided amongst 8,000 Tinners is but £40,338, which comes to be about £5 0s. 10d. per man." On these starvation wages "each Tinner hath to maintain himself and family, for his whole year's hard Labour, not only under Ground, but under God knows how many grievances. But, indeed," adds the writer, "they have been better able to bear them as being the most Herculean and stoutest men upon Earth; and for their most faithful and loyal services, have the greatest Privileges of Liberty and Property of any people in the Kingdom."

Both liberty and property, however, must have been more

apparent than real to men who at this time, "in some of the greatest Tin-Parishes, were forced to keep two Doles, and to work Day and Night in order to earn 14s. or 15s. per month." (20) When the mines or tin-works closed down, as they frequently did, "those who were ashamed to beg lay under the temptation of stealing or almost starving." "I have ordinarily seen such men," continues the same writer, "save sheep and Bullocks that have dyed in the fields by accident, tho' poor and lean (not being able to afford even salt to preserve the flesh). I am persuaded a great many families in the neighbourhood I live in do not make use of any other Flesh at their own tables twice in the year, their ordinary food being Potatoes and Barley-bread (as coarse as horse bread), with gruel thickened oftener with barley meal than oat meal. In summer they have the same sort of bread with milk only. And I have farther observed, in twenty or thirty years last past (by reason of the cold and hunger their youth suffer, having not rags enough to cover them), men are so reduced from well-grown persons to be now (comparatively) meer Pigmies in stature and strength, which is lamentable to behold." (21)

In 1703 a new offer of pre-emption, made by Queen Anne, was accepted with acclamation by the tinners, who thought they saw in it a salvation from their distress. This order remained in force for fourteen years, and with its lapse in 1717, pre-emption finally disappeared from the history of Cornish mining. How much good it did to the tinners it is hard to say, but, at any rate, the wave of depression which had mounted so high at the end of the seventeenth century subsided from one cause or another, and with it came a betterment of the tinners' condition. According to Tonkin, the best miners about 1730 were receiving 20s. to 27s. per month, all tools found, with additional pay when they made extra stems drawing water or stuff, or working at the capstan. "The miners' toil," he wrote, "is so far from being extreme, as Mr. Carew represents it, that few labourers I believe work so little, except when they draw water, for which there are so many engines now invented, that their labour is in a great measure taken off. For what between their numerous holidays, holiday eves, feasts, account days (once a month), yw-whiddns or one way or another they do not work half of their month for their owners and employers. It is further observable," he continues, "that once a fellow has taken to work tin, he shall hardly be persuaded to do anything else, though it were to keep his family from starving. In which respect the tinners are followed by the fishermen, of whom I have seen twenty or thirty together, basking themselves in the sun, when there has been no fish upon the coast, rather than they would go to earn a penny at husbandry work to buy bread for their wives and children who were at the same time starving for want." (22)

This picture of the miner of the early eighteenth century has doubtless something of a class bias about it, although the substance of the remarks is borne out by the statements of other writers. The feasts and holidays against which Tonkin inveighed (like other mineral lords who drew their fortunes from the mines) were festivals of ancient standing and in some cases seem to have been peculiar to the tinners. Those of St. Perran's Day (March 5th) and Chewidden (23) (the Thursday clear before Christmas) are the best known. According to a cost-book of Great Work Mine for the years 1759–62, the allowance for the men "at Perrantide" was 6d. and for the captains 1s. Of Chewidden there is no mention, although Borlase in 1758 stated that money was allowed "in all considerable mines" on both these days for the men to make merry. A similar amount was likewise always given at midsummer. The mines, however, were by this time evidently attempting to reduce the number of days which the men took off, and those who still persisted in observing "old Christmas Day" were "spaled" or fined for their absence.

It is, on the whole, a matter for marvel that any observation of ancient custom has survived in Cornwall, where, ever since the eighteenth century, any amusement of the working classes which was not discouraged by the gentry as tending to idleness was condemned by latter-day religionists as incompatible with the Christian calling. So one by one the old national pastimes of Cornwall—hurling, wrestling, running, guise-dancing, May games, Christmas plays, and many more—instead of being modified in character to suit the changing standards of civilization, were frowned upon and discouraged almost to the point of extinction, although, as Westcote said, "no better nor any so good have been substituted in their stead." So likewise have passed many of the old-time feasts, including those of St. Perran and Chewidden. The latter is now no longer heard on the tongue of the living; the former only remained until recently in the term "Perraner," which, used as a reproach to those whose footsteps were festive rather than steady, showed clearly enough the level to which the Saint's Day had sunk before its observance ceased altogether. Both feasts, it should be said, were throughout their hey-day regarded as commemorations of the first smelting of tin in Cornwall, the banner of St. Perran, with its white cross on a black ground, being, according to Gilbert's perhaps farfetched statement, an allusion to the black ore and white metal of tin.

In earlier times there is little doubt that such holidays were sometimes the occasion of bloody fights and pitched battles between parishes or the miners of different mines, a relic, as it is thought, of those ancient tribal feuds originally common amongst most Celtic peoples. One of the most serious or, at any rate, best remembered of the affrays which took place in later times was that known as the "St. Day Fight." What was the immediate cause of the quarrel between the inhabitants of Gwennap and Redruth or who were the real aggressors does not now appear; but the Redruth men, it is said, vowed on the occasion to take the life of the first living thing that they should meet in Gwennap. At Vogue they met a dog, which they killed, and, dyeing a handkerchief in its blood, carried it before them as a flag of defiance. In the contention which followed, at St. Day, many persons were severely wounded on both sides, and a man of Redruth, known by the name of Doctor Cock, lost his life. Victory is said, in the end, to have been assured for the St. Day men by certain women, who, leaning from the windows of the houses, shouted, "Hurrah! Gwennap men, Redruth men are running," a statement which, being taken seriously by the more timid of Uny's sons, led to their final rout. (24) Such affairs as these belong strictly to the older and rougher days and, together with cock-fighting and other brutal sports, had become of comparatively rare occurrence when Warner visited the county in 1808. "In the course of a few years," he wrote, "such fights will only be remembered in tradition: the spots where the scenes of disorder were held being now enclosed and a great part of them covered with habitations of the miners." (25)

The fact that the mines in former days took sufficient interest in the men to dole out money for their amusements shows clearly enough the personal and friendly relationship between employers and employed, which, on the whole, has always distinguished the Cornish mining industry. Very little is known of this side of the miner's life before the beginning of the eighteenth century, probably because in earlier times the distinction between the working adventurer (tributer) and the non-working adventurer (shareholder) was not a hard and fast one. With the development of mining, however, on a larger scale and the growth of capital investment, a new light begins to be shed on the miner's relationship towards the mine in which he worked, and the old cost-books take on a very human interest. Living in scattered cottages, without any of the communal system of village life such as existed in rural England, the central focus of the miner's life was the mine in which he worked. In a certain sense the mine took the place in Cornwall of the great squire or landlord in an English village. A great mine dominated the lives of hundreds of men, women, and children who lived in the neighbourhood of it. Whole families looked to it for their sole support. At an early age, eight years and upwards, children of both sexes were apprenticed to it, doing light jobs about the surface. Schools were not, and often the only opportunity the children had for playing together was in the dinner-hours at the mine or after work in the long days of summer. At twelve or fourteen years of age the boys proceeded underground miners, going below with their fathers and learning from them that skill in a hard and dangerous calling which has made the Cornish miner famous. The girls, too, as they grew older, continued to work on surface as " bal maidens," doing the heavier work of " spalling " or breaking the copper ores, an occupation at which they generally remained until they were married.

A Cornish mine in the eighteenth century (and indeed throughout the nineteenth century until the decay of the cost-book system) had for its principal manager the purser or book-keeper, who kept the accounts, made the necessary calls, and paid out the dividends. The purser himself was generally one of the adventurers (shareholders) who was chosen by the rest for the administration of their affairs during the intervals of the monthly meetings, at each of which a statement of accounts of the mine was produced and passed, and the total charge divided among the adventurers in proportion to the dole or share which each one held in the interest. Many of the adventurers were also merchants and, independently of the fortunes of the mine, did very well by supplying the concern with coal, ropes, candles, timber, or other materials. These were termed "in-adventurers," the rest, who lived at a distance from the mine or had no immediate interest in it as merchants, being called "out-adventurers." The actual working of the mine was deputed to inferior captains—inferior to the purser, that is, in book knowledge and in salary, but in most cases men of great practical experience. Captains were divided into underground captains and grass captains, the latter being responsible for the preparation or dressing of the tin and copper ores after their arrival on surface. In most cases the captains, as well as having to keep the mine above and below ground in order and repair, were responsible for the delivery of materials, such as gunpowder, candles, shovels, pick hilts, etc., to the men, and in this connection, as in the setting of pitches and other matters, a great part of the adventurers' profits depended on their integrity. (26)

As a typical example of an eighteenth-century mine, we may quote from the cost-book of "Great Work" for the years 1759–64. The mine was in the hands of eleven adventurers, who held shares varying from 1/48th to 1/4th, the monthly cost being about £500. The employees consisted of a purser at 50s., who also got an extra guinea a month "for inspecting the engine," and four captains at 40s. a month. Four "binders," or, as they would now be called, timbermen, were, together with the pitman, the next most highly-paid men on the mine, receiving about 42s. a month each. Binders' tenders or assistants, five or six in number, received only 22s. to 24s. a month. Next came the carpenters, of whom three were employed at from 27s. to 36s. Sawyers (two) received 18s. to 24s.; smiths (seven) from 30s. to 35s. (the head one 42s.), and smiths' strikers (five) from 22s. to 24s. a month. The four engine-men employed received 10s. to 12s. a week, which was a good wage and much better, in proportion to the cost of living, than this class of men received seventy years later, when engine-men were generally both ill-paid and ignorant. In addition to these there was also a "coal-meter" at 21s. a month, who spent most of his time at Carnsew or Lelant Cellars, where the coal was bought. The miners in Great Work, who seem to have been mostly engaged on tutwork (contract), were the lowest paid of the lot. They were denominated according to the part of the mine in which they worked, as Engine Winns men, Crane Winns men, Pennecks, ... Westren, ... Wheal Blow, ... etc. Their wages varied from 16s. to 21s. a month. In common with the rest of the employees on the mine, the miners frequently made extra stems amounting to 1s. or 1s. 6d. a month, which were always entered in a separate column of the monthly cost. In connection with the raising of the ore, nine landers were employed at 24s. a month, and fourteen whim men, who were paid at rates varying from 5s. to 12s. per hundred kibbles, according to the depth of the level from which the stuff was being "haled." About twenty "grass men" were engaged at surface dressing the ore, at an average wage of 18s. a month. Low as the wages were, considerable "spales" or fines were often inflicted. In February 1760 no less than seventy-six men had deductions made, two of the captains being fined 15s. and 10s., and the others 5s., 4s., 3s., or 1s. respectively. This may have been because of a wet month, when the engine required much repairing and the men had refused attendance, or it may have resulted from some rich wreck in the neighbourhood, when the miners had gone off to join one of those plundering "bands 2,000 strong" of which we read, leaving the mine to take care of itself.

Pryce, who knew the conditions of all classes of miners well, was always strong in advocating their better payment. Of the mine "captains" he wrote: "Though it is much to be feared that adventurers are often injured by dishonest captains, in conniving at the impositions of the common men; yet I must declare my opinion that many private peculations originate from the parsimony of the masters themselves. It is an aphorism in mining that 'A Tinner has nothing to lose,' but upon tribute or searching for Tin upon the mere strength of his labour, he puts himself in the way of fortune, to enrich him by one lucky hit. I therefore reckon a Tinner upon Tribute, if he can clear 30s. monthly with the chance annexed of gaining four times as much, is better off than a captain at 40s. without any further chance." (27)

This system of tribute, which has already been several times referred to, seems to have existed in one form or another in almost every metalliferous mining district of the world. Under it the miner, in lieu of ordinary wages, agrees to work for a percentage of the total value of the ores he sends to surface, after paying the cost of all tools and material necessary for winning the same. In Cornwall, in the eighteenth century, a whole mine was occasionally set or leased on tribute, in some instances for several years, but generally for periods of three or six months at a time. Thus at a survey held at Wheal Busy, on Buswase in Ludgvan, in the year 1756, it was agreed to set the mine (a very small one) on tribute. In this instance the takers, who were required to be eight men at least, were "to be at the expense of all working charges except pumps and keeping the Ingen in good repair, . . . to work the mine regular, to give the owners liberty to go underground and inspect, to put in good timber, to secure the work, not to drive further than a certain point, and to have the use of tools and the running takel, yielding them up in the same repair as they received them." For all this the takers, " Will Curnow and partners, agreed to paye and laye out on the grass 2½ doals out of five doals of all tyn and tyn stuff they raised or broke out of the said mine, Spald and fit for stampin." (28)

More frequently this system was applied to the taking of small sets and bounds by parties of tributers, who either directly worked them themselves or again sublet them to others. Thus a set in " Carn Barges," St. Agnes, was granted in 1770 " to Wm. Moulsery and partners to drive seventy fathoms East in the said bounds on any Load or Loads they shall or may discover in driving their addit called by the name of Treasure Troy, and the said Wm. Moulsery to have all Backs and Bottoms . . . and to keep the mine in a constant source of working, for which they shall pay the said owner 1/12th part of all Tin they shall return in the above said set at the Smelting House free of

VARYING FORTUNES OF THE MINERS

all charge, and to give him or his agent twenty-four hours' notice for taking out the same."

The usual rate for the "lord's dish or dole" at this time was either, as stated above, " 1/12th in white tin at the smelting-house " or " 1/9th part in stone at grass." (29) Such doles or shares were generally measured out in barrows and actually placed in separate piles for each owner to remove himself. " Every mine," wrote Maton in 1794, "enjoys the privilege of having the ore distributed on the adjacent fields." The re-division of the doles and parts of doles amongst the tributers themselves was extremely complicated and would at first sight, says Pryce, " puzzle the most expert mathematician. Yet it is effected by our illiterate tinners upon the simplest plan and with the utmost dexterity, dispatch, and accuracy. To any other but a Cornish reader, it may appear strange that so much trouble should be taken in dividing and re-dividing the Tin stuff in this manner, when it might be carried and returned altogether and the proportions reckoned in money ; but this cannot always be done ; for stamping mills are numerous and the separate estates of several people, whose value rises in proportion to the use and employment they have for them ; therefore, if the Tin-stuff is rich, everyone is ready to carry off his respective Dole or share immediately after it is divided out." (30)

In the case of a copper-mine or set there was this difference, that the respective doles or shares belonging to the lord, the adventurers, and the tributers were divided in money and not, as in the case of tin stuff, in kind. Thus, as an example, it used to be said that " Petherick Kernick of Hantergantick, Abednego Baragwanath of Towednack, Dungey Crowgie of Carnalizzy, and Degory Tripconey of Gumford, have jointly taken a copper mine upon tribute for nine and sixpence out of the pound." (31)

The system of setting whole mines upon tribute died out about the beginning of the nineteenth century. What, however, had always been much more common was the setting on tribute of portions of ground in large mines called "pitches," and this remained general until recent years. A pitch consisted of a section of the mineralized ground, of strictly determined length and height, wherein the tributer and those working with him (called a "pare" of men) agreed to extract what they could, receiving so many shillings for every pound's worth of ore they sent to surface. Periodically the mine would be inspected by the captains and the price at which every part of the labour ought to be performed noted, and then, on a certain day in each month, known as "setting" day, all the tributers would assemble in front of the count-house, the steps or stairs to the upper story of which were generally on the outside and terminated by a sort of covered stand. Here the principal captain would take his station, accompanied by the mine clerk and frequently the underground captains. A handful of pebbles was given to him, and the auction began. The clerk read aloud the description of the work to be done in a certain pitch and the number of hands to be employed on it during the succeeding month or given period. A voice from the men below would propose, perhaps, to take it on condition of receiving 10s. in the £ of all the ores he might raise in the stated time. To this the captain would probably propose 7s., at which another voice from among the men might call 8s. 6d. The captain would then immediately recite aloud the proposition which he had received, at the same time taking a pebble and throwing it in the air. No other proposition being called by the time it reached the ground, the last bidder was considered to have secured the pitch, and as "taker" his name and the number of his companions were immediately entered by the clerk in the "bargain" book provided for this purpose. (32) Thus the "setting," as it was termed, would proceed till the majority of the pitches were taken, the rest being left for afterbargains. The remainder of the day, and sometimes the whole of the next, was idle for the underground miners, who, under pretence of preparing and sharpening their tools, rendered it practically a general holiday. (33)

The following serve as examples of the way in which tribute pitches were actually described :—

BRIGAN MINE, *June* 8, 1793.

A Pitch from Nancarrow's shaft so far east as to join Amos Nicholls' Pitch from the 55 fathom level as deep as the 61 fathom level.

2 men.   Thos. Cocking (Taker)
till August Sampling, 13s. 4d. (34)

Or again :—

WHEAL ROSE, 30 *December*, 1798.

A new pitch from the Ladder Winze as far West as Halebeagle East shaft, from the back of the Level so high as to join Henry Trezize's Pitch.

2 men.   Till sampling in Feb., 4s. 6d.

John Martin   } (Takers) (35)
James Williams

The meaning of this was that, in the first case, Thomas Cocking agreed to work on the lode or lodes for so many fathoms long and deep, receiving 13s. 4d. for every pound's worth of ore he raised, whilst in the second case, where the lode was evidently a rich one, John Martin and John Williams were willing to work under similar conditions, receiving only 4s. 6d. on every pound's worth of stuff they sent to surface.

The men so working provided their own tools and materials, such as gunpowder, candles, etc., and in some cases even paid for the cost of "haleing the ore to grass." Shops and stores being few and far between, the men generally got their tools from the mine, (36) and in earlier days, on the completion of the bargain, each man was given 6d. to drink. "If the tributer," wrote an observer in 1815, "after covering the cost of tools and repairing them, together with such candles and powder as he may use and the charge of drawing his work to surface and rendering it merchantable by the women and children whom he employs, contrives to gain 20s. a week for himself, he considers that he has made wages, i.e. a decent living. If his work allows him such wages, he is, commonly, at least as well satisfied as the ordinary run of men, the extent of his ambition being the attainment of an agency or captainship, captains being generally raised to the station from the ranks." (37)

It is clear, at any rate, that the miners were in no way dissatisfied with the tributing arrangement, nor had any wish to alter it, a fact which is proved by the continuance of the setting of pitches by auction, in which the whole value to the mine consisted in the men being willing to bid against themselves. Had there been the smallest spirit of combination amongst them, by refraining from underbidding each other, higher rates of tribute might have been exacted, since in no case would it have paid a large mine to leave many pitches unworked.

In the case of copper ores set on tribute, the value of the stuff raised, from the adventurer's point of view, largely depended on the care with which the tributer, when breaking it, had picked it clean from waste. Accordingly, before each tributer's small parcel of ore was mixed with the rest for the general sampling, a private sample was taken, and at the final reckoning the tributer's rate had either an increase or decrease made upon it, according to whether his ore was respectively of a higher or lower quality than the whole parcel sold from the mine. This was known as the "tributers' account of ores," and is found stated at regular intervals in all the older mine cost-books.

The "pile" of the ore, or rather "dole," from the mine, when ready for sale, was generally made in a circular form, two to three feet thick, with a flat summit, and consisted of 20 to 100 tons or upwards, according to circumstances. Notice of the sampling day having been given, the agents of the smelting companies (being about twelve in number) met on the mine to see the samples duly taken and to receive one each. The dole was then divided and subdivided, until by common consent the whole was turned over and mixed sufficiently to satisfy all that the few ounces taken by each was a fair sample of the whole. These samples having been tried in the "dry" way by each of the samplers, on a given day the agents of the companies and of the mines which were selling ore assembled at an inn, generally alternately in Truro and Redruth, the chair being taken by the agent for that mine which was selling the greatest quantity of ore. The agents of the smelting companies then wrote, each on a slip of paper or "ticket," the price they were prepared to offer for the various parcels of ore as they were announced in turn, the highest in each case being, of course, considered as the buyer. If, as was not uncommon, two companies happened to offer the same price, the parcel was divided between them. Provided no secret agreement existed between the smelters to regulate the price given for the ores, thsi method of selling copper and tin ores by "ticketing" was one of efficiency and dispatch, business involving the transaction of thousands of pounds being conducted in the course of an hour or two in almost complete silence. At the conclusion of the proceedings "a dinner almost equal to a city feast" was provided at the expense of the mines, the cost being divided according to the quantities of ore which each was selling. (38)

In addition to tributers' work, a large amount of the development underground was done by tutwork or contract. This especially applied to the sinking of shafts and driving of crosscuts, etc., through unpayable ground. Thus at another survey held at the aforementioned Wheal Busy in 1756, it was decided "to sink a whem shaught by the fathom." Two "pares" of men offered, the one at £7 per fathom, the other at £4, the latter naturally being accepted. The size of the shaft was to be $6\frac{1}{2} \times 4$ feet, and in order to prevent the men "running from their bargain" if the ground became more unfavourable in depth, it was stipulated that the takers should be "obliged to sink two fathoms sartain or forfeit four pounds and four shillings to the use of the adventurers. . . ."

Of the two sorts of underground labourers, tutworkers and tributers, the latter nearly always made better earnings. The wages of both, however, differed considerably in different areas. The average wages of a St. Just miner between 1780–90 was said to be 24s. a month. (39) Matthew Boulton (40), on the other hand, writing to Wilson in February 1786, says: "I observe in Poldice Expenses for December that there is 101 men working on Loads at £450 14s. 10d., which is £4 9s. 3d. per Man per Month on an average. I also observe that there is 128 Men working on deads (unpayable ground) at £244 16s. 4d., which is £1 18s. 0d. per Man per Month. Hence I remark more men on deads than on lodes, and that the men on lodes gain much more than double the wages of a man on deads. How is this to be accounted for? I have always heard that Poldice men gain great wages by good bargains." (41)

Boulton was certainly right when he spoke of the foregoing as "great wages" and the Poldice men as good bargain-makers. To reckon a tributer's wage by averages, however, is apt to be deceptive, since two or three men who might be earning £20 or £30 in a month would materially raise the average, though the majority might still only be earning 30s. or less.

Tutwork, however, was, on the whole, always less well paid

than tribute. In the case of a smaller and poorer mine, such as Carnkye, in the month of July 1771, the wages of the "tutwork" men were still as low as 19s. to 24s. per month. Only one man on the mine got 40s., and he was doubtless the head captain. (42) The lower-grade workers, chiefly women and children, received wages proportionately small. In 1773 the women breaking ores by hand at Wheal Unity (which Boulton asked should be pointed out to a visitor as a characteristic sight) were getting 5d. a day. The men on night-shift, watching the stamps or burning-houses generally, got 1s. a night. (43)

The greater part of the surface work was done on contract. Thus, in building an engine-house at Wheal Gorland, in 1795, "John Cornelius and pare" were paid £35 6s. 10d. for building the boiler-house and chimney 100 perch 15 feet, at 7s. Water was "forked" on contract, balk was generally sawn at the rate of 2s. 6d. a hundred feet—even leats and roads were made at so much per fathom. (44)

According to an inquiry into the copper trade in 1798, the average earnings of Cornish copper miners had advanced by 50 per cent. between the years 1791–8, varying from 30s. to 42s. in the former year and from 45s. to 63s. in the latter. (45) This appears to have been a somewhat generous estimate of the rate of wages at this time, and certainly did not hold true in the outlying areas, where, as late as 1838 in St. Just, 40s. to 45s. was still a common wage for a working miner. (46)

As an offset to this account of low wages, however, it must be remembered how cheap living was in eighteenth-century Cornwall, where, as Mrs. Watt described in a letter to a friend, she and her husband frequently paid but 2d. apiece for their dinner. (47) "The finest Cod, Ling, and fish of that kind is purchased at less than a penny a pound," wrote another traveller. (48) "In West Cornwall mackerel are frequently bought for 8d. a score. Beef and mutton at Penzance are from 3d. to 4d. a pound, butter from 5d. to 6d., wheat is 11s. a bushel, but barley 4s. 6d., and coals (which are brought from Wales) 9d. a Bushel. In most places, however, the country people used turves, which cost them nothing at all."

The smallness of the miners' wages was also, to a certain

extent, made up for by the number of petty gifts, doles, or bonuses granted to them by the mine on special occasions, such as the taking of a whim on contract, the cutting of a lode, or the dangerous work of holing into old workings, etc. Thus entries such as for "Liquor to the Men on going through the Adit" (in winter) or for "10s. paid in consideration of the men having had a poor bargain" are by no means uncommon in the old cost-books. Many of the men also got additional pay by working "extra stems" in drawing water, filling kibbles, and the like. Attendance at the mine on Saturday afternoons, Good Friday, and Christmas Day was always reckoned as an extra charge, (49) whilst the midsummer allowance to every man and boy on the mine was one which remained until recent years.

The mine which provided work and wages for its employees when in health attended to them also in sickness and in death. The system of "bal surgeons" is believed to have originated in the early years of the eighteenth century. The earliest costbooks, at any rate, show the men contributing a fixed sum per month (generally 2d.) out of their wages, in return for which they, and sometimes their families also, were entitled to free attendance from the mine doctor. As an adventurer in the mines, as well as being a "bal surgeon," Pryce saw many objections to such a system where all the men were forced into being attended by one particular surgeon. "The 'bal' surgeons, too," he says, "begin to be weary of such a practice where an accident of consequence may require at least six weeks' daily attendance five or six miles from his residence, whilst another of a like nature may require the same attendance five or six miles diametrically opposite." "When an accident happens on a mine," he continues, "the poor sufferer languishes till the arrival of the surgeon, who is generally sent for in such haste and confusion that it may happen he is not provided with everything proper to administer present relief. The patient is then conveyed six or seven miles to his own hut full of naked children, but destitute of all conveniences and almost of all necessaries. The whole, indeed, a scene of such complicated wretchedness and distress, as words have no power to describe." (50)

It was no proof of the wisdom or generosity of Cornwall's nobility and gentry at this time that the erection of a county hospital such as Pryce had so earnestly recommended was delayed till almost the end of the century. (51) The smallness of the contribution paid by the men makes it clear that before the erection of such a hospital the miners must often have been dependent on the generosity of adventurers or the doctor for expenses which their contribution could not have covered. Many entries in the cost-books illustrate this : " Horse-hire to fetch the doctor," " Paid for Baize for Wm. Lesson's leg when hurt," " paid for Doctor Price [the author of *Mineralogia Cornubiensis*], 10s. 6d.," " Expenses on wounded men," " paid John James, hurted by the Damp, £1 1s. 0d.," " paid for carrying home John Jeffery, hurt, 1s.," " paid a woman for tending Richard Whitford, hurted," and so on. One guinea a month was the usual allowance for a man who was laid up from an accident received at the mine. On the occasion of a fall of ground in Wheal Sparnon in 1766, special entries occur for " bread and brandy when the Men was stopt in." Generally, if a man was killed, the mine bore the expenses of his funeral, the charge varying from 12s. 4d. to £2. In Poldice Cost for April 1789 appear the brief entries : " paid for a shrowd for Chylew, 6s. 6d. ; paid Martha Higgs, striping him, 5s. ; Expence on his funeral, 11s. 3d." The widow also generally received some provision for a short time afterwards. (52)

In addition to the contribution known as " Doctor's Pence," the miners, from the latter years of the eighteenth century onwards, paid a like sum per month to a mine barber, who in return cut the men's hair and effected their weekly shave.

There were, of course, both good mines and bad mines, and in the case of the latter or of small mines of an uncertain standing the conditions of the men were often poor in the extreme. In any case, the smallness of their wages made them at all times too much dependent on favour for matters which were of common necessity. Looking back on it, as we do to-day, the miners' life in the eighteenth century seems an immeasurably hard and laborious one. Though their toil was perhaps less extreme than in Carew's day, owing to the introduction of gunpowder, the length of the working hours had been proportionately increased. From the four hours which were customary for underground labourers in Elizabethan times, cores of six, eight, or even twelve hours had been substituted in the eighteenth century. The old "long cores," however, were by 1778 generally abolished, being found little more than an excuse for idleness, since twelve hours were too many for any man to work underground without intermission. Formerly, when a "pare" of men went underground, they made it a rule, if their working-place was dry, to sleep out a candle (i.e. for as long as a candle took to burn through), then rise up and work for two or three hours pretty briskly ; after that rest themselves for half an hour to "touch a pipe of tobacco," and so play and sleep half their working time. "But mining," wrote Pryce, "being now more deep and expensive than it formerly was, those idle customs are superseded by more labour and industry." (53)

The march of industry, as it is sometimes called, has generally shown itself a pretty ruthless proceeding, benefiting humanity on the one hand, only to deprive them of freedom on the other. Hard as were the working lives of Cornish miners 170 years ago and slight as was their pay, they were, in a sense, far less tied and bound to their work than a highly-paid artisan in a great industrial system of to-day. With no high-powered and expensive machinery running on all the time and demanding to be fed with work, mines could be run then in a leisurely manner which would quickly bring them into the bankruptcy court to-day. The taking off of working days, therefore, on the occasion of feasts, holidays, holiday eves, and the like, apart from being highly beneficial to men who spent much of their time in smothering air underground, was not attended with the loss to the owners which it would mean in a modern mine. The dominion of wheel and steam and electric wire had not yet begun, and the miner's life, though hard in its toil, was to that extent free.

Though the earnings of the tinner by the mid-eighteenth century were certainly a good deal higher than they had been fifty years before, his livelihood continued to be almost as precarious as ever. The reason for this was not only that the metal he produced was subject to great fluctuations in price, but the supply of food itself was frequently inadequate in the mining areas. From Elizabethan times onwards many regulations were in force to establish control of the distribution of fish, which, together with barley-bread, formed the staple diet of the poor.

Yet in 1591 we find Thomas Celey, of St. Ives, complaining of the "pressing" of fishermen for sailors. "When they are pressed," he wrote, "the country lacks victuals; if the men do not continue their fishing the country round will miss their best relief. The country is poor, and there is little flesh and less butter or cheese." (54) This statement, as showing the scarcity of food in the western parts of Cornwall at this time, is confirmed by the account of two travellers, who, on reaching Mousehole one night in the year 1590, found that no food whatever could be had there, and were accordingly forced to return to Penzance. (55) Such a state of affairs, by which the arrival of two strangers could throw out the commissariat of a village, was produced by several causes, of which the restrictions on the distribution of food and the narrowness of the area from which the supply could come, on account of bad roads and lack of communications, were the chief. As Fitz-Geoffrey said, when preaching the Cornish Assize sermon in 1631, of the two difficulties of the poor labourer, "first to get a little money for Corne and then to get a little Corne for money," the latter was often the greatest. (56)

Though methods of transport were much improved in the course of the next 130 years, the population of the county had likewise so much increased that the relative position, when Borlase wrote in 1758, was still much the same. Speaking of the "multitude of the inhabitants" of Cornwall at this time, he wrote: "The inhabitants since Elizabethan times are more advanced in numbers than the tillage has encreased in proportion, and though the lowlands in Cornwall, especially along the Tamar and Alan, may yield more corn than the inhabitants of those parts and the less fruitful hundreds of Stratton and Lysnewyth can dispense with, yet the hundreds of Powder, Kerrier and Penwith, and the Western parts of Pyder (far the most populous tracts of our county) do not yield corn near sufficient to supply the inhabitants. Upon the whole, if those parts entirely addicted to husbandry will yield a sufficiency of grain to make up in a moderate year what is wanting in the parts less cultivated and more addicted to mining, this is full as much as can be effected in this particular. In a plentiful year we may spare a little quantity for exportation, in a moderate year have enough for ourselves, in a year of scarcity not near a competency." (57)

At the best of times the Cornish poor lived very hardly. Their staple diet was fish, chiefly pilchards, fresh or salted, potatoes, barley bread, and "pillez," the last a form of corn no longer cultivated but once considered as the oatmeal of the poor. Wheaten bread was almost untasted by many. Butcher's meat, likewise, could rarely be afforded by the poor tinners, though, in the rocky parishes of the west, goats were kept in large numbers and were sold in the markets from Michaelmas to Christmas, being in flavour not much inferior to venison. (58) In bad seasons the poor would be reduced to such straits that, as in 1784, a year when fish was very scarce, the families of the Fowey fishermen lived almost entirely on limpets. (59)

In an age in which the highest gentlemen of the land had frequently to be carried home from the debauches which constituted an eighteenth-century dinner-party, it is little wonder that the poor, hard-living tinners were given to similar excesses when they had the chance. Tonkin, writing of the mining areas at the beginning of the century, stated, with picturesque exaggeration, that "If there be but three houses together, two of them shall be alehouses." These "kiddlywinks," which were professedly only beer-shops, were, on occasions of a run of smuggled goods in the vicinity, supplied with far more ardent spirits, and here the ale-drawer, says Polwhele, working in conjunction with the candidates for Cornwall's rotten boroughs, found the tinners an easy prey, and drunkenness, venality, and political corruption danced hand in hand, whilst the poor man's families starved at home.

The following remarks extracted from the *St. James' Chronicle* in 1776 give, in spite of some amusing absurdities, an interesting picture of life among the mining population at that time, as it appeared to an outsider :—

"I make no doubt," says the writer, "that this will contribute to the information of thousands of your readers, who know no more of the scenes here described than if it were not a part of this country. Cornwall presents a wild and strange appearance. There are few signs of fertility or cultivation. On the contrary, the whole face of the country is rudely furrowed, dug up and turned over by many thousands of miners, so that the eye which is accustomed to and fond of beautiful prospects will here meet with no other entertainment than wonderful heaps of stones, refuse of the Tinners or people who work the mines. Nevertheless, these mining folk can often agreeably treat you with the sight of their works, especially their curious fire Engines. In other respects this County in general has nothing to bespeak the good opinion of Travellers. The West end of it must undoubtedly be very unhealthy, being but a few miles across from the Northern to the Southern Channel, by which means it is always subject to heavy, cloudy, rainy weather, so that those people whose Business or Calling oblige them to be much abroad are almost continually wet to the skin and over shoes in dirt. The Natives, indeed, through constant use, think little of this, but seem to be very happy when they can sit down to a furze blaze, wringing their shirts and pouring the Mud and Water out of their boots. But the common people here are a very strange kind of beings, half savages at the best. Many thousands of them live entirely underground, where they burrow and breed like Rabbits (!). (60) They are rough as Bears, selfish as Swine, obstinate as Mules and hard as the Native iron. Those of the very lowest sort live so wretchedly that our poor in the environs of London would soon perish if reduced to their condition. The Labourers in general bring up their families with only potatoes or turnips, or leeks or pepper grass rolled up in black barley crust and baked under the ashes, with now and then a little milk. Perhaps they do not taste a bit of Flesh-Meat in three months. Yet their children are healthy and strong, and look quite fresh and jolly."

Living under conditions such as these and accustomed to being regarded by other inhabitants of the county no less than by strangers as almost without the pale of civilization, it speaks well for the character of the Cornish tinners that more than one traveller should have particularly commented on their courtesy and politeness. "The people of Cornwall," wrote Pocock in 1750, "are very hospitable and exceedingly civil to strangers, and the common people are much polished and ready to do all kind offices, which I observed more especially among the tinners." (61)

It is only fair, however, to add that he also commented on their "violent manner in falling not only on wrecks, but on ships that are drove in with all people and might be saved, plundering and even breaking up the vessels."

The psychology of Cornish people towards wrecking requires perhaps a little explanation. Their attitude, being one of thankful acceptance, was long ago expressed in the localized version of the proverb, "It is an ill wind that blows no good to Cornwall." Thus, when the first lighthouse was erected on the Lizard Point, an outcry was not unnaturally raised amongst the people of the district, who complained, in righteous indignation, that such a course was depriving them of "God's blessing." Early in the nineteenth century, Parson Troutbeck, of the Scilly Isles, expressed the feelings of his parishioners very acceptably when he added to the Litany the clause, "We pray Thee, O Lord, not that wrecks should happen, but that if any wrecks do happen Thou wilt guide them into the Scilly Isles, for the benefit of the poor inhabitants."

Until recent years, when wrecks became less frequent, it is well known how eagerly all classes of Cornish people watched for this peculiar harvest of the sea. (62) The gentry, it is true, did not risk their necks or reputation by rising at midnight to descend precipitous cliffs or to fight their way into the beating surf of a south-west gale to rescue the valuable jetsam, nevertheless they guarded their rights and prerogatives to all wreckage coming in upon their beaches with a jealous eye, and woe betide the poor man who was caught poaching anything therefrom. The treasures of the sea, which were thus regarded as valuable perquisites even by the rich, were naturally still more sought after by men so poor as the great company of tinners. The mining parishes of Sithney, Breage and Germoe, adjoining the coastline of Mount's Bay, were always particularly noted for their wrecking and smuggling propensities.

The reputed prayer of sailors passing this coast,

> God keep us from rocks or shelving sands
> And save us from Breage and Germoe men's hands,

though it reads like an invention of the nineteenth century, was doubtless an echo of earlier times.

In the series known as the Lanisly letters, dating between 1750 and 1756, George Borlase, brother of Dr. William Borlase, of Ludgvan, gives a vivid picture of Mount's Bay wrecking as it existed in his day.

"The people who make it their business to attend these wrecks," he states, "are generally Tynners, and as soon as they observe a ship on the coast they first arm themselves with sharp axes and hatchetts and leave their tyn works to follow those ships. (63) Sometimes the ship is not wrack'd, but whether 'tis or not the mines suffer greatly, not only by the loss of their labour, which may be at about £100 per diem if they are 2,000 in quest of the ship, but where the water is quick the mine is entirely drowned. They seldom go in a less number than 2,000." It is to be feared that often small pity was shown by the roughest of the tinners towards the poor sailors who escaped the fury of the sea. "I have seen many a poor man," says the same writer, "half dead, cast ashore and crawling out of the reach of the waves, fallen upon and in a manner stripped naked by these villains, and if afterwards he has saved his chest or any more cloaths they have been taken from him." The haunts of the smugglers and wreckers lay more particularly around Helston and the neighbourhood, though they swarmed in all parts. It must be admitted that in many respects the tinners were artists in these adventures, and the energy, neatness, and dispatch with which they worked was worthy of a better cause. "They'll cut a large trading vessel to pieces in one tide," wrote Mr. Borlase, "and cut down everybody that offers to oppose them. Last Wednesday a Dutchman was stranded at Helston, every man saved and the ship whole, laden with claret. In twenty-four hours' time the Tinners cleared all." (64)

It is interesting to note in this account of wrecking given by a resident living on the spot (and one who certainly did not whitewash matters), that there is no mention whatever of the time-honoured fable of ships being lured on to the rocks. The foul deeds which were done, and they were doubtless many, were performed in the white heat of excitement which the atmosphere of a wreck breeds and not through any cold-blooded deliberation or scheming to deprive others of their lives and property.

II

It is a matter of frequent comment amongst writers that Cornwall, from early times to the present day, has so largely escaped the strikes, lock-outs, and disputes which from time to time have occurred in almost all other industrial areas. The reasons for this will be discussed later. It may be noted here, however, that such riots and disturbances as have disturbed the peace of Cornwall in times past have nearly always owed their origin to the dread of starvation consequent upon a fluctuating and frequently inadequate food supply rather than to any social or political unrest.

Already in the starvation years of the late seventeenth century we read of the tinners plundering a ship laden with salt at Falmouth, and generally causing much terror to the inhabitants by the desperate straits to which they were reduced. Though the higher rate of wages obtaining in the early years of the eighteenth century would seem to mark an improvement in the tinners' lot, the duty on candles had greatly increased the expense of raising the ores. Throughout this century the tinners' chief resentment was shown towards the corn factors, who, as already shown, were in the habit of still further imperilling the food supply in the scarce years by exporting what little corn there was to make higher prices overseas. Few winters seem to have passed at this time without some small disturbance on this account. Thus the year 1727 was marked by great distress in Cornwall, and riots broke out among the tinners in many districts on account of the scarcity of corn. It was at this juncture that Sir John St. Aubyn, "the little baronet," as he was called, came to the rescue by advancing to the tinners a "sufficient sum of money to prevent them from starving and from the necessity of plundering their neighbours." (65)

Two years later, riots again broke out in different parts of Cornwall, and this time the magistrates addressed a petition to the Secretary of State, begging that as "the said Tinners and others have ravaged up and down the Countrey in a very insolent manner and great numbers, presuming so far as to break open and to enter dwelling-houses and outhouses, out of which they have forcibly carried off great quantities of corn and other things," that His Majesty would cause to be issued Royal Proclamation, with the names of certain ringleaders inserted, "with such reward as shall be thought fitting for apprehending them, and a pardon to such as shall impeach their fellows concerned in the said riots." (66) As a result of such inducements several were caught and executed. "One of them," wrote Tonkin, "is now hanging in chains on St. Austell Downs," a terrible reminder to the poor miner as he went home from night core of the dangers of coming into conflict with law and "Justice." Still, even this severity failed to check men on the borders of starvation, for, as a contemporary writer said, " 'Tis an old saying that ' the belly hath no ears.' "

In 1748 an insurrection occurred at Penryn, "where the tinners, suspecting that some merchants had laid up vast quantities of corn for exportation, assembled in great numbers, men, women and children, and broke open one of the cellars and took thence 600 bushels of wheat. They then started to rob the country people carrying their corn to market, and afterwards returning to Penryn in great numbers, armed with clubs and bludgeons, threatened further mischief, till the soldiers sent for from Falmouth to quell the tumult fired upon them, by which two were killed and many wounded." (67)

In the beginning of the year 1757 there was yet another rising of the tinners on account of the same cause, as is shown by the following extracts from a contemporary journal :—

"From Padstow in Cornwall, we hear, that on Friday the 3rd inst., the inhabitants were all alarmed with an account that several hundred Tinners were assembled at a place call'd St. Agnes in order to proceed to Padstow to plunder the town of what corn was in it, and afterwards to set it on fire. The next day ten of them actually came into the Place, but committed no riot, but the day after sent away two of their number, as it was supposed to give notice to the rest that the inhabitants were not capable to resist them, as likewise that there was some barley in the town, which had been bought up for malting. Accordingly on Monday, the 6th instant, in the afternoon, about five or six hundred of them, with several women, and upwards of 100 horses, came into the town, and immediately began plundering, breaking open warehouses, etc., and carrying away all the grain they could meet with; and tho' the Proclamation was read to them by the Civil Magistrate, it was all in vain, for they loaded all their horses, and what they could not carry off with them they either sold or gave away. After they had broken open the Warehouses, they proceeded to the Key, where there happened to be a Sloop bound to Guiney, which they imagined had corn on board, and several of them endeavoured to board her, but on firing some Swivel Guns, tho' only with powder, they thought proper to desist; however, for their satisfaction, the Captain suffered two to come on board to see there was no corn in the vessel. They stayed all night in the Town huzzaing and carousing, and the Town was not quite clear of them until ten next morning. The inhabitants sometime before had petitioned the Secretary at War for a party of soldiers, which was immediately ordered, but they could not march in time enough to prevent the Town's being plundered. The Party came in two or three days after the Riot, and, it is to be hoped, will stay there during the time their Regiment is in the County."

Ten years later, in August 1766, a similar state of things was reported, and the tinners were clearly overawing the agriculturists in the market towns. The following is extracted from a newspaper cutting of that date :—

"Last Wednesday a party of tinners assembled at Truro, where the farmers insisted upon twenty-one and twenty-two shillings per Cornish bushel for wheat, and twelve shillings per bushel for barley, which is three Winchester bushels. By the prudence of the magistrates, they were prevailed upon to be quiet; and corn was sold to them at the following prices, viz. wheat at fourteen shillings per bushel, and barley at seven shillings. On Friday they came into Redruth, where the farmers demanded the same prices as at Truro for their corn; sevenpence half-penny per pound for butter, and four-pence per gallon, Winchester measure, for their potatoes; but the tinners obliged them to sell the wheat and barley at the same price as at Truro, that is to say, butter at six-pence per pound and potatoes two-pence half-penny per gallon."

In 1773 serious riots once again took place in different parts of the county. "We have had the devil and all of a riot at Padstow," wrote a correspondent from Bodmin at this time; "some of the people have run to too great lengths in exporting of corn, it being a great corn country. Seven or eight hundred tinners went thither, who first offered the corn factors 17s. for 24 gallons of wheat; but being told they should have none, they immediately broke open the cellar doors, and took away all in the place without money or price. About sixteen or eighteen soldiers were called out to stop their progress, but the Cornishmen rushed forward and wrested the firelocks out of the soldiers' hands: and from thence they went to Wadebridge, where they found a great deal of corn cellared for exportation, which they also took and carried away. This was the state of affairs, the poor people saying they could not get bread for themselves and their families at any price. We think 'tis but the beginning of a general insurrection, because as soon as the corn they have taken away is expended they will assemble in greater numbers armed." (68)

The fear of an insurrection of the tinners was, as may be seen, a constant one in eighteenth-century Cornwall. The alarm with which they were regarded is shown by Wesley on more than one occasion in his Journal. "I rode with Mr. Shepherd to Gwennap," he wrote in July 1745. "Here also I found the people in great consternation. Word was brought that a great company of tinners, made drunk on purpose, were coming to do terrible things. I laboured much to compose their minds, but fear had no ears: so that the abundance of people went away." (69)

It does not speak well for the social atmosphere of the time that so large a body as the tinners, consisting of the greater proportion of the population of West Cornwall, should have been regarded by the rest of the inhabitants as outside the bounds of society. No doubt the appearance of the tinners was wild, ragged, and unkempt, but, taken as a whole, their behaviour on these occasions was remarkably ordered and peaceable. They were, indeed, not so much rioters out to loot as a band of hardworking men seeking, at a fair price, bread to keep body and soul together. The prediction, however, that the above-mentioned riot at Padstow would spread was in this case justified.

"Last Saturday," wrote another correspondent from Penryn,

VARYING FORTUNES OF THE MINERS 153

I was eye witness of the Riots and Robberies that some hundreds of Tinners did commit in this parish. These tinners have been out for ten days past in divers parts of the County and have committed many robberies on the high roads. They have plundered farmers' houses, many Malt houses and Cellars, and last Saturday at Ruan nigh Tregony I saw the tinners break open many houses and cellars and carry off great quantities of corn which was going to supply the markets of Falmouth, Penryn, and Truro. They have knocked down and beat everybody that opposed them. Some of our people had their bones broken, and some it is thought will not recover their wounds. As soon as they had the corn into their sacks they offered it for sale at one shilling a sack on the road to everybody they could get to buy of them." The letter ends with a petition for soldiers to protect the inhabitants of the town, and adduces, as a guarantee of good faith, the name of a famous landlord who "can inform you what sort of people these tinners are." If this was so it can only be said that the gentleman in question was a striking exception, since at this time most of the really great mineral owners of Cornwall, as elsewhere, though deriving their wealth from the mines, left all but the spending of it to their agents and had little first-hand knowledge of the poor workers who laboured beneath their estates. The authorities in Plymouth, whence this letter was addressed, seem hardly to have regarded the matter with the same degree of alarm as the writer, but order was nevertheless given that a party of "Invalids" quartered at Pendennis Castle should proceed to the defence of Penryn. This they did, and, after the manner of old soldiers, took up their station "at the King's Arms Inn." Here they were attacked by a party of the tinners and a skirmish ensued in which "one tinner and one poor woman were shot dead." The tinners, however, were not without a sense of military tactics, for when, at length, the "Invalids" were induced by their officers to leave the "King's Arms" for a short time to give chase to the first lot, "the town was visited by a fresh party of about 300 more of these Banditti, with whom the townspeople were forced to beat a Parley and let them have corn for one-third less than the prime cost to the Proprietors." (70)

What Pryce pointed out one hundred and fifty years ago

is at length, in our day, becoming recognized as a social and economic truth in industry as a whole. The Cornish tinners of his day and long after were too poor—poor beyond the point where poverty remains an incentive to industrious toil. With the least drop in the price of tin their condition at once attained to that desperateness where the remuneration of labour, however prolonged, was still insufficient to support life (71) and when the honest and hardworking poor became the wolfish desperadoes whose destination was, formerly, the gallows. What wonder indeed that to such as these a wreck appeared in very truth a godsend, to be fallen upon with all the frightful eagerness of starving men upon food.

Considering the conditions under which they lived and the way in which they were regarded by the rest of society, it is, indeed, remarkable how loyal the mining population of Cornwall remained, as a whole, to King and Country. Yet there is evidence on more than one occasion of the good spirit which they evinced in times of national peril. In 1745 we read of a company known as the "Independent Company of the Stout, True, and Hearty Tinners within and belonging to our said parish of Redruth" being raised to assist King George in opposing the invasion of the so-called Pretender. In 1794 another force was recruited under the name of the "Royal Redruth Infantry," and in 1803 the Miners of Pednandrea and New Wheal Virgin voluntarily engaged to serve under their mine captains as pioneers in case of invasion. (72) These are only a few instances of what was happening on similar occasions in all parts of the mining areas. In 1806 the return to the House of Commons on the Volunteer Corps of Great Britain shows companies of men in being in all the mining districts of Cornwall. Thus there were the Loyal Meneage and the Mount's Bay Cavalry—the Royal Cornish Stannary, Portreath, Crinnis Cliff, and Mount's Bay Artillery—as well as the 1st Mount's Bay, 2nd Mount's Bay, Breage, Redruth, Truro, and many other companies of infantry. The Royal Cornish Stannary Artillery were, at this time, 1,113 in number, divided into ten troops or companies. It is true that they are described as "having no guns attached to them," which must admittedly have been an inconvenience to a company of artillery, and they are also said

VARYING FORTUNES OF THE MINERS 155

to have been "very much dispersed," but neither fact was the fault of the poor tinner, who then, as now, was forced to seek a living where he could find it, often throughout a lonely countryside and obviously with little money to spare to provide the necessary arms for himself.

Already in 1772 the price of tin had fallen lower than it should have done, "owing to the consignments of tin on commission for foreign markets having fallen, through a species of infatuation, into the hands of the London pewterers." Their interest as consumers in keeping down the price of block tin, of course, infinitely exceeded any degree of percentage they could expect on commission for exportation. By this means they were able to dictate to their principals and fix the price of the commodity to their own standards. The producers, whether working tinners or owners of minerals, were invariably the chief sufferers from the lowered prices.

"The smelters who stand between the real and original proprietors of the tin stuff and the exporters," wrote the same pamphleteer, "though they usually have the greatest share of white tin (metal) in their possession, are not looked on as the real sufferers of the low price it bears ; since they take care to make all proper deductions on that account when the tin is brought to them to be sampled and the discount on the Tin Bills is an additional douceur. However much the smelters may join the general cry on account of the low price of tin, no thinking person will ever set them down as sufferers thereby." (73)

Indeed, in the imagination of the tinners, which saw not beyond the limits of the county and knew nothing of the complex influences affecting tin prices in London, the Cornish smelters were invariably considered as the prime causers of their distress. In 1784 "a petition from the distressed tinners of Wendron, Sithney, and Germoe to the gentlemen of Cornwall" stated that they had long been toiling half-naked in the vain endeavour to procure a subsistence for their families, and begged "that they would assist them against the tyranny of their oppressors, the tin smelters." (74) This is one of the earliest allusions to the much-vexed question of the rights of the miner versus the smelter to which so much prominence was given in the 'eighties of the last century. The petition resulted in a meeting of mining and smelting men in the neighbourhood of Hayle, where some steps are said to have been taken towards redress.

It should be borne in mind that the problem of unemployment in the eighteenth century was even more acute than it is to-day, owing to the fact that emigration on a large scale was still a closed door. Though the Cornish mining areas have known more than one bad period of depression in latter years, the knowledge that work can now almost always be obtained in foreign fields has relieved the situation from that desperateness which it formerly assumed. The last twelve or fourteen years of the eighteenth century saw the condition of the tinners at the very worst that has ever been known in the history of Cornish mining. In the opinion of all parties the men at this time were an object of pity and their distresses were felt to be a matter of national concern. A notice in the *Gentleman's Magazine* for June 24, 1789, stating that there had been a rising among the tinners near Truro owing to their want of work and the high price of bread, adds: "A party of the 38th Regiment was ordered out against them on Wednesday last and, after some expostulation between them and the Justices, the officers were ordered to fire, which, highly to their honour, they refused to do, and the people dispersed. On Friday, however, they rose again, and on Sunday a party of the same regiment was ordered again to march to assist the magistrates to keep peace."

In the same year Mr. Nicholas Donnithorne, chairman of the Quarterly Tin Meetings in Cornwall, wrote to the Directors of the East India Company: "I am acting in behalf of many thousands who at this time are destitute of even the most common necessaries of life. I am lately returned from the mining parishes in Cornwall, where I have been witness to the greatest imaginable poverty and distress, insomuch that I have seen women gathering snails to make broth for the support of their families. It is true that the Cornish tinners have lately been very riotous, and the gentlemen of the county have been obliged to call in the aid of the military, but, when the extremely low price of Tin and the very high price of corn are considered, much may be said in defence of these poor industrious labourers. For the last three years," he continued, "the quantity of Tin annually risen has averaged 21,000 blocks, and the European markets scarce equal to the consumption of 17,000 blocks. Consequently there has been a surplus of one-fifth. This has reduced the price from £84 to £58 a ton, and I do solemnly aver that with some thousands of distressed Tinners hourly expected to rise, unless some plan can be adopted for almost instant relief, the consequences will be dreadful." (75)

The chief reason for the increased output of tin at this time was (indirectly) the flooding of the copper market by the enormous output of cheap ore from the Parys Mine in Anglesea. This, by adversely affecting the Cornish copper-mines, induced many of the miners to turn to tin for their support, thereby increasing the production and decreasing the price of that metal also. "The annals of mining," said a writer in 1827, "exhibit no instance of a mine so productive as the Parys copper-mine has been, accompanied with so little expense in working. The labour consisted in quarrying an immense mass of ore which rose to the surface of the ground on the summit of a hill of moderate elevation. Here no hydraulic machinery was necessary for the drainage of the mine, a solid body of copper ore of prodigious extent was exposed to the glare of day, tempting the labour of the miner. There was no useless rubbish to remove, no toil in descending, no risk of life; nor was it possible after many years employed in excavating to calculate its extent or probable duration. (76) The quantity of copper which this single mine poured into the market for twelve years in succession, from the year 1773 to 1785, made such an impression as to lower the price of this metal throughout Europe, and to threaten the ruin and subversion of all the poorer mines of the Kingdom; This state of things continued for some years, to the great loss of the proprietors both of the Anglesea Mine and of the Cornish mines, before any endeavours were used to put a stop to so ruinous a competition. Nor was it possible, while the quantity of copper which was offered for sale continued undiminished, to find a remedy for the evil. At length the mineral riches of Anglesea began to show very plain symptoms of decline; the quantity of copper which it produced gradually became less, and in the year 1791 the reduced produce of this mine, in conjunction with the ruin of several Cornish mines, had the effect of raising the price of copper from £80 per ton to £90, and in 1792 to £100. It continued mounting in rapid progression until, in 1796, it reached the price of £118, and in 1799, when the Parys mountain mine was nearly exhausted, the price of copper was as high as £128 per ton, and had then attained what might be denominated its proper level."

In the meantime, however, disaster had followed in Cornwall. In 1787 the loss of the Consolidated Mines near St. Day was £8,000, on the United Mines £11,000, Chasewater Mine £2,500, Poldice £560, Crenver £1,350, North Downs £5,350, Dolcoath £4,000. (77) Many lesser mines (78) were likewise thrown idle about this time from the same cause—North Roskeer, Pednandrea, Tresavean, Trevenson, Treleigh Wood, Wheal Hawke, Wheal Raven, etc., all of which are stated by R. Thomas in his Report of 1819 as having been "long idle." On the first feeling of the pinch the mining interests in Cornwall had immediately appealed to Boulton and Watt for an abatement of their engine premiums. To this neither one of the partners was inclined to agree. "I don't see why we should be the only persons that should be asked to give up the profits of their trade," wrote Boulton in February 1786. "Whenever the merchants will give up their 20 or 30 per cent. profit or the Lords give up their dues, then will Boulton and Watt give up their profits for the good of the mines and the county. Compare the profits that the merchants have received from Polgooth or North Downs with those which have been received by Boulton and Watt and you will find the former exceed the latter out of all comparison, and yet there are plenty of men who can write a letter and buy and sell materials but none that could draw the water of a great mine 150 fathoms deep with one engine before we visited Cornwall." A year later, Boulton wrote to Wilson, their Cornish agent : "The abateing of lords' dues and engine premiums would only make matters worse, because anything which could enable them to get more copper would certainly decrease the value of what is already got, without they could procure sales for it. At present the best thing that can happen to the County is half of the mines stopping till better times, and as neither we nor anybody can dictate who shall stop, the weakest must go to the wall. . . ." (79)

As at all such times of trade depression, the wildest rumours

VARYING FORTUNES OF THE MINERS 159

were current. On August 7th of the same year Watt wrote to Wilson : " It is said that Mr. Raby has bought above 2/3 of the slags in England and that he has already made 50 tons of copper out of them and gets 25 per cent. and more from some of them—in short, more copper than was originally got from the ores. He says the slags alone will furnish copper enough for the sales of Europe for 100 years to come. If true, it would seem that all hell is broke loose against the copper trade, or, rather, against the Cornish mines. On the other side it is said that the Anglesea ores grow poorer and poorer but still there is enough and rich enough to ruin Cornwall." In May of the following year Boulton wrote to Wilson : " I am sorry to say the Commercial horizon looks darker and darker every day. I hope this will find the Miners turned their hands to other employ and reconciled to their fate." (80)

Owing to the continued low price of copper, Dolcoath, North Downs, Chasewater Mine, and Wheal Towan all ceased working about this time and several thousand more miners were thrown out of employment. The majority of the men thus discharged turned, as already stated, to the tin-mines for their support and consequently increased the production and lowered the price of that metal also. Various suggestions were made as a consequence for artificially raising the price of tin, but, in the opinion of experts, such methods for re-establishing the industry were doomed to failure. It is sometimes not fully realized that competition from the Eastern tin producers is no new feature in Cornish mining, and that the great periods of prosperity in Cornwall have been not for want of it, but in despite of it. That the production of foreign tin had a very controlling influence, at any rate, on the home price in the latter years of the eighteenth century is clear from Watt's statement on the subject. " I apprehend," he wrote, " the raising the price of Tin is very wrong and an unnecessary step as it must open the market for the Malacca Tin, which can be bought there for 50s. or 56s. per cwt., and may be brought to the Continent of Europe as cheap as the Cornish tin at 70s., Coinage price. . . . The freight home is a mere trifle, coming as ballast, so that the Insurance would be the principal charge."

A still further set-back was given to tin producers at this

time by the fact that pewter, which had formerly consumed vast quantities of tin, was going out of fashion and earthenware was being substituted in its stead. So much did the tinners resent this new introduction that cartloads of "clomen ware" taken through the county at this time had actually to be protected by guards of soldiers to prevent them from being smashed by the outraged Cornishmen.

Thus, with copper and tin at starvation prices and a decreasing market, with costs high and trade dislocated by the long war with France, the industrial horizon in Cornwall has never looked blacker. Added to all this, many of the mines were still further embarrassed by the action of the engineering firm of Boulton and Watt, who, in the course of a ten years' lawsuit, were vindicating the patent rights connected with the pumping engines which they had erected and were beginning to press for the settlement of premiums, which in some cases were long overdue. The storm of ill-feeling aroused on the occasion of this lawsuit has hardly yet died away in the mining towns, where the descendants of families, whose great-grandfathers championed respectively the cause of Boulton and Watt or their Cornish rivals, Trevithick and Hornblower, still bear in remembrance the ancient feud. The central mining area where the battle raged was divided into two camps, the Gwennap district being mainly for Watt, whilst the Western Mines round Camborne supported their local champion, Trevithick. In the course of the long-drawn contest much underhand dealing took place on both sides, and the more unscrupulous mine-owners lost no opportunity for reprisal. Realizing that in the hordes of distressed and out-of-work miners they possessed a useful pawn, they diligently set themselves to excite their tempers against the patentees, alleging that such men would rather close down the mines and deprive the poor of their livelihood than surrender one jot or tittle of their monopoly. To such calumnies, more than to any natural malice amongst the miners, must be ascribed the cause of the riots which occurred at Poldice Mine in 1787 and 1789. (81)

On these Watt and Boulton both comment in a characteristic manner. After the first, Watt wrote to Wilson : " I am very much alarmed at this fresh rising of the miners, who are certainly

VARYING FORTUNES OF THE MINERS

instigated by some enemy to the county and to you. I hope you will avoid going in their way again and to prevent surprises that you will pack up your books and papers and send them to Truro. Indeed, I wish you would remove yourself and your family there until matters are quieted. I hope no improper concessions will be made to them, and that some body of authority will interpose in time, soldiers should be quartered at Truro and Redruth." (82) After a similar disturbance two years later, Watt wrote again to Wilson : "We had it in the newspapers that the military were desired to fire upon the Tinners but would not. I hope it is not so, otherwise we are going the same road as the French are, that is to the devil."

Very different to the embittered and alarmist attitude of Watt are the letters of Boulton addressed to Wilson on the same subject. On April 18, 1788, he wrote : "We have not the least idea of the cause of the Tinners being violently prejudiced against you, and in your next pray tell us the grounds of it. We are certain of one thing, which is that they do not distinguish between those who are their real friends and those who are not." In the same year, when there was talk of the necessity of closing down Chasewater Mine on account of the low price of copper, Boulton wrote : "I am not insensible to the distress and inconveniences that will arise to many poor people who are dependent on that mine and would go to great lengths to mitigate their distress, but I have not the divine power of feeding a great multitude with five barley loaves and a few fishes, besides you may readily guess what all the adventurers will say when it is proposed to continue the mine at a certain loss." In a letter of the following year he wrote again : "I am sorry to learn the disposition for mobbing prevails in Cornwall on account of Flower (*sic*), and though I wish to contribute to their relief, yet I dare not send any Flower from London to them lest they should talk again of Arsenick." (83) This last remark forms sufficient comment in itself on the nature of the various defamations spread against Boulton and Watt in Cornwall.

As regards the starving tinners in the meantime, such measures as could were being taken for their relief. (84) In many of the mines of the great Gwennap district, notably at Wheal Unity, Treskerby, Wheal Damsel, and Tresavean, the men were subsisted with barley and fish, accounts of which were kept in the cost-books, and any deficiency or excess accounted for with the overseers of the parish. (85) Many Cornish mineral lords, too, unselfishly forwent the whole of their dues (particularly in such mines as in any case could not have paid them), whilst others who spent the great part of their life in London, and who therefore could hardly be expected to relinquish their sole interest in the county, instructed their agents to distribute doles amongst the starving poor. One of them, writing to his agent in 1797, acknowledging the receipt of dues, added : " I observe the very considerable remittance you have made my bankers of £1,530 7s. 8d., considerable indeed ! which prompts me to make a little offering to those poor wretches the Tinners to whom in a great measure Cornish Landholders owe their affluence. As you therefore mentioned to me some time ago what a number of miserable poor creatures there were in and about Redruth and the neighbourhood, without covering, shoes, stockings and blankets, etc., I should be glad if you would dispose of twenty guineas from me among the wives and children. I don't limit you to a few guineas if you should want a few more." (86)

This and other gifts of charity, though on, perhaps, an even more munificent scale, served as temporary expedients only. That the poor were in the most miserable condition imaginable at this time there can be no doubt. The following account, based on the Farington Diary and the tradition of certain old Camborne residents, shows that even in those days, when brutal disciplinary methods were most commonly accepted, the action of the magistrates in quelling any consequent disturbances often exceeded the limits prescribed by public opinion. " I observed," wrote Joseph Farington, the artist, on a visit to Cornwall in 1810, " that the impression on the minds of those who inhabit other parts of the kingdom is that the Cornish miner has something of the savage character, but that I, on the other hand, found them civil and obliging and not at all of the description supposed. Thus on one occasion, whilst trying to sketch in a cold north wind at Carclaze, one of the miners threw his thick waistcoat over me, another held my umbrella over me, and I was thus enabled to remain a considerable time and finish what I should not otherwise have been able to do. Lord de Dunstanville said

VARYING FORTUNES OF THE MINERS 163

that when assembled in bodies they were rough when moved by some occasion, but individually were sufficiently peaceful. He added, however, that in the year 1795 an insubordinate disposition rose to such a height as to cause a body of men to assemble and by threats to oblige millers and dealers in grain to do their business at certain prices fixed by these rioters. This happened whilst Lord de Dunstanville was in London, and when his Lordship returned to Tehidy no opposition had been made to their demands, the magistrates being afraid to act. He told them he would show what could be done, and finding their timid dispositions had recourse to his brother-in-law only, who, at his Lordship's request, came over to Tehidy and, after taking the depositions of the Millers, immediately swore in eighty constables, who, according to a plan formed, proceeded to take up from their beds at 2 o'clock in the morning fifty of the most noted of the rioters, who were without delay conveyed to Bodmin Gaol. At the Assizes which followed they were tried, and three of them were condemned to die—some were ordered to be transported and others were sentenced to be imprisoned. After the trials were over Lord de D. had a private conversation with the Judge, who remarked to him that the execution of one of the three might have a sufficient effect and the punishment of the other two might be mitigated. In this his Lordship fully concurred, and there being one more vicious and profligate than the rest, he was left for execution. After the trials were over and sentence had been passed, the Magistrates addressed his L'ship to obtain a remission of the punishment. He replied that they had done that which was very painfull to him, for that in refusing to make the application they wished him to do, it would seem to be fixing upon him the death of anyone who might suffer. He added that notwithstanding this he would not prevent an example being made which was highly necessary for the benefit of Society. The effect of this resolution was soon visible throughout the county, and the manners of the people were suddenly changed from rudeness and disrespect to proper obedience. *For a very short time there was some agitation, and the body of the man* who had been executed was brought to Camborne, about four miles from Tehidy, attended by a thousand persons to witness the funeral and show their respect. (87) It happened that at the time when they were thus assembled Lord de D., having occasion to go that way, passed through the place and stopped at the house of a Clergyman there, who warned him of his danger. To this he replied, loud enough to be heard by many of the Mob, that the danger would be with them if they acted improperly. No attempt was made to molest him, and the people dispersed quietly, after which order was generally restored." (88) Though such measures as these might serve to enforce peace by intimidation, the more difficult task of showing how the thousands of poor with their families might earn their bread rather than steal it fell upon other shoulders. Many were the suggestions made at this time for dealing with the problem of unemployment, and so closely has history repeated itself in the annals of this ancient industry, that nearly all of them found an echo in the mining depression of our own time in 1920–3.

The following remarks, in particular, from the *Political Magazine* of 1788 might, with but a few changes, be taken from any newspaper account of the last slump. "I allude," says the writer, "to the distressful situation into which many thousands of miners and their families will soon be permanently thrown by the expence of working the mines becoming heavier and the profits being counterbalanced. . . . Some of the deep copper-mines in Cornwall must very soon be abandoned, as the Anglesea mines can much undersell us." With the substitution only of tin for copper and the Malay States for Anglesea, how persistently have such remarks been put forward by the pessimists of latter years! "The parishes in which the mines are," continues the old writer, "already are heavily burthened with poor-rates" (89); and again (how familiar this sounds!): "It is a national concern and Parliament alone will be able to the task of remedying so very serious an evil." As in 1920, so in 1788, the same substitutes for the reopening of the mines were suggested. "Is it possible," it was asked, "that the miners could be employed in enclosing waste lands, the Crown lands of the Duchy, or Dartmoor, for instance (!), or could these poor creatures be rendered serviceable in any way to the new fishery establishments in Scotland?"

It is with a sense of relief that the reader turns from the panic attitude which is here displayed to the letters of Matthew Boulton, who, perhaps more than any man of his time, combined with a complete grasp of the economic situation a genuine desire to help the miners. His letters commenting on the conditions in Cornwall are always to the point. In 1788 (90) he wrote: "We conceive the most effectual means (of relieving the situation) is to extend and promote the consumption and sales of copper and to raise the price and to lessen the dead stock, all which we are silently doing to the best of our power. As the quantity of Copper and Tin lately raised in Cornwall is much too great for all the markets to take off, the Miners and Adventurers should turn their eyes to Lead, as the price of that Metal is almost double what it was some years ago, it being now from £21 to £23 a Ton, and we have no doubt from what we have heard that there are Lead Mines in several parts of Cornwall (91) that will at this time pay much better than most of the Copper and Tin Mines now working. . . . Setting aside the Lead Mines in Cornwall and Devonshire it is certain that all the Lead Mines now working in England and Scotland are desirous of putting into the mines all the miners they can get, and consequently most of your young men may find employment in them if they are disposed to be active. There is also a want of miners in the Shropshire and Staffordshire Collieries. It appears to us that it would be much better to provide for the miners in either of these ways than to open new tin or copper mines and thereby endanger the total ruin of the County by overloading the Markets."

In the end, however, then, as again in 1923, the problem was only solved by the gradual fall in the price of materials and the rise to economic value in the price of metals, the two factors causing forthwith a re-opening of the mines. The suggestion made by Mr. Donnithorne to the East India Company some years before had likewise borne good effect and a new market for the surplus Cornish tin had been found in China, where, in the form of tin leaf, "the people burn it morning and evening before their idols." In the last letter which he addressed on the subject, Mr. Donnithorne stated that "we may flatter ourselves with distressed Cornwall getting still further relief from the increase of exports." (92)

Could the mining men of the last years of the eighteenth century have foreseen that they were on the eve of a period of prosperity such as Cornwall had never known before, what a feeling of buoyancy there might have been! But the future then was veiled as closely as it is to-day, and doubtless then as to-day men were glad enough to see only a partial resumption of the industry, so long as the spectacle of hungry men in the streets and smokeless stacks in the country-side was gradually done away.

NOTES.

1. Lewis, 168. The single Stannary law that ordered that "the moiety or halfendeale that shall accrue to the stannaries from fines imposed shall be for defraying the common burthen that shall come upon them and for the relief of the decrepit, maimed, or decayed tinners," seems in this respect to have been quite exceptional in character, since the tinner, as a rule, in his work as in his home-life for ever "played a lone hand."—*Laws of the Stannaries*, 53.
2. Lewis, 211.
3. Cf. Lewis, 212.
4. Cf. Lewis, 213.
5. S.P. Dom. Eliz., 243, fol. 333.
6. Cal. S.P. Dom. Eliz., 250, fol. 46.
7. It is only the fact that they were able to turn from one occupation to another which explains how the tinners of the sixteenth and seventeenth centuries were able to live at all. The dual occupation of farming and streaming to which they had accustomed themselves is illustrated by the nature of one of their proverbial sayings, which was to the effect that an ox lying down in the rich stream moors would cover tin enough to buy it. This was variously said of Bostraze Moor in St. Just, Roseworthy in Camborne, and parts of Dartmoor, too.
8. B.M., Lansdowne MS., xviii, fol. 52.
9. Hist. MSS. Comm., Cecil, v, 160.
10. Hist. MSS. Comm., Cecil, vii, ref. 181.
11. Harl. MS. 6380.
12. For an account of tribute see later.
13. Lewis, Appendix, 254.
14. Cal. S.P. Dom. (1635-6), 450.
15. Further light is thrown on the conditions of a miner's life at this time by the proposals made about 1660 by Thomas Bushell, the famous seventeenth-century promoter of mines and mineral works, who was at that time lying a debtor in Newgate. In attempting to induce his fellow-

prisoners to join him in the working of his mines he promised them that they should be "cloathed in good Canvas or Welsh Cottons, their food Bisket, Beaf, Pease, and Bacon thrice a week, the other days, White-meat, Oyl, and Roots; the Drink of allowance for the most part to be water, though not to be barr'd Beer or Ale in orderly proportion. They are to lie on Mats, unless they rather choose a clean Plank; Lots and Delves being assigned to them, in which if God bless their honest diligence, they shall comfortably participate, whereby at last they may make themselves free."—Cf. "Devon and Cornwall," *Notes and Queries*, x, part ii, 40.

16. *View of Devonshire* (edit. 1845), 53–4.
17. Lewis, 220.
18. Tinners' Grievance, 1697.
19. Lewis, 220.
20. Tinners' Grievance, 1697.
21. Tinners' Grievance, 1697.
22. Carew (edit. 1811), 35 *n*.
23. Cornish, Deyow-widn = White Thursday, sometimes spelt "Yw-Whiddn," as above.
24. W. Francis, *Gwennap*, 123 *n*.
25. *Tour through Cornwall*, 301.
26. Cf. Pryce, iv.
27. Mr. Jonathan Hornblower, the engineer and inventor, was receiving £2 a month from Wheal Sparnon in 1765 for looking after the engine, and, as late as the end of the century, Richard Trevithick's father, a noted mine captain, got only £2 a month each for managing Dolcoath, Cook's Kitchen, and Roskear, three of the largest mines in Cornwall.—F. Trevithick, *Life of R. Trevithick*. Wages, however, increased rapidly in the next ten or fifteen years. In 1808–9 the manager of Cook's Kitchen was getting £11 a month and the other captains £6.
28. Extract from Wheal Busy Cost-Book, 1755–64, by the kind permission of Dr. Hambly Row.
29. MS. in Chyandour Office.
30. Pryce, 188.
31. Pryce, 188.
32. The custom of using a pebble instead of a hammer for such auctions was in use at the Providence Mines, Lelant, within living memory.
33. W. Phillips, *Mineralogy*, 204–5.
34. Brigan Pitches Book. Seen by permission of Mr. J. T. Letcher, of St. Day.
35. Wheal Rose Pitches Book.
36. Picks and gads were sold according to the weight of the iron in them—at $3\frac{1}{2}$d. per lb. in 1756. Pick-hilts cost 2d. each.—Cf. Wheal Busy Cost-Book.
37. W. Phillips, *Mineralogy*, 204, 206.
38. W. Phillips, *Mineralogy* (1815), 209.

39. R.C.P.S. (1838), 105, etc.
40. Boulton and Watt MSS. at Falmouth.
41. Cf.
    At Poldice, the men are like mice,
    The Tin is very plenty.
    Capun Teague is one from Breague
    And he'll give ten for twenty.
i.e., the price of 10 cwt. of white tin for 20 cwt. of black tin—very rich values.
42. Carnkye Cost-Book.
43. Cost-Books, St. Day Mines.
44. Various eighteenth-century cost-books, notably Godolphin Great Work, Carnkye Mine, Wheal Sparnon, Wheal Towan, Wheal Unity, Wheal Gorland, Poldice, etc.
45. Parl. Pap. (1799), x.
46. R.C.P.S. (1838), 105.
47. Smiles, *Life of Boulton and Watt*.
48. Forbes, *Tour into Cornwall*, 1794. MS.
49. Various eighteenth-century cost-books.
50. Pryce, 177.
51. In 1799 a county infirmary was erected, not at Redruth, as Pryce had suggested, but at Truro. The hospital at Redruth, which has latterly done so much for the mining population, was not opened until 1863.
52. Various eighteenth-century cost-books.
53. Pryce, 178.
54. Cal. S.P. Dom. (1591–4), 73.
55. Ferris, *Dangerous and Memorable Adventure in a Wherry Boat*.
56. *Curse of Corne-hoarders* (1631), 37.
57. *Nat. Hist. of Cornwall*, 89–90. Carew says that " in times past the Cornish people gave themselves so wholly to the seeking of Tin and neglected husbandry that their neighbours of Devon and Somerset hired their pastures at a rent and stored them with their own cattle " (p. 19, edit. 1769).
58. Tonkin, Notes to the 1811 edition of Carew's *Survey of Cornwall*.
59. Maton, i, 143.
60. Amusing errors of this kind were by no means confined to the journalist class of writer. Miss Edgeworth, even, that patient instructor of the young, in her tale of *Lame Jervas*, assumes him to have been born in a Cornish mine, and not to have seen daylight until the age of fourteen years! It will suffice to say that no child was ever born in a Cornish mine, into which no woman has ever entered but from motives of curiosity and of her own free will.
61. Richard Pococke, Camden Soc., N.S. xlii, 136.
62.   Then full against his Cornish lands they roar,
    And two rich shipwrecks bless the lucky shore.—Pope.

63. Praa Sands was formerly amongst the most notorious resorts of such wreckers, hence the old saying, when a gale of wind was blowing—
Get hatchet and saa (saw),
And away to Praa.

64. R.I.C. Journal (1881), xxiii, 374–9. In the home of the Borlase family at Castle Horneck, near Penzance, was preserved a rapier, bearing the inscription, " Given to Captain Samuel Borlase, by R. Gould, N. Holmes, and B. Hammatt, merchants at Boston, New England, for bravely keeping the tinners from plundering their ship (*Mercy*), stranded in Mount's Bay, 14th July, 1763."—*Cornish Notes and Queries* (1906), 294.

65. W. C. Borlase, *Sketch of the Tin Trade*, 54.
66. Brit. Mus. Add. MS., 32, 687, fol. 337.
67. *Gentleman's Magazine*, October 31, 1748.
68. S.P. Dom. George III, January 24, 1772.
69. *Journal*, i, 506–7.
70. S.P. Dom. (Military), 1773–7.

71. On the occasion also of any " lett " or misfortune in the tin-works where he normally found employment, the tinner of these days immediately found himself reduced to the point of starvation. George Borlase, agent to Lieut.-General Onslow, writing from near Gulval, January 30, 1748–9, says, " We have had the greatest floods of rain here that has ever been seen in any man's remembrance now living. The Tynworks are all drowned almost and many thousand tynners by that means deprived of employ and starving, ours amongst the rest."

72. Thurstan Peter, Notes in *Mate's Guide to Redruth*.
73. Address on Present State of Mines, 1772.
74. R. Cunnack, cf. H. Thomas, *Cornish Mining Interviews* (1896).
75. Cf. G. Unwin, *Letters and Remarks on Tin* (1790).
76. R.G.S.C., iii, 284
77. Boulton and Watt MSS.
78. Lesser mines still at this date, though some of them destined shortly afterwards to prove great prizes when vigorously worked.
79. Boulton and Watt MSS.
80. Boulton and Watt MSS.
81. Boulton and Watt MSS.
82. Letter, April 17, 1787.
83. Letter, September 5, 1789.
84. Amongst other well-intentioned efforts, Dr. James Adair, of Bath, published a dramatic dialogue (consisting chiefly of abuse of one of his fellow-practitioners) in aid of the starving tin-miners in Cornwall.—Cf. Boase and Courtney, *Bibliotheca Cornubiensis*, iii, 1023.
85. R. Cunnack, cf. H. Thomas, *Mining Interviews*.
86. Private Letters.
87. According to the tradition of a certain old Camborne family residing at Troon, the man who suffered execution was called Hosking

and lived at Carwinion. So strong was public feeling on the matter that Captain Andrew Vivian, the partner of Richard Trevithick, well known and respected in Camborne as " old Capun Andrew," went up to Bodmin to beg the body for burial. My informant's grandmother remembered being taken as a child to Roskear, where great crowds were assembled to witness the body being brought home.

88. Joseph Farington, *Diary*, vi, 119 and 133–4.
89. The poor-rate assessment for St. Agnes parish in 1790 was £1,173 8s. Rates were 8s. in the £.—Papers at Chyandour.
90. Letter, April 18th.
91. The mines at Wadebridge, Penrose, near Helston, and Combe-Martin, in Devon, are particularly mentioned.
92. Cf. G. Unwin, *Letters and Remarks on Tin* (1790).

CHAPTER V

MINERS AND ADVENTURERS DURING THE GREAT REVIVAL

AFTER the period of lean years which marked the closing of the eighteenth century, the rise of Cornish mining to its full tide of prosperity reads like an epic tale.

"The West of England mining district," wrote a well-known authority in 1897, "has yielded metallic minerals to the value of upwards of two hundred millions sterling. In getting this, hundreds of miles of shafts have been sunk and thousands of miles of galleries driven. Forests of timber have been used to support the ground, while mountains of ore and rivers of water have been brought to surface by the aid of fleets laden with coal." (1)

In 1801 there were 75 mines at work in Cornwall, the number of people employed in connection with them being in all about 16,000. (2) In 1818 the mines of the area between Camborne and Chasewater alone were employing 8,000, (3) whilst by 1838 more than 200 mines were being worked by the aid of 170 steam pumping engines and 120 steam stamps and whims, and a population of more than 30,000 persons. Of these some 18,000 were men, 5,000 women, and 5,000 children of both sexes. (4) Throughout the 'forties and 'fifties the numbers steadily increased. No less than 340 working mines are described in Williams's *Mining Directory* of 1862, at which time the population employed was close on 50,000. (5) One share-broker alone, Mr. Peter Watson, stated, in 1896, that he had formerly held shares in no less than 264 different Cornish mines at one time. (6) It must, of course, be remembered that mines were originally worked on a smaller scale than obtains to-day, and some of the larger properties at present working in Cornwall under a single name would perhaps have been registered as half a dozen different concerns in the 'fifties. Yet, taken all round, the mining development which took place in the first half of the nineteenth century was a truly remarkable one.

The increase in the population of Cornwall, which went hand in hand with the development of the mines, may best be judged from the tables published in the Registrar's Reports on the census between the years 1800 and 1860.

1801–11	1811–21	1821–31	1831–41	1841–51	1851–61
+ 14 %	+ 18 %	+ 16 %	+ 13 %	+ 3 %	+ 3 %

The rapid growth of population in a hitherto lightly peopled district such as Cornwall brought with it many changes. Between 1800 and 1840 the number of inhabitants in many of the mining areas more than doubled. The parish of Gwennap, which had once barely supported four or five thousand scattered inhabitants, now boasted such crowded centres as Carharrack and St. Day, whose teeming populations almost rivalled that of Redruth itself. (7) Throughout the country-side whitewashed cottages and little chapels sprang up like mushrooms amidst the surrounding wastes. Places which had once been sleepy villages, visited only by a lumbering van or strings of ponies and mules, developed into bustling towns. In 1800 Camborne, now, together with Redruth, the centre of the mining industry, was a mere hamlet, consisting of a dozen cottages. Treswithian Downs were at this time still unenclosed, and a regiment of yeomanry are said to have coursed a hare on them. The village itself was visited twice a week only by a wheeled conveyance called a "kitarine," which was driven by a man named Thomas from Penzance to Truro every Friday, and passed by Camborne again on its return on the following day. Camborne first became a regular post-town in 1800, but even then, and for many years later, the London Western Mail was carried to Penzance by way of Falmouth and Helston, (8) a fact of which the Falmouth Packet and the Coach and Horses inns on the South Coast Road bear witness to this day.

The restarting, about 1800–10, of several of the large and prosperous "Western Mines," as those round Camborne were called, was responsible for a great activity in road-making and traffic communication. Hitherto transport had been chiefly

MINERS AND ADVENTURERS 173

effected on the backs of ponies and mules, a method so slow and expensive that, in 1797, one of the copper companies refused to buy any more ore from Tresavean Mine on account of the cost of transporting it to the coast. (9) In 1806 a great meeting was held at Camborne to apply to Parliament for making a turnpike road from Redruth to Penzance ; (10) and this resulted in the present highroad, which linked up the mining areas with the works and foundries of busy Copperhouse and the growing port of Hayle. In 1809 the first tram-road in Cornwall was opened, (11) communicating between Portreath and Poldice Mine. Of this innovation Hitchens and Drew wrote : "The wheels of the carriage run on cast iron, which facilitates in an extraordinary manner the progress of the vehicles and greatly lessens the force of animal exertion." Following on this was incorporated, in 1824, the Redruth and Chasewater Railway, with powers for making and maintaining a railway or tramroad from Redruth to Point Quay, with several branches therefrom ; and also for restoring, improving, and maintaining the navigation of Restronguet Creek. The length of this line, with its branches, amounted to fourteen or fifteen miles, and the capital of the company was £22,500. (12) The sleepers of the permanent way were of stone and were bought from all and sundry at 1s. each, to the utter destruction of any remains of prehistoric antiquity which might have remained in the neighbouring hill of Carnmarth. The largest undertaking of all, however, was the inauguration, in 1834, of the Hayle (afterwards West Cornwall) Railway, which ran from the port of Hayle (Foundry) to Tresavean Mine in Gwennap, passing through or near all the principal mines of Camborne and Redruth, and extending its branches to the town of Redruth and the port of Portreath. (13) As in the earlier railways, horses were at first the only " power " used, save at one place, where a stationary engine on top of " Steamers Hill " drew the trucks up the steep incline from Angarrack to the present Gwinear Road. With the exception of the Bodmin and Wadebridge Railway, where steam was first used in the west in 1834, almost all the railways of Cornwall owed their beginnings to mining enterprise, the latest being the Treffry Railway from Par to Newquay, which was opened about 1842. (14)

The extension of steam-power in the mining areas had in the meantime been much more rapid in pumping and winding than in railway locomotion, and foundries and engineering works had sprung up in considerable numbers since the beginning of the century. Of all the Cornish foundries, Harvey's, at Hayle, and the old Perran Foundry alone date their beginnings from the latter years of the eighteenth century. (15) Of the origin of the Hayle Foundry a picturesque story is told in the *Life of Richard Trevithick*, the famous Cornish engineer. On a Sunday morning in the year 1770, a rich friend of the original Mr. John Harvey came into his smith's shop at Carnhell Green, having lost one of his silver shoe-buckles when taking a run with his beagles before church time. He said, " How can I go to church with one buckle ? "

" Give me one of your old silver spoons and lend me that buckle, and I'll soon set you up again," said John Harvey.

The rich man was pleased and asked what his friend would do if he had some of his money. " Why, go down to Foundry and make cast-iron pumps for Trevithick's mines in place of wooden ones," (16) was the reply. The up-country ironfounders, however, guarded the secrets of their trade very jealously, and another story says that Mr. Harvey had much difficulty in first learning how iron castings were made. Having been refused admittance on more than one occasion, he took to dressing in rude clothes, feigned to be half-witted, used to idle about the doors of the foundries singing songs and now and then venturing in on the pretext of carrying water for the men or doing errands, and so at length discovered how to make iron pipes. (17)

Second to Hayle Foundry was probably that at Perran, originally started by George Fox, of Perran Wharf, in the year 1791. (18)

The Cornish foundries, however, were still very small and primitive affairs at the beginning of the last century, and though it is true that the parts for Richard Trevithick's steam carriage were made in Hayle in 1800–1, much difficulty was experienced in getting them to fit, and the high-pressure whim-engine erected by him at Wheal Crenver and Abram in 1806 was made at Neath Abbey. (19)

Prior to this date practically the whole of the castings of the engines had been made in the Midlands or Lancashire. Even the timber (oak) for the working beams or " bobs " of the Boulton and Watt engines was cut and shaped by the firm's own carpenters in the woods near Birmingham. (20) For transport to Cornwall the goods were placed on canal-boats at Stourbridge, and brought by inland waterways to Bristol or to Chester, from whence they were shipped to Portreath, Hayle, or the Fal. Often in winter, when the Midland canals were frozen hard, the machinery would be delayed for six weeks at a time waiting for the frost to break. Considerable feeling used to be expressed both by the firm and the mine adventurers in Cornwall at the delays which were constantly occurring in canal transport. In answer to the charge of delay in erecting one of their engines at North Downs Mine, Boulton wrote to the Adventurers: (21) " We know that the parts we had the charge of were compleated and put on board a boat in the beginning of June, but it was not possible that we could foresee that it would prove so dry a summer and that these goods would have been stopped at Stourport and other places for want of water in the Severn. Neither can we suffer the delays that happened at Chester in the shipping to be placed to our account nor the further delay in the voyage, as we have not taken upon us to govern the Winds or Tides." " After all," he wrote to Wilson, " if you have done as I requested and set all our men to work at the mine that can be employed there, I will venture to predict you will find either the Carpenter's or Smith's work behind or water not brought to the engine, or something else that doth not depend on our men." (22)

The actual erecting of the engines was superintended by men sent down from Birmingham, of whom William Murdock, who resided at Redruth, was the chief. The shortage of men, however, both in Cornwall and the Midlands, who were capable of erecting engines was a constant anxiety to the new firm. " As to men," wrote Watt to Wilson on June 21, 1785, " we are extremely deficient in that article even for the works we have in hand here (Soho). We have only three men who can put an engine together, and each of these must do at least three engines this season. The inferior hands we have are very few and at such wages as would probably be grudged in Cornwall. We are constantly in quest of more hands, but there is so much machinery going forward all over the nation that it is difficult to get any that are worth having." This shortage laid an immense amount of work on Boulton and Watt and their indefatigable assistant, Murdock, the latter sometimes working almost day and night in order to cope with the Cornish orders, which were "constantly increasing." (23)

Such a state of affairs could not last for long, and the number of mines starting up after 1800 made it beyond the powers of any one firm (and that at a distance) to supply all the machinery required. Year by year the growing foundries at Hayle and Perran had been pressing to the front and turning out more and more heavy machinery from their premises. By the middle of the century Hayle Foundry had risen to be one of the greatest engineering firms in the country, and at home or abroad there were few mining districts where Hayle engines were not to be found. Side by side with this foundry had grown up, as its keen rival, the Copperhouse Foundry, started by Messrs. Sandys, Carne & Vivian on the premises of the old Copperhouse Smelting-Works after their abandonment. Though smaller than Hayle Foundry, from 300 to 350 men were frequently employed there. (24) In its earlier days the Copperhouse Foundry kept fifty or more of its own horses to do the haulage work necessary in delivering goods at the mines. Down to 1840, when the present foundry was started in Nancherrow, all the heavy castings for the St. Just mines had to be brought from Copperhouse or Hayle, and old inhabitants would formerly describe the scene which took place when a 30-ton "bob" or a 90-inch cylinder, rocking and towering on its wagon, was drawn through the narrow lanes by a team of twenty horses, whose drivers ran by their sides and urged them on with cracking whips. (25)

The demands of the Gwennap mines in the meantime and the increasing skill and enterprise of the Cornish engineers had enabled the Perran Foundry likewise to begin to undertake heavy work about 1828–30, and from this time on Perran Foundry ranked equally with Hayle as one of the great engineering firms of the country. Down to 1870, when many of the Gwennap mines were closed, work flowed in upon the Perran Foundry, for on such a gigantic scale were the Clifford Amalgamated

MINERS AND ADVENTURERS 177

Mines carried on, with nearly a score of large engines and an enormous quantity of pitwork, that, with the other Gwennap mines, they were well-nigh sufficient of themselves to keep a moderate-sized foundry running.

Other well-known engineering firms also sprang up in different parts of Cornwall as the mining developed. The Cornwall Boiler Works were started at Roskear in 1802, Messrs. Holman's Mining Machinery Works at Camborne in 1839, and the St. Blazey Foundry in 1848. (26)

Though copper smelting was removed in the early part of the century from Cornwall to South Wales, tin continued all along to be "whitened" in Cornwall, and many new smelting-works were built at this time in different parts of the country to deal with the increased production of tin ore from the mines. Each of these "houses" in turn seems to have been built chiefly with a view to cutting off the tin from the mines and preventing it going to either of the others. Truro had three smelting-works, one near the railway viaduct called Carvedras, belonging to the Daubuz family, a much older one near Tregolls called Truro Smelting-House (held at one time by the Roberts family), and a third called Trethellan, near the present gasworks, under the control of Williams, Harvey, of Hayle. Further east, Charlestown Smelting-House was built to prevent the St. Austell tin from going to either of the three Truro houses. Charlestown ostensibly belonged to the Enthovens and Brasseys, of London, but the Bolithos, of Chyandour, held a half-share in it unknown to the world at large. To the west of Truro was Calenick Smelting-House, at the top of the Calenick estuary, a well-known works which were built about 1703 by Francis Moult & Co., of London, to succeed much older ones at Newham. At first sight it would seem strange that these works should have been moved from alongside Truro River to a spot further inland, but the reason was in order to be near the main road to Truro, by which means they were able to intercept the tin from the eastern portion of the Gwennap mines and Chacewater, Kea, Baldhu, etc., from going to the three Truro houses. The Moults were succeeded by the Daniell family, of Trelissick and Truro, and later by the Michells, but, during the latter regime, the Bolithos also had an interest in the business, although, as at Charlestown, unknown to the outside world. The old clock-tower surmounting Calenick Works may still be seen by passers-by on the Truro to Falmouth road. Calenick itself had a rival in the Penpoll Works at Point, whilst in the Carnon Valley were two more smelters situated at Bissoe and Cons. (27)

Coming to West Cornwall, the principal function of Angarrack Smelting-House was to intercept the tin from the Camborne district and prevent it going to Williams, Harvey's Mellanear Works at Hayle ! Treloweth, adjoining the " Lamb and Flag " public-house near the present St. Erth station, belonged to the Daubuzes, of Truro, and was a branch of their Carvedras Works, and was so situated as to intercept some of the tin from St. Ives, Lelant, Towednack, and Nancledra, which might otherwise have gone to either Williams, Harvey's Mellanear Works at Hayle or to Angarrack or Chyandour. The public-house at each place was supposed to assist therein ! In later times Trereiffe Smelting-Works were built to prevent the St. Just tin from reaching Chyandour. (28)

Such small houses as Angarrack and Treloweth did not, of course, get the tin from the large mines, which usually sold by ticketing or private treaty, on the results of assays made at each mine a few days before. What kept the lesser smelting-houses alive were the little mines and scores of stamps and stream works, which simply sent out their tin on one day in each month and made the best bargains they could at their favourite smelting-house. The bargaining over the price often took a whole day and went on till night, with intervening visits to the pub., with the smelting-works manager. In order to attract sellers, a dinner was provided free at the inn by most smelting-works, this custom only ceasing at the " Three Tuns," Chyandour, when the works there were closed in 1912 and the " Three Tuns " pulled down.

In the case of a large mine selling tin, the mine manager or secretary himself would generally attend at the " weighing off " at the smelting-works, since this was a transaction which frequently involved several thousands of pounds. These great men, however, were no less keen on their perquisites than the working tinners, and every smelting-works, in addition to tipping the wagoners 2s. each, presented the mine purser himself with a douceur of 5s., not to mention numerous glasses of grog. This almost Oriental interchange of presents, however, was as long as it was short, since the mine, in its turn, gave a " drop allowance " of 2s. each to the smelting-house men who tipped the sacks, and to the smelter himself more allowances in kind than the donor was ever aware of, or, if aware, a willing party to !

Cast in 3-cwt. blocks to prevent them from being stolen, and each one stamped with the Lamb and Flag or other smelter's device, the ingots of silvery-looking tin might, until recent years, be seen stacked up on the mineral railways awaiting transport to the coast, (29) a convincing proof to all that passed by that tin, in conjunction with fish and copper, was no empty part of the county's toast to its famous productions.

The increase of engineering knowledge and the abounding prosperity of many of the mines brought with it, if slowly, many improvements in mining methods and machinery. The waste and extravagance connected with many of the early engines had been enormous. Previous to 1812 immense boiler-fires were frequently used, those at Poldice and the United Mines being sometimes seven and eight feet in depth. (30) Many of the earlier engines, too, were so badly made and miserably looked after that the whole of the engine-house was generally filled with steam exuding from crevices in the machinery and from almost every part of the boiler which was exposed to the air.

"A few years back," wrote Carne in 1824, "to go into an engine-house was to go into a hog's-stye; every part of the machinery was covered with dirt and the stench was intolerable. Thirty years ago," he continued, "it was a rare circumstance to erect a second engine on a mine before the first had arrived at the full extent of its power, or even to provide a spare boiler for the engine, in case of failure of the working boiler." In addition to this, pumps were in many cases allowed to remain when quite worn out, spurting water through numerous small apertures on to the men as they climbed the ladders; whilst the adits were frequently in such a slovenly state with the accumulation of mud, which was suffered to remain in them, that a part of the water drawn from the mine usually found its way back again to the deep levels. No care was taken either to prevent the rain-water from collecting in the "old men's workings" which pitted the surface, and so finding its way down into the mines. "The consequence was that the lower levels of deep mines were generally flooded at some period of the winter, whilst the stamps and various water-engines, from lack of surface water, were frequently suspended during the summer months. Consequently thirty years ago hardly any mine produced 500 tons of ore in a month, but lately we have seen a produce of nearly 1,500 tons in the same period." (31)

Improvements, of course, came gradually, and they came later in some districts than in others. Shortly after 1800, when Mr. Michael Williams was managing the United Mines, he found the surface indented by innumerable shallow pits, formerly sunk by the old men in pursuit of the tin ore in the backs of the lodes. By ordering these pits, which absorbed immense quantities of rain-water, to be filled with clay, by cutting channels to aid surface drainage, and by greater attention to the adits, a remarkable saving to the pumping engines was found to be effected. (32) "The quantity of water now drawn out of most deep mines," wrote Carne in 1824, "is much less than it was twenty years ago, although the mines are deeper. In Wheal Unity and Poldice, and also in the Consolidated Mines, the water now drawn to the adit is estimated at about three-fifths of the quantity which was drawn under the old system : and the water of Treskerby, Huel Chance, and North Downs is not now so much as was formerly drawn from North Downs alone."

Another innovation which greatly lessened the work of the engines was that of picking up the water at shallow levels and conducting it to the nearest "lift" instead of allowing it all to go down to the deep levels before pumping it, as had often been the case in former times. (33) The water thus naturally collected at each lift of pumps was not, of course, always, or indeed commonly, just sufficient to fill the pumps and no more. Thus whilst the water was in excess at one level and for its drainage the pump should be worked rapidly, at others it might be insufficient. To remedy this an artificial supply was allowed to descend to keep the pumps always "solid" (i.e. filled), lest the buckets and clacks (valves) should be injured by the irregular action of the engine and other apparatus "going into fork." (34)

The greatest stimulus of all to improvement in mine drainage was given by Captain Joel Lean, who, in 1813, inaugurated the system of "duty reporting" of engines, which was afterwards continued by his son and grandson. The use of the "counter" for ascertaining the "duty" of engines had been introduced by Watt, in order to ascertain the excess of work performed by his engines over what had been done by the old engines, as he was, by agreement, to receive a third part of the sum which might be saved. As, however, no publication was made of these figures, no comparison could be made of the respective merits of the different engines, and, on the expiration of Watt's patent, the counter, although retained in some mines for the satisfaction of the agents, was generally given up, and the duty of the engines appears to have greatly declined. (35)

The object of Lean's monthly engine reports was to compare the consumption of fuel of one engine with another, the standard of comparison being the number of pounds of water raised one foot high with the consumption of one bushel (? ninety-four pounds) of coal. The number was expressed in millions, hence the term "millions duty" as applied to pumping engines. (36) By the periodical publication of the "duty" done by engines in various mines, so much emulation was excited in the engineers and engine-men that, by keeping the machinery in better order —by close attention to the fires—and other improvements, the benefits of this measure were almost immediately felt. (37) In 1813 the average duty of the twenty-four engines reported was about twenty millions. By 1826 the number of engines reported had risen to forty-eight, with an average duty of over thirty millions, whilst in 1834, of the fifty-two engines reported, the average duty was nearly forty-eight millions. (38) This efficiency increased rather than lessened as years went on, so that seventy years ago Cornish engines had reached such a pitch of perfection that they were able to raise a ton of water 450 feet high by means of the steam produced by burning only one pound of coal, and at a cost of about half a farthing. (39)

"The construction of the Cornish engine which performed these duties is," says Mr. Davey, "precisely that of the Watt engine." How, then, did later Cornish engineers manage to get with the Watt engine a threefold duty? The answer is chiefly by two developments, the use of the plunger-pump instead of the bucket-pump, and Trevithick's new Cornish boiler with internal tubes. (40) By an ingenious device, known as the parallel motion, Watt had first contrived to do away with the old wheel and chain method of applying power to the shaft rods, but down to 1806 the water from the mine still continued to be drawn by suction on the upstroke of the engine, to assist which, in lifting the combined weight of the rods and the various columns of water, balance-bobs were employed at different depths. (41) About 1806, however, Captain Joel Lean, the manager of Crenver and Oatfield Mines, substituted a plunger in place of a bucket-pump, with a view merely to lessening the wear and tear on the pumps. (42) These plunger-pumps, worked from the main rods by offsets, forced the water up by the down stroke of the engine, or, in other words, the weight of the pump-rods descending the length of the stroke forced the various columns of water upwards. This alteration was found so advantageous that it was ultimately brought into general use, the whole of the pumps in the shaft being made of the plunger description, except the bottom one, which for various reasons is still a lifting pump. (43)

The modern Cornish engine still has its balance-bobs at surface and at various depths in the shaft, but their office now is to assist the engine in raising the weight of the rods only, whilst the water is raised by the downward or "out-door" stroke. As one watches to-day the perfect rhythmical motion of the 40-ton engine "bob" from which the pump-rods, 2,000 feet or more in length, depend into the shaft, one may see the dream of many generations of Cornish and up-country engineers come true. The inside of the engine-houses, no longer filled with steam and reeking like a hog-sty, as of old, are clean and burnished, the metal-work shining and the floor of holystoned whiteness. Overhead Watt's parallel motion still works on, undisplaced by any later invention, whilst Trevithick's boiler has but lately given way to others of a slightly different type.

Not, however, in the pumping-engine alone, but in many other ways the spread of mechanical knowledge was being shown in Cornwall in the early decades of the nineteenth century. Whilst Watt had been busy with his low-pressure pumps, Trevithick was developing the "puffer" or high-pressure winding-engine, and from 1810 (44) onwards "fire whims," as they were known, slowly began to come into use in the larger and deeper Cornish mines, displacing the older horse-engines for hoisting.

Down to the 'sixties, and in some cases much later, the stuff was nearly all raised in kibbles or iron buckets, of a shape which from time immemorial has been used in Cornwall. The carrying capacity of these had, of course, gradually increased. Those in use at Dolcoath in 1864 drew 12 cwt. at a time, and, according to Captain Charles Thomas, in a good underlying shaft, well-timbered with birch plank, the kibbles ran up and down like bottles, with scarcely any friction at all, never touching one another as the up-coming passed the descending one in the centre of the shaft.

The substitution of iron chains for ropes in hauling was made quite early in some of the mines. In 1825 the cost for rope for two whims at Binner Downs Mine was £996, but by 1830, owing to the introduction of chains, the cost for rope had decreased to £275, although three or four whims were then in use. The noise of these chains could often be heard miles away from the mine on calm summer nights. Where ropes remained in use they were sometimes of great size, those used within living memory for the capstans at Wheal Vor being six inches in diameter. (45)

Mechanical development, however, was not entirely confined to such matters as affected the adventurers' pockets. In one or two instances the more enterprising mines were beginning to study the miners' health and comfort to the extent of introducing machines for lowering and raising the men from their work. In 1841 the Royal Cornwall Polytechnic Society offered a prize for the best model of a machine for lifting miners to the surface. The prize was awarded to the distinguished engineer, Michael Loam, and an engine built on his design was shortly afterwards erected by him at Tresavean Mine. This machine, known as the "man-engine," was a double rotary, 36-inch cylinder, acting upon two small wheels, which acted on two larger ones. In ascending or descending the men stood upon small platforms attached to rods which depended into the shaft. At every stroke of the engine the men were raised twelve feet, and thus by alternately stepping from one rod to the other, if the man-engine was a double one, they soon reached surface. This innovation proved an incalculable boon to the men in the deep mines where it was introduced, and inspired the Gwennap poet to write :—

> "The engine by which he is raised from below
> Now supersedes climbing, health's deadliest foe—
> This miners know well and their gratitude show.
> Their core being o'er from labour they cease,
> And delighted avail them, O Loam, of the ease
> Thy genius procured them and joyful ride
> On the rod, while others descend by their side."(46)

The use of mechanical power for dressing tin and copper ores was likewise beginning to find its way into Cornwall throughout the early years of the nineteenth century, although it was not until 1830 (47) that it can be said to have become at all general ; whilst many of the mines west of Hayle clung to old-fashioned ways much later. The first steam stamps are said to have been erected at Wheal Fanny (part of the Carn Brea Mines) as early as 1813. (48) There were two at work on Wheal Vor by 1818, and another at Wheal Reeth before 1824. (49) Small water-wheel stamps, however, were still the only ones in use in many mines in 1828, though in cases where steam had been applied, the number of heads at work had been increased in some cases to thirty-six, and even to forty-eight. The lifters of these stamps were still made of wood, the iron "heads" varying in weight from $1\frac{1}{2}$ cwt. to $4\frac{1}{4}$ cwt. (50)

Underground, meanwhile, the old method of underhand stoping was gradually giving way to that of overhead or back stoping, (51) tram roads were being introduced in place of wheelbarrows, and more attention was being given to the size and drainage of levels and the art of ventilation. In earlier times, however, the methods employed in the various mining districts differed far more from one another than they do to-day, and thus improvements introduced in the Gwennap or Camborne mines might take thirty years before they were generally adopted in the outlying districts. (52) Thus, in spite of the many changes which were taking place elsewhere, Carne described the mining practices in St. Just in 1822 as still being old-fashioned and uneconomical to a degree. Lodes, for instance, which had been heaved (faulted) were rarely searched for with any determination beyond the heave, and practically no cross-cutting was ever done to the north and south of the principal lodes to discover fresh ones. If a level in a mine became unproductive it was abandoned almost at once, and instead of keeping the sump the deepest part of the mine, it was not uncommon to sink winzes in many places deeper than the main shaft and to draw the water from these to the sump by manual labour. In addition to this, shaft sinking was hardly ever continued until the bottom level was almost worked out, with the result that many mines were abandoned purely on account of the hand-to-mouth policy under which they had been worked. (53)

Yet in spite of the long lingering of antiquated methods in the outlying districts, the prosperity and importance of Cornish mining throughout the early decades o the nineteenth century were all the time increasing. Astounding, indeed, were many of the discoveries and fortunes now being made in mines which a former generation had believed to be already exhausted. An old St. Just miner informed Mr. Courtney that when he was a boy, about 1790, he remembered hearing the old men say that mining would soon come to an end in their parish, as the mines were becoming poor and getting deeper every day, and that as to a " fire-engine " (i.e. steam-pump), all the lodes in St. Just would not maintain one. By 1837 ten steam pumping engines and nine stamping and winding engines were at work in this one parish.

In the year 1820 a company was started to re-work the Levant lodes on the cliffs in the parish of St. Just. Twenty shares were issued, on each of which a call of £20 was made. Before this £400 had been spent, a rich band of copper was cut within twenty-four feet from the surface, from which the adventurers were able to purchase all the plant. The clear profits in the first twenty years of working were £200,000. Speaking of this mine in 1865, Spargo wrote : " On an outlay of £7 10s. a share the shareholders have received £1,091 per share. Every person who invested money in this mine received it back 449 times over in forty-four years." (54) Levant Mine is still working to-day (1927), and with its engine-houses perched upon the cliff's edge and its levels now extending for over half a mile beneath the bed of the Atlantic, it forms an interesting and almost historic link with the past.

Not, however, on the fortunes of the mines of any one locality was the fame of Cornish mining based. The Penstruthal and Tresavean lodes near Gwennap for a distance of 600 fathoms, or three-quarters of a mile, yielded the enormous amount of £4,000,000 (million) worth of tin and copper, and divided amongst the shareholders upwards of £1,000,000 in the shape of profit, on an outlay, as far as Tresavean was concerned, of about £3,000, and probably in both mines not exceeding £10,000. For about twenty-five years these mines paid interest at the rate of about 400 per cent. (55) Beneath this enormous course of copper ore, tin has been proved in depth, and Tresavean Mine also is working to-day. Another mine hardly less famous for its great riches of copper ore was the Devon Great Consols, situated on the Tamar, on the Devon borders of the county. In the year 1844 the shares in this mine rose from £1 to £800, and in the six years which followed, 90,000 tons of copper ore were sold and the lucky original shareholders received more than £200 per share on £1 paid. (56)

"Some idea of the great extent of these mines," wrote Mr. J. H. Collins, "may be gathered from the following particulars. The area of the setts was three miles by two miles. There were eleven large waterwheels employed for pumping and other purposes which were supplied with water through $8\frac{1}{2}$ miles of leat. Twelve main shafts were in use, in which were fixed 2,097 fathoms of pitwork operated by means of massive 'flat rods' from the waterwheels and with the aid from several steam-engines. Underground there were forty-six miles of levels and nearly three miles of tramways. At surface, eleven large steam-engines were employed in pumping, hauling, crushing, etc., and there were also three locomotives running on lines connecting the different parts of the mines with each other and the quays at Morwellham. Up to their abandonment in 1903 (57) the mines were still producing largely, and might have been working to-day but for a certain disastrous disagreement amongst the shareholders which led to the stoppage of the whole concern."

As Henwood had truly declared in 1854, "more mines have been discontinued from want of management than from want of mineral, jealousy and petty squabblings being fertile sources of failure. This is not mining, nor should it be laid to the fault of mining, as is too frequently the case." (58)

Coming now to the central area between the towns of Redruth and Camborne, the famous Dolcoath Mine has long overshadowed a district where numbers of rich mines have together contributed more wealth than any piece of ground of similar extent in the Old World. Throughout the eighteenth century, Dolcoath was looked upon as one of the most considerable mines of Cornwall, and when she stopped working in 1787—owing to the low price of copper resulting from the heavy output of the Anglesea Mines—she was already 132 fathoms deep and had yielded over £1,250,000. Started again about 1800, Dolcoath continued to make great profits on her copper, selling, in the year 1805, over £114,000 worth of ore at a clear profit of £36,000, and giving employment to 1,600 men, women, and children.

It is sometimes stated that at the mine meetings in these days the ruddy faces of the adventurers beamed through the steam of many grogs from midday until far into the night. Whether this was so or not, the Dolcoath Counts in 1805 must have been very interesting meetings. (59) Owing to the enormous extent of its underground excavations, a subsidence of the ground took place at Dolcoath about 1828. The movement—which continued for several weeks—was so slow that the miners who at its commencement were employed in the deep levels, by climbing uncrushed portions of the ladders in some places and waiting their opportunity and creeping through crevices between moving rocks in others, managed to reach surface at the west part of the mine in safety. (60) About 1832 the copper lodes began to grow poor, and the more timid adventurers talked of an early abandonment of the mine. The manager, however, persuaded the company to sink deeper, with the result that tin deposits almost equally rich were discovered below the zone of copper. This discovery of the presence of tin below copper has proved a most significant one for Cornwall, though its import is only now beginning to be fully appreciated. In the case of Dolcoath alone it meant the continuation of the mine for another eighty years, during which time another £1,000,000 profits were divided amongst the shareholders in respect of tin. (61)

The value of such properties as these to the mineral owners can well be imagined when it is realized that, in the space of ten years, one mine (Tresavean) gave to the lords (who frequently bore no risk) the sum of £36,331, whilst Dolcoath, in sixty-six years, paid to the Basset family no less than £119,355. (62)

Striking increases in the value of property sometimes occurred in the mining districts. Downhill, a small coarse tenement in St. Cleer, near Liskeard, which had been purchased thirty years before for £200, suddenly rose, in 1844, to great value owing to the discovery of copper lodes and the opening of West Caradon Mine, and for many years afterwards paid to its lucky owner a regular income of £2,000 a year in dues, without the least risk on his part. (63) Concerning the first discovery of one of the Caradon Mines, an interesting story used to be told around Liskeard. Two maiden ladies who had long owned a part of the wild moorland of this district decided to sell off some of their land which was so poor in value as to be scarcely suitable even for rough grazing. It was bought for a small sum by a well-known lawyer in Liskeard. Hardly had the transaction been completed, however, before private word was brought to the two ladies of the discovery of rich copper in the district. That very night their solicitor was instructed to post off to meet the lawyer who had bought the ground. After much general conversation the solicitor brought the talk round to the property which had lately changed hands, and, after dilating on the inconsistency of women and the way in which they never knew their own minds, etc., mentioned casually that his clients were willing to buy the property back for the same sum, having conceived a sentimental attachment for land which had been so long in their family. Lawyer —— had the reputation of being no fool, but in this case he consented to the proposition, and somehow or other the business was effected then and there at midnight. The next morning Lawyer —— was greeted by a friend in the street.

"Hullo ——, heard the news?"

"No," he replied; "what news?"

"Why, the great discovery of copper up to Caradon!"

It is said that Lawyer —— from that day registered a vow never to part with property in a hurry again.

Not infrequently it happened in those days of cost-book companies that mines which had yielded immense profits to one set of adventurers were abandoned all of a sudden when some temporary change of conditions necessitated the call of a few pounds per share, although the same mine might see within a few weeks or months afterwards another set of owners reaping a rich reward on their outlay. As an example of this the shares in the Gwennap United Mines, which for many years had been worked at a great profit, were actually being sold at one period for the mere value of the machinery and materials. Within a few weeks, however, in consequence of a discovery in one of the lower levels, the position had so altered that the same shares were selling at £420 apiece and the mine was shortly after paying handsome dividends again. In the 208 Fathom East, the Hot Lode was stated by Henwood in 1854 to be 17 feet big, a solid course of yellow ore, yielding 35 tons per fathom, or £300. The temperature of the water issuing was 114°. The men worked nearly naked, and even so it was found necessary to bring cold water in pipes from surface to pour over them whilst engaged in their labours. (64)

Of all Cornish tin-mines, probably the most productive was the world-famed Wheal Vor, situated in the parish of Breage, near Helston. Restarted in 1814 by the Gundry family of Goldsithney, after she had been idle for nearly a hundred years, Wheal Vor jogged along very quietly to begin with. So quietly, indeed, that the unredeemed outlay necessary in opening so large a mine became too great for the proprietors, who, like many another Cornish family, were bankers and merchants as well as being adventurers, and had innumerable irons in the fire. The result was that, to the general regret of West Country folk, the enterprising Gundry family became bankrupt. (65) The principal firm of lawyers and bankers who had been their rivals became trustees for the estate, and in a moment of weakness committed themselves to the illegal act of purchasing the mine. This act unfortunately not only cost them dear, but ultimately ruined the adventure, in spite of all its marvellous resources. About 1820, in one of the shafts, at 155 fathoms from the surface, the beginning of a course of tin ore was discovered, which proved the richest ever known in Cornwall. The great shoot was stoped away by the miners underhand to nearly the 310-fathom level. Sometimes the lode would squeeze in and then shortly afterwards open out again, the rich portions descending in a series of step-like formation. In some parts of this mine the riches of the ground were reckoned at £500 per fathom.

A law-suit, however, instituted by the representatives of the Gundry family, was drawing to an issue, and every means possible was taken to exhaust the reserves before the decision of the judges was given. Two steam-whims were put up, all exploratory operations were stopped, and orders were given to Captain Mark Reed, the manager of the mine, to exhaust her with all speed. Even so, the reserve ground already explored lasted almost exactly seven years from the time when orders were given to exhaust the mine to the day when the water was allowed to rise and the levels returned once more to their natural silence. The appearance of Wheal Vor in the hey-day of her working was said to have resembled a town. Nearly eleven hundred persons were employed on the mine in 1838 and sixteen steam-engines were at work, of which six were pumps. During a great part of this working the tin was smelted on the mine, six furnaces being in use. About 1832 the number of blocks of smelted tin sent out in one month was over eighteen hundred. For a long time, indeed, one-third to one-fourth of all the tin raised in Cornwall was the produce of Wheal Vor. (66)

Much space might be devoted to the recording of many other great prizes in Cornish mining similar to these, was not the purpose of this book more concerned with the lives and character of the men who worked the mines than with actual fortunes made or lost by the adventurers. It is interesting to note, however, that in the earliest part of the century the government of the mines was extraordinarily local, and nearly all the adventurers were personally interested in the well-being of the mines, either as part-owners of the mineral rights or as merchants supplying machinery or stores. Quite large mines were frequently held by only eight adventurers; and out of forty adventurers in one of the Western Mines in 1842, thirty-nine were inhabitants of the town of Penzance. The few mines which were run entirely as outside enterprises, and supported only by London adventurers, were by no means regarded favourably by those who had the welfare of the industry at heart. Salmon, the editor of the well-known *Mining and Smelting Magazine*, thus wrote in 1862 : " The re-working of Crenver and Abraham Mines seems now definitely abandoned, a most wise determination, for sufficient money has been squandered on similar concerns to show the folly of other attempts by ' London Companies.' " Again, on another occasion, he wrote : " North Pool ought to be worked, but with great prudence ; in the hands of an ' outside' Company, who never can (or at least never do) get good management, a disastrous failure would probably be the result." " Mines," he further added, " are sometimes conducted in a reckless, gambling spirit, but the public opinion of the metallic mining districts utterly disavows this class of mining, which is supported by—and, indeed, owes its existence to—the unreasoning credulity and cupidity of London or ' outside ' speculators." (67)

As has already been said, down to the mid 'sixties the prosperity of Cornish mining was ever increasing. These were the days when messengers were sent posting off on horseback in the middle of the night to tell some lucky owner of a new lode of great riches cut by the night " coor." During such a time which followed, when the mine was " cutting rich," an ensign was frequently kept flying from the top of the headgear, and throughout the local mining circles and in the Exchange at Redruth the talk was all of the great prices being fetched by the coveted shares. During these years, too, brokers and share-dealers of all sorts dashed about the country from mine to mine, making lightning inspections and reports, on which the more credulous of their clients in London and the great towns up the country hung in joyful expectation. Sound business men like Spargo or Mr. Joseph Yallowly Watson were unable to exclude from their reports the atmosphere of bustle and excitement which reigned in the mining areas. Their personal pleasure in going about Cornwall and visiting the mines is everywhere apparent in their writings. " You must excuse errors and omissions in these Notes," wrote Mr. Watson in 1863. " I have to write them hastily, when and where I can, in engine-houses, in count-houses, on dressing-floors ; standing in the rain at times (Cornwall had not yet become ' England's Riviera ' !), and at others writing in fly and railway carriages and, I may add also, sometimes in bed."

On one occasion Mr. Watson arrived all dripping wet at Drake Walls tin-mine, near Gunnislake, after a fourteen-mile ride across country, over the Downs. The captain was underground, and he sat alone in the count-house looking out into the mist and rain and listening to the roar of the stamps outside the window.

" 'Give us a good report,' they seem to say, as their heads keep rising and falling. 'We must have tin for pay-day, we must have tin for pay-day.'

" But here comes the captain in his flannel dress of the colour of gossan, and a candle stuck in his cap in a plaster of clay, and I hope he can do that." (68)

" The rage of the ' Roses,' " continues Mr. Watson, in the same chatty way on another occasion, " was a memorable time in Cornish mining. East Wheal Rose was then the richest mine in Cornwall and paying £50,000 a year to her fortunate shareholders. After a short but brilliant career she was exhausted (?) and stopped. Great as her profits were, it was calculated that still more money was lost in new mines around her. The discovery of a stone of ore in the neighbourhood of Newlyn, St. Columb, or Perran was a fortune to a man in the way of premium, and there arose West, North, and South, and a perfect host of other Roses, all at high premiums. I remember, in 1845, there was a great discovery of lead somewhere about Perran, and I passed it on the road to Truro. I think it was the Virgin Perran, and great care was taken of her in her early days. In stepping into the adit, open to the road, I alighted on a magnificent rock of lead ; and at the end of an almost open cutting, peeped (through a grating, padlocked) at the beautiful lode. If I remember rightly, shares went to £50 premium in the Perran Wheal Virgin."

Quite apart from the good dividends which many of them paid, it was a pleasant thing to be an adventurer in one of the old-style Cornish mines, in the hearty days of the 'forties, 'fifties, and 'sixties, when the monthly, quarterly, or biannual examination of the books was made the occasion of a scene of eating, drinking, and merrymaking which would have warmed the heart of Falstaff. From early times this jovial way of combining pleasure with business was customary in Cornwall, and throughout the eighteenth century the cost-book's record of "Meat for the account" is a regularly recurring one. It is true that a more parsimonious attitude was occasionally shown, and, on the ruling of some careful adventurer, it was agreed in one mine "that not more than six pence to one sixty-fourth share be expended at any meeting of the adventurers for refreshments," but this was in the case of a small concern near Zennor, where they doubtless knew no better and where nobody of importance was an adventurer! Much more frequent were such entries, made suspiciously near the day of the account, as "for 4 doz. Porter and Ale and 4 Gallons Brandy and Rum," or else for "2 Gallons of Gin for the Count House."

In most cases the adventurers arrived at the mine early in the morning and, having seen their horses placed in the stables and admired the splendid piles of copper ore placed best side out before the door, would pass in to the business of examining the books. A Cornish count-house even to-day has a character of its own not to be found in any ordinary business office. The bare holystoned floors, the clerks working at huge ledgers on their tall stools, are as reminiscent as the pictures on the walls of the captains, merchants, and adventurers of bygone days; whilst the sight of men passing by outside in their ruddy underground clothes and the roar of the stamps, which is heard immediately the door opens, proclaims to all the business of a Cornish mine.

In early times the conduct of many of the Cornish mine meetings appeared somewhat disorderly to at least one business man, who used to attend them from up the country. "Boulton," says Smiles, "found the proceedings conducted without regard to order. The principal attention was paid to the dividing, and after dinner and drink little real business could be done. No minutes were made of the proceedings. Half the company were talking at the same time on different subjects." (69) Boulton, we are told, changed all this. In any case, it did not apply to the mine meetings of later times, when business involving the loss or gain of many thousands of pounds was transacted with due seriousness and decorum.

In most cases, however, the drinking and feasting maintained their importance down to the final abolition of the cost-book system. Thus, as soon as the business part of the meeting was finished, a dinner consisting of roast beef, giblet pie, or other delicacies would be served by the count-house woman and her assistants in some long, low room adjoining, where the trestle tables, covered with rough but snow-white cloths, and the clean, holystoned floor set off a scene of homely festivity hard to describe to those who have never seen it for themselves. In many mines the dinner was eaten off services made from block tin or pewter, the mine's own produce and stamped with the company's seal. So clean and burnished was the set in use at Botallack that it was constantly mistaken by visitors for silver. (70)

After the dinner, which was well qualified with brandy, rum, and gin, jugs of steaming punch were brought in, and the drinking went on far into the afternoon. In the dining-room at Levant Mine are yet to be seen, especially beside two chairs, the marks which the cigar-ends burnt into the floor when the smokers' actions had become too uncertain to hold them. If any liquor remained over at the end it used to be placed in bottles, sealed with the mine seal, and carried home by the adventurers to their wives, who in some cases were no mean judges of the excellences of Major Dick White's punch.

The cost of dinners such as these sometimes created a mild scandal among such of the adventurers as were no drinkers, (71) and at such times it was left to the discretion of the purser to manipulate the entry in the books, many of the older men being very expert at inserting such costs without giving them too much prominence.

"I don't see the entry for that last count dinner," said an adventurer on one occasion, after looking through the books.

"No, my dear," was the prompt reply from the purser, "thee cusn't see un, but 'tes in theer alright."

The old-style Cornish count dinner is now, happily or unhappily, a thing of the past, and those who have attended them have experienced something which will never come again. The conversion of all the Cornish mines into limited liability companies has done away with the regularly recurring examination of the books. Gone, too, or fast disappearing, is the old type of adventurer, the local magnates, the mine doctor, the purser, and the underground captains, who sat down together to those dinners. Very mixed company was often to be found sitting side by side in the old days. At one dinner at North Roskear Mine, a peer of the realm, a new-comer in Cornish mining circles, found himself seated beside a burly underground captain, whose homely appearance he regarded with some amusement—if not contempt. Towards the end of dinner, however, a spirit of condescension making itself felt in the noble lord, he turned to his companion and said :—

"Captain—be pleased to drink with me."

"Thankee," was the captain's brief reply, "I aren't athirst."

On many occasions the quickness in repartee shown by some apparently stolid and illiterate miner proved more than a match for those who were their betters in education. The story is told how Dick Hampton, sometimes called Foolish Dick, the Cornish pilgrim preacher, was called into a count dinner for the amusement of two London adventurers, between whom he was put to sit. After several queer questions and more queer replies, the right-hand man said :—

"Dick, they say that you are more R than F."

"What do 'ee main, plaise?" asked Richard.

"Mean?" said the one on his left. "We want to know whether you are a rogue or a fool?"

"Why," said Dick, casting a squint first on one side and then on the other, "'tween the two, I reck'n!" (72)

As the drink circulated, story after story would go its round, remembrances of bygone captains and adventurers in the famous mines of former days, stories full of shrewd Cornish humour, racily told. Tales of adventure, too, might frequently be heard from men who even in those days had been in the pioneer movements of miners across the globe and who had returned, still Cornish to the backbone, to life in the local mining towns of their birth.

The day following the "account" was known in some districts as St. Aubyn's Day. On this occasion the captains and lesser officials of the mine had a dinner of their own off what remained from the account dinner of the previous day, and to it they were allowed to invite some of their special friends. Great was the merriment which took place at such times, especially among the younger captains, who, though responsible men at their work, were high-spirited as boys at heart and always out for fun when they could get it. Boot-marks were sometimes shown on the ceilings of the count-houses, where a captain had been "skied" by his companions on some occasion such as this, and one old man used to describe how he had seen four or five of them carrying each other up and down the stairs when too drunk almost to find the steps. Among the many practical jokes that used to be played off was that of inducing anyone who looked a bit green to test the strength of the count-house cat, telling him that the animal was strong enough to pull him through the engine-pool. If he agreed to try, a rope would be brought, one end of which would be tied to the man's waist and the other to the cat's tail, the two being placed on opposite sides of the pool. In the meantime, one or two men who had lain in ambush behind a bush of furze or other obstacle on the cat's side of the pool would seize upon the rope and, without showing themselves, give such impetus to it as quickly drew their unsuspecting victim into the pond, much to his unwilling amazement and ever subsequent respect for the strength of Cornish cats.

At times like these the most reckless wagers would sometimes be taken on. Two St. Day captains, boasting once of their underground knowledge of the district, agreed to put out their lights at a certain point in the mine and race through the levels in darkness and up to surface by two different shafts. In spite of the appalling risks from unfenced winzes and other pitfalls, the bet was undertaken and actually carried through, one of the men coming up near Poldory and the other near the United Mines.

Often the captains would play off elaborate hoaxes upon one another. "Capun ———, of St. Day, who was getting up in years, thought of retiring from mining and taking a small farm stocked with a few cows. Knowing little about farming himself, however, he got a friend to buy the cows for him. One evening some of the other men came up to see how the captain's cows were getting on. One of them, approaching the newly bought animals, solemnly inspected the mouth of each, and then, turning round very gravely, he exclaimed :—

"'Why, Capun, my dear, you've ben put through this time, sure 'nuff. Why, they're all ould cows. Seemin' to me they

MINERS AND ADVENTURERS

couldn't clunk a bit of mait to saave their lives—don't 'ee see, they 'aven't goat one full raw of teeth among them.'

"'Goos 'ome,' said the Capun, 'tedn't no such thing. Why, the man what bot they cows said they was young traade and I was fooced to pay a braave price for 'un.'"

All the same, when Captain Billy went to turn the cows in that night he did just take a look inside one of their mouths, and was disgusted to find that what the miner had said about the missing teeth was true, nor was it until after several days of suspense that he at length discovered that this was indeed the normal state of such animals. (73)

The working miners themselves, though they saw little of the feasting and jollity which went on at the monthly accounts, were fêted sometimes on the occasion of the opening of a new mine. The starting of a new engine was a ceremony attended with almost incredible pomp. By four o'clock in the morning the inns would all be astir with preparations for the numbers of guests who attended on such occasions, bands would be playing, and flags flying. When the time came, not only the officials of the mine but the parson, the squire, and the local magistrates might be seen assembled on the "bob plats," protruding from the tall three-storied engine-house. "Presently the engineer steps forward and begs to know what the name of the engine was to be, and who would stand sponsor. The Lord of the Manor requests it should be named after the Chairman, and that he would stand Sponsor. 'Then please, gentlemen, to stand here and when she makes her first stroke, throw this bottle of port wine over her, (74) christen her, and wish her success,' replies the engineer. A quarter of an hour after, the mine bell tolls for dinner, and whilst the adventurers are enjoying the good things inside the count-house, an ox, which had previously been roasted whole, is served up for the men, and champagne for the one and beer for the others flows freely. The rest of the day was generally given up to games and other festivities arranged to put the miners in good humour."

However inadequately the foregoing picture may represent the social side of Cornish mining in the hey-day of its prosperity, one has only to turn from it and consider the state of labour and capital (or "masters and men") in the industrial areas of the

North to see how far more happily placed was Cornwall, how much better fitted the spirit of its people and its local economic system to ride out the storminess of the times. A writer, reviewing the question of "Work and Wages in Cornish Mines," in 1888, spoke of Cornish mining as an industry "which seems to have escaped the disturbing influences of the Industrial Revolution." (75) In the instructive magazines and journals of the 'forties and 'fifties of the last century, the Cornish miner, his habits and system of work and wages, provided a frequent topic for discussion, and Cornwall itself was almost invariably alluded to as a district "where strikes are said to be unknown and no combinations or unions exist." What, it may be asked, was the reason or reasons for this? Doubtless the racial characteristic of the Celt, whose clannishness rarely embraces anything wider than his immediate neighbours, as well as the scatteredness of the areas where the miners dwelt, was partly responsible for preventing any fixed idea of combination amongst them. So, too, the familiarity of all classes, living continuously "cheek by jowl" in a society where the families of adventurers, merchants, captains, and miners were all inextricably related by generations of inter-marriage, made poor ground for the labours of a "foreign" agitator. Added to this, the spirit of local patriotism was strong, and the miners, though frank and independent in their ways and speech, still felt at heart a certain reluctance to break down the respectful relationship born out of long familiarity between themselves and the older Cornish landowning families who drew their incomes from the mines. There were, however, yet more tangible reasons why the times did not breed the same industrial disputes in Cornwall as they did elsewhere.

In the first place, the introduction of steam and machinery into Cornish mines, so far from displacing labour, had, as we have shown, the effect of enormously increasing employment. The introduction of steam for pumping, and, later, for winding and stamping, not only made it possible for scores of new mines to be opened up and thousands of hands to be taken on, but relieved the miners themselves from the almost intolerable labour of the hand-pumps and much of the work of winding stuff by hand. Thus one of the chief causes of discord which affected the manufacturing areas of the Midlands was obviated in Cornwall.

Foremost of all, however, among the reasons for the peaceableness of the Cornish miner was the peculiar system of wages under which he habitually worked. As we have already shown in a former chapter, the men made their own contracts, contending against themselves and not, as in other industries, against a ring of employers. For the month, or often longer period, during which he contracted to work a pitch, the Cornish miner was his own capitalist, and practically his own master. It is easy to see how different from that of the ordinary weekly wage the effect of this system must have been upon the men. A good pay-day for the Cornish tributer depended not on any decision of a wages board, but on the miner's own skill and judgment or the bounty of Nature. If the lode suddenly grew poor or the ground became hard and the men's takings dwindled to nothing, it was not any employer that was to blame. The realization of this bred in Cornish miners a great skill and judgment in their calling, combined with a hardy independence which carried them through the times when even the finest vision errs in piercing the secrets of the earth. On such occasions, when his earnings were "slight," the Cornish miner called philosophy to his aid, and, hoping only for better times, worked on—poor, hardy, and independent as his forefathers for countless generations had been before him.

NOTES.

1. J. H. Collins, R.C.P.S. (1900), 73.
2. R.C.P.S. (1900), 71.
3. R. Thomas, Report on Mining Area, 1819.
4. The average monthly wage at this date was: men, £2 12s. 6d.; women and children, 14s. 6d.—Cf. W. J. Henwood, R.C.G.S., v, 480.
5. Cf. J. Williams, *Mining Directory*, 1862. According to this authority, the number employed on the mines was approximately 41,000, leaving (as a moderate estimate) 9,000 for foundries, tin-streams, smelting-works, explosive factories, etc. If, in addition to these, the people employed in the ports, shipping, and other subsidiary trades were reckoned, the number would, of course, be very much larger.
6. Herbert Thomas, *Mining Interviews*, 259.
7. W. Francis, *Gwennap* (1845), 129.

8. R.C.P.S. (1841).
9. Letters at Trewirgie.
10. Thurstan Peter, *Mate's Guide to Redruth.*
11. The earliest tram road in the west dates from about 1803, being an inclined one to connect the mouth of the Tamar and Tavistock Canal with the river at Morwellham.—Cf. Plymouth Instit. (1887–90), 90, etc.
12. Plymouth Instit. (1887–90), 90, etc.
13. Cf. Parl. Papers (1834).
14. Plymouth Instit. (1887–90), 90.
15. A cost-book of Great Work Mine for 1759–64 shows, however, that more work was done in Cornwall than is commonly supposed. "George Johns, of Camborne, Engineer," was part paid for "casting Brass work for the engine, £30"; "for a Brass cylinder, 10 cwt. (odd) at 1s. per lb., £59"; "for a Brass working Barrell, £70"; as well as smaller work. William Jordan also did Brass casting. Copper work, however, was bought in Bristol, and an "iron pump with a Buckett door" from Colebrook Dale Company.
16. At this period the pumps used in Cornish mines were practically all composed of wood, hollowed out lengthwise and fitted together again to form a smooth and regular bore. The cost-books show that one or two coopers at least were employed in this connection in every large mine, the price paid for such work in 1760 at Great Work Mine being 10s. 6d. a fathom.
17. *Life of G. Francis Trevithick,* i, 88.
18. Michell, "Foundries," *Vict. Hist. of Cornwall.*
19. Cf. Michell, "Foundries," *Vict. Hist. of Cornwall.*
20. Boulton and Watt MSS., January 7, 1794.
21. Boulton and Watt MSS., January 23, 1786.
22. Boulton and Watt MSS.
23. Boulton and Watt MSS.
24. So great was the number of Cornish pumping-engines in use at this time that the price-lists of these two foundries in 1856 show that 80-inch cylinders were actually kept in stock, ready to be "reached down from the shelf" for any chance customer dropping in. The price worked out at 30s. per cwt.
25. Old St. Ives people would likewise tell of the difficulties experienced in taking the bob down Hellesveor Lane to Captain Martin Dunn's engine-house at Hor Bal. Sixteen horses were employed, but, owing to the twists in the lane, the front ones were pulling into the hedges as the others were trying to pull forward. It took several days to get it down, and all the neighbourhood turned out to see it.—Per R. J. Noall, Esq.
26. Cf. Michell, "Foundries and Engineering," *Vict. Hist. of Cornwall.*
27. Bissoe was an old works revived in the late 'nineties, and then dropped, and later turned into an arsenic works. Cons is also generally thought to have been an arsenic works, but I have it on good authority that traces of tin smelting may be seen there.

28. In addition to these and other lesser works, tin smelting was at one time carried on at one or two of the mines, notably at Wheal Vor and Wheal Reeth.—Cf. Stephens, R.C.P.S. (1904), 109.
29. The coming of the heavy road motor has done away with this sight. Until the war, however, the tin from the Redruth smelters was carried to Devoran on the old mineral railway, in open trucks with wooden blocks for buffers and drawn by antique-looking engines with tall funnels, called " Spitfire," " Miner," and " Smelter."
30. Carne, R.G.S.C. (1828), iii, 55.
31. R.G.S.C., iii, 72-4.
32. R.G.S.C., v, 425.
33. R.G.S.C., iii, 67.
34. W. J. Henwood, R.G.S.C., v, 429.
35. Lean, *Historical Statement of Steam Engines in Cornwall*, 8.
36. Davie, R.C.P.S. (1910), 285.
37. R.G.S.C., iii, 57.
38. Davey, R.C.P.S. (1910), 292-5.
39. Collins, R.C.P.S. (1897), 69.
40. Davey, R.C.P.S. (1910), 284.
41. The 100-inch engine at Wheal Vor had a water load of 72 tons, but the total weight of pit work, etc., set in motion at each stroke was 800 tons.—R.C.P.S. (1910), 288.
42. A plunger pump was in use at the United Mines in 1796.—R.C.P.S. (1872), 91.
43. " Formerly, when the engine shaft was sunk below the cistern which was connected with the lowest lift of pumps, the water was drawn to that cistern from the bottom, by manual labour, until the shaft became deep enough for another lift of pumps and another cistern, but for several years past this work is done more easily by very small pumps connected with the rod of the engine and known by the name of Puppy-lift."—R.G.S.C. (1824), iii, 60.
44. Two steam-whims were working at Cook's Kitchen Mine in 1808-9.—Cf. Cost-Book.
45. R.C.P.S. (1907), 33.
46. W. Francis, *Gwennap*, 17.
47. R.G.S.C., iv, 145.
48. R.C.P.S. (1872), 100.
49. R.G.S.C., iii, 62.
50. R.G.S.C., iv, 147.
51. For an explanation of the respective merits of these two methods, cf. R.C.P.S., iii, 68-72.
52. Thus " trams " for wheeling the ore underground were in use in several of the Gwennap mines as early as 1824 (R.G.C.S., iii, 65), whilst Great Work Mine, near Godolphin, was still using only wheelbarrows when it stopped in the tin slump of the 'nineties.
53. Carne, R.G.S.C. (1822), ii.

54. Spargo, *Mines of Cornwall and Devon*, 13.
55. Spargo, 99.
56. Spargo, 158. Amongst the famous shareholders and directors of this mine was William Morris, the craftsman and poet, whose family fortune was largely bound up with D.G.C. between 1850–80. The shares had originally been assigned to his father as part payment of a debt, rising within a few years to the value of £200,000.
57. Collins, *West of England Mining*, 263.
58. *Lectures on Mining and Geology* (1854), 17.
59. *Cornish Magazine*, i, 169.
60. R.G.S.C., viii, 666.
61. *Cornish Magazine*, i.
62. Henwood, R.I.C. (1871), 37.
63. Allen, *Hist. of Liskeard*, 297.
64. G. Henwood, *Lectures on Mining and Geology*, 21.
65. R. Cunnack MS.
66. Richard Cunnack MS. Cf. also J. H. Collins, *West of England Mining*, 165–71.
67. December 1862.
68. *Cornish Mining Notes*, 1863.
69. Smiles, *Life of Boulton and Watt* (1904), 245.

70. The making of plates, spoons, cups, buckles, etc., by the mines, from Cornish silver won on their own property, was at one time quite a fashion. The Basset family possessed a splendid piece of plate made from silver raised at North Dolcoath.—R.G.S.C., viii, 113. John Trewennack, the purser of Wheal Pool, Helston, had several articles made from silver raised there about 1800. One of these, a milk-cup weighing 6 or 8 oz., was in Cornwall about 1883, but, on the death of Mr. Trewennack's daughter, is said to have been taken to Australia by a relative, where it is probably irretrievably lost.—R. Cunnack MS. Notes.

71. And no wonder either, in some cases a "call" to liquidate the dinner being considered as necessary as a call to work the mine!
72. G. S. W. Christophers, *Foolish Dick*, 34.
73. Per Mr. Stephen Michell.
74. So, at least, it is said, but generally some economical person had already emptied the bottle and refilled it with water for this purpose.
75. L. L. Price, Stat. Soc., 1888.

CHAPTER VI

THE MINER AT WORK, 1800-1870

I.

FIFTY or sixty years ago anyone happening to be in the neighbourhood of the mines round about the inconvenient hours of six in the morning, two in the afternoon, or ten at night could not fail to be impressed by the sudden awakening of the countryside. This was the more noticeable because at other times of the day a remarkable stillness was seen to prevail in the mining areas, where, though everything proclaimed the country to be a populous one, the inhabitants were generally lost to view, being either underground or in bed, and only old people and children were to be met with along the roads or in the cottages.

At the stated hours, however, all this was changed. From every direction, along the roads, across the field-paths, and over the downs, scattered groups of men might be seen approaching the tall engine-houses which, like sentinels, stand on guard about the mining areas. As the hands of the clock approached the hour, the clanging of bells would begin, some near at hand, others sounding from far on the wind, as they called the men to their labour beneath the hill-sides or the bed of the sea. This was the signal for changing "cores." Shortly afterwards the men might be seen assembled round the mouths of the different shafts, changed into their underground clothes, consisting of jacket, shirt, and trousers of coarse drill, red-stained and tattered, hard hats to which a guttering candle was attached with a lump of clay, and stockingless feet shod with low-quartered shoes. Thus equipped, each man and boy, with his apportioned allowances of candles suspended to a button of his coat, began the long descent. Half-way down on the ladders they would meet the last "core" panting up towards the day, tired out after their six or eight hours in the hot, moist atmosphere of the deep levels, their faces pallid in the candle-light and their skin covered with perspiration and the red ochreous distillations of the mine.

The term "miner," as loosely applied to the whole class of men employed underground, included, besides the men actually breaking ground, many different grades of workmen, such as trammers, or men rolling barrows of stuff, kibble-fillers, pitmen, sumpmen, carpenters, and binders. The pitmen, whose duty it was to superintend the pumps underground, and the carpenters and binders, who "bound" or kept the mine timbered and supported, generally received monthly wages. In earlier times barrow-men and kibble-fillers were paid by piecework, but latterly these also came to be paid by the month. Throughout the period now under description the old Cornish system of reckoning by the calendar or "five-week month" was maintained, and down to 1872, whatever wages were paid, the miner, it must be remembered, had every three months to put in an extra week to earn them. (1)

The actual miners in Cornwall were, as already explained, paid either by tutwork (contract) or tribute (share of profit). Generally speaking, the development of the mine, such as shaft-sinking, cross-cutting, and other work necessary for reaching and opening up the mineralized ground, was done by tutworkers, who contracted to break the ground at so much per fathom, the price agreed on varying according to the nature of the ground.

The tributer, on the other hand, was employed on the lode only and worked, not at so much per fathom, but for a certain percentage of every pound's worth of stuff he sent to surface. The actual value of this (to the owners) was determined by the sampler or "tryer," who had to be a man of skill and judgment in showing the best values possible in the tributers' ores, "for else," as an old tin-dresser used to say, "a poor tryer might be throwing away a man's livelihood off the vanning shovel." In a matter of such vital importance as this the tributer in most cases had the right to take his sample elsewhere if he found cause for dissatisfaction in the sampler employed by the mine. (2) Both tutwork and tribute were to a certain extent a gamble; the former depending on the nature of the country rock and the latter on the quality of the mineral vein or lode.

"You set a pare of men and give them £4 a fathom," said a captain in 1864, speaking of tutwork, "and before they have driven six feet the ground will become such that they ought to have £7 or £8 to make a living." (3)

In spite of his nearly equal risks and hardships, the tutworker was generally looked upon as a slightly inferior grade of miner, and the ambition of the more intelligent boys was always to become tributers. As we have seen in an earlier chapter, the wages of the tutworkers in the eighteenth century were, on an average, less than those of the tributers, and this distinction still held good in the nineteenth century, as the following table, prepared in 1837, shows:—

AVERAGE MONTHLY WAGES EARNED BY THREE CLASSES OF MINE LABOURERS IN THE YEAR 1836-7.

	West of Penzance.			Mid-Cornwall.			St. Austell.			Average.		
	£	s.	d.	£	s.	d.	£	s.	d.	£	s.	d.
Tributers	2	7	6	3	8	0	2	19	0	2	18	2
Tutworkers ...	2	5	0	2	17	2	2	19	0	2	13	8
Dressing Labourers ... (i.e. Surface workers)	2	2	0	2	1	0	2	5	0	2	2	8

The tributer may best be compared to a small farmer who rents his land from a big owner and makes a living from such produce of the land as remains over after he has paid his rent. The tributer's rent was one which varied according to the richness or poorness of his (underground) farm. Thus, if a tributer agreed to work a pitch for 12s. in the £, the remaining 8s. may be considered as his rent paid to the adventurers of the mine. (4) Like a small working landholder, too, the tributer paid all the expenses connected with the winning of his produce, these including not only the cost of stoping the ore underground, but frequently that of bringing it to surface also. The following are two typical examples of tributers' "bal bills" (i.e. mine paybills) of sixty or seventy years ago :—

TINCROFT MINE. Tribute Pay. (1)

For February Ores, 1850.
Paid the 4th May, 1850.
——————— & Co. (2 men).

Real Amount, £13 11s. at 13s. 4d. in £ = £9 os. 8d.

The following were the deductions :—

	£	s.	d.
To Subsist	4	0	0
,, Materials	1	0	0
,, Smith's Cost	0	12	9
,, Drawing	0	3	3
,, Dividing	0	1	9
,, Dressing	0	19	1
,, Assaying	0	6	0
,, Debt	1	12	1
,, Spale	—		
,, Barrow	—		
,, Doctor and Club	0	3	0
,, Clay and Barber	0	1	3
	£8	19	2

Which left them a balance of 1s. 6d.

Cook's Kitchen Mine. (6)

Pay for August, 1863.
Paid 19th September, 1863.
————— and Partners (6 men).

Amount earned at 11s. 6d. in £ = £51 9 9

Deductions.

	£	s.	d.	£	s.	d.
Candles per lb.	2	15	6			
Powder ditto	1	3	4			
Fuse, Hilts, Shovels, Cans, Clay	0	11	2			
Smith Cost	1	0	5			
Drawing	2	12	9			
Weighing, Mixing, and Dividing	—					
Tramming	—					
Sample	0	9	0			
Subsist	16	14	0			
Doctor and Club	0	8	0			
Barber and Box	0	4	0			
				25	18	2
Debt				1	18	0
				£23	13	7

THE MINER AT WORK

As may be seen from a reference to these bills, the cost deducted from the total earnings of the "pares" or companies of tributers included not only candles, powder, fuse, barrels, nails, pick-hilts, shovels, and other materials necessary for breaking the ore, but the tramming of it to the shaft, the drawing to surface, and the subsequent crushing, weighing, mixing, dividing, and sampling of the ores by which the tributers' earnings were determined. It will further be seen that in the first case the earnings of the two Tincroft Tributers for February 1850, after all deductions had been made, amounted to exactly 1s. 6d. To meet such cases as this, which were by no means infrequent in the tributers' gambling existence, a system known as "subsist" was instituted, by which the men could claim an advance of ready money (in this case £2 per man), which was deducted from their next month's earnings.

A tributer's run of ill-luck might in some cases continue thus for many months on end. "We have a first-rate old man who has been working in North Roskear for thirty years," stated Captain Joseph Vivian before the Commissioners in 1864. "The last two years he has always been speculating and has done badly. I said to him the other day, 'You are doing badly?' 'Yes,' said he. 'I never had such a long run before, but I shall make it up again soon.'

"On the whole he has not done badly. He is worth £200 or £300 probably. He has one or two cottages and keeps a cow, and so on. We never let him go upon less than £2 5s. a month, though for a long time he has not earned any money." (7)

In the case of a good mine, with a good manager, the system worked out well enough for the tributer, but in other instances it left him too much dependent on favour for the living wage which should have been his right. David Buzza, for instance, a tributer working at Caradon, stated the opposite side of the case before the same Commission.

"I worked in a mine called Devon Great Consols, and my family is now residing at Tavistock. I have quarters here (Liskeard). I have been turned away, after I had done very badly for some months. In fourteen months all that I earned was £15 1s. 4d."

"You gave up work there?"

"I complained that I had not got money enough, and it was in their power to let me get more, and because I complained they turned me away out of that mine and would not let me work in any mine in the district. And so this is how a miner is tossed about. I went to the different mines in the district and I could not get any more work. 'I have no work for you,' they said." (8)

In order to keep a greater hold over the tributers, who were in many respects an independent class of men, a system known as the "month in hand" was general in many mines. This meant that a man, on coming to the mine, would not, in fact, receive any wages till after he had been working there for two months. If he came straight from another mine he should, by this system, have had a month's wages already in hand, whilst if he had previously been out of employment he would be entitled to "draw 'sist" at the end of his first month's work. (9) In addition to this, the shopkeeper would nearly always credit an industrious miner with goods in the intervals between paydays. A political orator on one occasion concluded his speech in a mining district with the leading question: "Now, gentlemen, can you tell me who is your best friend?" "The shopkeeper," came the prompt but unexpected reply.

It is true that a contrary view was expressed by one witness in 1864, who stated that a good many shopkeepers got 20s. for every 15s. worth of goods they sold. "Because if you are in debt to them you must take the article which they wish to sell or get nothing." Yet, on the whole, the miner rightly looked on the small shopkeeper, who, it must be remembered, was often not much better off than himself, as one of his best friends.

If, however, some shopkeepers made high profits on the goods they sold, so it must be admitted did the mines. Most materials, and especially candles and gunpowder, were supplied to the tributers by the mine adventurers at considerably above cost price. Candles were almost invariably charged to the men at 1d. or 2d. a pound more than the mines themselves gave to the merchants. The reason assigned for this was that if these goods could be procured at the mines at a cheaper rate than in the shops, the miners would take them away and sell them. This was, to a certain extent, true. For even as it was, the miners would go to the pitch of stealing candles from each other in order to exchange them at the shops for tobacco, etc., such being a means of gaining ready money, though at an ultimate loss to themselves. (10) But why, under these conditions, the adventurers could not have been content with selling their goods at the same price as in the shops it is hard to say, unless the £300 or £400 a year profit which many large mines made out of candles alone had anything to do with it !

In addition to materials, as the pay-bills show, various other deductions were formerly made from the wages of all classes of underground workers, the chief being for the doctor and the mine club. Towards the first the men contributed from their earnings at the rate of 6d. or 9d. a month, and towards the sick club 6d. In addition to these, in some mines a curious levy of 2d. or 3d. a month was made for the mine barber, who effected the men's weekly shave. It was stated, however, in 1864 that some of the boys at the age of fifteen or sixteen were beginning to resent this continued impertinence to their beardlessness.

In many mines also, as may be seen above, a system of "spale" or fines was in force, which, in certain instances, caused considerable resentment amongst the men. One of the chief misdemeanours was that of allowing attle (deads) to accumulate in the levels, thereby causing inconvenience to other workers and interrupting the natural ventilation of the mine. In some instances "spale" would be inflicted, too, if the miners were caught coming up from underground before time. As few of them at this date possessed watches and the passage of the hours underground was reckoned entirely by candles, which were irregular in their burning, it not unfrequently happened that the men found themselves leaving work too soon. Then, to avoid being spaled, many of them would stand patiently on the ladders or else lie about somewhere in a shallow level, as often as not shivering with the cold after coming up from the hot ends below. (11)

It was not always, however, that the miners found themselves coming to grass too early, for in those days many of the men were very indifferent about the time they came up. Towards the beginning of the month or the time of taking up a new pitch, stated a captain in 1864, "the tributers are often inclined to leave work early, but as the time draws to an end, unless the pitch has proved a very bad one, they work on steadily." In many cases where a tributer had cut rich and had but a short time left before surrendering his pitch, he would work the last few weeks like a slave, doing twelve or sixteen hours a day, instead of the normal eight. (12) The sight of the rich ore continually before them and the growing pile of "best work" exercised such a fascination over some tributers that it was with difficulty that they could tear themselves away to go home to sleep. (13)

Very frequently a miner's work in those days led him into the loneliest situations underground. Even in a great mine where several hundred men went down on each shift, a tributer, whose comrade was at home sick, might find himself for eight hours at a time in a place so far removed from the rest that nothing but a distant booming occasionally reminded him that other human beings like himself were passing the night in lonely labour fifteen hundred feet or more below the sleeping world. Strange adventures have been known to happen to men so placed.

One afternoon core a man named 'Lisha Billing was at work by himself filling kibbles at one of the levels in Cornish's shaft at Poldice Mine. Night came on and by half-past ten the other men were all "to grass," but 'Lisha Billing had not been seen. The night passed, and next morning counsel was taken what might have happened to the man and what ought to be done.

The agent, Captain Boundey, said: "If anyone can find him it is my son Andrew, who is working up to Creegbrawse."

The young man was accordingly sent for, and the matter having been explained, he set off on his search, taking two men with him. On arriving at the place where 'Lisha Billing had been working, they found the level blocked by a fall of ground. Realizing that the man had thus lost his candles and had probably been trying to find his way up by some other route, they searched about and found his tracks in the soft mud. Up through raises, along cross-cuts and old levels they followed his wandering tracks, till at last they found him lying in a level on the extreme verge of Harris shaft. Though lost and utterly bewildered, the man had felt instinctively that he was near a shaft and had crawled the last part of the way till, pushing a stone before him with one hand, he suddenly heard it fall away into water seventy feet beneath. (14)

Perhaps of all work in the mine the shaftmen's duty was the loneliest. The following reminiscences of a Camborne miner illustrate the way in which underground work sometimes played upon the nerves of the less experienced men. The man, who may be called Thomas, started as a shaftman's assistant in West Seton Mine at the age of seventeen. Unlike most boys of this neighbourhood, he went to work late, and this was his first experience of underground. One Saturday night, after everyone else had left the mine, he and the shaftman went down together to examine the pumps. At that time the miners were sinking below the 264-fathom level. Before they had got far down it was evident from his movements that the older man had been celebrating pay-day too well, and at last, when they had reached the 150, he stopped and said: "Boay, thee'st 'll have to go to bottom by thyself, I caent go no further." Thomas, being only a lad and new to the job, did not like it at all, but go he had to. The silence and utter loneliness of the black shaft once he was out of sight of the other man's candle oppressed him. However, he reached the bottom at last and found all fair. He looked to the lift to see if the engine was in fork and found it covered over with water and no air bubbles appearing. The engine had just finished her indoor stroke as he turned to ascend the ladders. Suddenly, without the least warning, the most frightful whistling shriek he had ever known rent the air. . . . Without waiting to consider, he set foot to the ladders and tore up the four hundred feet to the 200-fathom level as if all the fiends of hell had been after him; and only then did he pause to consider that what he had heard was nothing more than the engine going into fork and the rush of escaping air as it bubbled through the water.

Such experiences as these were not always confined to young or new hands. There was working at one time at Stray Park Mine a shaftman called Chenoweth, a steady, quiet, God-fearing man, a teetotaler and a bit of a local preacher. During the week-end it was the custom for the shaftmen to be divided into two "watches," the one from midday on Saturday (when the miners left work) till six on Sunday morning, the other from six till Sunday night. There were two shaftmen on each watch, but, except in emergencies, only one used to go through the shaft, his duty being merely to see if the rollers, etc., wanted greasing.

In deep shafts it was usual to have a sitting-down place on the underlie at some point below the vertical part. One night Chenoweth was sitting on such a spot "touching his pipe" and resting a while on his way up from the bottom. All of a sudden he said to himself, "Hullo, what's up now?" Far above him he could hear, as he supposed, his partner coming down. There was, first of all, the sound of his "hobs" grating against the iron "rungs" of the ladder, and then the tap of his boots as he stepped on to the wooden "sollar." Then the grating of iron against iron started again. Down and down came the footsteps, until of a sudden Chenoweth realized that they were now beneath him. Whoever or whatever it was must have passed by the actual spot where he was sitting, but of the strange visitant to the otherwise empty mine he saw absolutely nothing. When Chenoweth gained surface he found his comrade sitting where he had left him, having never moved from the spot. The incident played so strongly upon Chenoweth's nerves that it is said that he refused ever afterwards to go through that shaft again. (15)

Miners in those days were frequently employed on tasks which it is doubtful if their descendants could now be induced to undertake. On one occasion a lot of surface water appeared to be finding its way into Poldice Mine and search was made everywhere to discover where the leakage could be. Amongst other places, a man was sent up beneath the streets of St. Day, through some old shallow workings which had long been used as a general sewer for the town.

The old miner used to vividly describe, in language more graphic than printable, the going through these, the awful stench and the general discomfort when wading sometimes up to his chest. Not having found the leakage, he came up at last through a small shaft in the middle of St. Day and, going into a small general shop, all dripping as he was, asked for some tobacco to drown the smell. "Here, take so much bacca as you mind to," exclaimed the woman, "and git out of my shop quickly before you turn the meat bad!" (16)

Though willing to perform tasks such as these when properly approached by those who understood them, the miners were capable on other occasions of showing themselves very independent in their bearing towards their supervisors.

THE MINER AT WORK

"If you found deads accumulating in the levels, what would you do?" it was asked of a captain from the St. Just district in 1864. "Would a man be spaled?"

"I do not think you can spale any man in this place," was the reply; "they would be off to another place. They are just as independent as yourself. (17) The men are masters here; they have been masters for years."

"How do you account for this?"

"I believe we have been in want of men here for many years."

"Have you ever taken steps to induce them to come from other parts?"

"Perhaps we have quietly. If you want men you dare not say so in the mine. Our men are remarkable for their independence. And there is another thing, our men all work single-handed; we have not two men in an end here at a time. They hold the borer with one hand and beat with the other, and when the hand gets tired with the hammer the man changes it. That is a reason why the eastern man (i.e. from Camborne or Redruth) cannot work with our men here. They must all go double-handed. Single-handed men get more money; two single-handed men in an end will get as much as three double-handed men. Single-handed men are the most paying to the adventurers." (18)

The distinctions herein stated still hold good to a large extent, and to this day a St. Just miner beats his boryer single-handed and has, on the whole, but a slight opinion of the miner of other districts!

Most of the other outlying mining districts had at this time distinctive features of their own which made it difficult for men from other areas to work in them.

"Nobody will come out here to St. Agnes," stated another witness before the same Commission, "except those who are born and bred here. The mode of working here is peculiar. Our lodes are so 'flat' that strangers require some time to get acquainted with it." (19)

The result was that when the mines were booming, as they were in St. Agnes in 1864, the competition among the miners was small, and the comparative rate of wages paid to them was higher than in other districts. In some areas, however, this position was reversed and, according to a statement of one of the captains in the Providence Mines, Lelant, at this time, they were "so swarmed with men that they hardly knew what to do with them." Thus throughout the districts the miners' wages depended largely on the size of the population and the fluctuating prosperity of the mines. On the stoppage of one of these or the falling off of work in his own district a miner would sometimes take quarters with a family in another area, paying 6d. a week for his lodging and returning to his own home in the week-ends for a supply of food on which he kept himself. In most cases, however, if work could be got at all, the men not unnaturally preferred remaining at home to seeking it in another district, even at higher wages, a fact which accounts for the considerable variations in the rates paid in different areas.

Though a lucky tributer might now and then make £50 in a month, or even higher earnings, he much more frequently only succeeded in deserving them. In following the course of a small lode or pocket of tin, the tributer would sometimes be a hundred fathoms or more from the nearest shaft from which air could circulate into his working place. Often a candle would not burn at all in the ends where some of the men were working, but had to be placed twelve or eighteen feet behind them, and even then on one side or with a pin stuck through it to help the grease to run off more easily. (20)

In a mine called Wheal Devonshire, in the Perranzabuloe district, many years ago, the heat was so great in a particular level that the miners were said to be unable to keep their candles from melting away unless surrounded with water. (21)

"The closest place I ever worked in," said an old St. Just miner on a recent occasion, "was in a shallow level at Wheal Cunning, where there was a bunch of tin in an end far from the shaft. Even with a fan going all the time the candles would only burn right over on one side, and when the boy working it fell asleep, as he frequently did with the heat, the lights went out at once and we had to stumble out of the level as best we could in the darkness."

In some places such as this a lucifer match, if struck, would not even set fire to the wood, and in close ends it was not infrequent for the miners, before they could get their candles to burn,

THE MINER AT WORK   215

to have to take their coats and beat them about, to create a little current of air. (22) Strange stories the old tributers used to tell of putting out their candles at "crowst" time in order to save air, it being a saying amongst them that a "candle will eat so much air as a man."

In earlier times the poorness of the air resulting from bad ventilation was greatly increased by the use of hempen candles, which were so smoky that four or five burning in a confined space were sufficient of themselves to make the air almost suffocating. (23) Such candles, however, had one advantage, that they could be blown up again if the flame went out, a matter of great importance in the days before lucifer matches had been introduced, when the dark levels of the mines presented many pitfalls of the most literal kind in the way of unprotected shafts and winzes. By 1860 Palmer's candles, made by the merchants in the neighbourhood, were coming into general use and, together with the new lucifer match, served to relieve the miners from many of the perils of darkness underground.

Powder smoke, however, the worst contaminator of air, continued for long afterwards to be the bane of miners' health. The statement of a young miner aged seventeen, engaged in Fowey Consols Copper Mine in 1842, shows something of the conditions under which the men worked.

"The air," he said, "was 'poor' where he then was and he had a pain in the head after working some time, which lasted for hours after he came to surface. Almost every morning he had a cough and brought up some stuff as black as ink. In the place where he was working they used to 'shoot' (i.e. blast) three or four times a day, after which they could not go into the end for half an hour, as it was full of smoke. He would then eat his pasty in the level, where there was better air. Though he sweated a great deal and was very thirsty he could not generally get water underground." Another miner in Wheal Jewell described how he felt the air scalding down his throat, burning as though it had been hot water in his stomach. The end in which he worked was 170 fathoms (340 yards) from any ventilating shaft. The candle would not burn here for hours on end. (24)

It is interesting, in the light of such declarations as these, to hear the statements made by the manager of the Consolidated Mines on ventilation some years earlier.

"Do you consider," he was asked, "that the mines in the West of England are well and wholesomely ventilated?"

"I think they are perfectly well ventilated," was the reply; "indeed, it would be impossible to work them if they were not so."

This was, in a sense, true, since, as subsequently appeared, the manager's definition of an ill-ventilated mine was one where the air had become so vitiated as to extinguish all lights. The possibility that the air might become a trifle unhealthy without actually reaching this point does not seem to have occurred to the Commissioners, some of whom, one might judge, had never been underground. (25) At any rate, it was not suggested either by them or the manager, and in the latter's case with good reason, since the richest levels in the Consolidated Mines were at that time peculiarly unhealthy and the miners were working in temperatures varying between 90° and 100° F. (26)

Only one question seems to have shown that the Commission had any notion of what conditions in many of the mines really were: "You do not think," they asked tentatively, "that any unreasonable anxiety to save expense leads the masters to place their men in situations in which they ought not to be placed?"

"I do not," was the glib reply, "because it would be against the interests of the masters to do so." (27)

"In actual places where candles will not burn, and where no work can therefore be done, we believe you," they might well have replied, "but in air just breathable to-day, but which will entail years of ill-health and suffering on the men hereafter—what of those?" they might fairly have asked.

As has already been said, the chief cause of bad air in the mines at this date was the use of black powder for blasting. The actual methods employed were generally as follows: A hole having first been driven to the depth of two feet or more by the aid of a steel-capped "boryer" beaten with sledge-hammers, was cleaned out by a wooden staff known as a "swab stick," the ends of which were beaten open to form something like a brush. Into the hole thus cleaned and dried so many "inches" of powder were poured from the miner's "can" or flask, the

THE MINER AT WORK

quantity being in most cases estimated by guess-work only. If, as was frequent, it exceeded the desired amount, the surplus powder was removed by dipping into it a wet reed (i.e. straw), or perhaps the swab-stick itself, and shaking off the grains which adhered. When the hole was a "back hole" or "upper," that is, one in a vertical position or inclined above the miner's head, a frail cartridge of paper was concocted, the edges of which were cemented together with the greasy tallow of the men's "snoff" candles. Into this "paperen" cartridge the powder was placed, and the whole, after being well greased over to prevent its being affected by the damp, was pushed into the hole with the tamping-bar or any other tool that came to hand.

In the case of side holes, the powder was generally inserted by a "scraper" or iron bar having at one end a concave surface, somewhat like a marrow-spoon. Much of the powder inserted thus stuck to the sides of the hole and was thrust right back by the miners with their iron tamping-bars. (28)

Though a bar sheathed with copper had been suggested by Sir Rose Price as a safer tool as early as 1814, iron ones were still in general use in the St. Austell mining district in 1870. (29)

Of the two methods employed in firing the powder-charged hole, the older one was commonly known in Cornwall as "blasting with the nail." The latter consisted of a round rod of iron or copper half or three-quarters of an inch diameter at the top and tapering to a point at the bottom, which was placed with its point in the charge of powder, so as to pass quite through it and to rest on the bottom of the hole. The tamping was then laid on the powder (the first portion or layer being frequently of clay) and beaten hard with an iron mallet and an iron bar with a flat end, called a "ramming-bar." When the hole was filled with tamping, the nail was drawn out easily on account of its tapering figure. In some cases the entire aperture was then filled with powder; but this great waste was generally avoided by inserting a rush filled with powder into the nail-hole, to which fire was then communicated with a touch-paper or snuff of candle.

By another mode of firing, at one time extensively employed in Cornwall, the use of the nail or "neele" was entirely superseded. In this case the tubular parts of quills (called by the miners "queells") (30) were cut off and inserted into each other, as long as the hole was deep. This tube, which was called "a rod of quills," was filled with bruised gunpowder and placed in the hole instead of the nail. The tamping was then proceeded with as in the first case, but great care was necessary, as rough or stony matter was liable to separate the powder by the inequality of its pressure or to cut the quills by its sharp edges. (31) This fuse was similarly ignited with touch-paper or a snuff of candle.

The dangers attending the "shooting" of rocks with gunpowder were obviously manifold, arising not only from premature explosion, but from picking out the holes, which frequently misfired. Dr. Paris, in a paper which has already been quoted, describes more than eighty accidents from this source which occurred in a short space in the Hundred of Penwith alone. Unlike the blasting accidents of to-day, the sufferers were more often mangled than killed outright. The numbers of men in the mining districts with faces blackened and blinded in one or both eyes, or else lacking two fingers of the right hand, used formerly to be very great, and it was frequent in West Cornwall to meet the former being led about by boys as they eked out a livelihood in selling tea from house to house.

The greatest advance towards the protection of miners in Cornwall and throughout the world came with the invention of Bickford's Safety Fuse about the year 1830. (32) The gradual introduction of this into the mines did away from henceforth with the old powder-filled reed and quill and a great many of the dangers attendant on the old mode of blasting. The use of powder, however, remained throughout the working lives of most of the old miners who may be met with in West Cornwall to-day. The conclusion to be drawn from conversations with these men is that, though the unavoidable dangers of the old way of blasting were considerable, they were more strictly in proportion to the skilfulness and care of the individual men than is always realized.

Amongst the many hardships experienced by all classes of underground workers in the wet mines of Cornwall were the frequent transitions from heat to cold. A miner, speaking before the 1842 Commission, described how sometimes he would be working in a place to get at which he would be obliged to wade for a considerable distance up to his breast in cold water. At other times he worked in a very hot place from which they were obliged to retreat very frequently into the level as the water gained upon them. Here they would get all huddled together, "creeming with cold," then, "as the water was in fork once more" (i.e. removed by the engine), they would go in again and drive at their work as hard as they could. (33)

In some copper-mines phenomenal temperatures were experienced, occasioned, it is thought, by chemical action of the rich copper ores. Amongst the highest underground temperatures recorded in Cornwall were those at Poldice and the Consolidated Mines during the 'thirties, when the great St. Day mining area was rising to its splendour. The water issuing out of the lode (in the slate) at the 184-fathom level in the first mine registered 100° F. In the Consolidated Mines near-by, the temperature of the air at the 294-fathom level on Taylor's lode was 96° F., and in some of the ends 105° F. or 108° F. The water collected at the bottom of Davey's engine-shaft was 92·5° F., and into this the men working in the bottom levels actually plunged to cool themselves! At a later date than this, the water issuing out of a hot spring at Wheal Clifford showed the record temperature of 125° F. (34), whilst the air in the deep levels was always between 80° and 100° F. (35)

At the time when these great temperatures were being met with many of the mines were without any proper "dries" or changing-houses. Long draughty sheds without doors or windows, where the wind whistled through on the half-naked men, were frequently the only places provided for the miners on coming up from the great heat below. As late as 1842, the men in a great mine like Fowey Consols had no real "dry," no warm water to wash with, whilst in winter their shoes were sometimes frozen up in the chests. (36)

Twenty-two years later, a miner working in South Caradon, on the bleak exposed heights of the Liskeard moors, told the Commissioners that he had gone to work sometimes in the afternoon in cold weather when there had been a little rain and "I have come up at ten o'clock and put on my clothes when they have been frozen hard and my trousers would stand up as stiff as a stock." (37) Another witness from the Yarner Mine, near

Bovey Tracey, added : "Many of the men have to walk two miles to the mine over an exposed road. They frequently get wet through. They then go underground for eight hours, come up fatigued and freely perspiring, and have to put on their wet and cold clothes."

Very often the only way the miners had of ever drying their saturated underground garments was by "venturing" into the boiler-house and hanging them over the boilers. In this there was always an element of risk, the bursting of a boiler being by no means infrequent in cases where the latter possessed no water-gauges and were worked continuously without cleaning or inspection. (38)

An old Lelant miner used frequently to relate to me his experiences of working in a small mine (Wheal Margery) near St. Ives, about 1860, he being then a boy of thirteen years of age. The mine, which was being driven in some places 120 fathoms under the sea, was a very wet one, and the miners were continually drenched to the skin with the salt-water which found its way in from the shallow workings. Their clothes, when they came to put them on before going underground, were frequently so stiff and brittle with the salt that care had to be taken not to "break" them, as the old man would say. The miners' hands and all parts of their bodies were generally red and raw from the rubbing and the action of the salt. When the wind blew hard from the east, with a rising tide, the sea frequently entered the mine through the adit, which emptied on the beach, endangering the lives of the miners who were working below, far out beneath the bottom of the bay. On more than one occasion my informant, with other men, only escaped with his life by racing up the ladders in inky darkness whilst the salt-water poured in upon them from above and mounted in the shaft behind them almost more quickly than they could climb. The mine being a small and poor one, there was no dry for the men when they reached surface, and all hands changed their clothes on top of the boilers. One day, just after they had come up and were starting to change, the engine-man came into the boiler-house to put coal into the fire. Hardly had he opened the fire-doors before he perceived that one of the boiler tubes was dropping. "Men and boys," he cried, "run for your lives, the boiler's going to bust." Half-dressed as they were, and some with nothing on at all, the men jumped out through a little window on to a pile of ashes outside, and so fled into the fields. They had scarcely got clear before the boiler burst, indeed, in a cloud of steam, scattering mud and slime and stones far around. None of the men were seriously hurt, but many went home very scantily clad, and the loss of a coat or a pair of trousers was a serious thing to men earning only 10s. or 12s. a week. Such a story is typical of the reminiscences of many of the old miners who worked in the poorer mines of Cornwall sixty or seventy years ago. "'Twill lev'ee knaw what maining was, back in they days," as the old man would say.

The length of the cores which the miners worked under such conditions varied in different mines. "In Levant," said a captain in 1842, "they work six-hour cores. The mine is hot and deep, and it is considered that six hours will work a man down." (39)

The actual length of the cores, however, very much depended on whether the parties relieved each other "in place" (i.e. underground) or at surface. In mines where the latter was customary the one core coming up met the other going down. Old miners, in 1842, said that the practice of relieving "in place" was not so general in their boyhood as it then was. (40) Where this system was in force in deep mines, the normal eight-hour shift had often become ten hours by the time the men reached surface again, after climbing from the bottom levels.

In these days of quick transport and easy locomotion, it is hard to imagine the life eighty years ago of a Cornish miner, who, as often as not, walked five or six miles across rough country, at all hours of the day and night, to reach his work, climbed down 200 fathoms of ladders, and, after working an eight-hour core underground, repeated the climb to surface and the walk home once more to his cottage across the moors. In mines such as Wheal Vor, Dolcoath, Cook's Kitchen, Gwennap United, and Fowey Consols, all of which were close on 300 fathoms deep, "it takes the men three-quarters of an hour to descend and an hour and a quarter to ascend the perpendicular ladders to and from their work," wrote G. Henwood in 1854. "Sometimes, in addition to all this, they are obliged to carry tools and borers also to the weight of 14 or 19 lbs. Such labour can only be undertaken by robust youth and at high prices, so that if the mineral be not very valuable, it will not pay for working in such situations; but so strong a stimulant is the hope of gain (or perhaps one might add the fear of unemployment) that, despite the fatigue and loss of health, ardent youths are found daring enough to undertake the difficult and dangerous task." Rightly, indeed, did a petition of the Cornish miners to the Queen in 1842 submit that none of Her Majesty's subjects earned their livelihood by more severe bodily exertion.

As we shall show later, the tax which this excessive climbing imposed on the strength of the older men was a terrible one. The younger ones, however, made light of it, and in shallower mines it was a matter of honour amongst them never to give way to one another nor to pause for breath in climbing from the bottoms to grass. "When I was a boy," said Captain Rutter in 1864, "we did not think of stopping anywhere. We ran up 100 to 120 fathoms like a cat." The climbing of ladders in mines of depths such as this did not, in fact, prove of much hardship to those who had been accustomed to doing it from boyhood.

"I am now seventy years of age," stated Captain Joseph Vivian, of North Roskear, before the same Commission, "and I have been in the mines ever since I was twelve years old. I find no difficulty in climbing 200 fathoms of ladders." (41)

The men, indeed, throughout the mining districts of Cornwall were inured to the hardships of underground labour at an early age. As has been shown elsewhere, the tributers worked in most cases in "pares" or parties, consisting of two or more men and one or two boy assistants. The ages at which these boys were taken underground varied in different instances. The youngest child whom the Commissioners found working underground in Cornwall in 1842 was eight years of age, and it seems that this was an unusual case. One miner, indeed, stated that he was often taken down on his father's back when he was not eight years old to a depth of seventy fathoms, and would stay down till his father went up again, being too small to walk the ladders himself. (42) The commonest age for going underground, however, was between nine and twelve years, if the boys were well grown. (43) The principal occupation of these children was working air-machines or fans at the entrance to close unventilated ends. (44)

When the tributers themselves were cutting rich (or in certain cases to relieve a friend), the boys would greatly overtax their strength by working "a double core or stem." One witness said in 1842 : " I remember myself, when about fifteen, I used to stay once or twice a month for three twelve-hour courses in succession, merely coming to surface for a short time between each stem of twelve hours to take some food. At that time nobody took any food down with them. I was so much fatigued at the end of the time that when I got home to bed I often found it impossible to get to sleep for hours. I do not know that this is done anywhere now." (45) Yet before the same Commission the case of a boy was stated who had worked " five double stems out of six days last week," probably in all about eighty hours. Exceptional cases like this were commonly incurred by the boys as an act of kindness to a comrade, to prevent him losing his place, as he would probably do if the men were obliged to supply it by a stranger. (46)

In proportion to their strength, boys were also employed in " rolling " or wheeling stuff in barrows in places where underground tram-roads had not been laid down. (47) " I have wheeled many a time," said a witness in 1864, " when my fingers have been ready to go right out, when I was not able to hold anything and the weight was supported by a sling round my neck."

Although tram-roads had been introduced into some mines (notably the Gwennap Consols, Poldice, Treskerby, and Wheal Damsel) as early as 1824, (48) it was long before they became general, and less than forty years ago barrows were still being used in many places. Many a miner can still speak feelingly of the raw knuckles which were got when wheeling these through narrow levels, and the wiser ones nearly all wore strips of leather to protect the backs of the hands. When the level was a long one, the empty barrow from the shaft met the outgoing one halfway and had to be lifted over it.

Laborious, however, as much of the work was, conditions such as disgraced the collieries, where half-deformed children " hurried " the coal through passages eighteen inches high or sat ten hours on end in the darkness tending doors, were totally unknown in the Cornish mines. In most cases, indeed, in Cornwall it was the ambition of the boys themselves to go underground, where higher wages and shorter hours obtained than at surface work. (49) " On the whole," wrote the Commissioners of 1842, " the testimony of the mine agents and other well-informed parties shows that not only is no tyranny exercised by the men over the boys, but that there is a very general consideration, on the part of the men, of the age and powers of their young fellow-labourers, and a disposition to relieve them from any excess of toil even at the expense of increased exertion of their own. The very frequent association in work of children with their parents or near relatives contributes to the promotion of this generous and manly feeling." (50)

The anxiety which many miners displayed on first taking their children underground bears out the substance of this statement. A miner from Fowey Consols described to the same Commissioners how he was working in a part of the mine one day when the news was brought him that his son, a fine, strong boy of twelve years old, had fallen off a ladder and was hurt :—

" When I was told what had happened," he said, " I travelled as fast as I could to the place ; and I seemed to see, every few fathoms as I went, the body of my poor boy all crushed together ; it was so clear that I stopped and rubbed my eyes and asked myself if I was in my right mind or no. When I got to the place, the boy was sitting upon a man's knee, looking up quite cheerful, only crying a little." (51)

Under the tributing system the boys thus started at an early age to acquire that knowledge of their dangerous calling which afterwards made many of them miners of unrivalled skill and intelligence. In many instances to-day the men who are working the machine-drills, removing ground by contract at so much a fathom, are not so much miners as underground labourers. Very different to this were the conditions which produced the fine old race of tributers in the past. In most cases the Cornish tributer's very existence depended on his knowledge of the lode on which he was working, and an error of judgment in making his two- or three-monthly bargain might entail semi-starvation to himself and his wife and family and the swallowing up in a short space of time of the hard-earned gainings of years. From the point

THE MINER AT WORK

of view of the adventurers, tributers were an invaluable asset. It is true that in certain cases where large bodies of ore have been opened out, the lode itself may be extracted with the greatest advantage by tutwork or contract, but in mines which have been partially exhausted, or where the lodes are small or rich in bunches, with barren parts between, tributers have always shown themselves the most valuable miners. In them a large mine formerly possessed the unpaid services of several hundred practical geologists, men whose knowledge of the lode features peculiar to each mine was absolutely unrivalled.

Many a mine has been saved at the eleventh hour by some skilful tributer following up an indication of a lode and thereby discovering fresh mineral deposits; and many poor mines have been worked on tribute for years at a considerable profit, when on tutwork they could not have existed for six months without loss. The discoveries made many years ago in Wheal Towan provide a good instance of the value of tributers. In this mine the adventurers had for years been following a string of quartz accompanied by a small quantity of rich copper ore. The walls of the lode, however, were so hard as to deter them from crosscutting into them, till at length, one day, a man, to preserve his tobacco-pipe, made a small hole in which to place it, when, to his great surprise, a quantity of water of a black colour issued—which he tried by the usual miner's test, viz. wetting his fingers in the substance and applying them to his candle. The colour immediately gave unmistakable indications of copper. This discovery laid the foundations of two of the largest fortunes Cornwall has ever boasted, and it came just at the very time when the proprietary had determined to stop the mine, having long worked it "hoping against hope." It is said the mine after this cleared a guinea a minute for years both night and day, and the tributers broke and raised the ores to grass for 1d. in the £1.

Basset and Grylls, in Wendron parish, was another mine which owes its present existence to the discovery of a working tributer —a certain Henry Jenkin—who, whilst streaming in the valley below Porkellis village in the year 1845, laid bare the outcrop of the lode. Jenkin and his partners, under the circumstances, thought they would have been permitted to work their discovery on the grounds of their "streamers' lease" (in accordance with the custom which had previously prevailed). Such, however, was not the case, for the lords granted a "mining lease" to another set of adventurers, and the streamers were accordingly ousted, with presumably but scant reward for their labours. (53)

Probably the tributing "find" which has proved in the long run to be of the greatest importance to Cornish mining was that of the Great Flat Lode, which was discovered by men working in one of the Basset mines many years ago. (54) Not only did this discovery benefit the particular mine in which it was first made but through its later development it affected the whole of that important group of mines which now includes such well-known properties as Grenville and South Condurrow. Of these, Grenville, it may be noted, has more than once practically owed its existence to the fine body of tributers formerly employed there. In as recent years as those of Captain Bishop, the mine arrived at a point where it was practically abandoned by the adventurers, nor is it yet forgotten in Camborne how on that occasion the manager called the men together and explained that he was going to set the mine on tribute, with the result that such good discoveries were very shortly made that the mine was put firmly on its feet once more, the company was reconstructed, and Grenville entered on a new lease of life in which she continued prosperously down to the slump in 1922. (55)

Such were some of the discoveries of the palmy days of tributing. That the system, on the other hand, had its defects all who know the internal history of the mines will admit. The policy of the adventurers themselves was sometimes dishonest and often short-sighted. The agents, too, in their anxiety not to be "baffled" by the miners, occasionally engendered hostility and distrust. The "capuns," so the old tributers will say, often went too much by the books, that is to say, the average earnings of those who had previously worked the pitches on particular lodes, and too little by the actual condition of the lode at the time of resetting. Owing to a still more short-sighted policy which obtained in some mines, the tributers were not *permitted* to earn more than a certain sum per month, with the result that in many instances the men refrained from sending their best work to grass, knowing that if they did so their rate of tribute would be reduced on the next setting day. (56)

As a case in point an old tributer, working on one occasion in Wheal Fortune (Sithney), put aside his best work beneath a pile of dirt, intending to send it up by degrees. The mine stopped, however, very suddenly, just after this, and the old man never recovered his savings. Before he died he described to his son exactly where it was, so that he might get it if ever there was a chance. The son himself is now an old man drawing near his end and the rich pile of ore still remains buried beneath the hundreds of feet of water which fill Wheal Fortune to her adit. When the mine will be unwatered again and who will at last stumble by chance on the old man's savings is a matter of interesting speculation. The result, however, of such a policy was an ultimate loss to men and adventurers alike. Worse than this, instances have not been wanting, as every old tributer knows, where contracts have been interrupted simply because the men " were doing too well." This was especially the case in instances where the mine itself was losing money and where the agents, as a result, professed themselves unable to go before the adventurers with a high wage-bill.

Nor was the treatment of the tutworkers, or men on contract, in many cases any less unfair. A correspondent to the *Cornish Magazine* described how, on one occasion, he, in company with another miner, was employed in driving a drift, in alternate shifts, each with a youngster for a comrade. They began the month at a certain price per fathom. They knew exactly how much ground to drive to get the wages allowed them for a month ; and in about two weeks, or sometimes three, they could finish, and for the remainder of the month they did little or nothing. His youngster would often bring down a book of music, and so they sang the time away ; whilst in afternoon shifts they would frequently bribe the " dry-man " with a few candles to change their clothes, in order that they might go back home and not be reported ! On one occasion the captain was asked for a longer contract. He complied. The men and boys went to work with a will ; but what was the result ? For every pound they earned they could not get more than 10s., as they had wheelbarrows and other things they had never ordered or received charged to them ! In this mine it was useless to try to get more than they were " allowed." (57)

But if the adventurers and their agents, the captains, were sometimes sharp in their practices, so, it must be admitted, were the men. In some mines it was quite a regular custom among the tributers to go to work early and leave late under the pretext of having to make up time on a poor pitch, but in reality in order that they might have the opportunity of going into the "owners' stopes" (58) after blasting and carrying away the best ore into their own working places. Amongst other slippery practices common among the tributers was that of "kitting," or the mixing of ores by two parties, one of whom was working a very rich and the other a very poor pitch. The tributer who was working poor ores might perhaps have bargained to receive thirteen shillings out of every twenty shillings' worth raised for the owners, whilst his friend who was working rich ores was to get only one shilling out of twenty. In the dark levels of the mine two such men would secretly agree to exchange some of their ores and then divide the gross profits, which were, of course, very large; for by this arrangement, instead of one shilling they got thirteen shillings out of twenty for a portion of the rich ores, whilst losing but a trifle on a corresponding portion of the poor ores. (59)

On one occasion in the Gwennap mines an old man and his comrade, working at the 190-fathom level in Poldory, were doing "very slight." The lode was hard and the produce poor, so that a bad pay-day was in prospect. In the level above them, on the other hand, the lode was standing so rich that the men there were working on day's pay, in order that the full benefit might go to the adventurers. At last the old man said, "This edn't no good, booy, what we got here. Gos' thee the way up to next level and thraw down a barrow or two from the awners' petch." The younger man did as he was bid, shinning up a chain through the rise to the level above. The old man waited impatiently for what appeared to him a long time, and at last went out to the foot of the rise to discover what was happening. As he did so there was a thundering roar and down came a barrow-load of rich ore, striking out the old man's light and sending him flying backwards into the level.

"Aw, Billy boy, my dear son, what ast thee done?" groaned the old man, as the younger one came sliding down once more in great alarm; "if tes good hure, maybe tes alright, but if tes 'attle' theest killed me sure enough!"

Various other tricks were occasionally employed by the men to try to get the better of the captains, if they thought it in their power to do so. Sometimes, for instance, when the lode was standing well in their pitch just before setting day and the men were afraid of having their rate of tribute cut, they would smoke over the best part with a candle or else beat their dusty coats against it, thereby hoping to deceive the captains into thinking the lode had gone poor and letting them have the pitch again at a high tribute. A miner was recounting not long ago of how, as a boy, he worked with another man in a winze in Wheal Sisters. On one occasion the captain was coming down just before setting day to look at the pitch. Before he came the man instructed the boy how to cover up the good ore they had broken beneath a pile of dirt. Presently the "capun" came down and found the boy by himself. Looking around and up and down, with something of a twinkle in his eye, he remarked :—

"Well, booy, thee're doin' very well; we'll make a good tributer of 'ee yet, I reckon."

"Aw, Capun Nickey," said the boy, quite creening like, though at the same time busily piling up the deads in the bottom of the winze, "tes a wisht poor place we got here, sure enuff."

The captain looked at the part indicated by the boy, which was indeed singularly poor. But being himself no fool, he had already guessed what was under the pile of deads. So he said :—

"I do see one thing, booy, theest got a good maister."

And of this he had no doubt, for the man with whom the boy was working was a nephew to the "capun" himself and a tributer of his own training!

So important was it, indeed, to tributers to know the nature of the ground ahead of them at the time of the resetting of their pitch, that cases have actually occurred where men have gone to the labour of sinking down and driving a second drift beneath the level in order to prove the lode beyond the boundary.

In the diamond-cut-diamond method of Cornish mining, a fairly effective check was put upon such practices by the appointment of underground captains, who, having themselves been working miners, had full knowledge of the tricks of the trade.

These men generally had fixed salaries of about £80 or £90 a year, and it speaks well for their honesty as a class that in spite of such low wages they did not more often fall to bribery and connivance of the tricks of the men.

In many respects the old "bal capuns," recognizable throughout Cornwall by their white drill coats and high pole-hats, were a class to themselves. Though in most cases not possessed of any great degree of book-learning, they had a natural shrewdness and an almost instinctive knowledge in mining affairs, which was inherited from generations of those who had preceded them in the same calling. "A stranger," wrote Hitchens and Drew in 1824, "is instantly at home in the presence of these men, and, in proportion to his own attainments, is frequently highly gratified with the vigour of their intellects, the readiness of their calculations, the extent of their scientific acquirements, and their mathematical knowledge. It is much to be doubted if in any walks of life similar to theirs a race of men more hospitable, polite, communicative, and intelligent than the captains of the Cornish mines are can be found in England." Their method of dealing with the men, too, was generally found to be extremely effective, and though the position of a young captain newly raised to the rank was not, on the face of it, an easy one, their eminent good sense generally overcame any initial awkwardness.

Certain of the smelting agents, however, who attended at the mines were not always so much "on the spot" as the captains, and were occasionally "put through" by the men. Those who remember the sampling of copper ore in the days which are now past will remember the advice given to young samplers: "Never mind the owners' ores, but keep a sharp look out on the tributers'." "Never walk in front of your barrow" was likewise another piece of advice given by samplers who had grown old in tributers' ways. Amusing scenes often took place on the occasion of sampling days at the mines. The various "parcels" of ore, crushed down to correct size and made up into "doles" or circular piles two to three feet thick with a flat summit, would be laid out near the top of the shaft. Here the samplers, representing the various copper buyers, would attend and, agreeable to their direction, one of the "doles" would be cut across and samples taken from the "rill" on both sides of the cut. These, being placed in a hand-barrow, would be seized upon by two tributers and raced off at top speed to the sampling-house, followed by the perhaps elderly and perspiring sampler, who was afraid to let the samples out of his sight for a moment, lest round the corner they might be hastily "prilled" or doctored with some richer fragments of ore before reaching their destination.

In respect of tin-sampling, many of the methods were also extremely tortuous. The case of miner versus tin-smelter has occupied much-heated discussion from time to time in the annals of Cornish mining, but it is safe to say that down to the beginning of the War very few of those who attended regularly at the weighing-off of mine tin at the smelting-house understood in the least how the smelters' complicated figures were arrived at. They did know, however, that the smelters claimed many privileged customs; and that, in addition to the $6\frac{1}{4}$ per cent. normally deducted from the assay value for returning charges, a ton of 2,300 lb. (or 115 lb. to the cwt.) was demanded, the extra 3 lb. to the cwt. being for an allowance known as the "breaking of the balance." (60) On all low-grade ores (usually below 60 per cent. tin) still higher returning charges were made, in order, it is said, to discourage the practice of sending to the smelting-houses parcels not sufficiently cleansed and concentrated.

The smelters, on their part, could not have remained entirely ignorant of certain practices which went on at the mines. Until recent years it was the custom in the Redruth-Camborne area for a sampler to attend at the mines on Friday to take samples for the smelter, on the assay of which depended the prices offered for the various parcels of tin put up at the ticketing or sale which took place (at Tabb's Hotel, Redruth) on the following Tuesday. After the sampling the parcels of tin should, of course, have been left untouched until the sale, but such, in many mines, was far from being the case, for throughout the intervening days tin, invariably of a poorer quality, was continuously added. Further than this, owing to difficulties of transport, not a few mines in the outlying district were trusted by the smelters to make up their own samples, and these might commonly be seen drying by a fire in the count-house before going to the smelter, though with the full knowledge on the part of the mines that the tin itself would subsequently be bought according to its wet weight.

The old system and all that went with it depended largely for its success on the local understanding of its working. There was often, it is true, a little cheating on both sides, but both sides knew the rules of the game, and generally knew where to stop. It was not until the London adventurer came into Cornwall and a new generation of mining men arose "that knew not Joseph" that the tributing system, together with many other customs once general in Cornish mining, began to fall into decay.

II

The tribute system, though commonest in its application to the miners, had at no time been confined to underground working, but was applied to the more skilled work at surface also.

The term "surface worker," like that of "underground man," included, of course, many different classes of workmen, such as engine-men, firemen, kibble-landers, whim-drivers, stamp-watchers, burning-house men, etc., not to mention the carpenters, masons, smiths, and others who were immediately employed about the mines. Generally speaking, however, a surface man or one who "worked to grass" was understood to be employed about the actual preparation or "dressing" of the tin and copper ores for the smelter after they had been sent to surface.

The dressing of copper ores was almost entirely performed by hand in the older Cornish mines, and consisted firstly of breaking the rock down to the required size, and afterwards of "jigging" or washing it in water to free it from its earthy impurities. (61) This work was performed by low-paid workers, chiefly women and children, of whom great numbers were formerly employed on the surface.

Similarly, a great deal of the work connected with tin-dressing was also performed by hand seventy or eighty years ago. On being raised from the mine, tin ore was first broken into pieces as large as a man's fist, and then picked over by hand and the worthless stones rejected before being sent to the stamps. After stamping, the "crop tin" was taken to a Cornish square buddle, an inclined plane over which water was allowed to flow. The man or "stout boy" who performed this work stood in the buddle, assisting the action of the water by passing his foot from side to side. If the ore was rough this operation was generally performed with the naked feet, even in the coldest weather of winter, but when the particles were very fine the foot was shod with a smooth piece of wood called a "brogue" (locally "broog") The subsequent processes to which the ore was subjected—tying, jigging, trunking, framing, chimming, dilluing, tozing, packing, and others too numerous to mention—were performed by armies of surface workers whose remuneration varied according to the degree of laboriousness or skill required by their tasks. (62)

Very frequently the whole work of dressing both tin and copper ores was undertaken by some enterprising surface tributer, who agreed to render so many tons fit for smelting, in return for a percentage of their vanning assay. In this case the tributer himself would employ women and children to act as his assistants, the ages at which such children were engaged varying from seven or eight to twelve or fourteen years.

"There are a few at nine years of age," stated Captain Charles Thomas, at Dolcoath, in 1864, "but very few indeed. At the age of ten or eleven there are great numbers." There was no particular limit to the age at which children were received on the dressing-floors. "Sometimes," said the same witness, "a father or mother will come and say, 'I have this little child, and I do not know what to do with it; I can scarcely get bread for it: will you take it?' We sometimes yield to that and take the child in to such work as it can do, but it is very light work." (63)

Children of this class would receive perhaps 2d. or 3d. a day on first coming to the mine, "afterwards making their own contracts," so the Commissioners were told. (64) It is pleasing to find that the precocity which was supposed to enable children at the age of nine or ten to "make their own contracts" did not extend to their pleasures also. Thus there is no hint of the children rioting with their money on tobacco or raw spirits; on the contrary, it was stated that their habit was to carry their earnings home to their parents in a most exemplary manner.

The work of the youngest girls employed consisted chiefly in picking the pieces of copper ore, and that of the youngest boys in washing it. The hardest work undertaken by the children was the "jigging" or sieving of the copper ore in water, a work which necessitated standing in a doubled-up position. Some of the boys brought up blood after working thus. (65)

Though in the majority of cases the work performed by the children was not very laborious, the hours were long, being for the most part ten in summer and nine in winter. In summer, work began at seven in the morning and stopped at five, five-thirty, or six at night. In winter it began with daylight and ended with dusk. In most mines an hour was allowed for dinner, but in some only half that time was permitted. Only in a few cases was a short interval allowed about 10 a.m. Sometimes, when engaged in piecework, the surface hands would get off at two or three in the afternoon once or twice a week. At other times, however, especially before sampling day, the hours of work were often greatly prolonged. At such times a boy or girl from nine to twelve years old was obliged to rise at about four o'clock in the morning, get a hasty breakfast, and, after a walk of an hour or more—three, four, or even five miles—reached the mine at six. Work was here continued till twelve without intermission or refreshment, save what might be got by stealth. Half an hour was then allowed for dinner. After this the child worked on again without interruption till eight, got home after repeating the walk of the morning, and may have had supper and got to bed about ten. According to the evidence of some of the children employed at a great mine, they worked in this way for about a third of each month during the summer. (66) In other mines a system of overtime was occasionally adopted, which overtasked the children's strength still more, though it was not imposed on so great a number nor continued so long. At such times certain of the boys were employed in preparing the ore from seven in the morning of one day till two in the afternoon of the following, working throughout the whole night. (67)

In exceptional cases, prolonged labour of this sort was occasionally enforced on other surface workers, such, for instance, as the horse "whim" drivers, who were generally boys. The "whim plats," where the horses walked their rounds in turning the machine which drew the kibbles up the shaft, had generally low walls around them and, the horses knowing their duty so well, very little was required of the boys, save to stop or start the animals when the kibbles reached the top or bottom of the shaft. On ordinary occasions the boy drivers worked from seven in the morning till six at night, sitting for the most part on a seat slung from the capstan bar, half asleep and sometimes so stiff with the cold that they could hardly get down. One of them, however, an old man now, remembered a time when they were "stripping" the mine in which he worked that they had trouble in raising one of the pump lifts and, owing to the water gaining upon them, he, with the rest of the men and horses, was kept at his post from seven one morning until 3 a.m. of the next.

It should be understood, however, that as a general rule it was not usual in Cornwall for children or young persons to be employed on the surface by night. Conditions of life for the mine children of Cornwall in earlier days were certainly rough and hard, and only the fittest perhaps survived. Yet those who did grew up strong and hardy, to labour as few of their descendants have done. They worked long hours in the cold and wet, and on apparently insufficient food. On going home in the evening they rarely changed or dried their clothes, but started the next day in the damp garments of overnight.

It was those, of course, whom hereditary disease or other causes had rendered delicate who really suffered from the hardness of the struggle for life.

"I was 'bout eleven 'eers ould when I was hired out to tend the Rickers at the stampses, for three shellin' and sexpence a month," wrote Richard Hampton of his early childhood, about 1790, when both his body and mind were "shuck to rags," as he termed it, by the fits to which he was subject. "I was awnly glad to git anything for faather an' mother, the deears. But aw, my time was spent in laabour and sorrow, sure 'nough. Many times ded I go and cum from work weth baare feet, and my poor thin body with nothin' but rags upon me. Some people did pity me, they that had feelin'. But the wicked boays ded nothin' but loff, and everything they cud do they ded to maake my sufferin's bitterer. They would scat (strike) my lembs an' teear my cloase. . . . Then they wud tie my hands behind my back, an' put a hank'shuff ovver my eyes, an' caal me haaf-saaved, and foach (push) agen me, an' then they wud say that ef I wud but sweear they wud lev me go. But I wud'n." (68)

At a later date poor Richard went to another kind of work, which he found equally bad. "My maaster," he wrote, "keept a lot of moyles (mules) to car cawls (coals) and copper oore, an' my work was to go weth the caryer to fill the sacks and help un to git the moyles along. Here I got the wecked boays an' girls round me agen; they knackt me about, thrawed stones at me, shoved me into mud pools: and waun day, as I was going along by a church, I was draaged into the tower and locked up ever so long. Many, many miles have I lemped along arter the moyles ovver the stony roads with not a shoe to my foot nor a bit of anything pon my back that wud keep out the cowld and wet." (69)

Hard as the conditions of life and work were, the state of the child-worker in Cornwall was incomparably better than in the industrial and mining areas of England at the same period. The advance of money to parents on the credit of the future labour of their children was in Cornwall totally unknown. No system of apprenticeship was practised anywhere, and the obligation of giving one month's notice of the intention to quit a mine was the most stringent condition under which any class of labourer was bound. Corporal punishment of the children was a thing unheard of in the Cornish mines, and "would certainly be resented by recourse to legal process on the part of the friends," stated one of the Captains. (70) At the most, an occasional "spale" or fine was inflicted for late attendance, but generally the word of the agent was sufficient check on indolence or misconduct. In a few mines, notably at Wheal Vor, premiums of 1s. and 6d. a month were given to girls of different classes who had attended at their work without interruption during the whole month. (71)

Most of the work in connection with the dressing of tin and copper ores, which was too heavy for the children, was given to older women and girls known as "bal maidens," great numbers of whom were always employed on the surface of Cornish mines. The work of "spalling" or breaking up the larger rocks was performed by the women with long-handled hammers, standing out of doors. (72) These stones, if they consisted of copper ore, were subsequently broken down into pieces about the size of a walnut by a process known as "bucking" on an anvil. Bucking, though performed with lighter tools than "spalling," was really the hardest work in which the "bal maidens" were engaged. The girls sat to this work in cramped positions which allowed little or no movement to the lower limbs. The sheds in which they worked, being open on one side, were draughty and cold, and often ran with water when the rain beat in that way. The exposure to cold and its effects were accordingly much complained of, though not so much as the exposed situations of many of the mines on bleak hill-sides or on the tops of cliffs might have led one to expect. The pay for this kind of work varied, but in 1842 the Commissioners learnt that it was only by the utmost industry that a girl could earn 1s. a day, (73) whilst 8d. or 9d. would probably have been a fairer average.

Twenty-four years later the position of the "bal maidens" seems to have been little changed. In many of the mines they still worked with practically no cover over them, or without any place to sit and eat their meals in, though in Dolcoath and a few of the larger mines more comfortable conditions prevailed.

"We have four mine establishments," stated the manager of the first in 1864, "with an oven in each of them, large enough to contain two hundred pasties or hoggans. We have benches round a long room where they can sit down, and hot water is always prepared for dinner-time. As soon as the bell rings they rush to get their dinner, and so many as like to do so join together. Half a dozen perhaps purchase a tin kettle, and everyone brings a cup, and if they join together they get a little tea with the water." (74) Many of them were very poor, however, and found it hard indeed to make both ends meet. But, like the miners, the bal maidens were generally proud and independent and hated to show their poverty. The agent in one mine stated that "the women commonly collected in groups for their dinner, but he had observed some of the girls steal away at such times to eat their meal behind a hedge, being ashamed of the meanness of their fare." (75)

The Cornish bal maidens formed a class of workwomen to themselves, a class, as a whole, shrewd, honest, respectable, and hard-working. Though sometimes rough in speech and generally plain-spoken enough in repartee, as anyone who addressed them disrespectfully soon found, their work brought with it no demoralization of character. In their dress, too, they were clean and neat, and generally very particular about their appearance. "They wrap their legs in woollen bands in winter, and in summer many of them envelop their faces and throats in handkerchiefs to prevent them getting sunburnt," said the Commissioners in 1842, "whilst on Sundays and holidays they appear in apparel of a showy and often expensive description." (76)

The sight of the bal maidens at work spalling stone in the long open sheds or doing lighter "chares" on the tin-dressing floors was a familiar one to all who knew the Cornish mines even twenty years ago. The peculiar headdress of the bal maiden, known in some districts as a "yard of cardboard," consisted of a piece of cardboard placed across the head with a curtain of print which fell down on the shoulders. In this it differed slightly from the ordinary "gook" or sunbonnet, which comes forward over the head in front. Below this the "maidens" wore a bodice called a Garboldi (i.e. Garibaldi), which was tucked inside the skirt, and over the skirt a clean white pinafore, in which they walked to and from the mine. During working hours a hessian "towser" or rough apron would be substituted for the pinafore. In winter-time, or when engaged on rough work, many of them used to cut up a stocking, which they used as a sort of mitten. Most of them brought their crochet or knitting in their pockets and would be seen industriously employing their spare moments at croust and dinner-time.

The spread of cheap education and the substitution of machinery for human labour has caused a complete disappearance of the bal maiden, although a few were employed at the Carn Brea Mines as recently as fourteen or fifteen years ago. Their disappearance has robbed the surface of a Cornish mine of one of its most picturesque and characteristic features; and never again, one supposes, will the sound of them going by singing at six o'clock in the summer mornings be heard in the mining areas.

The employment of women in any other office save that of dressing the tin and copper ores was very exceptional in Cornwall, and there is no evidence of their having ever been employed at any period underground. "In one instance, and I think the only one known, the strenuous and exposed task of kibble-lander was attended to by a woman," wrote a correspondent in 1885. "She was a Cornish celebrity, known by the name of Gracey Briney, who resided at the East End of Redruth for years. A frequent visitor at the Pick and Gad Inn with the miners on pay-days, she smoked, drank beer, and talked in common with the rest. Her dress consisted of a man's high pole-hat, known amongst her fellow-workers as a 'long sliver,' 'bell topper,' and, more recently, 'Par stack'; a blue clawed-hammer coat (called so from the shape of its tails) having a thick, deep collar and brass buttons; under this a blue frock with white spots, and very thick, nailed boots. She invariably, when walking, carried a stick. Her hair flowed carelessly down her back, and she had a grey moustache. After ceasing to work at the mine, and perhaps before, she sold fish, driving a horse and cart, with the whip tied across her shoulders when not in use. She was a constant attendant at Redruth weekly market—was always most industrious. She died at an advanced age." (77)

As a rule, the heaviest and most exposed labour on the surface was performed by men known as "owners' account men." These generally received a low monthly wage, though a few, taken on at special times of emergency, might be paid by the "stem" or working day. Having little of either the tributer's or tutworker's incentive for showing skill or intelligence in their work, those who never broke away from the "Awners' Count Stap" were regarded for the most part as an inferior grade of workmen.

Much as may be learnt from printed documents, those who have taken the trouble to compare them with the recollections of old people yet living will have gained a better proportioned picture of mining life in Cornwall seventy years ago than the reading of any number of Commissioners' Reports alone could give. What does become clear to all who have studied both sides of the case is that the old people were hardy and strong to labour, to a degree which seems scarcely credible to the generation of to-day. Much of the hand labour which a mechanical age has now rendered obsolete was performed in the past cheerfully as a matter of course. The working people of Cornwall were naturally not without some grievances. Injustice in the payment of wages they frequently resented, likewise the exportation of cereal crops affecting their daily bread. Such abuses are not forgotten. But of the mere hardness of their labour they rarely complained. Indeed, what really broke their spirit was not so much *work* as the times when industry flagged and sufficient employment could not be found.

The old type of Cornish miner, though generally short-lived, was hardy to a degree, going out in frosty nights in winter with a shirt open at the neck and his chest quite bare. (78) "They have a pallor," stated one witness in 1864, "but they are very wiry men, capable of enduring a great deal of fatigue and possessed of great muscular power. They will beat a boryer in some close confined place underground for ten minutes on end, without ceasing, calling not only the chest into play but the muscles of the abdomen." (1)

Many of the men were very proud of their great physical strength and delighted in opportunities for displaying it. On one occasion, for instance, a young miner, for a wager, ran from Wheal Vor to Helston Market House, a distance of 3½ miles, in fifty-six minutes, wheeling a barrow of stamps sand weighing 160 lb. (80) At shows in the mining or quarrying districts drilling contests were, and to a lesser extent still are, a popular feature. The speed with which holes were drilled by a "pare" of skilful miners was often amazing. At a hand-boring contest held at Camborne in 1888, a "pare" of three men from Tincroft Mine, two beating the boryer and one turning it, put down a hole thirteen inches deep into close granite in six minutes forty-three seconds. (81)

"Nearly all the work was piecework," said an old St. Ives man, speaking of the tin-streams seventy years ago, "and we boys would race against each other, running 1 cwt. and ½ cwt. barrows up and down planks only six inches wide. We were so strong we thought nothing of it." As a proof of this the bal boys were commonly in the habit of spending a part of their dinner-hour "trying a hitch to wrastling" and in other strenuous games, which showed them little exhausted by their long hours of labour. (82)

In spite, therefore, of the many hardships and dangers connected with the old ways of mining, those who once started to work "to bal" rarely afterwards changed their occupation.

" I would rather see a good bal than a good farm any day " is a statement which might frequently be heard from the older miners.

" They have a great dislike to agricultural work," wrote the Commissioners of 1864 ; " they think farmers' wages insufficient." Seeing that down to the 'fifties the regular wage of a Cornish agricultural labourer was 7s. a week, this was not to be wondered at, and in comparison to them the mine workers were not badly off. Even the mining children employed at surface got more wages than those employed in agriculture. (83)

To the tributer accustomed to the gambling chances of mining, where he might at any time earn £50 in a month, the life of a farm-labourer seemed dull and uninteresting.

Added to all this, the miners' hours of work were short in comparison with workmen in other trades. In the foundries, for instance, the men worked from 6 a.m. to 6 p.m., with an hour and a half for meals. (84) The miner, on the other hand, working in six- or at most eight-hour " coors," found himself for a considerable portion of his day a free man. The varying ways in which he employed this freedom will form part of the subject of the following chapter.

NOTES.

1. The present year is memorable for the abolition of the system of payment by calendar months—commonly called the five-week month—and the substitution of the payment for four weeks.—Worth, R.C.P.S. (1872), 119.

2. A tributer generally only paid 6d. for having his sample tried (W. Michell). Most of the tryers were skilful enough men with the vanning shovel, but the actual method by which the sample was taken in the first place often left much to be desired. Forty years ago, in one of the largest of the Camborne mines, the rock was broken down simply on a " bucking iron," with the result that the large pieces which flew off were neglected, and the fine stuff only got sampled. The " pigeons flying away," however, as the hard stuff was facetiously called, proved at a later date to contain good tin values, a fact of which the mine had for many years been blissfully ignorant !

3. Commission Appointed to Enquire into the Condition of All Mines in Great Britain (not Coal), 1864. Hereinafter referred to as Parl. Pap. (1864).

4. The adventurers themselves, of course, farmed the mine in the first place from the mineral lord, paying him " dish " or dole on all mineral raised from his ground. These dues varied from one-sixth to one-thirtieth.

5. Parl. Pap. (1864), Appendix B, 445. Hereinafter referred to as Parl. Pap. (1864).

6. Parl. Pap. (1864), Appendix B, 446.

7. Parl. Pap. (1864), 97.

8. Parl. Pap. (1864), 24.

9. The tutwork men were also granted subsist on occasion, but more by favour and less by right than the tributers. Both classes of miners, however, were entirely in the hands of the purser in this respect, who thereby exercised an unobtrusive but none the less powerful hold over the conduct of the men. The " month in hand " system died out in the " western mines " about sixty years ago. Since that time tributers as well as tutworkers were always paid monthly, subsist being commonly granted at the end of the first fortnight. Samples, however, were generally taken from the tributers' work each week to make sure that the stuff they were breaking warranted the granting of a cash advance.

10. Years later than this, the system still obtained in many mines of *making* the men take up so many pounds of candles a week whether they needed them or not. A respectable inhabitant of Camborne told me recently that he well remembered working as a boy in a shallow level at West Frances, and how the men would often send him up " to grass " with 2 lb. of candles to exchange for " bacca " at the village shop. The whole system barely escaped infringing on the Truck Act.

11. Parl. Pap. (1864), 98.

12. Parl. Pap. (1864).

13. *Cornish Magazine*, i, 179.

14. Per Mr. Michell, of Hayle, related to him by Captain Boundey, now an old man living far away from Cornwall, in Montana.

15. Per Mr. Veal, of St. Ives.

16. Per Mr. Michell, of Hayle.

17. " Independent as Members of Parliament," another captain described them.—Parl. Pap. (1864), 261.

18. Parl. Pap. (1864), 167.

19. Parl. Pap. (1864), 261.

20. Per old tributers who formerly worked on the pockets of tin in the Providence Mines, Lelant.

21. F. J. Stephens, R.C.P.S. (1889), 108.

22. Parl. Pap. (1864).

23. Parl. Pap. (1864), 102.

24. Parl. Pap. (1842), xvi, 840. Children's Employment Commission. Hereinafter referred to as Parl. Pap. (1842). " They offered us more wages to ' hole ' to a certain point," explained a dying miner in 1893,

"and said it would cost too much to pump air into the end; and the last three cores I worked there the air was so bad that the candles repeatedly went out. When I came out I was trembling like an aspen-leaf, and that was the beginning of my breaking-up."—H. Thomas, *Entombed*, p. 28.

25. The nature of some of the questions asked by them seems to warrant this supposition.
26. Cf. Henwood, R.G.S.C. (1848), v, 387.
27. Parl. Pap. (1845), Report on Accidents in Mines, 123, 142, 144, etc.
28. J. A. Paris, *Accidents in Mines of Cornwall through Blasting*, 1817.
29. Worth, R.C.P.S. (1872), 98.
30. Large stocks of quills used formerly to be disposed of to the miners at Goldsithney Fair.—Per R. Cunnack.
31. W. Bickford, *Safety Fuse*, 1832 (pamphlet).
32. R.C.P.S. (1872), 79.
33. Parl. Pap. (1842), 854.
34. Henwood, R.G.S.C., v, 397, and viii, 586.
35. When this great run of mines closed down in the 'seventies, many of the miners were forced to seek work in the colder granite mines round Carn Brea, where the majority are said to have soon died off.
36. Parl. Pap. (1842), 852.
37. Parl. Pap. (1864), 92.
38. Parl. Pap. (1864), 87.
39. Parl. Pap. (1842), 848. These were known as "Forenoon core," 6 a.m. till noon; "Afternoon core," noon till 6 p.m.; "First core by night," 6 p.m. till midnight; "Last core by night," midnight till 6 a.m.
40. Parl. Pap. (1842), 772.
41. Parl. Pap. (1864), 11.
42. Parl. Pap. (1864), 851.
43. Parl. Pap. (1864), 765.
44. Parl. Pap. (1864), 765.
45. Parl. Pap. (1842), 772. After "working a doubler," an old St. Just miner told me that he has walked home three miles, frequently falling asleep as he went, and, on getting in to supper, has sat half dozing whilst his wife put food into his mouth.
46. Parl. Pap. (1842), 773.
47. Parl. Pap. (1842), 765.
48. R.G.S.C., iii, 65.
49. Parl. Pap. (1842), 851.
50. Parl. Pap. (1842), 789.
51. Parl. Pap. (1842), 854.
52. G. Henwood, *Lectures on Mining* (1854), 9.
53. R. Cunnack MS.
54. Per Captain W. Thomas, of Perranporth.
55. Per Captain Nile.
56. One day, many years ago now, a captain in one of the Perranporth silver lead mines came across a boy "cobbing" down a lot of very poor

stuff in one of the levels. "Why that's no good what thee'st got there, boy," said the captain, glancing over the pile. "How long hast 'a ben working on that?" "Aw, I ben doin' this for months," innocently replied the lad, "but I tell 'ee tes nothen to the stuff in Dad's pass" (per Captain Cann). The father was doubtless not pleased at his son's candour, as he had a lot of rich stuff put aside out of sight, which he was sending up gradually, thereby maintaining good average earnings without having his rate of tribute reduced.

57. *Cornish Magazine*, ii, 155.

58. I.e. portions of the mine not set on tribute but being worked for the owners by men receiving daily or weekly wages. Amongst themselves, however, the tributers, on the whole, were very honest. Thirty years ago it was a common sight to see the tribute pitches scattered thickly along the line of underground workings on the "Great Flat Lode." These pitches were separated only by a board or two placed lengthwise. Thus any man coming to work early or leaving late could easily have helped himself (if he had been so disposed) from his neighbour's ore on the other side of the board—yet on the whole few complaints arose.

59. *Quarterly Review* (1827), 86.

60. The mines had little right to complain of this, since they themselves demanded 21 cwt. to the ton of ores raised by the tutwork men.

61. Copper ores when brought to surface were divided into three parts, denominated according to lessening size as *spalling* stuff, *picking rough*, and *shaft small*. The larger pieces, being broken to about $1\frac{1}{2}$ in. square, were mixed with the picking rough, and the whole then divided into: (1) *Prills*, or lumps of pure ore; (2) *Dradge*, or ore mixed with other substances; (3) *Halvans, hennaways*, or *leavings*, which contained but a small quantity of copper. The *prills* were bucked only with flat-polled hammers and were then fit for sale, the *dradge* was also bucked, and then jigged in a sieve, the poorer grades requiring more than one treatment. The *shaft small* was jigged, and that which came through was called *hutchwork* and was ready for sale. A part of what remained in the sieve was then treated with the halvans, which frequently had to be cobbed and picked by hand, to render the better parts fit for sale.—R.G.S.C. (1828), iv, 160–2.

62. For a complete description of the dressing of tin ores in 1828, cf. Henwood, R.G.S.C., iv, 146.

63. Parl. Pap. (1864), 121.

64. Parl. Pap. (1842), 786.

65. Parl. Pap. (1842), 776.

66. Parl. Pap. (1842).

67. Parl. Pap. (1842), 771.

68. *Life of Foolish Dick*, 21.

69. *Life of Foolish Dick*, 28.

70. Parl. Pap. (1842), 786.

71. Parl. Pap. (1842), 788.

72. Parl. Pap. (1842), 775.

73. Parl. Pap. (1842), 775.
74. Parl. Pap. (1864), 122.
75. Parl. Pap. (1842), 821.
76. Parl. Pap. (1842), 791.
77. *Cornish Magazine (and Devon Miscellany)*, 1885.
78. *Western Morning News*, September 20, 1865.
79. Parl. Pap. (1864), 84.
80. *Royal Cornwall Gazette*, February 11, 1832.
81. Burrows and Thomas, *'Mongst Mines and Miners*, 24. This book contains the best selection of Cornish underground photos in existence.
82. Parl. Pap. (1842), 784.
83. Parl. Pap. (1842), 807.
84. Parl. Pap. (1842), 807.

CHAPTER VII

THE MINER AT HOME, 1800-1870

I

NIGHT descending over a mining area brings out its picturesque features most strongly. The lurid glare of the pit-heads in the northern collieries, where flaming baskets of coal were formerly kept alight by night to guide the pitman to his work, has attracted the notice of many writers. The scene in Cornwall, though not so startling, is scarcely less mysterious. The numberless headgears outlined against the evening sky, the rising and falling beams of the "fire whims" or the bulky "cages" (winding drums) of the older horse-engines, the cries of the landers, the glare from boiler-house doors, and the lights showing dimly in the arched windows of the great three-storied engine-houses, all combine to make up a scene not easily forgotten, whilst more than all these the rattling din of the stamps, which throughout the noonday and midnight never cease in their work of pounding up the ores which unseen miners are raising from the shafts, serves to increase the mystery of night. Chimneys everywhere, new and old, broken and split, point like fingers to the sky, whilst the smeech which pervades the air tells the night traveller of the deadly fumes of arsenic escaping from the flues of some burning-house close at hand. Day and night work has never ceased in these busy areas between Camborne and Redruth, where so long and so persistently have the miners laboured in extracting the treasures of the earth that the old unchanging hill above, in its solitude and peace alone, can number their generations.

Let us suppose a winter's night in the 'fifties and the time nearing ten o'clock as we approach the confines of one of the larger mines. The creaking of the flat rods and the rattle of the geared wheels proclaim the "man-engine" at work and the time that of "changing cores." Peering into the black abyss of the shaft, the dim lights of the miners' candles may be seen, as they leisurely ascend from their labours on the moving rods of the man-engine. The ascent from a deep mine in this way takes nearly half an hour and the miners beguile their time by singing. Nearer and nearer come the lights "to grass," and the sound of the men's voices, taking parts in some favourite Wesleyan hymn or psalm tune, strikes upon the ear in its full manly strength. At last the foremost reach surface and, stepping off the beam, pass a friendly "Good night, capun," to the stranger standing beside the shaft, and betake themselves to the "dry" or moorhouse, where they change their saturated garments.

In the old drinking days it was the habit of many of the men, on coming to surface, to resort to one of the innumerable "winks" or dram-shops which at one time dotted the country-side, there to stimulate themselves with spirits and beer, which, taken at such times, was said to produce fevers and tended to shorten their lives.

"The ardent spirits to which the vulgar Cornish (and not only the vulgar, it might be added) are habituated, are unquestionably prejudicial to health," wrote Polwhele in 1817. "On our farms the women as well as the men have, at particular seasons, their morning drams before the commencement of work. And the brandy-glass circulates briskly among the farmers before any occasional dinner, immediately after the dinner, and a third time before the breaking up of the company."

What wonder, then, that among the miners spirituous liquors were equally in repute, being employed to support them in their laborious calling when, owing to disease, their appetite for solid food had already begun to fail. (1)

The temperance movement, however, was already at work in Cornwall in these days to check such practices amongst the poor and vulgar, though it was some time before its influence reached their betters. A Society for the Suppression of Drunkenness was started in Redruth in 1805, and from small beginnings such as this the cause has gained such power and influence that it may perhaps be said that to-day no class of workers in the country is so temperate as the Cornish miner, nor any district so largely "teetotal" as Cornwall.

It was partly with a view to encouraging temperance that the experiment was tried in the 'sixties at Dolcoath Mine and Wheal Uny (Liskeard) of providing the miners with hot soup immediately on their coming up from underground. The benefit to the men's health which resulted is said to have been very noticeable, but the practice never became general, probably owing quite as much to prejudice on the men's part as parsimony in the owners. As it was, only too frequently a man would set off from the mine in the darkness of a winter's night in the pelting rain, and, pursuing his intricate course amidst burrows and streams and unfenced shafts by the light of a glimmering lantern, would at last arrive at his journey's end without finding any comfortable meal awaiting him. (2) "I have known instances," wrote Mr. Jory Henwood to the Commissioners in 1842, "where men who had to remain in an atmosphere of 96° F. whilst at their employ, at a late hour of the night had to walk three miles to their homes. Some of these were too poor to be well clad ; (4) and after so frightful a transition of temperature and so long a walk against a fierce and biting wind have often reached home without a fire and had to creep to bed with no more nourishing food and drink than barley-bread or potatoes with cold water." (4)

What walks many of these must have been only those who knew the former wildness of the mining districts and the situation of such mines as Botallack, Ding Dong, or Perran Wheal Golden can realize. Over the exposed downs, round the foot of the carns, down the faces of cliffs, the old men's paths can still be traced, though in places time is blotting out their tracks. Through the cold blustering nights of winter, with the beating pitiless rain, and in the misty nights of autumn, when the air was so still that the creak of the flat rods and the rattle of chains could be heard a mile away, the miners came and went to their labours. In past times, when there was more working by night than there is to-day, hundreds of men were coming and going every night along the cliff-paths leading to Wheal Castle, Wheal Owles, Wheal Edward, Botallack, Wheal Cock, Levant, and other mines in the parish of St. Just. Some used to carry a miner's lantern, that is, a candle placed in an old "slowg" (miner's boot, St. Just) or a treacle-tin pierced with holes, others stumbled home in the dark as best they could. It was at times like this that a miner's wife would sit listening for every step, a candle burning dimly in the cottage window long after the rest of the population was wrapped in darkness and sleep. Often in the darkest nights of winter, in a blustering gale, women would be out on the cliffs with lanterns, waiting for their husbands to come up.

The sort of home and conditions to which a miner arrived back after his work depended on many circumstances, but first and foremost on the character of his wife. This was especially so with men who were tributers and whose earnings were consequently fluctuating and uncertain. "You will find two men," stated a witness in 1864, "and one has got a clean, decent, wholesome, industrious wife, and that man's children will be kept as clean and comfortable as possible. You will then see one of the same 'pare' who has got a dirty, careless wife, and that family will be in rags, and yet that man will make the same earnings. One man will be well off and the other always in misery." (5) "There is a woman living about four or five miles from Penzance," added Dr. Quiller Couch; "she has a husband and four or five boys who are all working in a mine, and I calculate that they are earning from £11 to £13 or £14 a month, and yet they have not got a chair to sit down upon; there is scarcely a cup or saucer in the place, and as for a bed, what they have would disgrace the poorest persons in the kingdom." (6) In this case poverty was not attributable to intemperance or any accidental cause, but merely to a lack of management on the part of the miner's wife.

That there were such cases is perhaps hardly to be wondered at when one considers the woman's task in a household of four or five men living in a tiny cottage, one rising before daylight, another going to work at ten at night or arriving back to dinner at three in the afternoon, almost all requiring meals at separate times and "crowst" to be prepared for each. In spite of all this, and the fact that in the poorer households the women themselves were sometimes out all day working on farms or the tin-streams, the Cornish miner's home was generally clean and well ordered. "It was exceedingly rare, too," the Commissioners of 1842 noted, "to meet with an example of squalid filthiness in any members of a Cornish miner's family." (6)

The miner's usual dinner, which he took with his family on his arrival home (if he had been working first core by day), consisted of fish, generally salted, potatoes, and tea. The latter, however, being very dear, the dried leaves of mugwort were frequently substituted for it. This meal was varied sometimes by a slice of fried green pork (i.e. home-cured bacon) with eggs and potatoes; or else a small lump of meat put into a great dish of potatoes; little enough in many cases by the time nine or ten children had all had a share.

Pork used everywhere to be more commonly eaten in the mining districts than beef or mutton, because many of the miners kept their own pigs. On the whole, the Cornish miners ate far less butcher's-meat than other classes of labourers, such as navvies, and much less than was customary amongst the pitmen in the North of England. (8) "We cannot afford more than 3 or $3\frac{1}{2}$ lb. of butcher's-meat a week," said one man, before the Commissioners in 1864. "With the miner," stated another witness, "it is generally a feast or a fast. One day he will have his beefsteaks and his good living, and the next day he will have his broth. They live upon broth for some days after, and they only throw in a bone or perhaps a bit of pork to make it." The lack of butcher's-meat was especially noticeable in the outlying districts. "In the Lelant Hills, and the high country especially, there is a great deal of gruel and vegetable food and not much animal food. In the western districts from St. Ives to the Land's End or at St. Just, they are men who do not eat much animal food. They take more gruel and vegetables, and yet they are strong men." (9)

The actual shortage of butcher's-meat did not, perhaps, tell so much upon the miner's health as the roughness and unsuitability of much of the food he ate, either through choice or necessity. In many cases where the miner rose at 4.30 in order to get to the mine and be underground by 6 a.m., his breakfast would consist only of a cup of tea and bread and butter. (10) As the price of wheat was formerly nearly double that of barley, both bread and pastry were made from the latter, wheaten loaves being generally indulged in by the working classes only at feast times or Christmas. (11) In earlier times neither food nor drink was taken by the miners underground, (12) but at a later date it became the custom for the men to take down a "mossel" (i.e. bread and butter) with them, and in some cases a "kag" of water also. On account of its convenience for carrying underground, many miners preferred the "hoggan," a solid mass of flour mixed with water and baked without any leavening—a heavy enough fare to kill anyone not accustomed to it from youth.

There is little doubt that, as a whole, the miners often wanted a better class of food than they got. "They cannot eat, as a rule, like agricultural labourers," said a doctor in the mining districts. "Many of them have delicate, picking appetites." (13)

"More died there from slow starvation than from poor air," said an old tributer to me in speaking of a set of mines which were formerly notorious for their unhealthiness. There is little doubt that he was right. One witness, in 1842, said he knew a man in Wheal Jewell who was laid up for five years from the effects of "poor air" and was afterwards restored by being allowed a quantity of beef and beer daily by the adventurers, " he being sent to the inn to eat it, as it was known that if he took it to his own house he would share it with his family." (14)

"The hungry 'forties," indeed, were hardly less deserving of their name in Cornwall than in the rest of England. The following reminiscences of an old miner give a picture of Cornish working-class life in those days which tells more than pages of statistics. "Everything was very dear," he wrote, "and the working people were half-starved. My father had the standard wages for surface hands, which was £2 5s. a month, and I was earning 10s. a month, so that £2 15s. a month had to provide for five of us. For our breakfast we had barley gruel, which consisted of about three quarts of water and a halfpenny-worth of skimmed milk thickened with barley flour, a concoction which went by the name of 'sky-blue and sinker.' We lived about half a mile from the mine, and I had to go home to dinner. I can assure the reader that I was sometimes so feeble that I could scarcely crawl along. For dinner we had sometimes a barley pasty with a bit or two of fat pork on the potatoes, and for supper a barley cake or stewed potatoes or turnips with a barley cover. Everything was very dear; groceries such as raisins and currants were 10d. per pound, tea 4s. a pound and the common brown sugar 5d. a pound. I never saw at that time such a thing as jam. Barley flour was £2 per bag of 240 lb., and wheat flour £4 per bag of 280 lb." (15)

"The working miner is attached to his calling because it gives him more leisure time than a day labourer enjoys," so wrote Buller in his *History of St. Just* in 1842. The way in which these "leisure" hours were spent varied much according to the character of the men themselves, but even in the out of the way parts like St. Just, the once prevailing pastimes of drinking and fighting were giving way to civilizing influences. An improvement also began to be noticeable in the general conditions of the miner's home about this time. "Formerly," wrote Buller, "no vegetable (besides potatoes), and not a single flower, enlivened the miner's dirty hovel, now neatness prevails within and without, and there are many gay flowers in their gardens."

To the industrious miner of eighty years ago, "a change of work was as good as a touch-pipe," as he himself would have put it, and on returning home from the mine he as often as not merely transferred his energies from one sort of work to another. Chief among these "out of core" occupations was that of building a cottage for himself and of clearing land for a garden. "I think there are some 800 houses in this town," said a witness from Camborne in 1864, "the property almost entirely of labouring miners, which they have built themselves and which they have on a lease of three lives."

"I am told that the aggregate amount of house property belonging to labouring miners in Camborne exceeds £50,000."

"Do you consider this an evidence of their prudent habits?" inquired one of the Commissioners.

"Of their prudent habits—yes—and of their temperate, orderly, and good conduct."

"Do you think that miners are more in the habit of living in their own houses now than they were thirty years ago?"

"Yes, beyond all comparison."

The cost of building these houses was estimated in the Camborne area at this time as being from £50 to £80. (16) In the country districts it was, of course, very much less. (17)

The miners very seldom borrowed money in order to set about building these houses. "The fluctuations in miners', that is, in tributers', wages are such," explained a witness in 1864, "as to give almost every good miner once or twice in his lifetime, at least, an opportunity of getting £40 or £50 in a month or so." The whole thing, then, depended on whether the miner's wife had previously managed to live without going deeply into debt. If they were badly in debt, every one of these "sturts," as the miners call them, was swallowed up in clearing their liabilities. If this was not the case they straightway set about building a house in their spare time. (18)

The benefit of such a system to the landowners is clear. The ground on which the miners built their cottages was, in most cases, waste croft land, too poor in the first instance to repay the farmer or anyone else but an industrious miner to bring it in. Mining, indeed, in Cornwall, so far from being prejudicial to surface-owners' interests, has proved, in the long run, of the greatest benefit to them.

"Thousands of acres of downs, commons, and wastes," wrote Mr. Richard Thomas in 1819, "have been enclosed and are continually being enclosed by the miners and others on a small scale, generally from three to six acres in a tenement, on each of which one or two cottages are erected. The soils on the granite hills are generally better than on the killas downs, especially for grass, but in many situations cost immense time and labour in clearing away the rocks and stones. This has been particularly so on the south-west slope of Carn Marth, where the enclosing tenants (chiefly miners and labourers) have had to blow the rocks in pieces with gunpowder before they could remove them to where they are collected and heaped up to form fences to their little plots. Two or three thousand tons per acre are thus removed from some spots before the ground is cleared. About thirty tenements of this sort are enclosed on the south and west sides of Carn Marth, containing about 150 acres all together. Many more would have been enclosed had not the land been divided among so many owners. The cost of so many leases, which the tenants have to pay, amounts to more than the freehold of the surface is worth; without reckoning the circumstances of being compelled in some cases to attend the Lord's Court at loss of time and labour or else to pay a fine." (19)

It may appear somewhat hard to the impartial reader that

the property which he thus helped to render so much more valuable, and on which he spent so many laborious hours, should, in most cases, have remained the miner's own for the term of three lives only. But thus it stood. The most serious drawback, however, to the miner owning his own cottage lay in the fact that he was thereafter tied to a fixed abode. "A miner will travel (i.e. walk) six or even eight miles between the mine and his home twice in the day in cases where he has built a house near a mine which has ceased to give him work," wrote the Commissioners in 1842. (19) Such an added labour at the beginning and end of a day's work would now appear almost insupportable, but fifty years ago many miners performed it regularly, and in some cases voluntarily. At the time when the St. Ives mines were in their glory, it was no unusual thing for a St. Just man working there to walk home on a Sunday morning to see his friends and return the same night ready for work the next day.

The cottages which the miners built varied much according to the character and means of their occupants. "Miners' houses are much cleaner and more comfortable than agriculturists'," stated one witness in Camborne in 1864. "In the Camborne and Redruth districts the modern cottages are well and substantially built, much better than those inhabited by labourers in the Midland counties. They contain two, three, four, or six rooms, in the former cases being occupied by one, in the latter by two families. They have usually garden plots before or behind in which vegetables and potatoes are cultivated."

The older cottages were for the most thatched and contained only two rooms, the upper one being in the slanting, high-pitched roof. Few, if any, of the cottages at this time were provided with privies or possessed any system of under-drainage. The floors were generally of lime ash and apt to be very damp. Little room existed in the older and smaller cottages for the washing of clothes indoors, and hot-water systems were, of course, totally unknown. "The water from most of the mines, however," wrote a visitor to St. Just in 1843, "is used for domestic purposes, and sometimes fifty women may be seen at once standing round an engine-house, washing the linen of their families in the warm water from the steam-engine. This particularly

THE MINER AT HOME

occurs at Boscean, Boscaswell Downs, and Wheal Owls; and it is rather a singular sight of a Monday morning to see the females hastening to the mines, bearing on their heads their washing trays and the linen of their respective families." (21)

Water itself was often a scarcity in the mining districts, where many of the ancient wells were drained dry by the surrounding mines. At the time when the Marazion mining area was in full swing during the 'thirties of the last century, the parish of Perranuthnoe, which was formerly noted for its excellent streams of water, was reduced to such a condition that people were obliged for some time to go as far as Germoe, nearly three miles, for their supplies. (22) At a later date the large 90-inch engine erected on the west part of Mellanear Mine, near Hayle, is said by old miners to have " raised such revurs of water when she was forking " that all the plumps (i.e. wells) in the immediate neighbourhood went dry. The fetching of water was thus another of the miner's many " chares " which had to be performed out of core.

Except in districts where loose stone, suitable for building, was particularly plentiful, the miner generally built the walls of his house of cob or clob, that is, a mixture of clay stiffened with chopped straw and beaten hard like concrete. Owing to prejudice and the opposition of the building trade, the use of cob has now practically become a lost art, and only the standing walls of the old cottages bear witness to its sturdy qualities. But, as a miner who had lived for years in one of these home-made cottages used to say, "they auld housen built of clob and thatch was so loo as a box inside, and so dry that if you was to jump out the bed any time of the night you could strike a match up agin the walls"—a pretty strong testimonial, considering the damp atmosphere of West Cornwall. Houses built in this way had the additional advantage of cheapness. Many years ago now a gentleman from Camborne was passing by a spot on Horse Downs, in Crowan, where he found an old man putting the finishing touches to a small cottage he had just completed.

" I suppose you find house-building expensive," said the gentleman.

" I do ! I do, sir ! " he replied.

" Well, how much do you think your house will cost ? "

"Why, I reckon, sir, by the time I have turned kay in the door, 'twill haa cost me fifty shellan," was the answer. (23)

In many cases the inside of the miners' cottages was as clean and spotless then as it is to-day, and the inhabitants, in spite of cramped conditions, a contented and happy lot. Seated of an evening round the open hearth, with a fire of blazing furze, the whole family would be assembled, with perhaps a neighbour or two on his way to night core. The Cornish miners are generally fond of children, and a father would often on such occasions take a child on his knees and amuse it by recounting stories of the knackers and small people who worked in the old mines long ago, telling them how, when they were old enough, he would take them himself to hear them and show them the rich places down below where the tin was "sparklin' like dimonds." And then perhaps, placing the child "athurt the knees" and lowering it backwards and forwards by the arms, the father would croon to it some purely local nursery rhyme, such as only a Cornish miner's child would appreciate :—

> Balance-bob work up and down,
> Pumping the water from underground,
> Over a while the inion (engine) do lash,
> Scat the old man (or woman) back in the shaft.

So the old life would go on its simple, homely way, till ten o'clock came, and those who were working night core went off to bal and the rest of the household to bed.

In cases, however, where the miner's wife happened to be a slut or a bad manager, dirt and crowded conditions soon aggravated the original poverty of their lives. In some places—in the St. Just district especially—very miserable and filthy conditions at one time prevailed. The attention of the Commissioners in 1864 was particularly called to one settlement of cottages in which, in spite of its healthy situation, conditions were the most squalid imaginable. "The cottages," they wrote, "are built on the open downs, two or three hundred feet above the sea, which is two miles distant. They are exposed in every direction, with a dry, shallow, and rocky soil beneath, covered with heath. In situation nothing could be healthier, yet the conditions are utterly pestilential, the houses being surrounded with shallow pools of water, covered with green slime, through which it is often necessary to pick one's way in order to reach the door. There is no drainage whatever, and all the refuse of the cottages is thrown out on dust-heaps situated in front of the doors. In one of these habitations lives a butcher, who kills his meat on the spot." (24) As a consequence of the prevailing squalor, fevers of one sort or another were more or less endemic among the labouring population here.

Bad housing conditions and overcrowding were nearly always worse in the country districts than in the towns. Dr. Richard Couch, in 1858, vividly described the miserable dwellings of the miners situated on Rocky Downs and the slopes of Trink, Nancledrea, Trencrom, and Castle an Dinas, in the Lelant district. "If they are not in swampy situations," he wrote, "they are as exposed as possible, their only protection being the undulations of the ground. Many of them have only one floor and only two rooms, the bedroom and the kitchen. The kitchens have only earth floors, the doors so dilapidated or so badly made as to admit every wind that blows, and the rooms are consequently cold and comfortless." (25) In the bedroom it was general for the whole family to sleep, however numerous, and as hardly any were ceiled, the temperature sometimes varied 25° F. between night and day in the cottages with slate roofs. In a two-roomed cottage at Wendron, nine persons were found living in 1864. In the small bedroom upstairs, slanting to the roof, were three beds. The two small windows were both incapable of being opened. In this room slept the father, who was ill, his wife and a small baby, a married daughter and baby, the son-in-law, a daughter of sixteen and two sons of fourteen and twelve." (26) Generally, however, a married child was accommodated by building on a linney, or lean-to, to the original cottage where the parents dwelt. (27)

Overcrowding in the cottages was, indeed, very general seventy or eighty years ago, when the country-side was humming with life and every village was packed with men. Writing at this time from East Gunnislake, on the extreme border of the county, a mine manager said: "The miners are too much crowded, and the sanitary condition of the village is very bad. When a man gets home he has a miserable place to sleep in; he may be sleeping in the same room as that in which his wife has been washing all the day." (28)

Very often, of course, the men were out by night, which made the crowding less except on Saturday and Sunday nights, but throughout the week it may be said that the beds in many of the cottages were never empty, since as one arose to go to bal, another, who had been working night core, returned. Undesirable as such a state of affairs certainly was, the Cornish miner crowded in his little cottage was at least better off than the miner in the outlying districts of the North of England, who was forced to pass the week in the horrible lodging-shops provided by the mines, where thirty or forty men, packed three in a bed with a boy across the feet, slept in small rooms, suffocatingly hot, and reeking with the smell of cooking, perspiration, and the steam of drying clothes. (29)

Such lodging-shops were, in Cornwall, quite unknown, and where the distance to the mine was too great for the men to walk daily, they would bring their own food and lodge with another miner's family, returning home on the Saturday night to see their own people.

II.

Much of the discomfort and ill consequences from overcrowding in the cottages in Cornwall was, in a sense, the result of the miners' own choice. "The miners often marry young, many of them at the age of sixteen," wrote the Commissioners, "although, as is frequent in Celtic communities, the matter is often delayed till the circumstances of the girl with whom they have been 'keeping company' render marriage indispensable." Desertion, however, in such cases was rare, whilst prostitution was almost unknown in the mining areas. (30) In all respects the standard of morals amongst Cornish miners was far higher than among the pitmen of the North. (31)

As a result, however, of early marriages, long families were general in Cornwall, and children consequently had to be sent to work at an early age. "It is common here to send boys underground at ten years of age," stated a St. Just captain in 1842, "but parents would not send them so early except for their necessities." (32) Both in these children and their parents slight indispositions were often aggravated into fatal illnesses through the impossibility of taking any respite from their work. "The necessities of home, a widowed mother or a consumptive father, often force a boy to work on, without sufficient food or nutriment, till at last he, too, reaches a sudden crisis and dies," said one witness in 1842.

As was to be expected under such conditions, the toll of infant mortality was also high. "Fifty-five deaths in every hundred in a mining parish are found to be under the age of five years," wrote Dr. Richard Couch. "A large proportion die from debility within the first year of their existence: and no one who has not seen these miserable specimens of humanity can have the slightest idea of their diseased appearance; small, thin, and shrivelled, with scarcely strength to cry, it seems sometimes almost a crime to attempt to prolong their existence." (33) Very frequently, under these conditions, a doctor would not be sent for at all. "They say, 'Let the will of the Almighty work its way'—that is very common. They say, 'An infant of this size a medical man cannot do much for.'" (34)

Many poor human atoms were called, but few chosen for that battle of life where only the fittest could survive. Those that did seemed for the most part unaffected by hereditary disease, and, until they had been for some time working underground, were strong and healthy.

"You see the children in Wendron parish going about without any stockings or shoes and the picture of health, though they live in the wildest places," stated a witness in 1864. (35)

"Those on the surface, taken as a class, have the appearance of robust health; those who go underground soon become pale or show signs of impeded development."

"When I visited a large school for miners' children at Pool," stated the same authority, "I have certainly never seen a more healthy lot of children collected together. The children and young women who are employed in picking the ore on the surface have remarkably clear, bright, healthy complexions. The married women who are seen in the cottages are also very healthy-looking. The men, on the other hand, have often the appearance of being thoroughly worn out and decrepit when their wives, at about the same age, are healthy and young-looking. Cornish miners are not an intemperate race, when compared with the working population of London and the other large towns. They rarely drink spirits. But, working as the men do in eight-hour spells, in winter they scarcely have any sunlight at all. This will go far to explain the peculiar blanched appearance, the glassy eyes and pale lips, which are constant among the miners." (36)

These statements are fully confirmed by other accounts of the health of the Cornish miners at this time.

"Examples of longevity must not be sought among the miners," wrote a visitor to Cornwall in 1865. "On an average, they do not live beyond forty years. The vicar of St. Just said : ' I have seen many widows among the miners but not a single widower. Those who are not killed by accident, perish of exhaustion and excessive toil.'" (37) "Very admirable is the stoical coldness with which they regard their fate," continues the same writer. "Cornwall is proud, and justly so, of her miners. Who can say what England owes to these men ? They produce riches and scarcely enjoy common necessaries themselves." (38)

Such is a typical statement of what was the attitude, not only of the governing classes, but of the more patient of the labouring masses themselves, who were content to regard it as an incontrovertible act of Providence that the majority should work for a bare living under conditions not only dangerous but so unhealthy as to shorten the normal span of life by half, with the added infliction of untold misery and suffering. Long indeed was the time to wait before public opinion at length realized that life under such conditions was not only wrong but foolish and unnecessary, and that the better compliment to Providence was not to submit to remediable evils but to remove them, as in recent years has in a great measure been done.

Generally speaking, the conditions of life in Camborne and Redruth in the 'sixties were ahead of those in other districts, so that, in spite of the greater depth of the mines in that area, the men's health was better on the whole than in the outlying places, where more primitive conditions in housing and work still prevailed. Captain Joseph Vivian, in 1864, attributed the better health of the miners round Camborne to their taking water and food with them underground, which, it was stated, "they never used to do," and also to their having warm, comfortable dries. "Here they keep their own soap and towel, and every man is expected to go away clean. Formerly they went away dirty, and they used to be without stockings and things of that sort. I should think that nearly fifty years ago," he continued, "there were a great many young fellows that went off in decline. You used to see them about the streets in the summer-time with greatcoats on, laid up with the miners' disease." (39)

As against this testimony of improvement, another captain said: "We have many men home for years who have been fairly worn out in the mine, because miners do not live to be very old. I have stood upon the hill, just where we cross North and South Crofty, many times, to look at the faces of the miners as they come up, and you will see very few old men. It has been sometimes complained of when men have a holiday. I have said you cannot err much in that. When I heard people complaining of a Whit-Monday or Whit-Tuesday, which are holidays with us, and that they do more harm than good, I have not thought so. With all their holidays they die off very early." (40)

Some mines were, of course, more unhealthy to work in than others, owing to peculiar local conditions. The Great Beam Mine, near St. Austell, was so damp that the timber would often become loaded with fungous growths after it had been in a short time, and the air in the levels was dead and heavy. The running of the white clay through the fissures of the soft growan in which the mine was sunk, was such that the miners were obliged to caulk all the boards of the shafts with heath, sedge, grass, and moss. (41) This was about 1840. "In those days," said a witness from St. Austell, "the men were in the habit of drinking more in that district and would often go down half-drunk and sleep underground. Nearly all who worked in the Beam Mine suffered from miners' consumption. They were all old men in the Beam Mine at the age of forty, but I should not call all our miners old at that age. In fact, riding through the district, if you saw them you would say, 'That is a Beam man.'" (42)

In mines such as these, where the air was poor and stagnant, black spitting came on almost at once as the result of the powder smoke which the men were continually forced to inhale. (43)

"Miners are never very florid or robust," wrote Dr. Couch, "but to see the men from such mines arriving at surface after eight hours' work is a most sickening sight. Thin, haggard, with arms apparently very much lengthened and hanging almost uselessly by their sides, they seem like men worn out rather than tired." (44)

It is a curious fact that the older writers, though frequently dilating on the hardships of Cornish mining, never seem to have regarded it as a peculiarly unhealthy occupation. Carew, indeed, in 1602, stated that "while the miners play the Moldwarps, unsavourie Damps doe here and there distemper their heads," but, he added, "not with so much daunger in the consequence as annoyance for the present."

A hundred years later the Hon. Robert Boyle, whose acquaintance with mining, it is true, was probably not extensive, went so far as to note that "over some tin-mines in the West of England not only trees but plants flourish . . . 'tis likewise observable of such as constantly dig in those tin-mines that they arrive at a great and vigorous age." (45)

Borlase, who, as a Cornishman living in West Cornwall amongst the mixed population of miners and fishermen, ought to have known the truth, wrote: "The inhabitants are usually of middle stature, healthy, strong, and active, mining and fishing enabling them to bear watching, cold and wet much better than where there are no such occupations: the miners, particularly, who escape accidents and live temperately, generally live to a great age; the alternate daily use of cold and heat, wet and dry, hardening their bodies equally against the different extremes of weather." (46)

Even Pryce, a resident doctor in the mining areas and one keenly interested in the welfare of the miners, does not seem to have attributed any excess of disease among them as directly occasioned by their work, although he noted that fevers, probably the result of poor food, were more or less endemic. (47)

Maton alone of the eighteenth-century writers called attention to the "wretched and emaciated appearance" of the miners whom he saw round Camborne. (48)

That the growing depth of the mines, and the consequently increased strain on heart and lungs in climbing, rendered the miners' occupation increasingly unhealthy as time went on may well be, yet, considering the known conditions under which the men worked underground in the eighteenth century, it seems scarcely possible that the miners can have been so immune from disease as the older writers supposed. How easy it was, however, for those in high places either to hoodwink themselves or others appears from statements made as late as 1835 by the manager of the United Mines, who, not content with stating that the number of casualties attending a Cornish miner's life would compare favourably with that of the surrounding population and that the copper-mines were well and wholesomely ventilated, went on to affirm that " the tin-mines are perhaps the most healthy of all." (49)

Serious attention was first called to the dangers of the miners' life and the alarming statistics of his health by the action of the Royal Cornwall Polytechnic Society, which, during the 'forties and 'fifties, published many papers on this subject :—

" Think of the fact," said one writer in 1847 (and think of it particularly, we might add, in the light of the manager's statement concerning the miners of this same district only twelve years before), " that nearly one out of every five Gwennap miners incurs a violent death to produce the staple commodity which most contributes to the wealth of this county. . . . About one in every million railway travellers has been stated to be killed by railway accidents and the country rings with demands for inquiry and prevention, the Press gives minute particulars of the causes of the accidents, governmental and parliamentary investigations are instituted . . . while of the miners working in a single parish of this county, nineteen in every hundred die a violent death, and it has only been by your Society that attention has been called to the subject or active measures encouraged to remedy the evil." (50)

It must, of course, be admitted that a number of fatal accidents occurring in the mines were directly occasioned by the indifference shown by the men themselves to the dangers which encompassed them in the course of their daily work. Familiarity with such dangers only too often bred contempt. " They will seldom keep their ladders in proper repair, unless absolutely compelled to do so," stated one writer; whilst in the deep mines the men would frequently leap by the light of a glimmering candle into a passing kibble as it came bumping and banging up the shaft and so save themselves the added labour of a climb to surface, though at the risk of their lives. Again, stated the same writer, " I have actually seen a man sitting on a powder-barrel smoking his pipe and a candle merely stuck against the wall by a bit of damp clay, when, from the quantity of loose powder strewed about, had a spark fallen he and his companions must have been blown to atoms."

If, however, the miners were responsible for some of the accidents which befell them, the same could not be said of the great toll of ill-health and suffering which was directly resultant from their work. Further systematic inquiry only served to show the more convincingly how fearful was the mortality from these causes. During the years 1857, 1858, 1859, investigations were carried out by Dr. Richard Couch in the outlying mining districts of West Cornwall, where, as a mine surgeon, he had many opportunities for investigation. In one particular mine (Balleswidden) he found the average age of the 303 men and boys employed underground to be 29 years 4 months. In a neighbouring mine (Levant) the average age of the 206 persons underground was 28 years 10 months, whilst in a third mine of the same district (Ding Dong) the average age was but 26 years 1 month. (51) As Couch shows, these averages might very easily have been compiled in such a way as to show an even worse state of affairs. They may, at any rate, be taken as representing the highest average age that could be possibly found underground in any of these mines. Experiments made in the Lelant and Nancledrea Mines in the following year showed the average age of the miners working there to be thirty, whilst their average death-age was the same as in the St. Just area—forty-seven years. (52) " The active life of a miner," Dr. Couch concluded, " supposing it to commence at ten years of age, terminates in eighteen years, at the very early age of twenty-eight, when, in most other occupations, he would be in the prime of manhood and vigour." This, taken together with the average death-age, which was reckoned at forty-seven, gave a period of nineteen years of unproductive life, during which the miner was incapacitated from work either by accident or disease. Some men, of course, failed sooner than others, but nearly all were obliged, as they advanced in age, to seek to perform lighter and more healthy duties at the surface, leaving the more laborious and unhealthy work to younger men. Many, however, were incapacitated from work altogether and were often compelled, for the last twenty years of their existence, to depend either on the precarious mine club or to fall at once, with their families, on the union. (53)

The mine club, to which, as already stated, the men paid a monthly subscription throughout their working lives, varied very much in different mines in the benefits which it conferred on the men. In many, if not in most mines, the club granted only what was known as "hurt pay," that is, relief at the rate of 1s. a day or 30s. a month for "external and visible hurts" contracted by the miners at their work. "We do not allow any sick pay," said one manager, "for this reason, that very often in a mine old men come in whose constitutions are already broken, they get laid up, and then there is so much taken away from the fund which would otherwise go towards the man who is hurt, who naturally wants all you can give him." (54)

In some mines, however, the relief was wider in its extent, especially in the large mines of the Camborne-Redruth district.

"Never in any case is the club money confined to visible hurt," said Captain W. Rutter, the manager of East Crofty, in 1864. "The rule says it must be visible hurt, but we have always slipped it over as a matter of philanthropy, and we have relieved men when they have been home with severe colds, and so on, and have continued to do it all the way throughout. If a man has a broken leg, for example, we pay for persons watching him and bandages and anything that he wants. If he wants a bed or a mattress, or anything of that sort, we have always given it. We have many men home for years who have been fairly worn out in the mine, because miners do not live to be very old." (55) In this mine, when the club fund became exhausted, an appeal would be made to the men to pay 2d. in £ more for a little while, "and they do it with great pleasure."

"I have always recommended liberality with regard to club money," stated the purser of Carn Brea Mines, before the same Commission. "We apply it to pensioning off old men who are unable to work any longer on the mine, who have been there for many years, and whose money is spent. We always make them some allowance, and we are not particular about the injury or illness which is occasioned by their work. We treat an illness brought on by working in the mine as a visible hurt. Then, again, out of the club fund we bury the men, and if a man dies from an ordinary illness, not at all connected with his duty in the mine, we always pay for the coffin. Any man working in the mine has his coffin from the mine, and that is always charged to the club at Carn Brea." Ten pounds also was generally allowed to the widow out of the club money. (56) Such talk of allowances for worn-out men, with the added charm of a nice free coffin when the painful business of dying was over, sounds so benevolent and liberal that the reader might almost be led to suppose that it was something especially arranged through the kindness of the purser, and not merely his common honesty in dealing with money which was not his own but the men's. It was not in all mines, however, that the men got what they did in Carn Brea, and the management of club money was, on the whole, perhaps one of the greatest scandals of the old regime.

"I have often observed," stated one witness, "that when mines have been abandoned the men who have been permanently injured there have no means of getting their club money, notwithstanding that the mines may have produced a large sum of money which has been placed in these clubs. It has been taken by the purser or the secretary or otherwise disposed of."

Q. "Do you think, upon the whole, that the club is a matter of profit to the men or to the adventurers?"

A. "I am afraid that it is to the adventurers in jobbing mines."

Q. "Is this money ever applied to purposes connected with the mine?"

A. GEORGE SMITH, Esq.: "Yes, I have seen £300 or £400 balance of the money in the club appropriated to pay merchants' bills."

Q. "Do you know of any case, when a mine has stopped working, of the club money being divided?"

A. "I know of a case in which a mine has stopped when the club money and the doctor's money (a surgeon never having been appointed) have been thrown back among the parties to pay for a dinner that was given at the closing of the affair." (57)

"What became of the club money?" it was asked of another —a mine captain.

CAPTAIN W. RUTTER: "I am very sorry to say that the adventurers devoted some of it to working the mine afterwards. I told the purser, then and there, tooth and nail, that they were taking the blood and bones of the men." (58)

The extent to which this practice prevailed varied much in different localities. One witness from St. Just (Mr. Alfred Chennalls) said: "The miners have recently taken upon themselves to conduct the clubs. They have insisted, by a sort of rise in one or two cases, upon having control of their own moneys, and that the agents should no longer govern them, nor the adventurers in that respect." (59) This was in the mines of Balleswidden, Boscean, and Wheal Castle. In the St. Ives and Lelant area, where the men were probably less powerful on account of the supply of labour being greater than the demand, the club money "was invariably considered as the property of the adventurers." "At Providence Mine," stated the purser, "we have a balance in hand for the club of £268 13s. 5d. Twelve or fourteen years ago we transferred £100 to the credit of the adventurers." (60)

The defence of such a policy was a plausible one, it being argued that when the club was in debt the adventurers stood by it and went on paying the sick or hurt men, and that, therefore, conversely, they had a right to any surplus money when the mine stopped. The crux of the matter lay in the fact that the men had no representation amongst those who controlled the club moneys, and though in some cases the system worked well enough, it left the men too much dependent on persons whose honesty they had no previous means of ascertaining.

In addition to the club, a further subscription of 6d. or 9d. a month was levied from the miners' wages for the mine doctor, who in return took on a contract to attend the men, and in some instances their families also, in cases of sickness or accident. Here again the actual benefits which the men received from such a system varied much. The doctor or doctors were generally appointed by the adventurers, though sometimes the mineral lords or owners of the mine inserted a clause into the lease giving them the power of appointment. Only in a few large mines, where more than one doctor was appointed, had the men any choice in deciding by whom they should be attended, although it was generally agreed by all that " to be pleased with the doctor is half the cure."

Striking evidence of how distasteful this system generally was to the men is afforded by the following letter from a witness, who had previously spoken entirely in its favour.

My Lord,
Since giving my evidence before your Lordship and the other members of the Mines Commission, I have been led to inquire into the opinions and feelings of the miners on the matter of appointing the mine surgeons, and the extent to which they are satisfied with the existing arrangements in use for that purpose.

And from careful and extensive enquiry, I find that I was much mistaken in the evidence I then gave on this subject. Although the men but seldom loudly complain, and are not forward, for obvious reasons, to speak on the subject, I am convinced that there is among them an extensive and deep-seated dissatisfaction with the manner of these appointments, and not unfrequently with the professional men who are so appointed.

I have now no doubt whatever that any measure which would give every man the free choice of a surgeon in any case of accident or illness would be hailed by them as a great boon. (61)

(*Signed*) George Smith.

That the system proved lucrative to all but the most conscientious doctors is clear from the fact that much canvassing of the adventurers went on to gain the post and many medical men took shares in mines solely with a view to rendering themselves the more eligible. Having once gained the position, however, the actual work of attending the miners was only too frequently left to some low-paid assistant of whose medical qualifications no security would be given. In some cases even, doctors living at a distance would be appointed and receive their 6d. a month whilst all the work was done by some surgeon residing in the neighbourhood, the sick men, so we are told, " not finding it *worth their while* to go five, six, or nine miles to the doctor." (62)

To the really conscientious mine doctor, on the other hand, the system was highly unsatisfactory on account of the obliga-

THE MINER AT HOME 269

tions, which he felt the impossibility of fulfilling. Speaking of the fearful mortality and also of the blindness resulting from accidents in the Marazion mining area in 1860, Dr. Couch wrote : " Much of the consequences of this evil might be remedied if they had hospital accommodation and careful nursing. But the men live so far apart and are separated by such barren wastes that the time occupied in visiting is so great as to preclude the possibility of their having so much care as would most willingly be bestowed upon them." (63)

III.

Some miners, of course, were more fortunate than these, and either by working in healthier and better-ventilated mines or by retiring from underground work sufficiently early, escaped the fatal " miners' disease " and other dangers, and were able to live out their latter years independent of bal club or doctors.

"What happens to the miners after forty?" the Commissioners inquired in the St. Agnes district in 1864.

"Many of them go away upon the burrows," was the answer, " picking a little tin. Many of them have help from their friends and retire. There are a great many old men who are not working living in the parish. They take little tenements and work them after they have trained up their children to work at the mines. Whilst they are still young they take a little farm, perhaps at a time when they are unable to get work, and they build a cottage and take in a few fields, and then they have that to fall back on. I suppose that three-quarters of the working men in this parish have money accumulated in the Savings Bank. They are continually paying into the Savings Bank. There is very little drunkenness here. They get a cow or two and a horse, and pick up a living in many ways when they cease to be miners after forty." (64)

"The intermixture of employments is great in all the mining and maritime parts of the county," wrote a correspondent to the *Quarterly Review* of 1857. "The small trader and the farmer are habitually speculators in mines and fisheries. That strange-looking individual whom you, an eastern visitor, may observe in swallow-tailed coat, rusty silk hat, black trousers and stockings, and low-quartered shoes, at work in his croft of potatoes or cultivating a pretty luxuriant two-acre field of wheat in the half-reclaimed flats about Tregonning Hill or St. Agnes Beacon, seems a very heterodox specimen of the British agriculturist ; but if you knew his history you would probably find that he has shares in a drift-boat, a seine, and a neighbouring mine or two, and his soul is at this moment far away from his dirty acres, wandering in El Dorado." (65)

It used to be said that every Cornishman was born and bred with the conviction that he would one day make his fortune by speculating in the local mines. The miners themselves, if they were tributers, generally possessed this feeling no less strongly than the adventuring class, and many of them invested their small savings in the same mine which gave them work.

The lifelong search for tin began when, as little boys, they were first sent to the river for water, and returned with some " slocking stone " in their pocket to ask of father or grandfather whether it might not be tin. This spirit continued throughout life. Tributers, indeed, were " always on the scran," and until death itself removed them at last from their native moors, the prospector's fever never properly left their blood. Nothing delighted the old miners more than of an evening in their little cottages to work over the day's core again, in the presence of wife and children or a few admiring neighbours. Especially would they boast of their own and other men's skill in beating the boryer (drill) in awkward positions underground, no empty boasting, as anyone who has seen them do it will affirm. " He's the prettiest man in Cornwall to use a drill," I have heard miners say ; " single or double hand, 'tes all the same to he. Put the hole downright, cundit, cundit side tosser, brist hole or upper, he can beat 'un faster than any man in the parish."

Many a Cornish miner's wife was, and still is, a good judge of tin, and will speak of her husband's doings with a knowledge which shows her fully conversant with his way of work. " Often," wrote Mr. Bottrell, in his *Hearthside Tales and Traditions of West Cornwall*, " a wife would humour her husband on his return from bal by beginning, ' Well, Tom, my son, and what hast a ben doan to-day ? ' ' What use for me to tell 'e ; I can never make thee understand anything,' he'd say, 'but look here, boys!' At the same time he would take out an old boryer, hammer, gads, and other tools such as used to be kept under the chimney stool in a miner's cottage and, quite pleased, draw out the form of his end in the back of the old-fashioned open chimney, and all would be told to 'look on, say nothan, and learn.' When he had marked out, to his mind, how the end stood, he would say to his wife, 'Now thee cust see the end es about square as a was this mornan, take the boryer and show me where thee west go for a hole.' 'Well, I shud put down a hole there,' she would say, pointing with the boryer in the most seemly place to her. 'Now gos't away, thou great Paddy! I tell thee, Betty, thee doesn't knaw more about such work than a Buryan man! (66) Thee west never larn anything! Give me the tools,' he'd say, and show them all with pride sure nuf, how he'd stand and strike the boryer in the different positions ground is subject to, and so he wed keep on for hours. The way in which Tom and his wife amused themselves was not singular amongst tinners, who, as a rule, took great pride in their work and passed hours showing their family or comrades how they worked the last core and what they purposed to do next."

Many of the miners in the maritime districts, especially around Lelant, St. Ives, and St. Just, held shares in fishing-boats and at certain seasons of the year passed much of their time on the water. Amongst several fragmentary pieces of the Cornish language picked up by Lhuyd in the early eighteenth century, in the parish of St. Just, was the saying:—

> *Sâv a man, kebner tha li, ha ker tha'n hâl;*
> *Mor-teed a metten travyth ne dâl.*
>
> Get up, take thy breakfast, and go to the moor; (67)
> The sea-tide of the morning is nothing worth.

Showing clearly enough that from early times this intermixture of employments was to be found, among the ancient alluvial tin-stream workers no less than the latter-day miners. More than half a century later Pryce, in his *Mineralogia Cornubiensis*, called attention to the same fact. "Our county being altogether maritime and the mines being situated in the most narrow part of it, between the two channels, many of our adroit tinners are equally conversant with naval and subterranean affairs. So true is this that, in St. Ives and Lelant, during the fishing season, they are wholly employed upon the water, to the great hindrance of the adjacent mines; and when the fishing craft is laid up against the next season, the fishermen again become tinners and dive for employment into the depths of the earth. . . . This may seem strange to some of our readers, but we could make it appear that there is in some parts of the two employments a great analogy. It is a maxim among us, that a good tinner makes a handy sailor." The foregoing account may be said to still apply to the parish of St. Just, where, within recent years at any rate, quite a number of small fishing-boats belonging to miners might be seen at Priest and Pendeen Coves, (68) and it is only the temporary depression of mining in the St. Ives district which prevents it from being equally applicable there also.

In many other respects the Cornish miner of eighty years ago was a remarkably independent character, whose life in the outlying districts was as nearly self-supporting and self-sufficing as is compatible with the modern structure of civilization. Having built his own house and cleared his land, the miner, who was also a small farmer, would kill his own pigs and cure them. Milk being, somewhat curiously, a scarce commodity even in the country, many families held a cow, or a share in a cow, and perhaps even made a little butter. In the rough land which surrounded his house, the miner very frequently grew a quantity of potatoes, which, together with abundance of salted fish, supported himself and his family; whilst the furzy crofts gave a sustenance to the donkey which, perhaps, carried him and one or two comrades on a miners' shay to bal. In addition to such occupations as these almost every miner could turn his hand to odd jobs, such as mending his own shoes. "A man," wrote the Commissioners in 1842, "would think it a disgrace not to be able to do this. They do it as well as a cobbler, the father teaching his boys." (69)

Almost every writer on Cornwall, from Carew onwards, has called attention to the high level of intelligence common amongst Cornish miners. "Amongst themselves," wrote Hitchens and Drew in 1824, " they use the greatest familiarity, expressing their ideas without flattery or fear. On many occasions their language abounds with lively sallies of poignant wit, and their sarcasms are frequently keen and pointed. (70) To strangers they are civil in a high degree ; being always ready to communicate the information they desire and sometimes astonishing those with whom they converse by the promptitude of their replies and the quickness of their apprehension." (71)

"When a man is not only a miner but a builder, a farmer, and a fisherman as well, no surprise will be felt at his being both intelligent and well-informed," wrote the Commissioners in 1842. "Miners in Cornwall never appeared to be so deficient in education as in most other counties," said Mr. Taylor, manager of the Consolidated Mines, commenting on the same fact in 1835. "I never knew the time when many of our common people could not read and write, and in fact their business rather requires it, and though I am not very clear how they acquire the knowledge, considering how young they go to work, yet I have always observed the quantity of knowledge they possessed was remarkable. Many of them are tolerable mathematicians in the lower departments of that science." (72) "It has been said of the Cornish miners," wrote a traveller in 1865, "that they possess the mathematics of the mole. Endowed with a species of instinct and an admirable judgment, they find means, practically, of solving certain problems which seem to demand all the calculations of geometry." (73)

"However did you arrive at your results?" asked a Government surveyor on one occasion, with some astonishment, on being told by a working miner the solution of a problem which he himself had figured out by the aid of trigonometry. "Why, sir," replied the man, giving a slight nudge to one of his companions, "I tell 'ee I mizured un up braave and careful, and I found the length of un was two showl hilts, three picks, a mallet, four lil' stoans and so far as I cud spit, jus' zackly."

How and when the Cornish miner of the past found time to acquire even the slight theoretical knowledge that he possessed is a mystery, seeing that many never went to school in childhood at all, and that the majority even of those that did left at the age of seven or eight for work on the mines, where they continued to be thereafter occupied for nine or ten hours a day. The following recollections of Dick Hampton, the Cornish Pilgrim preacher, concerning schooling in the year 1790, would have applied in most respects for quite a generation later.

"When I was eight years owld my paarents sent me to a raiding school, keept by a poor owld man caaled Stephen Martin. My schoolin' cost three a'pence a-week. I was keept theere for seven months, and so my edication was worth no less than three shellin' and sixpence—theere's for 'ee ! When my edication was fenished, as they do say, I was took hum, seven months' larning being aull that my poor paarents cud afford for me. But I shall have to bless God to aull eternaty for that eddication. At that deear owld man's school I larnt to raid a book they caaled a Psalter; and havin' larnt so fur, when I got hum I gave myself to raidin', and keept on keepin' on tell I cud raid a chaapter in the Testament or Bible. Aw, my dear ! what a blessin' thes heere larnin' a ben." (74)

An old miner of my acquaintance used frequently to describe the small dame-school to which he was sent as a child about the year 1850. The school consisted of five or six little boys and a similar number of girls. The course of instruction did not go much beyond the alphabet, which was chalked up on a large blackboard in the old lady's kitchen. Her son was an engine-driver at one of the neighbouring mines and usually returned from work about half-past three or four in the afternoon. The old lady would always have a "fuggan" (heavy cake) made hot and ready for him, and this he used to eat as a dessert after his dinner of broth or pasty. The cake was always divided into little squares, one of which was given to each child as a taste if he or she had been good. Some schools were more ambitious in their course of instruction than this one and included even geography in their curriculum.

"'Hes Coornwall a nashion, hes a a Hiland, or hes a ferren country?' an old school-dame, Peggy Combellack, would ask.

"'He hedn't no nashon, he hedn't no highlan, nor he hedn't no ferren country,' the brightest of the scholars on one occasion answered.

"'What hes a then?' asked Peggy.

"'Why he's kidged to a furren country from the top hand,' was the reply, which was heard by the whole school with much approval, including old Peggy herself. On Saturday mornings 'Peggy' would always give out about the school-money which had to be paid before work commenced on the following Monday. 'Now mind the money, Monday, cheldren,' she would say, 'if you haant got a penny, high'd taake candels or a corner of a pasty. They that come weth nort, 'll be sent home agen.' Strange to say, on the Monday morning, out of fifteen scholars, only three, perhaps, brought pence, twelve bringing pieces of pasty or candles. Peggy was not particular so long as they brought something. She usually sent one of the children shopping in order to 'swap' her candles for tea, sugar, treacle, or snuff. The old lady was not singular in this, as in those days everybody did the same, for there was very little small change passing." (75)

In addition to the dame-schools such as these, there were, in 1840, about twenty-seven small day-schools scattered throughout the length of Cornwall. To these a few of the children found their way for a short period. The knowledge of many of the teachers themselves was often extremely limited, whilst some were grossly ignorant and, like those in the northern colliery areas, had apparently only "resorted to tuition as being easier than manual labour." (76)

The masterships, however, were generally too ill-paid to attract a better class. Such books as there were, were provided by the parents—a fragment of a Testament and a small spelling-book being the most usual; whilst for the few more advanced the Bible and the elementary books of Pinnock, Murray, and Goldsmith. (77)

In one or two districts evening-classes were also held, to which the boys paid 3d. a week if they brought their own candle and 3½d. (78) if this was provided for them. The mines themselves occasionally contributed towards the expense of the schools where the children of their employees attended, (79) but generally the evening-classes, like the day-schools, were endowed by private charity.

The majority of the children, after leaving the dame-schools (if they had been even there), received no further instruction except such as might be got at the Dissenting and Church Sunday Schools, which, however, taught little general knowledge except reading. As attendance at the Church schools often meant a two or three-mile walk, repeated twice in the day, in order to be at the two Church services, few children were anxious to avail themselves of this privilege.

Twenty-two years later, when the second Commission visited the Cornish mines, they found educational conditions little changed :—

"How many hours a day do the children of nine or ten work?" it was asked in 1864.

"They go to work at seven in the morning and leave work at five, and they stop for one hour in the middle of the day for dinner."

"They have not much time for education?"

"No."

"Do you find that the children in your mines can read or write?"

"They can all read, but they cannot all write."

"Are there any evening-schools established to which these children can go of an evening to receive instruction?"

"Some schools, but not enough to take one-tenth of them, I should think."

"So that many of these children have not an opportunity of obtaining any education if they go so early to work?"

"Not in the evening, except in the Sunday-schools; they are open to all." (80)

The matter and method of instruction afforded to the children in the Wesleyan schools at this time is worthy the attention of curious educationalists. "The children are taught reading, the Conference Catechism, spelling, and the recitation of verses learnt from the Gospels or the Psalms. For this last a reward is given at the rate of 5d. per hundred verses. The retentive memory evinced by some of the children is surprising. A boy aged twelve on one occasion recited 363 verses, and on another 400" (= 1s. 8d.).

"The prizes consist of books; some earn valuable ones—Josephus's *History of the Jews*, Watson's *Theological Dictionary*, Baxter's *Saint's Rest*, etc. One little boy, only ten years old, received from the Bible Christian Association a bible of the value of half a guinea!" (81)

What wonder, indeed, if religious education has latterly suffered some eclipse, when the music of the Psalms is no longer valued by the pennyworth in hard cash. Out of justice to the unconscious humourist here quoted, as well as to the, now old, men to whom it applied, it is but fair, perhaps, to add his conclusion, which was that the boys of St. Blazey, sixty years ago, were not the faultless beings described in story-books, that they liked marbles and "clidgy," and preferred changing their money, when they had any, for these delights rather than giving it all to alms-boxes.

Seeing the elementary nature of the little instruction they did get at school, the only explanation of the miners' sometimes unexpected degree of book knowledge lay in the fact that what they missed in opportunity they made up for in enthusiasm and intelligence. They could not all read the newspapers then, but they possessed something of the shrewd, discriminative faculty which enabled them to think clearly on many subjects for themselves. I well remember an old tin-dresser whom I frequently used to visit at his work. One morning I found him sitting beside his stamps reading, in the intervals of work, a tattered copy of the *History of the Reformation*. His remarks on Luther showed at once how clearly he had grasped the significance of the book he had been reading. His general keen intelligence showed itself in many other ways besides his work, the knowledge which he displayed of the history of his native parish alone entitling him to the appellation of no mean antiquary. Yet this man had started work as a buddle boy at the age of ten years, walking twice daily to a mine six miles away from his home! The comparison between himself and his son was a significant one. The latter had received a full Board School education and at a later date had gone out to work in America. Throughout the whole of his working life he had been in receipt of wages which to his father would have appeared princely, and yet (in the opinion of everyone except himself) as far as culture and general intelligence went, he was never fit to hold a candle to the older man.

The thirst for knowledge, indeed, which many of the older generation displayed cannot be recalled to-day without a sense of sadness by those who have witnessed how much cheap standardized education has done to destroy the very interests it was intended to promote. That many, on the other hand, in whom the wish for knowledge was strong in the past had to reach it by undesirably hard and laborious ways, must also be admitted. An old miner who died in recent times has thus described what was by no means an uncommon experience in the 'forties. "The first book of any account I purchased was Dr. Dick's *Christian Philosopher.* Oh! how proud I was to think I could now have some fine works I never formerly imagined was in existence. Then his *Celestial Scenery,* then followed his *Philosophy of a Future State,* and his *Philosophy of Religion.* I thought what a grand library I possessed. I used to read them to my mother. She was a very intelligent woman and was delighted to hear about the stars and especially about the planets. When reading about the distance of the earth from the sun, I was amazed and wondered how was it possible for any man to find that out. I concluded that if it was possible for one man it might be for another, and I determined I would not rest until I knew something about it. There were two good schools in Camborne; one was conducted by a man called Chatham, who was a kind of art teacher, that is, he used to teach drawing and beautiful writing. The other man was called John Thomas, and was more of a mathematician and could teach several languages. He was a brother to Captain Charles Thomas, who for several years was manager of Dolcoath Mine. I put myself under his tuition. I was working at Great Condurrow Mine, which was on the top of a range of granite hills about a mile from the town. I was working eight-hour shifts, and when forenoon shift I should go up a little after 2 p.m. There was no grand dry on the mine then, provided with a bath whereby the men could have a wash before going home. I had to go to the school with my dirty face and hands because I could not stay to go home to wash. At the other shift I had the chance to appear decent. I studied very hard and gained a knowledge of arithmetic, mensuration, geometry, algebra, conic sections, and the specific gravities of substance. When I left school I continued my studies at home and commenced the study of trigonometry, land surveying, and mine surveying. I did not smoke or drink intoxicants, I put my spare money to buy books, and in a few years I had a decent library. Shortly after this, I commenced the study of theology and joined the Methodist Church. I was asked to have my name put on the plan as a local preacher." (82) This simple relation of facts tells of the aspirations of one who was by no means a priggish exception (in spite of the theological bias of the writer's outlook), but who was representative of many Cornish miners of the last generation.

The system of "local preachers" here mentioned was one which trained many of the miners to be both fluent and original speakers. Mr. R. M. Ballantyne, in his justly famous novel, *Deep Down (A Tale of the Cornish Mines)*, has well described the eloquence of men of this type who were miners throughout the week and preachers in the chapels on Sunday. "It was a new and impressive thing," he wrote, "to hear the thrilling, earnest tones of the preacher as he offered up an eloquent extempore prayer—to the petitions in which many of the people in the congregation gave utterance at times to startlingly fervent and loud responses—not in set phraseology, but in words that were called forth by the nature of each petition, such as 'Glory to God,' 'Amen,' 'Thanks to Him'—showing that the worshippers followed and sympathized with their spokesman, thus making his prayer their own. But the newest thing of all was to hear the preacher deliver an eloquent, earnest sermon, without book or note, in the same natural tone of voice with which a man might address his fellow in the street—a style of address which riveted the attention of the hearers, induced them to expect that he had really something important to say to them, and that he thoroughly believed in the truth of what he said."

Fine and worthy men many of the local preachers undoubtedly were, living according to their lights throughout the week the doctrine that they preached on Sunday. Being, too, in direct contact with all the problems which beset the honest hard-working poor, they could speak of life in the exact terms and language of their hearers. That the local-preacher system had its meaner, pettier side, that jealousies often arose amongst those who had acquired a "little learning" and no more, and that the bandying about of questions of heterodoxy and theological dispute sometimes obscured the essentials of their mission, was, of course, as true in Methodism as in other denominations. The local-preacher system had its amusing side, too.

"While working at Dolcoath," wrote the before-quoted miner, "my father-in-law and myself employed a mason to build a house in one block for us; this man was a local preacher with the Bible Christians and not too honest (!). He put very bad work in the roof that could not stand an ordinary storm. About this time a great religious revival took place in the parish. There were prayer meetings held in the mines, on the surface and underground, in the shops and in the people's homes; men, women, and children were calling on the Lord to have mercy on them. There were midday prayer meetings carried on in the Town Hall by the various ministers in the town. At one of the meetings my father-in-law was standing beside the blessed mason that built our houses, and the mason got in an ecstasy and began to rub his hands and shout in a very loud voice, 'Glory, hallelujah, 'tis the sign of an abundance of rain,' and my father-in-law shouted in his ear, 'Then it will be a bad thing for our houses.' This was in October, and just immediately after this I could not sleep one night for the noise of the slates rattling and flying off the roof." (83)

Among the most famous of Cornwall's miner preachers was Billy Bray (1794–1868). Never was a preacher more calculated to attract audiences by his eccentricities or to hold them by his joyful intensity, as when he spoke to them in their own language of the presence of God in their everyday life. Very frequently his illustrations in preaching were directly taken from some local incident within the experience of all his listeners. "I remember once," wrote a friend, "hearing him speak with great effect to a large congregation, principally miners. In that neighbourhood there were two mines, one very prosperous, and the other quite the reverse, for the work was hard and the wages low. He represented himself as working at the latter mine, but on 'pay-day' going to the prosperous one for his wages. 'But had he not been at work at the other mine?' the manager inquired. He had, but he liked the wages at the good mine the best. He pleaded very earnestly, but in vain. He was dismissed at last with the remark, from which there was no appeal, that he must come there to work if he came there for his wages. And then," said the writer, "he turned upon his audience and the effect was almost irresistible, they must serve Christ here if they would share His glory hereafter, but if they would serve the devil now, to him they must go for their wages by and bye." (84)

"Oh, you Western men!" Billy would conclude at the end of some such "refreshing" meeting. "I am an old miner. Come to heaven. If there is one crown short I will willingly go without one. But there is no want there. I tell 'ee it is a good thing to change a miner's hat for a crown." (85)

Frequently, in the fervent days of Methodism, as has already been said, services were held on the mines. References to such meetings are not infrequent in the autobiographies of local preachers. "On one occasion," wrote Dick Hampton, "they broft me to Godolphin Mine, and theere, stannin' up in a buckin' house, the Lord gave me power to exhort hundreds of people." Such meetings were not always without interruptions, but these were frequently silenced by some apt quotation, for the local preacher's knowledge of the Bible was generally very intimate. "Just as I had stopped spaikin'," continued Richard Hampton, "a poor drunkard come foath with a glass of brandy in hes hand, and said a wud maake the praicher drink un. 'No,' says I, 'you wean't, an' let me tell 'ee what the wise man says, "The drunkard shall come to poverty, and drowsiness shall clothe a man with rags."' God's word was enough for he, so he went on hes way." (86) At another time, when on the eastern borders of the county, the same preacher went to the Canal Mine, near Gunnislake. "My pulp't," he wrote, "was the count-house stears; an' the miners behaaved very daisent, an' showed that they felt the word."

Not infrequently before going underground at the beginning of a shift, Billy Bray would kneel in the midst of the men who worked with him, and pray: "Lord, if any of us must be killed or die to-day, let it be me, for they are not happy; but I am, and if I die to-day I shall go to heaven." (87) Oftentimes impromptu services were held underground in the intervals of work. "I was grateful," wrote one Methodist parson, after visiting a mine, "to hear my guide speak of the 'wells of salvation,' at which down in that deep, dark, damp mine he and other pious miners often had 'times of refreshing from the presence of the Lord.' Billy Bray once referred to those mine services in a way I shall not soon forget. I was preaching at a camp meeting and, in the course of my remarks, said, 'The joys of religion are not all confined to heaven; many of them may be realized down here.' Billy, who was present, at once responded, 'Praise the Lord, I've felt them at 250'" (88) (i.e. at 250 fathoms underground).

Such was the simple, earnest, joyous faith of Cornish Methodism at its best. Many of the local preachers, it is true, were "fiery" enough in their discourses, and by nearly all the working classes of the last generation the doctrine of fire eternal was taken in its most literal sense. Yet, as a whole, Methodism in Cornwall has always shown itself kindlier and less "dour" than in its acceptance elsewhere, and frequently called forth a deep humour of its own, in its attempts to show the course to happiness in this world and the next, rather than to torment its followers with fears of death everlasting. It was this which caused men like Billy Bray to literally leap and dance for the inexpressible joy of their faith, often to the bewilderment and misunderstanding of those who did not fully appreciate how essentially local was this interpretation of Methodism to Cornwall.

Nothing short, however, of such a spirit could ever have supported those Cornish miners of the last generation in their hours of self-imposed labour which they spent in raising the little chapels of whitewashed stone which, until recently, were such a feature of the country-side in the mining areas. Though some of these have since been replaced by ecclesiastical imitations of the poorest kind, many of the older sort still remain, and by faraway roadsides and lonely crofts remind the traveller of the simple practical love of early Cornish Methodism. Few indeed, however, of those who pass by them in their cars to-day, or even of those who worship within their walls, realize at what sacrifice of time and strength much of the original work was done.

"I was a very poor man, with a wife and five small children, and worked in the mine underground," wrote Billy Bray concerning an occasion when he was building one of his chapels almost single-handed. "Sometimes I was forenoon 'core,' and when I had taken my dinner I should go to the chapel and work as long as I could see, and the next day do the same. The next week I should be afternoon 'core'; then I should go up to the chapel in the morning and work until the middle of the day, and then go home and away to the mine. The week following I should be night 'core,' I should then work about the chapel by day and go to mine by night; and had not the dear Lord greatly strengthened me for the work, I could not have done it. When I was about the chapel, I had potatoes to 'teel' in my garden and every Sunday I was 'planned.' Sometimes I had to walk twenty miles, and speak three times. I have worked twenty hours in the twenty-four." (89)

Nowhere, perhaps, could a better insight be gained into the simple dignity of Cornish Methodism than at a walking funeral of some miner as it passed along the open highroad towards one of these chapels, with granite hills ringed about. Looking down on the little procession as it passed along, the listener might catch the sound of the "burying tune," such as was always sung on the way by the mourners as their last tribute to the dead :—

> " Sing from the chamber to the grave,"
> I hear the dying miner say;
> "A sound of melody I crave
> Upon my burial day.
>
> " Sing sweetly whilst you travel on
> And keep the funeral slow;
> The angels sing where I am gone
> And you should sing below.
>
> " Then bear me gently to my grave,
> And as you pass along,
> Remember, 'twas my wish to have
> A pleasant funeral song." (90)

The influence of Methodism in Cornwall can be traced from its first inception by the gradual taming down of the mining population and the consequent falling off of fighting, wrecking, smuggling, and hard drinking. " I have known the miners for thirty-six years," wrote Mr. Taylor, manager of the Gwennap Consolidated Mines, in 1835. " I think their moral habits are generally improved. They are less inclined to drunkenness, I think, than they were thirty years ago. Methodism has had good effects. There is not now the fighting which was formerly prevalent." "Forty-five years ago," wrote a correspondent to the *Western Morning News* in 1865, "Sunday in the mining districts was a scene of debauchery, drinking going on from morning till night." Little change indeed seems to have been observable in the adventurer class at this date, and the "count" and ticketing dinners still retained their vinous character. As these, however, were confined to persons of a different social order, they were naturally described in the newspapers in much more flattering terms.

In the outlying districts, it is true, many of the miners were still a fairly rough lot. In 1842 it was stated that the men from Wheal Vor were considered less steady and industrious in their out-of-work hours than those to the eastward. The Monday after pay-day was customarily known here as Bad Monday or Maze Monday, on account of the men's habit of spending it in drinking. As late as 1850, we are told, a miner in the western districts, in Breage and Sithney especially, could hardly pass from his own parish to another without danger of being assaulted and maltreated. An old man, not so very long since dead, remembered in his youth funeral processions of miners brought to Breage from other parishes being assailed with showers of stones. Sunday, however, was kept as a day of truce, and on that day a miner from an outside parish might be borne to rest without danger of an assault to his friends as they followed him to the grave. (91) Those who remember St. Day as it was more than sixty years ago likewise recall the drinking and fighting which took place there when pay-day at Poldice and the Consolidated Mines chanced to fall on the same Saturday. On such occasions the miners would come to the public-houses in great numbers and generally take a room upstairs, where they divided the money of their month's tribute earnings. This was afterwards followed by a big feed, when the beer flowed in such a literal sense that it might often be seen running down the stairs and through the door into the street, as the drinking became wilder as night went on.

In spite of this, however, there is no doubt that the miners, as a whole, were taming down, and both drinking and fighting were becoming much less common than they had been in former days.

A very noticeable feature in the character of the Cornish

miner throughout these years was the smallness of the interest which he evinced in politics. This, too, has often been ascribed to the influence of Methodism, which, by means of the channel of the local-preacher system, absorbed much of that mental energy and need for self-expression which in other parts of England was devoted to social and political controversy. "We have few turbulent demagogues in Cornwall," stated a writer in 1865. "A miner who has any rhetorical powers and strong lungs prefers the pulpit to the platform." (92) In addition to this, the long course of neglect and indifference to their interests which the Cornishmen had experienced at the hands of many Governments had doubtless helped to cool what little political ardour they had, and had turned their main interests into other channels. Cornwall, as Boulton had pointed out long ago, was too far removed from the seat of government, and perhaps too independent in its attitude, ever to make its influence much felt, nor, whilst its many pocket boroughs were represented in Parliament by jobbing members who knew little and cared less for the interests of the constituencies they were supposed to represent, did any redress appear likely to be derived from attention to political matters. Nevertheless, "the miner of the West of England," as the Commissioners noted in 1842, "is a man of frank and independent manners. He is not often insolent, but he is usually blunt." It would be absurd, therefore, in the light of such statements and from what else we know of his character, to suppose that the older Cornish miner was in all respects perfectly satisfied with his lot, or that it never occurred to his shrewd judgment that something must be wrong with a system in which the mineral lord, without labour or risk, was drawing £20,000 a year from his dues, whilst he was earning £30 per annum under conditions always of hardship and often of peril. Yet, on the whole, the tendency of the best brains amongst the miners remained individualistic rather than socialist. A sturdy independence marked their character and the whole course of their working lives. The situation of their dwellings, the nature of their work, their system of earnings, their local patriotism—everything, in fact, within the Cornish miner's sphere was averse to the spirit of interdependence and outside interference which socialism compels.

But though not much interested in outside politics, certain fundamental measures affecting their daily lives, particularly in respect to the supply of food and the payment of wages, still roused the Cornish miners of the nineteenth century into forceful protest, as they had their forefathers in older times. How utterly different, however, such disturbances were in Cornwall from the spirit informing those in industrial England at this time may be judged from the following account of one which occurred in the Helston district in the year 1831.

"On the morning of February 22nd," states the writer, "a party of 3,000 miners collected from the parishes of Breage, Gwennap, Crowan, and Wendron passed through Helston in complete order for the avowed purpose of preventing further shipments of corn at Helford. Near Mawgan they were met by H. Grylls, Esq., who entreated them to return, but they would not. One of the leaders said, 'If you, sir, will go with us, we will not do any mischief; but if you do not, perhaps we shall be unruly.' They proceeded to Gear and to Treath, near Helford, where small quantities of corn were found which was promised them should not be shipped, but brought to market. From thence they went to Gilling, where they found in Mr. Roskruge's cellars several hundred bushels of barley and wheat. Four of the leaders entered the cellars and measured the depth, length, and breadth of each pile of corn and computed the quantity. Having been promised by the son of Mr. Roskruge that all the barley should be sent to the market, they set out for their homes without committing any acts of violence. About five o'clock in the evening they entered Helston in perfect order. They declared that their only object was to obtain an adequate supply of barley at the different markets on the 25th. On another occasion, a few days later, as some corn was being carried through Breage to Penzance, a great body of people, mostly females, supposing it was about to be shipped, stopped the wagons, from which they took the corn, but without committing any depredations on it. Subsequently, on finding that it was to be ground at a mill near Penzance, they carefully housed it, and on Monday delivered it to the persons sent to fetch it, without any part of it being missing." (93)

During the hungry 'forties, further disturbances of a like

nature took place. The following reminiscences of an old miner concerning the happenings of his boyhood are of interest in this connection. "The miners at this time," he wrote, "were maddened to think that their wives and children could not have their fill of bread. One Saturday I went with my Mother to Helston market, and it was the pay-day with the miners. I shall never forget what I saw on that Saturday afternoon. Coinage Hall Street was thronged with miners from the bottom to the Market House on the top of the street, all armed with shovel handles and pick handles. I saw the soldiers march with difficulty up the street; they were about sixty or seventy in number, very young men. They were so pressed by the miners that they could scarcely move along. I saw a gentleman on the Market House steps reading; my mother told me it was the Riot Act. I could not hear what was said because of the tumult. I was told that the commanding officer ordered his men to fire a volley in the air, but they refused, and no wonder. I should think the miners were twenty to one soldier. If they had fired, every man of them would have been killed or disarmed. I saw a great quantity of bread distributed among the hungry crowd. I was informed that the mine agents bought a great quantity of flour and sold it to the men at a cheaper rate." (94)

"Only once have I known anything like a political demonstration," stated another writer to the *Western Morning News* in 1865. "That was at the repeal of the Corn Laws. Some ingenious individual simplified the matter in the miners' eyes by having a large loaf and a very diminutive one carried on long poles, with the inquiry appended: 'Are you for the small or big loaf?'

"This was a very exciting question to a man who spends two-thirds of his income on bread and flour, and afterwards all who were deemed protectionists—squires, clergymen, or mine captains—men who had previously been held in estimation or even awe, became for some days subjected to every species of insult and annoyance."

In the year 1830 a rising of a somewhat different character occurred among the miners of Fowey Consols, who objected to the way in which their tribute pitches were at that time being set. Accordingly, on a certain day they assembled in great numbers on Par Green and held what was then considered a riotous combination, as the result of which seven of their leaders were seized and carried to Bodmin Gaol. "Next day," continues the chronicle, "having gathered in still greater force, they started off with hatchets and pick-hilts, determined to rescue their comrades. In the meantime, at Bodmin, thirty or forty special constables had been sworn in, and the Royal Cornwall Militia were placed in and around the prison. The rioters sent a deputation consisting of six or seven persons to the High Sheriff at the gaol, to explain their object. The Sheriff reasoned with them on the consequences of their conduct and sent them back to their comrades. On their return they were accompanied by some of the respectable inhabitants, who reasoned with the mob, and at length induced them to depart. As a reward for this peaceable demeanour, the persons who spoke to them gave each a pint of beer and a penny loaf, which they thankfully received." (95) Considering their numbers, the inhabitants of Bodmin were doubtless glad to be rid of them so easily, and, indeed, the poor men's price at a penny loaf and a pint of beer was not a high one.

As may thus be seen, such slight disturbances as these, however ominous they may have looked to the ruling authorities at the time, in reality possessed little or no political significance. In character and spirit they were in every way entirely local, owing nothing to outside instigation and amounting to little more in the long run than sober remonstrances against evils which could be, and afterwards were, locally remedied.

IV.

The miner's life of sixty years ago was not, of course, wholly without play-time nor necessarily one ceaseless round of work. It is true that holidays as they are understood to-day were practically non-existent, Christmas and Good Friday being then the only ones which were general in all mines. In some cases, as at St. Austell and St. Just, the day of the parish feast was added to these, whilst in other districts half a day was allowed at Whitsuntide and on Midsummer Day. (96) In one instance only, at Levant Mine, the men were allowed six days' holiday in the year (without pay), in accordance with an ancient custom. (97) This, however, does not by any means represent the full amount of time which the men took off from their work, for, in addition to Maze Monday, that is, the Monday after Saturday pay-day, few tributers worked every core throughout the month.

Down to recent years, Midsummer Day was observed with great festivity in all the mining districts of West Cornwall, when an allowance, generally at the rate of 1s. per man, was given by the mines for the men to make merry. Early in the morning on this day a flag was hoisted on top of the headgear or else at the corner of the engine-house, and those who were not working first core by day went up to the Carns to beat the "Midsummer holes." At twelve o'clock all work ceased and the men came up from underground. The holes, which had been charged with gunpowder (called "plugs" in the Wendron district), were then fired off in brisk succession, and by the time night came on bonfires would be seen blazing on all the hilltops and beacons around as far as eye could reach. Corpus Christi Day likewise was the occasion of great festivity, especially in Penzance, where tar-barrels were lighted in the streets and men and boys with flaming torches rushed through in wild procession. In the country-side of the western parishes scarcely a cottage, however poor, but would have its farthing dip placed in the window after dark to celebrate this day. So, too, St. Peter's Fair in Camborne and Whit-Monday Fair in Redruth (the latter preceded by the preaching and prayer meeting at Gwennap Pit) were time-honoured holidays which no miner would miss.

But best of all holidays in the miner's year was the day of the parish feast, which, until the middle of the century, at any rate, retained much of its old-time spirit of revelry. During the week-end of the feast open house was kept and friends and neighbours came from miles around, in sometimes embarrassing numbers, to share in the victuals and drink provided. Throughout the day hurling, wrastling, kailles (ninepins), and kook (quoits) were largely practised, beer and "moonshine" (spirit that had not paid the duty) were drunk in large quantities, and the sports often ended with a free fight. Though beginning to be looked upon askance by some of the busybody "reformers," the old traditional sports of Cornwall, wrestling and hurling, continued at this time to be still the most popular form of recreation in the mining areas of the West. Fifty years ago in St. Ives it was a regular custom during the winter months for the miners to come to town every Saturday afternoon and try a hitch with the fishermen on the sands below the wharf, whilst on every Feasten-tide the silver ball was "hove up" and the men of St. Ives, Towednack, and Lelant strove for the mastery of their parish in the old three-cornered "hurl to country." Nor were the amusements of the people entirely confined to physical sports and games. Sixty or seventy years ago, when nearly a hundred thousand persons were employed in connection with the mines, the country districts were packed with men, and every little village had its band, as well as its parties of "curl" singers and guise dancers, who enlivened the neighbouring farms and houses at Christmas-tide.

During the 'sixties and 'seventies, however, ways and manners were surely, if but slowly, altering and many of the old-time feasts and revels were giving way to temperance meetings and popular "tea-drinks," run by the chapels. (98) Throughout this period, indeed, nearly all the influences at work in Cornwall were adverse to the continuance of almost every form of amusement which was both local and popular. Those who, however misguidedly, had the moral welfare of the people at heart, and those in whom an affectation of gentility took the form of despising everything local, were at this time in unison in decrying what was considered to be the "barbarous" nature of Cornish recreations. So hurling was nearly wiped out altogether and wrestling was driven to seek refuge in public-house circles, where it, too, rapidly degenerated. (99) The would-be reformers, however, soon found that to eradicate all taste for sport was not so easy as it looked and, in place of the old local pastimes, football was introduced and soon acquired a more sinister reputation for roughness than even wrestling had held.

With the increasing number of social occasions and the opportunities for display provided by chapel-going, tea-drinks, Sunday-school treats, and the like, there developed among the Cornish people a great attention to dress and a love of finery undreamt of in earlier times. Sundays, in the mining districts of the 'sixties, saw the men coming forth in handsome black "surtouts" and the women in a perfect blaze of finery, whilst the poor bal maiden of the week had to regulate her expenditure with some care in order to put by the 10d. or 1s. a month at which the best seats in chapel were now valued. (100) Such changes, indeed, had religious fervour brought about that the really poor and destitute scarce dared to venture from their cottages on Sundays and their pains and poverty were thus kept comfortably out of sight and mind of their Sabbath-keeping neighbours. Curiously enough, the Cornish people, with all their newly acquired love of fashion, were peculiarly censorious of any signs of the same in their pastors. " Wesleyan ministers never dare to wear the gown or bands with us," wrote a newspaper correspondent in 1865, " though in other counties it is customary. A minister said : ' They would think it looked like pride and be injurious to our cause. They hate pomp and ceremony in religion.' " (101)

The attitude of the ruling classes towards this growing love of display was one of shocked disapproval. The days of drinking and wrestling had been bad enough, but now they found that the " packmen " who travelled the country-side were inflicting " serious injury upon the comforts and morals of the people." " They go round with the packs," wrote the Commissioners in 1864, " and exhibit their finery and coax the women to take it, telling them they may pay 6d. or 1s. a month, and when once the goods are received they have them entirely under their power, and summon them by a dozen at a time to the County Court." (102) With the unmarried girls the position was said to be still worse. " The girls have worked all day for a very small wage, generally seven or eight pence," wrote a visitor to Cornwall in 1865. " Sometimes this money is honourably employed to support an old mother, or else proportionately to augment the comfort of the family, but only too often this small sum is used to satisfy coquetry. In vain do the parents strive to combat this fatal inclination : the girls leave the cottage plainly dressed, but under the nearest hedge they take out of their pocket a veil, a brooch, or some other ornament. The workwomen of the mines have an inveterate foe in the packman. This name is given to a pedlar who sometimes sells everything—sugar, tea, coffee, but more especially feminine finery. As he comes back every fortnight, he is also called, in familiar language, Johnny Fortnight (Johnny-go-Fortnight). This man tempts the girls in their weak point—vanity. As he does not ask for cash payments, and, on the contrary, is satisfied with a small instalment every fortnight or month, the bargain is soon concluded. If a girl is on the eve of marriage, the packman persuades her that she wants a wedding outfit. 'She can pay this debt hereafter out of her husband's wages, and the transaction will be kept secret,' for Johnny Fortnight represents himself as a model of discretion. It is always the same story, the compact of the maiden who sells herself to the fiend." (103)

Notwithstanding the many modernizing influences and spread of religious teaching following on the introduction of Methodism, popular belief in ancient spirit influences unrecognized by church or chapel still remained. Down to recent times the belief in the power of white witches or "pellars" to cure many ills which lay beyond the reach of medical science has constantly been shown. Great distances were sometimes sent in order to consult these descendants of the ancient medicine-man. A writer in 1865 said that he knew of a case where a St. Austell miner, suffering from dropsy and heart disease and beyond the help of doctors, sent all the way to Redruth to consult a celebrated white witch, who ordered him to be touched with blood taken from his ill-wisher. (104) White witches made it their especial profession to stop bleeding and to cure external skin diseases simply by passing the finger with a circular movement over the part affected and making the sign of the cross. (105) There are many people still living who have seen this simple operation performed.

Considering the nature of their work, encompassed with darkness and dangers throughout long hours of labour amongst the silent dripping levels of the mine, followed by lonely walks at midnight to their scattered cottages across the downs, there is small wonder if belief in spirits and other supernatural phenomena remained late amongst Cornish miners. Certain mines in particular were said to be haunted by familiar spirits, the best authenticated being that of Dorcas, at Polbreen, the wraith of a woman who had committed suicide there long years ago. Her special delight, it was said, was to torment the miners when they were at work, by calling their names and in other ways enticing them to leave their occupations. Only on one occasion is Dorcas said to have acted kindly. Two miners were at work in an end, beating the borer, when the name of one of them was heard distinctly between the blows. They stopped and listened, but all was quiet. As soon as work was resumed the name was shouted again, but no notice was taken until it was pronounced more vehemently than before, when the man called threw down his hammer and went to see who wanted him. Immediately he did so a great mass of rock fell on the spot where he had been standing and enclosed his companion, who, happening to be protected by a projecting rock, was taken out alive. Dorcas was always credited with saving the life of the man who moved. (106) Dorcas's fame is not yet forgotten among the old miners of St. Agnes, though one who had worked in " Darkey's Shaft" as a boy informed me that he had never heard "mouth speech" from the old lady's spirit.

Still more remarkable is the story recorded in the *West Briton* of Mr. John Lean, a member of a well-known Cornish mining family, who, on one occasion, whilst walking through a level in Wheal Jewel (Gwennap), absorbed in examining a rich course of copper ore in the roof or back, was suddenly startled by the words, "You are in the winze," as though pronounced by a human voice. At the time when these words were uttered he was hundreds of fathoms distant from any other person in the mine. He at once, however, threw himself flat on his back in the bottom of the level and, on sitting up, discovered that his heels were, in truth, on the verge of a shaft or winze, left open and exposed, and communicating with the next level, ten fathoms below. When warned he was about to take a step that would have resulted in death. (107)

In addition to such phenomena as these, many stories are told of dead hands which have been seen holding candles in the shafts of certain old mines and portending death to the seers. At Wheal Vor the appearance of a black dog which haunted a certain engine, and of the white hare which appeared in another part of the mine, were likewise taken as certain portents of disaster. (108) So, too, before the great fall of ground which entombed eight men in Dolcoath in 1893, the miners heard "a God-send" in the form of cracking sounds and trickling fragments (109); whilst at the inquest on a miner killed in one of the St. Just mines a year or two ago it was affirmed that the deceased had received warning of the disaster in a dream on the previous night.

The horror which the fishermen of Cornwall, as elsewhere, showed towards the hare was also shared by the miners. Snails, too, or "bulorns," as they are known in Cornwall, had their peculiar folklore associations, and if they were met with by the miner on his way to work were propitiated by a bit of tallow dropped from a candle or else by a crumb of his dinner. (110)

These scraps of miners' folklore, however, are of small importance compared with the stories of the tribes of small people, known as "knackers" or "pick and gad men," who were thought to work in the mines. The belief in these little underground spirits is, of course, widespread, and the tales of the "knackers" of Cornwall have their counterpart in the mines of Wales, Germany, and Scandinavia, as well as in the collieries of the North of England. The Cornish "knackers" are generally described as "little withered, dried up creatures," of the size of children twelve months or two years old, with big, ugly heads, faces like old men, and ungainly limbs. Some think that these little creatures are the spirits of people who inhabited Cornwall thousands of years ago, and who, though too good to be condemned to hell, were not good enough for the joys of heaven. Formerly, it is said, they were much larger than children, but ever since the birth of Christ they have been getting smaller, and eventually would become "murrians" (Cornish *murionants*) and disappear. By others the knackers are spoken of as the spirits of the Jews who crucified Our Saviour; and, in confirmation of this, it was said that they never worked on Christmas Day, on the Jews' Sabbath, on Easter Day, or on All Saints' Day. Further, it was said that on Christmas Eve, when even the oxen in their stalls fell on their knees in praise to God, the knackers ceased from their labours and held midnight Mass in the deep levels of the mines. Those who have been underground at such times have heard melodious voices, sweeter than any earthly choir, singing "No well, no well! the angels did say," whilst at the same time deep-toned organs shook the rocks. (111) At ordinary times the knackers were heard by the miners only in the intervals of their own work, when the cries of the little people mingled with the beating of boryers, the falling of rock, and the rolling of barrows appeared to be going on, apparently in the solid rock, close by them. Amongst themselves the knackers were considered exceedingly playful, but a demureness came over them when they knew that they were being watched. Generally these little elves were considered friendly in a freakish way, and the miners thought they did especially meritorious service by leading them to valuable mineral, as "knackers" were rarely heard working except in rich ground. But they could be vindictive, too, and this a miner soon found if he shouted disrespectfully to them or neglected to follow the custom of leaving a part of his dinner on the ground for their enjoyment. "As stiff as Barker's knee" was once a common saying in Cornwall, said to commemorate a man named Barker who treated the knackers disrespectfully, and who in return lamed him for life by throwing all their tools in his lap. (112)

A story is told by Bottrell, in his *Traditions and Hearthside Stories of West Cornwall*, of a miner named Tom Trevorrow, who, hearing the knackers near him on one occasion as he was at work by night, roughly told them to "be quiet and go," upon which a shower of stones immediately fell about him, giving him some fright. Soon after this, while Tom was eating his croust, a number of squeaking voices sang :—

> Tom Trevorrow! Tom Trevorrow!
> Leave some of thy fuggan for bucca,
> Or bad luck to thee to-morrow!

But Tom was a scoffer and took no notice and ate up all he had brought, whereat the small people changed their tone and they sang :—

> Tommy Trevorrow! Tommy Trevorrow!
> We'll send thee bad luck to-morrow;
> Thou old curmudgeon to eat all thy fuggan,
> And not leave a didjan for bucca.

After which, it is said that ill-luck so continuously followed him that at last he was forced to leave the mine and take to farmer's work, which, to a born tinner like Tom, was almost as bad as going to the workhouse straight away.

In addition to such agelong beliefs as these, many natural phenomena were attributed by the old miners to supernatural agencies. Amongst these may be mentioned the small dancing lights generally known in Cornwall as Jack-o'-Lanterns, but in the Wendron district dignified into "Tin Lanterns," (113) on account of their supposed virtue in showing where metal exists. The most famous story connected with the appearance of these lights is that told of North Basset Mine, near Redruth, whose fortunes about 1850 were said to have been completely changed as the result of them. Copper was thought of chiefly in those days, but, search as they would, the miners could not discover sufficient mineral to meet costs; and as things went from bad to worse, the agents became full of gloomy forebodings. Casually, they would say to an elderly woman who lived close by, "Nothing can be done, Gracey; we shall have to knack the bal." But "Gracey Mill" always made the same reply, "Take'n try over there, do 'ee; that's where we seed the Jackey Lanterns." For a while no notice was taken of the advice, but when everything else had failed, miners were set to work in the place recommended by Grace, and in a short time they met with what has been described as one of the richest deposits of malachite, red oxide, and black and grey copper ore ever found in the county. From it profits amounting to over £90,000 were made, and "Grace's Shaft" is still well known on the property. The old lady, during her lifetime, was granted 5s. a month by the mine, in addition to being given a grand new dress annually in recognition of the value of her advice. (114)

Among curious practices still sometimes adopted in searching for lodes, "dowsing" (i.e. divining with the forked rod) should be mentioned, being one of those phenomena still only half on the borderland of accepted fact. Yet those who have frequently seen it practised and noted the score-marks left on the hands of the dowser as the rod turns irresistibly downward when passing over the place where metal or water exists cannot reasonably doubt that the gift is a perfectly authentic one in some persons.

Many ancient customs and curious practices observed by former generations of miners in Cornwall have only fallen into disuse within living memory. As an example, Mr. F. J. Stephens, of Reskadinnick, Camborne, tells me that within the last generation it was the habit amongst old miners to place a little image of clay over the first set of timbers on the entrance to a level, and that when the level was begun a curious formula was uttered, beginning: "Send for the merry curse and the priest." Though religious significance had long since departed from it, the rite is clearly one dating from before the Reformation, whilst the formula may well be, as Mr. Morton Nance suggests, a Cornish invocation to Camborne's patron saint.

> *Synt Meryasek ny a 'th prys* . . .
> Saint Meryasek we pray thee . . .

The horseshoe, on account of its shape (a crescent talisman), has always been regarded as an omen of good luck, and occasionally one used to be placed in the engine-house of a mine for the men to touch before going underground. Four men engaged in sinking a winze in Tincroft Mine in 1886 took a horseshoe underground and nailed it to the top of the brace. Each man touched the shoe four times and started work. One day the afternoon and forenoon "cores" met on the man-engine: "How did 'ee git on?" asked one of those going down. "Well, you," came the reply, "we touched the auld shoe four times, but didn't git on but slight." (115)

Other customs of a not dissimilar kind have lapsed in their observance within still more recent years. Amongst these may be mentioned the breaking of a bottle of whisky over the engine "bob" at the christening of a new mine, hanging up a bush of holly on the tackle of the headgear at Christmas-time, and in some districts the placing of a green bough on top of the shears on St. John's Day also. (116)

Customs such as these died late in West Cornwall, and they go far towards illustrating one side of the Cornish miner's character and his outlook on the mine in which he worked. For the miner, like the fisherman, was from the beginning of times a hunter—with all the hunter's feeling for omens and propitiatory ceremonies. Conservative by nature and deeply attached to the way of his own country, the chain of custom and tradition which linked the Cornish miner to his forefathers of untold generations was, until recent years, an unbroken one.

The imaginative instinct, it is true, which once peopled the dark underworld of the mines with spirit forms has now been gradually turned by the preaching of Wesley into other channels and its outward manifestations have changed, but the spirit itself not all the materialism of a machine-driven age has as yet been effectual in killing.

NOTES.

1. *Hist. of Cornwall* (1817), vii, 102.
2. R.C.P.S. (1835), 35.
3. About the beginning of the last century white shirts, stockings, and even cloth clothes could scarcely ever be afforded by miners (R.C.P.S., (1841), 100), whose garments were quite insufficient to keep them warm in winter. Old coats, dresses, petticoats, and even sacks were used as bed coverings in the cottages.—*Cornish Magazine*, ii, 114.
4. Parl. Pap. (1842), 813.
5. Parl. Pap. (1864), 43.
6. Parl. Pap. (1864), 146.
7. Parl. Pap. (1842), 792.
8. Cf. *Coal and Coal Pits.*
9. Parl. Pap. (1864), 101.
10. Parl. Pap. (1864), Appendix B, 6.
11. Cf. *Cornish Magazine*, ii, 110, etc.
12. Parl. Pap. (1864), 11, and Parl. Pap. (1842), 772.
13. Parl. Pap. (1864), 19 and 20.
14. Parl. Pap. (1842), 851.
15. T. Oliver, *Autobiography of a Cornish Miner*, 12.
16. Parl. Pap. (1864), 120–1.
17. Up to the period of the War, decent houses in West Cornwall were built for £60, stone being found on the site and the building partly done by the occupier himself.
18. Parl. Pap. (1864), 120.
19. R. Thomas, Report on Mining Area (1819), 15.
20. Parl. Pap. (1842), 753.
21. J. Y. Watson, *British Mining*, 40.
22. F. J. Stephens, R.C.P.S. (1893), 113–20.
23. Rev. Sims Carah, *Cornish Almanack*, 1926.
24. Parl. Pap. (1864), Appendix B, 5 and 11.
25. R.C.P.S. (1858), 3.
26. Parl. Pap. (1864), Appendix B, 5.

27. *Western Morning News*, January 28, 1865.
28. Parl. Pap. (1864), 15.
29. Parl. Pap., " Lead Mines of the North " (1864).
30. Parl. Pap. (1842), 806.
31. Engels, *Working Class in England* (1844), 250.
32. Parl. Pap. (1842), 848.
33. Manchester Statistical Society (1859), 4.
34. Parl. Pap. (1864), 240.
35. Parl. Pap. (1864), 240.
36. Parl. Pap. (1864), Appendix B, 6.
37. Esquiros, *Cornwall and its Coasts*, 63.
38. Esquiros, *Cornwall and its Coasts*, 63.
39. Parl. Pap. (1864), 11.
40. Parl. Pap. (1864), 111.
41. R.G.S.C. (1830).
42. Cf. Parl. Pap. (1864), 82.
43. Couch, R.C.P.S. (1858), 34.
44. R.C.P.S. (1858), 34.
45. *Works*, viii, 522 (edit. 1725).
46. *Nat. Hist.* (1758), 292.
47. *Mineralogia Cornubiensis*, 197, etc.
48. *Observations of the Western Counties* (1794–6), i, 238.
49. Parl. Pap., " Accidents in Mines " (1835), 275.
50. R. Blee, R.C.P.S. (1847), 15.
51. R.C.P.S. (1857), 37–40.
52. R.C.P.S. (1858), 26.
53. R.C.P.S. (1857), 39.
54. Parl. Pap. (1864), 115–20.
55. Parl. Pap. (1864), 111.
56. Parl. Pap. (1864), 110.
57. Parl. Pap. (1864), 108.
58. Parl. Pap. (1864), 114.
59. Parl. Pap. (1864), 109.
60. Parl. Pap. (1864), 177.
61. Parl. Pap. (1864), 238.
62. Parl. Pap. (1864), 118.
63. R.C.P.S. (1860), 35.
64. Parl. Pap. (1864), 261–3.
65. *Quarterly Review* (1857), 315.
66. A purely agricultural parish in West Cornwall.
67. That is, go and work to Tin; they call that especially going *to Moor*, when they work in the Stream Tin.—Pryce, " Archaeologia Cornu." *Britannica*, 1790.
68. " Priest " = *porth Just*—St. Just's Cove.
69. Parl. Pap. (1842), 839.
70. The use of family nicknames, frequently given in the first place

for some quite trivial cause, still continues strong in Cornwall. In the eighteenth century many of the tinners seemed to have been known by these names and nothing else, since they occur in the wage-bills of mine cost-books. Such were Thomas Edwards All-abroad, Sidney Scholar, Richard Tubby, John Lucky Buck, Will Rogers Sailor, William Cornish Hair-Lip, William Pearce Snuffler, etc. Many of the other nicknames were Cornish, as, for instance, Wella Govdrack, Will the Snubnose, etc.—Cf. Great Work Cost-Book, also Tonkin, *Notes to Carew*.

71. *Hist. of Cornwall*, i, 727.
72. Parl. Pap. (1835), v, 223.
73. Esquiros, *Cornwall and its Coasts*, 71.
74. *Life of Foolish Dick* (1873), 16.
75. Charles Bath, *Uncle Kit's Legacy*, 13–18.
76. Parl. Pap. (1842), 801.
77. Parl. Pap. (1842), 802.
78. Parl. Pap. (1842), 802.
79. Parl. Pap. (1842), 803. North Roskear Mine paid 1d. a week for each child.—Parl. Pap. (1864), 121.
80. Parl. Pap. (1864), 121.
81. *Western Morning News*, January 10, 1865.
82. *Autobiography of a Cornish Miner* (1914), 16–17.
83. Oliver, *Autobiography of a Cornish Miner*, 19.
84. Cf. *The King's Son*, 27.
85. Cf. *Life of Samuel Thorne*, 156–60.
86. *Foolish Dick*, 48.
87. *The King's Son*, 18 (2nd edit.).
88. C. G. Honor, *Fish, Tin, and Copper*, 25–6.
89. *The King's Son*, 56.
90. C. G. Honor, *Fish, Tin, and Copper*, 54.
91. Coulthard, *Breage with Germoe*, 79.
92. *Western Morning News*, June 16, 1865.
93. *Annual Register* (1831), 38–9.
94. *Autobiography of a Cornish Miner*, 12–13. About this period several cases of sheep-stealing occurred in the Gwennap district. On one occasion the men left the following notice on the gate of the field :—

> Dear Sir William, do not weep,
> We've had one of your fat sheep;
> You are rich and we're poor,
> When this is done we'll come for more.

95. *Annual Register*, February 22, 1831.
96. The old tinner holidays of St. Perran's Day and "Chewidden" seem to have quite gone by this time. As early as 1824 Hitchens and Drew wrote of them : "These days are now regarded with less veneration than formerly, many of the tinners knowing little about them and caring less."—*Hist. Cornwall*, i, 725.

97. Parl. Pap. (1842), 848.
98. *Western Morning News*, August 10, 1865.
99. From this unhappy state it has recently been set on a good basis again by the work of the Cornish Wrestling Association, whilst other of the ancient pastimes of Cornwall are now also being brought to notice by the spreading movement of the Old Cornwall Societies.
100. *Western Morning News*, August 23, 1865.
101. *Western Morning News*, September 20, 1865.
102. Parl. Pap. (1864), 101.
103. Esquiros, *Cornwall and its Coasts*, 74.
104. *Western Morning News*, April 6, 1865.
105. *Western Morning News*, April 6, 1865.
106. A. Bluett, *Cornish Magazine*, ii, 273.
107. *Cornish Magazine*, ii, 273.
108. *Cornish Magazine*, ii, 267.
109. Herbert Thomas, *Entombed* (1893).
110. Courtney, *Feasts and Folklore*, 131.
111. *Cornish Magazine*, ii, 269.
112. Courtney, *Feasts and Folklore*, 128.
113. R. Cunnack MS.
114. *Cornish Magazine*, ii, 268–9.
115. *Cornish Magazine*, ii, 274.
116. The latter is said to have been in commemoration of the Saint's preaching in the wilderness. A similar custom is still observed (1925) on Ascension Day by Breton quarrymen.

CHAPTER VIII

FIFTY YEARS OF CHANGE IN THE MINES

THE period of the 'fifties and early 'sixties saw Cornish mining at the floodtide of its prosperity, and this small corner of the British Isles heading the list of production of the copper and tin ores of the world. The earlier part of the nineteenth century was essentially the copper period in Cornwall. The opening up of Great Crinnis, Fowey Consols, South Caradon, Tresavean, Gwennap Consols and the United Mines, Penstruthal, Wheal Buller, Wheal Basset, South Frances, the Roskears, the Setons, and a host of others had all been on account of copper, and the fortunes made in these mines at this time were practically on copper alone.

Ever since the first decades of the eighteenth century the output of Cornish copper ore had been steadily on the increase. Between 1726 and 1735 it had averaged little more than 6,000 tons—by 1771-87 the annual production was over 30,000. During the years 1790-93 accounts are lacking, but by 1794 production had risen to over 43,000 tons. In the year 1798 more than seventy mines in Cornwall were engaged in working for copper. (1) During the first decade of the nineteenth century the price of copper began to rise again steadily and a greatly increased production resulted. In 1806 the output was 79,000 tons, in 1822 nearly 107,000 tons. By 1838, 151,000 tons had been reached, which, with the high standard then reigning, represented a money value of practically £1,000,000 sterling.

In comparison with these figures the output of tin was a small one. From 1750-85 the approximate annual production of metallic tin was 2,600 tons. In 1786, when the great output of Anglesea copper was adversely affecting the Cornish copper mines, many of the miners turned to tin, with the result that the production of that metal rose to over 3,000 tons. This figure was maintained until the year 1798, when it again dropped back to 2,800. It was not until 1815 that the output of tin started to rise once more, but from that year until the abolition of coinage in 1837 the production averaged a little over 4,500 tons. In the year 1838 Henwood calculated that from about two hundred mines at work the value of tin produced was only £462,000, as compared with nearly £1,000,000 worth of copper. To put it in another way, the combined output of black tin from ten large mines at work in 1914 and 1916 almost equalled the total production from Cornwall in 1837, when two hundred mines were working—the amount in 1914 being 6,500 tons and in 1837 not more than 7,000 tons. (2) These figures show clearly enough how comparatively small, according to modern standards, has been the production of Cornish tin in the past and confirm the statements of many eminent mining men and geologists, who claim that, in spite of centuries of working, more tin remains in Cornwall to-day than has ever been taken out of it.

Down to the late 'sixties, therefore, it is safe to say that, with certain exceptions, the mining industry still looked to copper as its mainstay and support. Then came the discovery of the great copper deposits of Lake Superior, combined with the increased productiveness of several of the Spanish Peninsular mines, in particular Rio Tinto. As a natural result a great fall in the price of copper took place, and, as when Anglesea was flooding the markets ninety years before, disaster followed in Cornwall. Many of the older generation who had so long seen Cornwall heading the list of the world's tin and copper producers once again became filled with the gloomiest forebodings, and not a few believed that the end of the industry was at hand and that the long course of Cornish mining was finished. Indeed, as the price of metal steadily dropped, there was good reason for depression. Whole mining areas, like that around Gwennap, which had once employed a population of 10,000 people, grew more and more insignificant, till finally the end came, and in all that district, once humming with human and mechanical activity, not a single mine remained at work. In the streets of St. Day, which formerly had been packed with miners on a Saturday evening, the grass now grew and broken shutters swung dismally on the windows of empty houses. Not only here but in many other of the one-time flourishing mining camps in the east as well as in the west parts of the county the same process was taking place.

Adversely, however, as foreign competition was affecting Cornish copper-mining, it is quite clear that it was not the sole cause of the depression, since many of the mines were becoming less productive for copper even before any serious fall in the price took place. "In ten years our production of copper ore has decreased from 147,330 to 88,603 tons," wrote the mining correspondent of the *Cornishman* newspaper on November 4, 1868. The time had come, indeed, when the supply of high-grade Cornish copper ore was pinching out, at an average depth of about 1,000 feet from surface. The fact which was really significant, however (though not fully appreciated at the time), was that many of the great copper-mines prior to their abandonment were beginning to make tin in their bottom levels, where the altering character of the lodes showed unmistakable signs of a change in mineral content. The transition stage, however, left the mines in most cases very poor, for in the palmiest copper days, when almost every mine had been worked under the cost-book system, profits had been divided up to the hilt, and no capital was placed in reserve for an emergency such as the industry was now faced with.

The mines thus situated, without any money for development, with old-fashioned machinery suitable only for the treatment of copper ore, and as often as not controlled by men who were "copperers rather than tinners," bowed to the inevitable and closed down. A few mines only, more fortunate or more provident than these, obtained the necessary capital to continue sinking and development and were able to prove a point which has since been of far-reaching importance to the industry, namely, that tin exists below the copper in the aureole of metamorphosed ground surrounding the granite. This accounts for the fact that several mines such as Dolcoath and Levant (already referred to in a former chapter) have continued in one unbroken course of working for a hundred years, and that the first mine, after yielding a profit of more than £1,000,000 on copper, has since gained a further sum of like amount from the working of the deeper tin grounds below. In a similar way, Wheal Kitty, Tincroft, Carn Brea, East Pool, Wheal Agar, South Crofty,

Botallack, and other mines in the parishes of St. Agnes, Illogan, and St. Just, all originated for copper and turned to tin producers in depth, owing their long continuance in working to the spirited recognition of the same fact on the part of the adventurers.

Compared with the number of mines formerly at work, however, those which succeeded in passing straight from the copper to the tin-producing stage were few. Those which did were still further embarrassed by the phenomenal drop in the price of tin which took place during the 'nineties, (3) when, after falling from £100 to £86 in 1891, the metal touched rock-bottom at £64 per ton in 1894. At this miserable figure it remained until 1898, when it suddenly recovered to £122 per ton. From that time until the Great War the price of tin never averaged less than £118 for the year. The damaging effect, however, on Cornish mining of the slump of 1894-8 was seen in the number of tin-producing mines which became derelict at this time, not in the least degree from exhaustion, but merely on account of the low prices temporarily ruling in the metal market. With the stoppage of such famous mines as Trumpet Consols, Great Work, Wheal Sisters, Ding Dong, Providence Mines, Giew, and St. Ives Consols, to mention but a few in the west, (4) work practically ceased in many of the parishes which had once lent their names to flourishing mining areas. Many of these mines would have paid to work again immediately the price of tin rose to over £100 a ton, and, still more, would give handsome returns with metallic tin at anything over £250. Mines once abandoned, however, require capital to unwater and re-develop them again, and for this not a few of them are still waiting. An effect of the slump of 1894 was, for the time being, to engender a complete loss of confidence in home mines among a public largely ignorant of economic causes and supposing the one cause for the abandonment of mines to be sudden poverty in their mineral resources. Those who took the trouble to inquire for themselves, however, then, as now, felt very differently about Cornwall's future. For as the figures already quoted have shown, tin-mining in Cornwall, owing to the smallness of its output in early times and the lack of vigour with which it was prosecuted during the copper period, may be said to be still in its infancy in many districts, and has undoubtedly a long future before it. (5)

It is, no doubt, true that Cornish mining in the last decades of the nineteenth century required a certain amount of speeding-up in order to hold its own with the outside tin producers with whom it now found itself in serious competition. The short-sighted policy of not allowing the men to earn more than a certain sum per month had induced a leisurely way of working which the costs of modern industry could not stand. A well-known Cornish mine manager stated in 1896 that he did not think the average Cornish miner at that time actually wielded his tools for more than $4\frac{1}{2}$ hours per day. "They start to go down at 6 a.m. perhaps. The last do not reach the bottom before 6.45. Then they wait for their tools to be sent down, and about 7 o'clock are getting to their places. Before working, however, they have 'croust.' I never saw men in Levant or in any mine in America or Africa eat underground before working, but here it seems to be the custom. After that they begin to work and keep it up till 10.30. Then they have more 'croust,' and resume work about 11.30. After another $2\frac{1}{2}$ hours at it they make their way towards the shaft and are ready for the first turn of the gig." (6) The actual amount of work performed largely depended, of course, on the energy and health of the individual men. Conditions underground, too, varied considerably. As late as the beginning of the present century, ventilation was, in some cases, extremely insufficient, and in mines where the temperature of the bottom levels was frequently over 90° F., and even seasoned miners were brought to surface in a state of collapse, little real work could be expected of the men. This, together with old-fashioned, or still more frequently worn-out, machinery, caused many companies to make a loss in working which could be, and subsequently has been, avoided.

One of the beneficial results, therefore, of the slump in Cornish mining in the 'nineties was that it taught the industry as a whole the necessity of a greater economy in working and the mode of reducing overhead costs by increasing output and replacing human labour by machinery. The taunt of being behind the times can no longer be held up against the industry as a whole to-day, and those who still persist in such an opinion are generally themselves about twenty years out of date and have little knowledge of the changes which have revolutionized Cornwall since the beginning of the present century. It is no exaggeration to say that a mining man of the last generation returning to Cornwall to-day (1927) would recognize few features at surface to remind him of the workings of a Cornish mine with which he was once so familiar. The Cornish beam pumping-engine, it is true, has retained a place on account of its proved efficiency and economy in working, and in some cases has been reinstated where electric pumps have been tried—and failed. Gone, however, are the lines of creaking flat rods which once drew the water from distant shafts or worked the man-engine, on whose slowly rising and descending beams the miners "rode" from work to surface. Gone, too, or almost gone, are the Cornish steam stamps, and with them the old "fire-whims." In consequence, therefore, the number of tall, gaunt engine-houses, once so characteristic a feature of the Cornish landscape, is rapidly diminishing, their disappearance not unregretted by many who recognized a grim beauty in their weathered strength. On the dressing-floors of the mines, too, the long sheds wherein the bal maidens used to be seen with their heavy hammers spaling ores, are now all swept away, and the bal maidens themselves are part and parcel of the past.

So likewise are the ramshackle wooden buildings below the stamps, where scores of women and children formerly earned a hardy living, shifting sand with their long-hilted shovels, or tending the jigs, trunks, strips, hand-frames, square buddles, and other paraphernalia of the old style of tin-dressing. In place of them have arisen crude buildings of galvanized iron and floors of concrete wherein elaborate machinery is driven by belts from a network of shafting overhead. Human labour, now become so expensive, is in the minority in these new surface-workings, and in great buildings wherein scores of persons would once have found employment the buzz of machinery has taken the place of the "maidens'" song and but two or three men may be seen, attendant on the engines. Among such new surroundings the old "grass capun," in his white coat and billycock hat, or the mine manager, in his "par stack," would look strangely out of place, and these, too, have given place to a new generation of mining men—machinists, electricians, surveyors, and geologists, each with a label and a specialized craft of his own.

Underground, amongst the miners, the tributer has, for the time at any rate, disappeared, and the ground, both lode and country, is now broken by the ton or fathom on contract only. The reason generally adduced for this is that the employment of tributers, each of whose ores have to be sampled separately, entails methods too slow to be adopted in modern mines. Dolcoath, however, until recently the largest of all Cornish mines, was employing very considerable numbers of tributers down to the stoppage after the War, and here it was generally agreed that in sections of the mine where the lodes were small, pockety, or partially worked out, such men were of great advantage to the company. Within recent years a combination of tribute and tutwork has been adopted with advantage in one or two mines for "driving ends." Thus, for example, if the contract price was estimated at £10 per fathom, the men in such cases have been allowed £7 per fathom, with an additional 3s. or 4s. in the pound on all the ore they picked clean and sent to surface. To-day, however, the usual method of payment of miners has become either by "ton work" when on development, such as shaft-sinking or cross-cutting in the country rock, or else by contract for the "running" fathom (i.e. fathom in length of height) when engaged on narrow lodes. This latter system has many advantages and, as the result of it, stopes of only two feet in width are being advantageously worked in the St. Just district by men with single hand-drills.

Many instances, however, have occurred where the lode itself has been set either on ton-work or by the cubic fathom, and in these cases it is no uncommon thing to hear the miners, among themselves, boast of how they have run the drills up into the hanging wall and sent away tons of clean granite to surface in order to make a good pay-day. Very properly does the Report of the Tin Tungsten Research Board (1922) state that, if the miners are not tributers but paid only by ton work, " the closest supervision has to be exercised in the mines to ensure that nothing but ore proper reaches the surface," but, in spite of such warnings and the most careful supervision on the part of the " shift bosses," there is no doubt that the system is still very open to abuse.

FIFTY YEARS OF CHANGE IN THE MINES 309

The modern "tutwork" men or contractors so far resemble the tributers in that they pay for their own materials, as in former times, buying candles, fuse, "dynamite," etc., from the mine at what is said to be practically cost price. In addition to these the men generally buy their own underground clothes, although in some cases the shaftmen engaged in very wet places are provided with a suit of oilskins each year.

Contract accounts are now usually settled up at the end of each month, though the men are entitled to receive "subsist" after the first fortnight. The payment of wages both to surface hands on day-work "at Company's account" and to miners on contract is thus made at shorter intervals than formerly. One man only in each of the "pares" of contractors is paid, the division of the money being afterwards made by the men themselves. The mines, in most cases, provide change, so that no resort to the public-house is necessary. As an incentive to good work, bonuses are given in some mines, arranged either on a scale of increased output or according to the monthly profits made by the Company. Boys no longer go to work underground at the early age which was formerly common. Few will now be found under sixteen years, whilst most of them are older. The desire for a "white collar" job, though less strong in Cornwall than in other parts of England, is gradually being felt even amongst Cornish miners, and a complaint is sometimes made that the boys are not coming forward to the extent they once did. The men on the whole, however, show themselves a sober and contented lot, and with reason, for though wages are somewhat lower than in other parts of England, living is decidedly cheaper. (7)

The number of hours worked underground is now less than frequently obtained in the past, being eight from surface to surface, but it may safely be said that during that time labour is more vigorously kept up. The days are past when men lay down and slept out a candle on first getting underground or carried a book of carols with them and waked the levels with melodious singing, "to put away the time." Even to-day, however, long cores are occasionally worked by the men, who will do a "doubler" of fifteen hours on end in lieu of going to work the next day. This, however, is not done by many. The number of paid holidays varies in different mines according to custom. Good Friday and Christmas Day are the only ones general in all, but August Bank Holiday, Whit-Monday, and half a day at Midsummer and on St. Just Feast are also allowed in some of the western mines. Through another excellent arrangement, it is being made possible in some cases for every employee to take off one day in each month if he so chooses. In addition to these, no work except that of attending to the stamps and pumping engines is done on Saturday afternoons or Sundays. It is to be noted also that there is now much less working by night than was formerly the case, the general experience being that the efficiency of the men at such times is not equal to that by day.

Underground, nearly all the work is now effected with machine-drills driven by compressed air, although in some instances stoping is still done on a large scale with single hand-drills, in the use of which St. Just men have always been celebrated. Owing to communications between levels being made at more frequent intervals than formerly, and the levels themselves being opened to a more or less standard width, ventilation is now much better than it used to be, and the miner's health ought in consequence to show an improvement.

Since the introduction of National Health Insurance, the old "bal clubs" on which the Cornish miner was formerly dependent in sickness have disappeared. By the payment of a small additional subscription the miner can now obtain medical aid not only for himself but for his family also, with the additional advantage of being able to choose his own doctor. In the St. Just mines alone the old system of "death money" is still voluntarily kept up amongst the men. By this, if any man employed at the mine dies or is killed, the men contribute at the rate of 1s. a man and 6d. a boy to the purser, who places the sum in the widow's hands on the first pay-day after the death.

During the same period which has witnessed so many alterations in the working of the mines, a change in management has also come about by the substitution of the limited liability company for the older cost-book system. This has resulted in what is usually considered a more cautious and stable method of working. How far, however, the cost-book system was to blame for the short-sighted way in which many of the mines had formerly been run is a moot-point. There are those who still hold that the older system had much in its favour, and that in cases where the bills were "paid up close," and the purserships were in the hands of men of integrity, considerable advantages accrued. Not the least of these was the fact that the adventurers could formerly keep a closer hold and inspection on the way in which their money was being spent than to-day, when a large capital is called up all at once. The much greater subdivision of the shares, however, and the increasing number of "out-adventurers," whose financial standing the rest had no means of ascertaining, led, in the first place to the general introduction of the limited liability company, and there is no doubt that it has now come to stay.

Nor were the mines the only ones who were brought face to face with new economic facts during the depression of the 'nineties. The mineral lords also were taught the lesson of greater reasonableness in the matter of dues. Many landowning families, who, in the eighteenth century, were exacting royalties amounting to as much as one-sixth from the mines working on their property, now signified their contentedness to receive one-thirty-second, or even temporarily to forgo such payments altogether. To-day, though prospecting and the taking up of setts by small parties of men is perhaps made more expensive than is always necessary, the mineral lords of Cornwall are generally reasonable enough in respect of their dues from working mines.

The result of returning interest in Cornish mining was seen in the activity which began to be shown throughout the county about 1904. In some respects this boom did good to Cornwall and led in more than one instance to the permanent and profitable re-working of abandoned mines. Side by side with this genuine mining, however, the combined circumstances of the high price of tin and the novelty of electric power provided just the opportunity desired by the company-promoting shark, who is ever on the watch. Tales of the Cornish "bal capun," and the way in which unfortunate London adventurers have been swindled at his hands, have long provided a favourite theme amongst raconteurs, but how rarely has the mirror been held up to show the reverse side of the picture ! Too often it is forgotten that in times of mining depression, such as the 'seventies and 'nineties, not only the outside shareholder suffered but many a Cornish family backed the local mines with almost the last penny of their capital, and lived or fell according to their fortunes. So again at other periods, when the mines have been booming in recent years, though it is not unnoticed that Cornwall still has many sinners (as well as saints) in its midst, it is generally found that the former resemble the older "saints" in being, at least nine times out of ten, of "furrin" extraction and of shady antecedents.

The boom of 1906, "the electric boom," as it is sometimes called in Cornwall, was one of these occasions which must always be regarded as a somewhat mixed blessing by those whose interests are concerned with genuine mining and not merely with the formation of companies or the selling of machinery. That neither electricity nor any other mechanical aid will render a poor mine rich or produce good lodes where none exist would seem to be a patent truth, (8) yet time and again it has been proved how attractive a bad investment can be made merely by the introduction of such "surface indications" as machinery. Cautions with regard to "sensation" mines have proved every bit as necessary in recent years as when Salmon wrote of them in the early 'sixties. He said: "The public opinion of the metallic mining districts utterly disavows this class of mining, which is supported by, and indeed owes its existence to, the unreasoning credulity and cupidity of 'outside' speculators." Almost every disaster in Cornish mining of later times has been attributable to this same reckless credulity. All who know the mining areas will recall instances of companies formed to work mines which seem almost to have been chosen for their depth, chargeableness, or poverty, and where, after money has been spent like water, almost all on the surface, affairs are wound up, and half-finished buildings and rusting parts of machinery alone remain to tell the tale of roguery or folly. Those who get their fingers cut in such enterprises can hardly execrate this kind of mining more bitterly than those who look on and see money thus wasted, whilst legitimate speculations containing lodes of proved values are only awaiting the "Open Sesame" of capital to convert them into what might be paying mines.

Mismanagement of capital, however, by those actually engaged in the running of the mines is probably a less frequent cause of mining failures than the deflection of unduly large sums into the pockets of individuals who hold mine setts or who engage in the promotion of new companies. This last abuse forms what is known in London as "office fees," or in Cornwall, less politely, as "plunder." In this connection it is well to give further publicity to a warning note recently struck in the columns of the *Western Morning News*. "A century ago," says the writer, "the beginning of a new venture was a simple and comparatively inexpensive incident of frequent occurrence, for the ventures of those days were small undertakings in their initial stages. The starting of a modern mining company is a different problem. It unfortunately opens out possibilities of abuse whereby locally one or more individuals who have been lazily 'sitting' on a sett, doing really nothing, may come in for a large unearned sum of purchase money; and whereby, at the same time, equally useless and non-productive individuals in London, or elsewhere, may make large encroachments on a new company's capital. The local 'sitter' may be regarded as an ancient relic or survival, but the receiver of unearned 'promotion' money is a more modern growth. Both are obstacles to success; both have injured the mining industry; both are still very much alive. How are the really interested parties affected? The lord sees his property lying idle. The merchant looks in vain for the market for his goods. The officials and employees have to seek a livelihood in foreign climes. The adventurer receives little or no dividend, even when the company continues in operation, for the company has become a victim to *over-capitalization* and finds it impossible to spread an appreciable dividend over the unduly inflated capital. Obviously, in the circumstances, a special responsibility rests upon the lords. The granting of a licence or a sett to an individual should be for a reasonably limited period only and subject to safeguarding restrictions till an approved company is in process of formation. 'Sitting' should be made impossible. In the matter of excessive 'promotion,' the responsibility mainly rests upon individual adventurers—in other words, the investing public. Each should exercise to the full his own discriminating powers, should carefully scrutinize the prospectus, and ascertain the location and prospects of the properties, as well as the standing of the directors and technical advisers. If he cannot do this for himself, he should not invest till he has had advice through reliable channels."

In spite of such abuses as these, however, which are equally attendant on mining enterprise in every part of the world, Cornwall continued to hold her own successfully throughout the years 1900–14. Worked on a much larger scale than hitherto and with cheaper and more efficient machinery, the panic of the 'nineties was proved an unnecessary one, and it was clearly shown that the home industry could well cope with her foreign competitors. In 1912, out of six large mines at work near Redruth and Camborne, five were dividend payers; (9) and others were operating with equal success in different parts of the county. In 1914 the output of black (unsmelted) tin from Cornwall amounted to something over 6,500 tons, which, though only a small part of the world's supply, was nevertheless won at a profit to the mines and gave a livelihood to six or seven thousand persons directly connected with them.

With the beginning of the War, Cornish mining entered upon a period of somewhat artificial prosperity. With wolfram (tungsten ore), a material of vital importance in the making of high-speed steel, a source of supply within the country was regarded by the Government as an asset of national importance. In 1915 the output of tin rose to over 8,000 tons, whilst the production of wolfram increased from 180 tons in 1913 to 347 tons in 1916, and that of arsenic from 1,500 tons in 1913 to nearly 2,300 tons in 1916. (10) This largely increased production, in spite of enhanced prices and the considerable profits made, was regarded by those who knew the internal economy of the mines as a not unmixed blessing. In the ordinary working of a mine fresh lodes of mineral are being continuously opened up whilst others are being worked. In other words, where the ground is crossed and recrossed with a network of mineral veins one section of the miners is employed in sinking shafts, driving cross-cuts, etc., through unpayable ground to reach them, whilst the rest are providing the income of the mine by extracting ore from such lodes as are already opened. The work of the first is called development. During the War, the demands of the Government, who called at the same time for many of the best miners for the Army and an increased production of tin, wolfram, and arsenic from the mines, could only result in a policy suicidal to sound mining. It meant that the highest-grade ore alone could be worked, that "the eyes of the mines had to be picked," and that the development and exploration of fresh ore reserves became a practical impossibility. It was not at the moment that the evil effects of this were felt. During the next year or two, tin rose steadily in price, though, owing to Government control, it never attained the figure it might otherwise have reached. In spite of control, however, in the early months of 1920 tin had risen to the phenomenal price of over £400 a ton. Hardly had it done so before a reaction set in. From April 1920 onwards the price of tin dropped steadily day by day, till by March 1922 it registered £141 a ton, or, in other words, £40 a ton lower than it was in 1914, whilst coal, in the meantime, had risen from 15s. to over 50s. a ton. With these two adverse conditions combined against them, the mines had either to cease working at once or else to receive some form of subsidy to carry them over the period whilst their ore reserves were being once more developed and working re-established on a normal economic basis. For such assistance the Cornish mining industry considered that it had a just claim, seeing that its then parlous position had been largely brought about by the demands made on it by the Government during the War. The help, however, which was granted for a similar purpose to the coal-miners who struck was refused to the Cornish miners who did not strike. The mines were accordingly closed down. Those who could afford to bear the pumping charges kept the workings drained in the hope of better times, and those who could not, abandoned them altogether, whilst the money which would have reinstated them and many more to an economic basis of working was given away in the form of dole to the miners who were thus thrown out of employ.

The poverty and distress which ensued in the mining districts during the next two years was perhaps hardly realized outside the immediate areas concerned. With the cessation of work in the mines many hundreds of men and their families were deprived of their only means of livelihood, the depression affecting not only the miners themselves but the employees in tin-streams, smelting-works, foundries, explosive manufactories, and numerous other trades and employments bound up with the mining industry. In the towns of Redruth, Camborne, and St. Just, an unprecedented slump in trade followed on the closing down of the mines, a depression which was felt most acutely, perhaps, by the smaller shopkeepers. The result was indeed appalling. For between two and three years an appearance of utter deadness reigned, in so much that the town of Camborne, which was flourishing and prosperous three years before, became so impoverished, through the inability of many of its inhabitants to pay any rates, that even street-lighting had to be dispensed with and night descended on pitch-black roads and a silent town. Hundreds of men left the county at this time for mining camps overseas, and almost every week saw Camborne and Redruth stations crowded with friends and relatives saying good-bye to further detachments of miners who were seeking work abroad. Many more, however, still remained at home, deterred by the reports of lack of employment oversea or unfitted by age or circumstances to start life again in a new country.

The dole system, in the meantime, evil in its influence and effect, did not even enable the men and their families to live without further aid from private charity. From all parts of the world Cornishmen and others came forward with contributions to the aid of the distressed areas. In the towns of Camborne and Redruth, soup-kitchens were opened and free dinners were provided for the families of the workless miners. Had it not been for such charitable response to appeals the position would have assumed an even greater seriousness than it did. Throughout this period, when semi-starvation stared them in the face, the quiet fortitude and orderly behaviour of the mining population won the tribute of all who knew them. In the worst period of their distress the Cornish miners never made the slightest attempt to make their claims felt except through the legitimate channels of peaceful (and entirely useless) delegations to the Government. As in 1788, so again in 1921-2, all sorts of proposals were put forward with a view to relieving unemployment, drainage schemes and the reclamation of land being among the commonest. In most cases such employment amounted only to a charity and could not have been sustained at all without aid, since it was economically unsound. In some cases land which had been originally either given, or let at a purely nominal rent, was cleared at a cost of £200 per acre and was finally let for £10 per annum, having provided employment for a couple of months only. All felt that such measures were but temporary expedients, and that while charity was a practical necessity for the moment, the resuscitation of the mining industry alone could permanently attain the solution of the problem. (11)

It was not, however, until the early months of 1923 that a rise in the price of tin, together with a fall in materials, made the resumption of mining an economic possibility once more. It was then soon discovered that the unprecedented depression through which the industry had passed had created a vast cloud of prejudice in the minds of those who had not studied the *causes* but had only heard of the fate which had temporarily eclipsed the mines. It must be admitted, too, that the choirs of Cornish miners still touring the country, begging money for their distressed companions at home, did not, on the face of it, provide a good advertisement for an investing public ignorant of many of the facts. Among such it was still assumed, as in 1894, that the mines had all closed down (practically at the same moment!) on account of a sudden and miraculous exhaustion of their lode deposits, and here, presumably, further inquiry was dismissed. The action of the Government, therefore, in guaranteeing loans to two or three of the larger mines, under the Trade Facilities Act, was a valuable, if tardy, recognition of the claims of the tin-mining industry and undoubtedly helped to create a certain outside confidence of which it was badly in need. Nor should the plucky action of several new companies at this time go unnoticed. Almost before the revival of prices had set in and it became apparent that Cornish mining was to have a fresh future before it, capital to the extent of £200,000 was being laid out in the opening up of the northern mineral areas of Camborne and Redruth alone. In this latter work the Cornish miner proved to be no less skilful and efficient than his forefathers, and showed conclusively that, given the opportunity, Cornwall could still sink shafts and equip and develop mines as quickly as any other mining camp in the world. These, together with the other mines which had managed to keep their pumps going during the slump, were, of course, the first to resume production and to benefit from the favourable price which tin has since maintained.

That Cornish mining has once more come back into existence is due solely to its own merits and the fact, which was emphasized in the case of the above five or six mines, that the temporary failure of the industry was not due to any exhaustion of its mineral deposits but to utterly abnormal conditions produced by the aftermath of war. The result of more systematic prospecting since that time has all been to prove that tin-mining in Cornwall is in many districts still in its infancy—a fact by no means so extraordinary as might at first appear, when one considers that, as already stated, copper was the main objective during the most fruitful period of mining activity in the last century. Added to this, many modern facilities for underground exploration, such as the diamond drill and cheap pumping-plant for prospecting shafts, are now for the first time only enabling miners to test the ground adequately, and in many cases such work is showing the existence of considerable ore bodies still remaining even at shallow depths.

Cornwall, indeed, can still offer to the mining investor a fine field for the judicious use of capital. Whole areas, like that of Gwennap and St. Day, have never really been worked for tin at all. Their reputation as the richest few square miles of ground in the Old World was made on copper alone ; below them, in all probability, lies a tin zone, in which their former fortunes have every likelihood of being repeated. Undertakings such as this, however, would undoubtedly involve the outlay of very large sums of capital, and for this they may have to wait some time. In the meanwhile, the number of fresh lodes at shallow levels which have actually come to light in the course of prospecting since the War have opened the eyes of many to Cornwall's existing ore deposits, and have shown that opportunities for the investment of small sums of capital are equally to be obtained within the Duchy.

From the point of view of the cautious investor, Cornwall has one great advantage over almost every other metalliferous mining field in the world, in that it is within a few hours' journey from London, from whence the business man can run down for a flying visit or a prolonged stay and see with his own eyes the nature of the speculation and the way in which his capital is being laid out.

That a returning confidence in home mines is following on the wider understanding of the problems which have beset the industry in the past is fully clear to all who visit Cornwall to-day. Many of the mines are once more working full bore and others are starting up, so that in a few years it may be assumed that Cornwall will have once more regained its pre-war measure of prosperity. Looking onward to the future, it may be asked, " Will it stop at this ? " The answer from every hand seems to be unanimously—No ! The drop in the price of tin in 1921-2 was an extraordinary feature, solely caused by the irregularity of the markets in the aftermath of war, and as unlikely, we may trust, as the War itself to ever occur again in our generation. With the consumption of tin in America and throughout the world steadily increasing, and many of the largest alluvial tin-fields already past their prime, the lode deposits of Cornwall seem likely to come into greater prominence in the near future than ever before.

Be that as it will, the roaring stamps and smoking chimneys of the western mining areas to-day are proof to all that pass by that a healthy resumption has been made, and that this ancient industry, as so often before, has once again weathered the storm, and is proceeding in full confidence into the uncharted future.

NOTES.

1. Parl. Pap. (Copper Com.), (1799).
2. The above statistics are gathered from the Appendices to the early volumes of the R.G.S.C. Reports; Henwood's Report on the Cornish Mines, 1838, R.G.S.C., v; Lewis, *Stannaries*, Appendix giving production of tin; and *Cornish Chamber of Mines Year Books*, 1917–21.
3. When Malay tin first began to find its way into this country in wholesale quantities.
4. " The rise of *the china clay* industry round St. Austell was the salvation of this district, coming as it did about the time that so many of the mines were stopping. It was not so thickly populated then. There were no bunches of mines such as there are around Redruth and Camborne, but the district had long been noted for its alluvial stream works, and the Great Beam Mine (to mention one) on the northern slope of Hensbarrow

could boast a history dating from the reign of Henry VII. In the first instance, however, clay was regarded by many of the miners as a bastard growth. The miner, indeed, with his pick and hammer and drill, was contemptuous of the 'clay' man with his dubber, and for a long time the expression 'so and so's gone to clay' was regarded as little better than 'so and so has gone to the workhouse.' The tinners' blood, however, long remained in the older generation, most of whom always showed greater interest in the finding of a small vein of tin ore than in the china clay which provided them their living."—Cf. H. Pascoe, *Cornwall " Education Week" Handbook*, 1927.

5. Cf. articles by the present writer in the *Economist*, April 12th and 19th, 1924.

6. *Mining Interviews* (1896), (153).

7. Cottages can still be rented in the western districts for £6 or £8 a year. A miner earning £14 to £16 a month in Cornwall is, in most cases, better off than one earning £18 or £20 abroad.

8. "What's the good of a rotary hairbrush to a man with a bald head?" as a miner put it.

9. Programme of Joint Meeting of Scientific Societies (1912), 39.

10. Cornish Chamber of Mines Year Books, 1919 and 1920.

11. Cf. an article by the present writer, on "The Cornish Mines," *Contemporary Review*, March 1923.

CHAPTER IX

THE EXODUS OF THE 'SEVENTIES AND THE MINER OF TO-DAY

"WHEREVER a hole is sunk in the ground to-day—no matter in what corner of the globe—you will be sure to find a Cornishman at the bottom of it, searching for metal," wrote a traveller not many years since. "From Nova Zembla to New Zealand, from Cape Horn to Korea, from Klondike to Cape Town; frozen in the Arctic snows, dried to the bone in tropical deserts, burnt out with fever in equatorial swamps, and broiled thin under equatorial suns—in every country of the New World and the Old the Cornish miner may be found at work"—so far-reaching have been the changes wrought by the depression which set in in local mining in the early 'seventies. During this period, the short space of a few years witnessed the breaking-up of the tradition of centuries. An essential local inheritance of skill and knowledge in mining affairs, gained from countless generations of those who had won their living in the local mines, was at last leaving the soil whence it had so long drawn its experience and, answering the call of necessity, was seeking new fields of action overseas, there to mingle with other men and other traditions.

Though the Cornishmen's birthright of mining experience at once placed them in the forefront of the pioneering movement, even they had lessons to learn from the varying conditions of the foreign fields in which they now found themselves placed, and in imbibing these they were destined to lose some of the most strongly local characteristics which had linked their fathers in an unbroken line with the Cornish tinners of the past. From the very start of the overseas movement there was, of course, a constant coming and going between Cornwall and the new mining camps. Few settled abroad in the early days, but those who returned, though Cornishmen still to the backbone, yet represented clearly enough the transition stage between the past and present race of Cornish miners.

In Cornwall, meanwhile, the face of a country-side was changing too, like the manners and modes of the people in it. With the cessation of mining in many districts, engine-houses were torn down, machinery and headgears removed, "count-houses" were converted into dwellings, water leats fell into decay, and lanes became grass-grown. On the wastes where the surface buildings of prosperous mines had once stood, red piles of stone and sand by hedged-in shafts alone remained to tell the tale. In the neighbourhood of the mines acres of land which were once under cultivation by the miners went back into croft, and hundreds of cottages fell into decay. In the seaboard districts the sites once occupied by these are to-day being rapidly covered again, but this time with the summer bungalows of London holiday-makers, to whom mines are either scars or curiosities, and who know still less of the but lately departed race of inhabitants on whose hearthstones they have planted their new rubble concrete and still newer and more foreign fashions and ideas.

Meanwhile, the descendants of the people who once inhabited the land and "teeled" the little wheelbarrow farms are now either living in countries overseas or have drifted away to the great towns. Many of them, perhaps, have forgotten now, but bitter leave-takings there must have been in those black years when the Cornish people, who still can love their home after a lifetime of separation, were first called upon to leave their natural inheritance. Many of the present generation who have won for themselves big positions in the mining world overseas have never even seen the old mines whose workings are scored for miles across the Cornish country-side, although it was in them that their fathers and grandfathers gained much of that skill and knowledge which they have inherited.

"It is not too much to say," wrote one writer, "that between the census of 1871–81 a third of the mining population of Cornwall left the county. The Registrar-General, in his Report on the census of 1881, says that the population of Cornwall had decreased by 8·9 per cent., and that it is probable that the miners diminished by 24 per cent." (1) "As a concrete instance of the process of depopulation, let me give the story of my family," wrote a correspondent to *Cornish Notes and Queries* circa 1904 (p. 52). "My paternal grandfather and grandmother, with

THE EXODUS OF THE 'SEVENTIES 323

their three sisters and three brothers, had a total issue of twenty-six, each of which had a family. My maternal grandparents, with their two sisters and four brothers, had a total issue of twenty-eight, each of which had a family. Of these fifty-four families with a total membership of considerably over two hundred, five only now live in the county. In other words, of four marriages that took place in Cornwall in the years 1795, 1806, 1816, and 1818, only about 2 per cent. of the descendants now live in the county. The rest are scattered all over the face of the earth, in London, South Africa, Australia, New Zealand, India, and America."

The seeking of work in foreign fields was no new conception even to the Cornish miner of the 'seventies, although it had never been necessary on such a wholesale scale before. Already prior to 1778, miners from Redruth had been sent to inspect the copper deposits of Lake Superior, (2) whilst in 1816 Richard Trevithick, Cornwall's great engineering genius, had sailed from Penzance for Chili and Peru, where eleven of the most adventurous years ever recorded in the life of one man were spent in erecting Cornish pumping-engines in the famous silver mines of those countries Again, in 1825, it will be remembered how Cornish miners (on board the *Cambria*) were to the fore in the rescue of the 547 persons taken off the *Kent*, East Indiaman, which was found on fire and sinking in the Bay of Biscay. The terrible difficulties experienced, owing to the seas which were running, in getting the women and children on board were largely overcome by the strength of two eminent Cornish wrestlers, Warren and Carkeek, who, standing in the chains of the vessel and availing themselves of the short intervals between the waves, drew up the sufferers from the boats and delivered them to their " comrades " on deck. The subsequent kindness of the Cornish miners in opening their stores and cheerfully giving up their clothing and beds to the destitute people was particularly noticed by the captain in his report (3) to the owners.

These miners, who had embarked from Falmouth but a few days before, formed the pioneers of the Anglo-Mexican Mining Association, which was, at this time, making attempts to work various gold and silver properties in Mexico, with the aid of Cornish miners. In the history of mining, few undertakings have proved more disastrous than this one, which owed its existence to the wildest stock-jobbing speculation, backed by the completest ignorance and credulity. The mines themselves were, in most instances, too poor to employ the attention of the natives, whilst to the indigent Guards officers and half-pay Navy captains who had been placed in charge of the mining operations their very situations were said to have been unknown ! Enormous were the salaries offered by the Company to induce the Cornishmen to leave their homes under such conditions. Working miners were to receive £15 a month and captains £1,000 a year. According to the rates of wages then being paid in Cornwall, such men would be getting 50s. a month and £80 a year, respectively. Those who fell to such inducements, however, paid dearly for it. Some, it is true, happily insisted on returning to Falmouth after a few days at sea, owing to their landman's disgust of the salt beef with which they were treated; others, after enduring unspeakable privations, arrived at last at Vera Cruz, where, out of the forty-four which formed one company, twenty-six died. Robbed and cheated on every side, unable to speak the language or withstand the climate, and leaving ponderous heaps of rusting machinery by the mule-tracks through the forests, those who were luckiest returned to Cornwall, whilst many found a foreign grave. (4)

In spite of this early failure, a small proportion of the more adventurous Cornish miners still continued to cross the Atlantic in search of work and higher wages, and by 1830 to 1840 Redruth and St. Just men were frequently to be found working in the copper-mines of Cuba, though, except in cases of shaft-sinking or other special work, as superintendents only. (5) The use of the pick and gad, however, with which he was accustomed to loosen the joints of the rocks and thus economize in blasting, made the day's work of the Cornish miner, where he was employed, nearly one-third greater than that of the native miner. (6)

Many of the Cornishmen who went out in these early days belonged to the old fighting, hard-drinking school. Magnificent men many of them were—tall, muscular, and upright, with a sort of swaggering gait about them as they used to appear in town on a Saturday night, dressed in their suits of corduroy with

THE EXODUS OF THE 'SEVENTIES

trousers buttoned up at the calf, according to the fashion of the time. "I would as soon have a kick from a horse as a blow from one of those men," said an old gentleman who had seen many of them in their prime. Trouble often occurred on the voyages between the Cornishmen of this type and the other races on board. One of the most pugnacious of the fighting families of St. Day, a man named Rowe, was going out to America on one occasion on a ship which had a lot of Irish on board. Some trouble having arisen between them and the Cornishmen, Rowe went up to the most offensive of the Irish and knocked him down with a blow which cut his cheek to the bone. His comrades drew him aside as soon as might be, but only just in time, and for the rest of the voyage he had to lie very low, for the Irishmen would have murdered him if they could. Strong as was their physique, however, the malign effect of the Cuban mines was stronger, and from them many a young Cornishman whose strength had once been the pride and boast of his parish returned home a yellow and emaciated wreck.

During the 'forties many miners embarked at Falmouth for service under companies in Brazil, where responsible positions sometimes carried the princely salary of £6 a month. Going abroad in those days, however, was not the easy undertaking that it has since become, and any responsible man with a family or dependents would then make arrangements before starting for all the contingencies which might occur during the long period of absence which had to be expected. The following is a typical document which explains itself :—

To All Whom these present may come.

John Chynoweth of the Parish of St. Agnes sends greeting. Whereas the said John Chynoweth is shortly going to the Province of New Granada, in Columbia, South America, as a stampsman under the employ of the Columbian Mining Association for the term of six years to commence from his arrival at the place of his destination in New Granada, at the monthly wages of Nine pounds, the same hath appointed Joseph Newtown and Martin Hitchins of the said parish of St. Agnes to receive for him and in his name the sum of Four pounds and ten shillings per month . . . upon trust that they the said J.N. and M.H. do pay out of the said sum unto his wife Clovina Chynoweth the sum of £2 per month for and towards the support of herself and her children. But in case his said Wife or Children shall be afflicted with sickness he does hereby further authorize his said Trustees to pay unto her such further sums of money as they may deem meet and proper . . . and upon trust that his said Trustees do place and lay out in the savings Bank or any other Bank the surplus moneys in his name and for his use.

Signed and Witnessed.

September 30, 1834.

It was not, however, until 1849, when gold was discovered in California, and later in the 'fifties, when it was discovered in Australia, that the first real exodus from the county began. One old gentleman living in Truro as recently as 1925 used to relate how his father went to California (round Cape Horn) in 1849 and saw San Francisco first when it was only a village of log huts. (7) It is probable, at a later date, that many Cornishmen heard Artemus Ward during his lecturing tour through the silver country of Nevada, may even have heard him in the saloon at Big Creek, where the bar-keeper applauded each point with a bang on the counter and a vociferous " Good boy from the New England States ! Listen to William W. Shakespeare ! "

In an excellent paper given in the county some time ago, Mr. Harry Pascoe has vividly pictured the mining exodus of those days. (8) " Some of us," he wrote, " can remember certain interesting old men—nearly all dead now—old men of iron, whose fiery youth had experience of gold and blood and lust and the wildest of lives in the mad rush to Western America seventy-five years ago. It was not then a fortnight's journey in a floating hotel steaming the 3,000 miles to New York and a comfortably upholstered railway carriage, fitted with every convenience for dashing across the States, which brought these early emigrants to the Far West. There being no railway then in Cornwall, Nicholas Penhaligon and Uncle Bill Trebilcock, each with bundle on shoulder, tramped from Carrigan Downs to Padstow Port, and went from there in a sailing-ship to California—spending thirteen weeks on the water." Sometimes a whole year elapsed from the Sunday evening when son or husband walked away from home to the nearest port before ever a word came back to the Cornish village, where news was being so anxiously awaited. Old people relate that owing to the cost of postage much letter-writing was impossible, and not infrequently unstamped letters would be sent with some pre-arranged device scrawled on them to denote good news, seeing which the relations would abstain from redeeming the letter, content with this slight token only.

"During these times," continued Mr. Pascoe, "many Cornish ports, such as Fowey, Falmouth, and Penzance, became collecting stations from which emigrants were forwarded in small sailing-ships to join the large sailing-liners at Bristol and Liverpool. Hundreds, and probably thousands, left the country from Hayle. Terrible hardships were frequently experienced by these early mining pioneers from Cornwall. Straight from some little village amongst the granite hills, without having ever spent an hour on the sea in his life, the young miner embarked on a voyage of four or even six horrible months (if he took the 16,000-mile sea-route to San Francisco) with all the hardships of a sailor's life, including salt junk and the terribe seas around Cape Horn. From the Californian landing port the miner made his way, by any primitive means and in any primitive company, to the gold diggings. If, on the other hand, he took the regular service between England and New York, he found himself on American soil with three thousand miles—plain, prairie, desert, and Rocky Mountains—between him and his objective." (9) Nor was the rate of pay gained by the miner when he did at last reach his destination so very princely. One dollar 75 cents a day was all that many men earned in the 'sixties, out of which they paid 20 dollars a month for their lodgings.

Yet during the 'fifties and 'sixties, and still more during the 'seventies and 'eighties, there was a steady stream of young Cornishmen carrying unique skill and knowledge to every mining camp in the North American continent, and to Australia. The returned miner of early days, with his broad-brimmed hat, red shirt, open at the neck, and big rolled top-boots, was a familiar sight in the Cornish mining towns, and their "heroic" figures acted as a call of the blood to many an adventurous young Cornishman. "And so in the pride of life and with his twenty-first birthday the event of yesterday, he turned his back on the little whitewashed cottage with the geraniums in the window—leaving his mother in a silent and strangely empty room—and keeping a stiff upper lip as he gripped the old man's hand, went off to the unknown future."

In some families the boys, as they grew up, took to foreign lands, one after the other, like ducks taking to water. One instance, mentioned by Mr. Pascoe, is a good example of this. The family consisted of nine sons:—

1. "William" went abroad as a boy of twenty. He paid his first and only visit to his Cornish home when he was a grey-haired man of fifty-five, and then disappeared again for good.
2. "Dave" died in New Zealand.
3. "Ki" travelled the world for thirty years and then settled down near his birthplace.
4. "Jerry" died in Butte City, Montana.
5. "Wazzy" died in Australia.
6. "Luther" left as a lad and never came back.
7. "Johnny" died in Cornwall of African phthisis.
8. "Martin" was killed in New Zealand.
9. "Willie," called after his eldest brother William, because, as his mother said, "Bill will never come home again, and I like the name," visited half the world, made a small fortune, and settled down alone, the only occupant of his father's cottage.

Well might this make the subject for another of Mrs. Hemans's poems :—

> Their graves are scattered far and wide,
> O'er mount and stream and sea.

The above, however, may be considered, as a whole, a rather exceptional case. In probably the greater majority of instances the early pioneers came back and settled—as one may see returned Cornish miners settled to-day—in some little farm or modern house to which is given an outlandish name—"Katoomba," "Esperanza," or "Geldenhuis Deep"—to remind them of the greater world which they once knew so well, but with which they since have severed all connection. Those who went out and never returned were chiefly older men, who transported themselves and their families, root and branch, and settled down for good in the "greater Cornwall" which for the last fifty years has been growing up overseas. Many of these men, after doing very well and winning responsible positions, retired from work and interested themselves in the public affairs of the new townships, wherein they often exercised considerable influence.

Curious meetings sometimes took place among Cornishmen in the most distant corners of the world in those days, as they doubtless still do. One story, told by Mr. Pascoe, concerns a voice only. "A Cornishman, nicknamed 'Chippy,' was a passenger in a train in Western America, and was showing considerable interest in the progress of the journey. 'Where are we to?' he bawled through the window, as the carriage drew up at a wayside station. 'Roche Rock,' came from a window at the other end of the train. 'And where av us got to now,' he shouted at the next stop. 'Goss Moor,' was the answer from the other end. 'And where's this to?' he called again at the third halt. 'St. Columb,' came the same mysterious voice. At the first opportunity Chippy started to look through the train for his fellow-countryman, but the other lay low and the mystery was never solved.

"By 1870 bullock-carts were jolting the Cornish miner from Cape Town to the newly-discovered fields at Kimberley. This was followed by the discovery of gold on the Rand, and soon after the great trek to the Transvaal was in full swing. There were Cornish miners at Johannesburg when that great city was just a couple of tin shacks and half a dozen tents. Near its centre, in the early days, was the well-known 'Cousin Jack's Corner,' where Cornishmen used to forgather on Saturday nights to exchange gossip, just as they do round some favourite spot in every town and village in Cornwall to-day. But as the vast buildings narrowed-in the streets, the cheery greetings and homely Cornish talk amid the glitter and roar of the gold-reef city became as the songs of Zion in a strange land. The rendezvous is now lost under bricks and mortar, and frequented only by poor wandering ghosts, in search of spirits long since departed.

"Every Friday morning (from 1890 to 1900) the up-train from West Cornwall included special cars labelled 'Southampton,' the embarkation port for South Africa. Each following Sunday night eyes were dimmed as congregations in the mining villages sang with deep feeling the hymn :—

> Eternal Father, strong to save,
> Whose arm doth bind the mighty wave,
> Oh, hear us when we cry to Thee
> For those in peril on the sea,

while 7,000 miles away, in the Joubert Park, kindred eyes were dimmed as the band played 'Lead, Kindly Light' (regarded by many as a kind of Cornish National Anthem) to hushed audiences. In those days one never heard 'For those in peril on the sea' without being impressed both by the fervour of the congregation and the 'fitness' of the hymn. But, strictly speaking, the 'peril' was not so much 'on the sea' as beyond the sea, where typhoid and phthisis claimed their victims by the score, by the hundred, by the thousand. The name 'South Africa' is cut deep in the heart of mining Cornwall, not so much engraved with an instrument of steel as jagged and ghastly with the malignant quartz that hid the gold and filled the lungs of the Cornish pioneers. Nevertheless, the allurements were strong. There was plenty of money, plenty of fun, plenty of 'life,' and niggers to do the work on the Rand, even though the dread scourge might be biding its time in the dust-filled stopes where the drills roared out unceasingly. 'Let us eat, drink, and be merry, for to-morrow we die,' was the one text faithfully followed by many a careless youngster. Even the women at home were in some cases demoralized by the weekly drafts from Johannesburg. They spent as they had never spent before—and probably never will again. When their man had got work, their fortune was made. One poor creature, unable to read and on the verge of extreme poverty, tore her first South African cheque from the envelope—the letter fluttering to the floor—and rushed off to spend right and left. Her excitement abated, she returned and saw the letter. She then learned that she was a widow and that the money she had just squandered was the few charitable pounds subscribed by her dead husband's comrades. Previous to the Boer War a common notice on the Rand mines was : '——, a Cornishman, will be buried to-morrow at 3 p.m. at —— Cemetery.' "

Still, for ten years, Cornish miners poured like a flood into

South Africa, till the settlements of families around the mines read like the roll-call of a Cornish village. One well-known mine at this time—Fereira Deep—was almost entirely manned with Dolcoath tributers, superintended by a captain who was himself a Camborne man and one of an old Dolcoath family. "A splendid mine of men they had," you will hear returned miners say, "a company which, for skill and steady reliability, it would be hard to find the equal of to-day." From Redruth, Camborne, St. Day, St. Agnes, Beacon, Troon, and all the mining villages of Cornwall, families were living out there side by side and intermarrying in the new country as closely as they do in the old. At Christmas-time the sound of Cornish voices singing the carols of their fathers came as naturally upon the ear as if the three thousand miles which separated them from home had never been. Local distinctions, too, were equally kept up. Even out there "Santusters" (St. Just men) retained their character for aloofness and independence, and St. Just feast was regularly celebrated by them on the very day that their relatives and neighbours were entertaining one another at home. On one occasion the manager of a Rand mine found one of his underground foremen, a St. Just man, absent. "Where's so-and-so to-day?" he inquired of one of the miners. "Why, sir," came the somewhat reluctant reply, "I reckon he've gone into Johannesburg to buy a glass eye. He aveant goat but wan eye, and last night was St. Just feast and they was 'aving drop of beer and got a bit merry, and time to go home, he found he'd ben and lost the glassen eye he do belong to have up. So I reckon he've gone into town to buy another."

A fine spirit of camaraderie existed among the picked Cornishmen who were to be found in the mining camps of those days. "'Twas one and all on the mines then," said one who knew them well. "Anyone could put his hand in another's pocket for anything," and a boy arriving out from his Cornish village, however poor, could rely on receiving not only hospitality but money itself to supply his needs. Those who were so helped rarely forgot the kindness done to them, and more than once, when in after years fate had altered the respective positions of helper and helped, the friendless boy was able to repay with interest the early kindness which he had received. (10)

Throughout the various changes in the fortunes of the industry, the condition of the Cornish miner who found work at home was not greatly affected. Up to the period of the war, wages remained low, as was only to be expected, though they were in a large measure counterbalanced by the cheap rate of living. In 1879 the miners at Devon Great Consols were getting 15s. or 16s. per week, but with the low price of copper it had become a question of that or none at all. (11) As a shareholder at one of the meetings remarked, " Devon Great Consols is not a philanthropic society, but a commercial undertaking. If it be commercially valueless it must be abandoned." (12) This point was one entirely appreciated by the men, who realized that the ruling economic conditions were outside the control of either themselves or their employers. (13) Rather than " knack the bals " altogether, most of them were content to work at home for low wages until better days came, varying this with periods of work in foreign mines, where their skill would always get them high wages, though at the cost of keeping two homes going and often at that of ruined health.

Chiefly on account of the Cornish miners' direct way of thus facing facts, trade unions have so far obtained small hold in the county. It was, indeed, stated in 1887 that a few of the younger men were in favour of the union, though none were willing to sacrifice themselves by being the first to join, (14) whilst fewer still would ever have consented to subscribe from their already small earnings. Added to this, the Cornish miner's locomotive habits, which land him at one time in Africa, at another in America, and then in Cornwall again, have hitherto precluded any serious spirit of combination amongst them. The lessening spirit of competition on setting days, however, showed the growth of a certain feeling of unionism even amongst Cornish miners, and accounts for the gradual discontinuance of putting up underground pitches for public auction and the adoption of the present-day mode of setting contracts by private arrangement between the captains and the men.

Notwithstanding the depressed state of the mines, the living conditions of the miners continued to show improvement, and the men were really becoming better off than in the hey-day of mining prosperity. The chief reason for this was the increased

THE EXODUS OF THE 'SEVENTIES

buying power of money consequent on the drop in the price of food-stuffs—an alteration clearly shown by the following table:—

	Prices in August 1841.	Prices in August 1871.
Flour, half peck ...	3s. 6d. to 4s.	2s. 6d. to 2s. 9d.
Tea, per lb.	6s. (good quality)	3s.
Sugar, per lb. ...	8d.	3½d.
Currants, per lb. ...	10d.	5d.
Soap, per lb. ...	6d.	3½d.
Starch, per lb. ...	6½d.	4d.

Animal food alone had increased in price during this period, but the increase was counterbalanced to a great extent by the lower cost of clothing. (15)

Yet, in spite of changes for the better in food and housing, the health of the Cornish miner continued to give cause for the gravest concern. During the years 1871–80, Cornwall headed the list of mortality from all causes amongst miners, and more than doubled the rate among colliers; (16) whilst the Report of the Registrar-General for 1885 stated that the number of Cornish miners suffering from phthisis and diseases of the respiratory organs was more than twice as much as the miners in any other district, and more than three times as much as the rest of Cornish males. (17) The reasons at that date suggested to account for the excessive mortality were partly innutritious food, but chiefly the climbing of nearly perpendicular ladders from great depths after putting in six or seven hours' work underground. The man-engine, it is true, had in certain cases done much to relieve the miners of the fearful labour of the ladders, but the number of mines into which it had been introduced was comparatively few. In 1862 only eight had been installed in the whole county. (18) It was all very well, however, for the Inspector of Mines in 1880-1 to describe the attitude of the Cornish companies as one of "disgraceful supineness," since, as was frequently the case, the old shafts were too crooked and narrow to admit of the introduction of a man-engine, and the mines were at this time too poor to sink new ones. Even in the mines where a man-engine had been installed there was often no single shaft which went to the bottom. Thus in Dolcoath, though the bottom of the mine was 362 fathoms, the man-engine only went down to the 240; in Carn Brea it went to the 170, though the mine was much deeper; whilst in Cook's Kitchen the man-engine descended to little more than a third of the depth of the mine. (19) As late as 1886-7 there were only ladders in West Wheal Seton, and the miners working in the bottom levels there had to climb 266 fathoms to surface.

Before the end of the century, however, the use of "gigs" drawn with wire rope had become general in all deep mines for raising the men—a method attended with less initial cost than the man-engine and possible to install in narrow, crooked, and inclined shafts. (20) Not only was the toil of the ladders obviated by this means, but commodious dries provided with boilers and steam pipes, and basins where the men could wash, had taken the place of the little exposed moor-houses to which the miners of past generations had had to walk in the teeth of gales on their arrival at surface. Improvements such as these, though undoubtedly adding to the miners' comfort and general well-being, scarcely benefited their health to the degree that might have been expected, and the additional fact that colliers and ironstone miners, who generally do not change at the mine but go home in their underground clothes, were yet far healthier than Cornish miners led to the conclusion that sudden changes of temperature on coming to the surface, though aggravating incipient lung troubles, could not be considered as the primary cause of the same. Neither could the miners' pulmonary complaints any longer be attributed to ladder climbing, seeing that the excessive mortality remained, though the men now in almost every case "rode" through the shafts to and from their work.

About 1900 the alarming increase in the death-rate of Cornish miners led to a Government inquiry. Excessive mortality from lung disease had, up till 1892, only seriously affected men over forty. "During the last few years, however," wrote the Commissioners, "there has been an enormous increase in the death-rate from lung diseases, particularly among younger men from about twenty-five–forty-five, with the result that the total death-rate at all ages from twenty-five–forty-five is now far greater than at any previous period during the last fifty years. Between the ages of twenty-five and forty-five the death-rate from lung diseases among miners living in Cornwall has recently been from eight to ten times the corresponding death-rate among coal miners and ironstone-miners." (21) As was further shown by the Report of the Commission, this increase in the death-rate corresponded with the general introduction of machine-drills into Cornish mines, the machine-men employed in driving levels, sinking winzes, and particularly in "raising" being more rapidly affected than the miners employed in stoping, which was still almost entirely done with hand-drills. (22) "The men working machine-drills," they wrote, "under present conditions are greatly exposed to dust, as the drill at work on dry rock gives off a lot from holes bored horizontally or upwards. Anyone standing in an 'end' or 'rise' with a drill at work boring dry holes becomes quickly covered with dust, and the grit is soon noticeable even in the mouth."

The problem before the Commissioners was considerably complicated by the fact that, bad as conditions were in Cornwall, the state of the notoriously dry Transvaal mines, where the men came up looking as white with dust as if they had been working in a flour-mill, was infinitely worse, and as Cornish miners were continually coming and going between these and the home mines, the high death-rate in Cornwall had largely to be attributed to the effect of the former. It having been once proved, however, that the stone dust which the miners inhaled was the cause of permanent injury to their lungs and enormously predisposed them to tuberculosis, various precautions were adopted which have since, in Cornwall at any rate, considerably altered this state of affairs. The prevention of dust has now become one of the most important features of mine sanitation. Jets and sprays of water are invariably used to prevent dust arising in drilling holes, the stopes and ore-shoots are kept damp, fans are used to draw out the dust and smoke released after blasting in confined spaces, and the men are forbidden to return to their working places until the "smeach" has in a large measure subsided. By adopting precautions such as these, and by hearty co-operation on the part of both managers and men in seeing that they are carried out, the conclusion of the Commissioners was that "there is no reason why work underground should not be a perfectly healthy employment, being wholesome to body and mind, and the special dangers associated with it being such that, if recognized and faced, can be avoided." (23) Whether this pious hope has been fully realized, lack of proper statistics makes it impossible to say; and whilst the Cornish miner continues to spend part of his working life in foreign camps and part at home, the difficulties of obtaining any comparative figures are obvious. It is clear, however, that in Cornish mining, as in every other branch of industrial life, the movement of the times has had effect in the increase of mechanical aids and the consequent lessening of the physical strain on the workman. The introduction of electricity, fast-moving hoists, compressed-air drills, and high explosives has rendered the miner's work much less laborious than of old, and although the general speeding up and increased attention required by machines may prove in the long run to have more of a counteracting effect on the human organism than is usually allowed for, a general improvement has certainly taken place.

So great, indeed, are the changes which have taken place in all the large mines, and the methods of working them, during the last thirty years, that many would be surprised to learn that the ancient ways are not yet altogether forgotten and that here and there may be discovered little backwaters in the industry where men of the old type are still working in ways and places scarcely changed from those in which the Cornish miner of centuries ago was earning his daily bread. As a result of the good average price which tin has latterly maintained, small parties of miners have been "free setting" again in the "backs" or shallow levels of certain of the old abandoned mines. Here they may be found to-day working away the small but frequently rich "stringers" of tin branching out from the main lodes, or else removing pillars of ground or stull fillings, left by former generations of miners to keep the workings open. In most cases these "free setting" lessees (often consisting of an old tributer and one or two sons) pay the owner of the sett a royalty of 2s. or 3s. in the £ and make what they can from the rest. Their method of going to work is to open up one of the "old men's" shafts (often a labour of several weeks), and then, lowering themselves down by rope or ladder through these gaping apertures, search among the rabbit warren of ancient workings below for likely places where pieces of standing ground may have been left.

Sometimes a month's labour under these conditions will prove entirely thrown away, but nothing daunted, like bees after pollen, they then apply themselves to some other hole, where, perhaps, their industry, patience, and skill are well rewarded. The fact that some of them have been engaged in this kind of work for many years shows that, with tin at a fair price they contrive, on the whole, to do well. The small droppers on to the main lodes, which are their best prizes, are frequently very rich, in some cases almost clean tin. The produce of their labour they sell to some "bargain buyer" in the neighbourhood, who, with metallic tin at £280, pays them, perhaps, £120 a ton for their stuff "in the stone," and afterwards crushes and makes it ready for the smelter.

The form of mining carried on by these men represents the genuine old-style tributing. Their shafts, when they sink them themselves, are in many cases mere chimneys, where there is just room for a ladder and the passage of a small bucket, the latter being frequently made from a carbide tin or other home-made contrivance. In some of the "levels" where many a man would find it difficult to turn, the tributers manage to sink small winzes—how small may be judged from the fact that the proximity of the hanging to the footwall in some places scarcely allows of the fixing of a ladder! In the bottom of these little crannies the men will work cheerfully enough when their gettings are their own. By the fixing of a cowl at surface, which they turn to face the wind, they contrive to render the air quite breathable, and by working away the lode in the richest parts only, with the aid of "hammer and moyles," and taking care to break no country rock, they generally contrive to make a living, if no more. Considering the nature of their employment, it might readily be supposed that men of this type would receive every encouragement from the mineral owners, who stand to benefit so largely by any discovery they may make, but this, strange to say, is far from being the case. In many instances working miners, on applying to the mineral lords for permission to enter upon their setts, receive no further encouragement than a curt reference to their lawyers. From these gentlemen they hear of fees for this and fees for that, until the men find, perhaps, that a sixth part of their total capital would have to go in preliminary expenses, and so the whole scheme is quashed at the very outset. At the same time, it may well be asked, what ordinary investor is prepared to risk so large a portion of his capital, to say nothing of the labour of his hands, as these men are? Be the sum large or small, it represents, in most cases, a very considerable proportion of such working miners' gross savings. If they lose it, they alone are the sufferers, whilst if their venture succeeds it must redound in every case to the benefit of the mineral lord. The opposition of a farmer may perhaps be excusable when it is a question of having his land disturbed, although he, in most cases, receives very good compensation for any damage which may be done. But the opposition, or at least the apathy, of the mineral owners is, to say the least of it, extraordinarily short-sighted. The result of such a policy is that the prospector or old free-setting tributer is being discouraged out of existence, and at the present rate will soon have disappeared altogether.

The same may be said, though in a lesser degree, of the small working tin-streamer, whose operations are still carried on in the old way in a few secluded valleys in the mining parts of Cornwall. These tin-streamers are either employed in working over the refuse sand washed down in the "red rivers" from large mines stamping their ores higher up or else in crushing and dressing tin-bearing stones, picked by hand from the waste burrows of abandoned mines in the neighbourhood. In the latter case the parties of men who own the stream require, in addition to their concentrating plant, a set of stamps. In almost every case these stamps are driven by water-power, through the aid perhaps of some moss-grown wheel erected by the tinner's father or grandfather a generation or more ago, and still doing yeoman service. All night long, in these valleys, the ear is greeted with the merry rattle of the iron lifters or the more serious thug-thug of the older wooden stamps, as they work on unattended throughout the hours of darkness. Such is the "music of the stamps," once so well known to almost every Cornishman that, on leaving home, many of them lay awake at night, missing this rhythmic accompaniment to their slumber, and of such I have heard men say: "When the stamps stopped we felt as if we had lost our best friend." Nowhere, indeed, can the continuity of economic process and the traditional nature of

THE EXODUS OF THE 'SEVENTIES 339

Cornish mining be better seen than in these secluded stream works. In four or five places, at least, the lifters of the stamps still consist of great logs of timber hardly stripped of their original bark, (84) their working stamp-heads being of much the same weight as those used in the eighteenth century. Here and there, too, the old Cornish square buddles may still be seen, differing hardly at all in design from those described by the anonymous writer of 1671, whilst one or two of the hand-frames mentioned by the same writer remained in use until a year or two ago. The speech of old streamers, too, is hardly less conservative than their ways, and amongst them may be heard terms and usages connected with tin-dressing which were current in Cornwall hundreds of years ago. Sitting in their little " croust-houses," on the wide settles made in past times for those who "watched" the stamps by night, a streamer will describe how he first "went buddly and packy down 'pon the floors when he was ten years ould," and will go on to speak of the intricacies of chimming, loobing, trunking, framing, searging, tozing, packing, and other processes to which tin sands are subjected. Apart from such merely old-fashioned words, many tin-dressing terms, like those used by the miner, are pure Celtic Cornish, and not English at all, but through the agency of Cornishmen have found their way into mining camps and the mining vocabulary of the world, where they may now be heard bandied about on the tongues of distant races who have never heard of Cornwall.

The tin-streamer, with his old-fashioned machinery and old-fashioned ways, has this much remarkable about him, that he contrives to make a decent living out of the low-grade ores which he treats, where those who have bought him out and erected expensive modern machinery have failed dismally. If a tin-dresser on a large mine requires to be a skilled worker to save the tin in ores averaging 28 lb. to the ton, how well must a man know his trade, and what care must he exercise in saving costs, if he is to make a living for himself and two or three dependents on ores which carry, perhaps, only four or five pounds of tin to the ton. Yet, thanks to an inherited skill which amounts almost to instinct, the streamer contrives to do this, and pay the mine or mineral owner a small royalty in addition. Show one of these men a stone with the smallest quantity of tin in it and he will crush it down on his broad "vanning" shovel, and with a drop of water swirl it round till the tin ore comes up to the point "as plain as a bullock's tongue," as he himself would say. As a Cornish farmer once said, "They've got a nause like a spannel dawg, they can 'most smell tin, I bla'."

In some instances the free-setting tin-streamer of to-day has shown an energy and determination in prosecuting his work equal to that of the Cornish miner of any time in the past. In such a case as that of the Portherras Tin Sands, near St. Just, six months of totally unremunerative labour were required in bringing waterwheels, pulverizers, timber, sheds, etc., down to a spot on the cliffs long rendered almost inaccessible by virgin growths of furze and other vegetation which had obliterated the "old men's" tracks. Once there, the machinery, buddles, waterwheels, etc., had to be fixed, a cable stretched to a rock, which was covered by almost every tide, on the beach below, and accumulations of sand to be gathered and carted some distance in hand-barrows, as often as not in the teeth of northwesterly gales. Men of this type, who prefer the independence, together with the risks, of working on their own to the usual wage-earning conditions of the modern industrial system, are the last of a fine tradition of miners, and they themselves stand upon the threshold of disappearance. In the large mines of to-day the new mechanical aids and innovations have bred a new class of men the very nature of whose occupation prevents them having the same outlook that was essential in their tributing forefathers.

Notwithstanding this, it may confidently be said that to-day, with the home industry once more steadily developing and with the abundant facilities for technical education now provided by the Cornwall School of Mines, the ideal combination of theory and practice may still be found in the Cornish miner—a man whose ancestors have taught the world to mine, and who is himself to be found in every mining camp, however remote—a reliable and resourceful workman, a genial and courageous companion, a friend to have with one in a tight corner.

NOTES.

1. L. L. Price, Roy. Stat. Soc. (1888), 15.
2. W. Pryce, *Mineralogia Cornubiensis* (1778), 61.
3. Pamphlet, *Morrab Lib.*, Penzance.
4. *Quarterly Review* (1827), xxxvi, 2.
5. Charles Darwin, in the *Voyage of the* "*Beagle*," 1834, describes how he found a man of this type settled at the mines of Jaguel, Central Chile, in a remote ravine at the flank of the great Cordillera chain. " I stayed here five days, my host, the superintendent of the mine, being a shrewd but rather ignorant *Cornish miner*. He had married a Spanish woman and did not mean to return home; but his admiration for the mines of Cornwall remained unbounded. Amongst many other questions, he asked me, ' Now that George Rex is dead, how many more of the Rexes are yet alive?' This Rex must certainly be a relative of the great author Finis, who wrote all books !"
6. Henwood, R.G.S.C., viii, 151.
7. Per Mr. Harry Pascoe, of Truro.
8. Cf. *Cornishman* newspaper, January 9, 1924. Also Cornwall "*Education Week*" *Handbook*, 1927.
9. There are still living in West Cornwall a few miners old enough to remember these days, when Buffalo Bill was real life for the pioneer, when the journey across the Rockies was made in a stage-coach with wooden seats and straw for the feet, and every passenger carried his life in his hands and a " six-shooter " at his hip, for fear of the Indians.
10. Of less size and importance than these foreign emigrations, but none the less interesting, are the little Cornish colonies or groups of settlers which may be found in various mining districts of Great Britain. During one period of depression in Cornwall, a number of Cornish miners obtained work in the lead-mines of the Isle of Man, the most important of which was managed by a Captain Richard Rowe, of St. Agnes. In Burnley, on the Accrington Road, is a cluster of houses still known by the name of " Little Cornwall " on account of the number of Cornish miners who settled there during a strike in the 'seventies. At Dalton-in-Furness is an old colony of Cornish miners who have long been engaged in the local Hæmatite-mines, whilst in 1867 *The Glasgow Herald* speaks of over 1,000 Cornish miners " having lately removed to the iron-works and coal-pits of Scotland." The latter seem to have settled, for the most part, about Gartsherrie, in North Lanarkshire, where, as in the other localities mentioned above, it is by no means an infrequent sight to see Penaluna, Tregenza, Veal, Tonkin, and other familiar Cornish names over the doors of shops, etc. (cf. *Western Morning News*, " Notes and Queries," February 22, 1926).
11. On an attempt, however, to reduce these wages by reintroducing

the payment by calendar months (the five-week month), the men struck. After staying out several months, they won their point, but at considerable pecuniary loss to themselves.—*Mining Journal*, January 11, 1879.

12. *Mining Journal*, April 19, 1879. In 1893 mine girls at Dolcoath were earning 1s. to 1s. 6d. a day, surface labourers £3 a month, and underground miners £3 10s. to £5 10s. a month. To-day (1927) the best men in the same mine are receiving £20 a month.

13. The so-called " Camborne Riots," the first of which took place in the autumn of 1873, had no more " political " significance than any of the other disturbances which in past times have roused the indignation of the mining population. The story, as told in Camborne, is that a certain Dolcoath miner, by name Bawden, walking one night on a narrow piece of pavement by the White Hart Inn, slipped on the curb. A certain police officer, well-known in the town for his overbearing and obnoxious behaviour, observed the scene and, declaring the man to be drunk, handcuffed him and carried him off to the " clink." His brother, hearing of this, attacked the policeman with his fists, and after a fight he, too, was taken off. Both brothers were known to be men of a somewhat rough type, but in this case the magistrates seem to have taken an unnecessarily severe view of the case. On learning that the men had been condemned to five and six months' imprisonment each, an excited crowd attacked the police station, town hall, etc. Considering the miners had the whole town at their mercy for several hours, little damage was done. The magistrates and police retired altogether for the time. Eventually red jackets were got on the spot and placed by the station, free library, etc. The next day, though great crowds were in the streets, the people were quiet and good-humoured.—Cf. also *The Times*, October 9, 1873. The second Camborne Riot was largely caused by the introduction of Irish labourers into some of the mines, which were controlled at that date by a Roman Catholic family named Pike, resident in Camborne. Little damage was done beyond the " looting " of the R.C. chapel. After one of these " riots," on the occasion of a small disturbance at Porthleven, the cry arose " Give 'em Camborne "—a saying not yet forgotten.

14. Report of Select Comm. on Stannaries Act (1887), 22, 92.
15. R.C.P.S. (1871), 51.
16. Price, Royal Stat. Soc. (1888), 49.
17. Price, Royal Stat. Soc. (1888), 51.
18. *Mining and Smelting Magazine*, June 1862.
19. Price, Royal Stat. Soc. (1888), 51.
20. Curiously enough, some of the miners, though inured to dangers all their lives, could never trust themselves to this new innovation. One man I knew, who formerly worked at the 200-fathom level in Wheal Sisters (Lelant), was so fearful of the " gig " that he preferred to climb the ladders, even when sometimes too tired almost to put one foot before another. His father, who used to ride, would be changed, home, had supper, and in bed before he got back.

21. Parl. Rep., " Health of Cornish Miners " (1904), 8.
22. Parl. Rep., " Health of Cornish Miners " (1904), 9.
23. Parl. Rep., " Health of Cornish Miners " (1904), 31.
24. In the St. Austell district as late as 1916 the " tongues " affixed to the lifters were made of oak, cut by the streamers themselves.

INDEX

My best thanks are due to Mr. Trelawny Roberts for the gift of this Index.—A. K. H. J.

ADITS—
   driving of, 93 et seq.
   earliest, 83
   references to particular, 93 et seq., 108, 109
AGE, average, of workers, 233, 260, 264
ALLUVIAL TIN, in early days, 41
ANGARRACK SMELTING HOUSE, 110, 178
ANTIQUITY, evidences of, 27–9
ARMADA, tinners' part in, 37
ARSENIC, 106, 314

BAL BILLS, 205
BAL MAIDENS, 131, 236–8, 291
   wages of, 140, 342
BAL SURGEON, 141, 267
BARBER, the mine, 142, 206
"BEELE," 86
"BEUHEYLE," 55
BICKFORD SAFETY FUSE, 218
"BINDERS," 132
BLACK DEATH, effect of, 30
"BLACK TIN," 81
BLASTING, 92, 217 et seq.
BLOWING-HOUSES, 69, 70, 78
BOULTON, Matthew, letters, 139, 158 et seq.
BOULTON AND WATT ENGINE, 101, 160
"BOUNDING," 31 et seq., 46
BOYS, employment of, 105, 222, 232
"BRAWS," 51
BRAY, Billy, 280
"BREAST," 58
"BUCKING," 241
BURNLEY, Little Cornwall in, 341

CALIFORNIA, Cornish miners in, 326
CAMBORNE RIOTS, 342
CANDLES—
   as timekeepers, 209
   duty on, 149

CANDLES—*continued*
   Hempen, 215
   sold by mines, 208, 209, 242
CAPONS as rent, 69
CAPTAINS—
   character of, 230
   introduction of term, 78
CAREW on tinners, 124, 126
CARNON " Stream," 59–60
CASTINGS, making of, 175
"CASTLE," 69
CHARACTER OF MINER—
   adaptability, 273
   contempt of danger, 263–4
   diet of, 249
   independence, 213, 272, 285
   liberality, 49, 51, 52, 146, 162
   mathematical aptitude, 273
   reading, fondness for, 277
   religious fervour, 279–83
   thrift, 61, 269, 340
CHARCOAL, use of, 72 et seq.
CHARTER, tinners', 30
CHEWIDDEN FEAST, 66, 80, 129, 300
CHITROOSE BLOWING HOUSE, 69
CHRISTENING A MINE, 197, 297
CHUN CASTLE, ancient smelting at, 28, 80
CHYANDOUR SMELTING WORKS, 178
CLUBS, miners', 265, 310
COAL, 101 et seq., 118, 120
   waste of, 179
COB HOUSES, 255
"COFFINS" or "GOFFINS," 43, 85
COINAGE—
   abolition, 39
   burden of, 39
   descriptions of, 38, 74
   pre-emption, 126
   under the Commonwealth, 40, 127
COINAGE TOWNS, 38
"COLLIERS," 73

CONDITIONS OF WORKERS—
  at end of eighteenth century, 161, 164
  diet of poor, 145
  in seventeenth century, 126, 127
  in smelting-works, 115
  juvenile, 233 et seq.
CONSUMPTION, see LUNG DISEASE
COPPER—
  depression of 1787, 158
  former neglect of, 91
  numbers employed in 1787, 91
  prices, 1710, 1758, 91
  prices, 1791–96, 157
  smelting conditions, 115
COPPERHOUSE FOUNDRY, HAYLE, 115, 177
"CORES"—
  length of, 142, 221, 241, 306, 309
  scene on changing, 203
CORNISH LANGUAGE—
  in mining terms, 55, 71, 80, 297, 339
  proverb in, 271, 297
CORPUS CHRISTI FAIR, 289
COST-BOOK SYSTEM, 304, 310
COSTAR, John, 91
"COUNT," The, 192–5
COUNTY ADIT, 93
"COW," 118
CRANYCE, Burchard, 108

DEPRESSION—
  after Great War, 315
  at end of eighteenth century, 164
  in 1787, 158
  periods of, 127, 149
  1860–70, 303
  1894–98, 305
DESCENT—
  accounts of, 102 et seq.
  old methods, 85
"DEVELOPMENT," 314
"DILLUER," 56, 105
DINNER, Count House, 194
DISASTERS, Mining, 95, 119
DISTURBANCES AND RIOTS, 149, 160, 163, 342
DOWSING, 43, 296
"DRADGE," 244
DRAINAGE METHODS, 83 et seq., 88 et seq., 98

EARLY WORKINGS, 41
EARNINGS OF MINERS, see WAGES
EASTERN TIN, import of, 159, 164, 319
EDUCATION, 274 et seq.
EMIGRATION AFTER 1870, 321 et seq.
ENGINE DUTY, 181
ENGINE-HOUSES, neglect in, 179
EPSLEY, Thomas, 92
EXPORT OF TIN, 27, 76, 112
"EYE," 57

FARINGTON DIARY, 162–3
"FARM TIN," 45
FARMER, miner as, 271
"FEASTS," tinners', 65, 126, 129 et seq., 288 et seq.
"FEATHERS," 92
FIGHTS AND FEUDS, 130, 284
FISHERMAN, miner as, 271
"FIVE-WEEK MONTH," 204
FLAT LODE, 226
"FLOAT," 70, 112
"FLOORS OF TIN," 44
FOLKLORE—
  animal taboos, 52
  belief in omens, 64, 294
  haunted mines, horseshoes, Jack-o'-Lantern, knackers, snails, witches, etc., 292 et seq.
FOOD—
  prices of, 140, 333
  riots, 149, 286 et seq.
  shortage of, 144
FOUNDRIES, 115, 174 et seq.
"FREE-SETTING," 336
FROSE, Ulrich, 53, 85, 115
FURNACE, first reverberatory, 71

"GADD," 86
"GARD," 58
GERMAN MINERS in Cornwall, 53, 92
GIBLET PIE at Count Dinner, 194
"GIG," 22, 335
GIRLS, see BAL MAIDENS
"GOAD," 49, 79
GODOLPHIN, Sir Francis, 53, 124
"GOFFINS," 43, 85
GOLD, 49, 80, 326
GOOL-PELLES LODE, 116
GOONLAZE ADIT, 96
"GOUNCE," 59

INDEX

GRAIN TIN, 70
" GUINEA-A-MINUTE " WHEAL TOWAN, 225

" HALVANS," 244
HAMPTON, Dick, tales of, 195, 235, 274, 281
" HARD TIN," 74
HARVEY FOUNDRY, Hayle, 174
HEALTH, miners', 258 et seq., 335
HEMPEN CANDLES, 215
" HENNAWAYS," 244
" HERIOT," or " FARLEIFE," 69
" HOGGAN," 89
HOME-LIFE, miner's, 249, 270
HORNBLOWER, Jonathan, 167
HORSE-WHIM, 88, 97
HOURS OF WORK, see CORES
HOUSE—
  miner's, 252 et seq.
  cost of, 298
HUBERT, Archbishop of Canterbury, 30
HURLING, 290
" HURT PAY," 265

" JEWS' HOUSES," 68
JOHANNESBURG, 329
JOHN THE ALMSGIVER, 29
JOSEPH OF ARIMATHEA, 29
JUVENILE LABOUR, 105, 222, 232, 258

" KIDDLYWINKS," 62, 145
" KITTING," 228

LADDERS FOR DESCENT, 103, 221, 222, 262, 333-4
" LADED," 55
" LAPPIOR," 105
LEAN, Capt. Joel, 180
LODES—
  marking, 47
  rich, 91, 185 et seq., 225
  tracing, 42
" LORD'S DISH," 33, 45, 135, 285, 311
LUNG DISEASE, 261, 333

MAN-ENGINE, 183, 333
MATON, 39, 101, 115
MECHANICAL POWER for ore dressing, 184

MEDICAL ATTENDANCE, see BAL SURGEON
MIDSUMMER DAY, 66, 289
MILITARY SERVICE, exemption from, 37
MINES, references to particular—
  Wheal Abram, 118, 174, 191
  Wheal Agar, 304
  Balcoath, 99
  Balleswidden, 264, 267
  Barncoose, 109
  Wheal Basset, 302
  North Basset, 296
  Basset and Grylls, 225
  Great Beam, 261, 319
  Wheal Beauchamp, 109
  Beer Ferris (Devon), 84
  Binner Downs, 183
  Boscaswell Downs, 255
  Boscean, 255, 267
  Botallack, 44, 194, 248, 305
  Brigan, 136, 167
  Wheal Buller, 302
  Wheal Busy, see also Chacewater, 100, 135, 136, 167
  Caradon, West and South, 188, 302
  Carharrack, 101
  Carn Brea, 265, 304, 334
  Wheal Carne, 117
  Carnkye, 140, 168
  Great Carnmeal, 34
  Wheal Castle, 98, 248, 267
  Chacewater, 119, 158, 159, 161
  Wheal Chance, 109, 180
  Wheal Clay, 110
  Wheal Clifford, 219
  Clifford Amalgamated, 176
  Wheal Cock, 248
  Great Condurrow, 279
  South Condurrow, 226
  Consolidated Mines, 91, 101, 158, 180, 216, 219, 284
  Cook's Kitchen, 98, 109, 167, 201, 221, 334
  Creegbrawse, 19, 29, 93, 210
  Crenver, 118, 158, 174, 182, 191
  Great Crinnis, 302
  East and South Crofty, 261, 265, 304
  Wheal Cunning, 214
  Wheal Damsel, 161, 223
  Devon Great Consols, 186, 207, 332
  Wheal Devonshire, 214

MINES, references to particular—*contd.*
  Ding Dong, 248, 264, 305
  Dolcoath, 108, 117, 118, 158, 159, 167, 183, 187, 221, 247, 304, 333
  North Dolcoath, 70
  Downhill, 188
  Drake Walls, 192
  Wheal Druid, 109
  Wheal Edward, 248
  Wheal Fanny, 109, 184
  Wheal Fortune, 87, 116, 227
  Fowey Consols, 215, 219, 221, 224, 287, 302
  South and West Frances, 242, 302
  Wheal Freedom, 47, 98
  Garden Mine, 68
  Geevor, 117
  Giew, 305
  Godolphin, 168, 281
  Wheal Gorland, 118, 140, 168
  Great Work, 87, 118, 119, 129, 132, 168, 200, 201, 305
  Grenville, 226
  Gwennap Consols, 223, 302
  Wheal Hawke, 109, 158
  Wheal Jewell, 215, 251, 293
  Wheal Kitty, 304
  Levant, 185, 221, 248, 264, 289, 304
  North Levant, 96
  Ludgvan Lees Mine, 118
  Wheal Maid, 101
  Wheal Margery, 220
  Mellanear, 255
  North Downs, 91, 158, 159, 175, 180
  Oatfield, 182
  Owan Vean, 100
  Wheal Owles, 118, 248, 255
  Pednandrea, 109, 158
  Wheal Peever, 109
  Penstruthal, 181, 302
  Perran Great St. George, 34
  Perran Wheal Golden, 248
  Polberro, 68
  Polbreen, 292
  Poldice, 19, 93, 136, 158, 160, 168, 179, 180, 210, 212, 219, 223, 284
  Poldory, 196, 228
  Polgooth, 98, 158
  East and North Pool, 191, 202, 304
  Wheal Providence, 109, 214, 267, 305
  Wheal Raven, 158
  Wheal Reeth, 98, 201

MINES, references to particular—*contd.*
  Wheal Rose, 100, 109, 167, 192
  Roskear and North Roskear, 118, 158, 167, 195, 302
  St. Ives Consols, 305
  Sealhole, 43
  West Seton, 211, 302, 334
  Wheal Sisters, 229, 305, 342
  Wheal Sparnon, 107, 109, 119, 167
  Stray Park, 211
  Ting Tang, 100
  Tincroft, 109, 118, 162, 205, 297, 304
  Wheal Towan, 159, 168, 225
  Tregajorran, 109
  Tregonebris, 99
  Tregurtha Downs, 100
  Treleigh Wood, 158
  Trenethick, 108
  Tresavean, 158, 161, 183, 186, 302
  Treskerby, 161, 180, 223
  Trevascus, 91
  Trevenen, 99, 108
  Trevenson, 94, 158
  Trevigha Bal, 93
  Trewirgie Downs, 109
  Trumpet Consols, 305
  United Mines, 158, 179, 180, 201, 302
  Wheal Unity, 109, 140, 161, 168, 180
  Wheal Uny, 247
  Wheal Virgin, 99, 101
  Perran Wheal Virgin, 192
  West Wheal Virgin, 101
  Wheal Vor, 99, 116, 183, 184, 190, 201, 221, 284, 293
  Yarner Mine, Bovey Tracey, 219
"MONTH IN HAND," 208
MOORHOUSE, 63
MORTALITY—
  infantile, 259
  among miners, 260, 334
MOULT, Francis, 71, 110
MULES, 67, 173
MURDOCK, William, 176

NAMES—
  bounds, 33
  pump lifts, 100
  streams, 72
NEWCOMEN ENGINE, 99
NICKNAMES, 299

INDEX

NUMBERS employed—
  in 1787, 91
  in 1801, 171, 199
NUMBERS of mines—
  in 1798 (copper), 302
  in nineteenth century, 171

ORE (see also Smelting)—
  dressing of, 105 et seq., 232
  hoisting, 89, 97
  mechanical power for dressing, 184
  sampling, 138, 204, 241
OUT-ADVENTURERS, 132
OUTPUT, see PRODUCTION

PACK-HORSES AND MULES, 68, 73, 173
" PARD," 49, 79
" PARE OF MEN," 61, 136
PARYS MINE, ANGLESEA, 157
PAUL'S PITCHER DAY, 65
" PEASER," 38
PEBBLES, at Tribute Auction, 136
PELL ADIT, 108
PENVENTON ADIT, 94
PERRAN FOUNDRY, 176
PEWTER—
  disuse of, 160
  tin for London, 74
PHŒNICIANS, the, 29
PICROUS DAY, 66
" PIGGAL," 64
PILLIAN TIN, 74
PIONEERS, 328, 341
PIPE ROLLS, record of output in, 29
PITCHES, letting of, 136
" PLOUGHS," 68
PREACHERS, local, 279
PRE-EMPTION by the Crown, 126 et seq.
PRICES—
  copper, 1710, 1758, 91
  copper, 1791–96, 157
  fall in, 1772 (tin), 155
  of tin in 1590, 123
  rise under Commonwealth, 127
  tin, 1891–98, 305
  tin, 1920–22, 315
" PRILLS," 80, 244
PRIVILEGES OF TINNERS, 31 et seq.
PRODUCTION—
  arsenic, 1913–16, 314
  at end of sixteenth century, 126

PRODUCTION—continued
  copper, 1726–35, 1771–87, 1794, 1806, 1822, 1838, 303
  excess, in 1788, 165
  record in Pipe Rolls, 29
  tin, 1750–85, 1786, 1798, 1815, 1837, 303
  tin, 1798, 156; 1914, 1915, 315
  tin coined in 1704, 46
  wolfram, 1913–16, 314
PRIVATEERS, 113
PUMPS, 89
  improvements, 181
  wooden, 98, 200
PURSER, the, 131
" PUPPY LIFT," 201

RAG-AND-CHAIN PUMP, 88, 97
  early example, 55
RAILWAYS, first, 173
RALEIGH, Sir Walter, 37, 48
RECREATIONS in seventeenth century, 129, 131, 288 et seq.
" RELISTIAN TIN," 74
REOPENING MINES IN 1923, 317
REVERBERATORY FURNACE, 71
RIVERS, silting up of, 56
ROCK CAVITIES for breaking tin, 57
ROMAN PERIOD, 28
ROPES, outlay on, 183
ROYALTIES, see LORD'S DISH
" RUDDLE," 59

ST. AUBYN'S DAY, 195
ST. BLAZEY FOUNDRY, 177
ST. DAY FIGHT, 130
ST. JUST, methods of work in, 185, 213
ST. PAUL, tradition of, 29
ST. PERRAN'S DAY, 300
SAMPLER, 204, 241
SAXON PERIOD, 28
" SCAWS," 47
SEAL HOLE ADIT, 95
SETTLEMENTS of Cornish Miners in other parts of England, 341
" SHODEING," 42
SILTING up of rivers, 56
" SINDER TIN," 74
SINGLEHAND WORKERS at St. Just, 213
SKILL—
  contests in, 240, 270

SKILL—*continued*
  produced by tribute system, 226
  testimony as to, 54
"SLOWG," 248
SMELTERS—
  deductions and additions by, 112, 230
  oppression by, 155
SMELTING—
  ancient, 28, 80
  charcoal for, 72 et seq.
  copper, 114 et seq.
  early methods, 69
SMELTING HOUSES, 111, 177–8
  Angarrack, 110, 178
  Calenick, 110, 178
  Chyandour, 178
  Newham, 110
  Treloweth, 178
  Trereiffe, 178
SMUGGLING—
  of export tin, 75
  regulation to prevent tin, 76
  tinners' part in, 62
SOLOMON'S TEMPLE, 29
"SPALE," 49
  (as a fine), 133, 209
"SPALIARS," 51
  condition of, in 1630, 126
"SPALLING," 131, 237
STAMPS, 107
  first stream, 184
STANNARIES—
  Courts, 35
  districts, 31
  first Charter, 30
  Gaol, 36
  Parliament, 36
  privileges, 31 et seq.
  warden, 31
STANNATORS, 36
STEAM—
  first utilization of, 99
  for stamps, 184
"STENT," 58
"STILLING," 58
STRABO and Tin Islands, 27
STREAMING—
  methods, 54 et seq.
  to-day, 339
SUBSIDENCE at Dolcoath, 187
SUBMARINE MINES, 59, 60, 185, 220

"SUBSIST," 207
"SWAB STICK," 216

"TEARER," 92
"TEEM," 55
TEMPERATURE OF MINES, 214, 219
TICKETING, 138
TINNERS—
  who were, 37
  description of, in 1586, 48
  grievances in sixteenth century, 123
  turbulence of, 149 et seq.
  see also CHARACTER, HOME LIFE, HOUSE, RECREATIONS
TOKENS, 100
TOLL TIN, 33, 45
"TOLLER," 34
TRADE UNIONS, 332
TRANSPORT—
  pack, 67, 73, 173
  to Cornwall, 175
TREVITHICK, Richard, 21, 323
TREVITHICK'S ENGINE, 182
TRIBUTE SYSTEM, 134
  abuses of, 308
  decay of, 308, 338
  defects and merits, 226
  differences for copper, 138
  dressing ore by, 232
  setting of pitches, 136
  skill produced by, 226
TRIBUTERS—
  diversion among, 135
  modern, 337
  tricks by, 228
  unfair treatment of, 227
"TRYER OF ORE," 204
"TUTWORK," 139, 204
  unfair treatment of workers under, 227
"TYE," 56

UNDERGROUND WORKING, earliest, 41, 84 et seq.
USES OF TIN in early days, 30

VENTILATION, 85, 96 et seq., 214
"VISGEY," 64
VIVIAN, "Old Capun Andrew," 170

INDEX

WAGES—
  allotment for dependents on emigration, 325
  in 1586, 50, 125
  in sixteenth century, 125
  in 1697, 127
  in 1730, 128
  in 1759, 132
  in 1771, 140
  in 1780–90, 139
  in 1791–8, 140
  in 1836–7, 205
  in 1838, 199
  in 1879, 332
  in 1893, 342
  to-day, 309
WAR, the effects of, 314

WATER—
  difficulties in sixteenth and seventeenth centuries, 97
  disaster, North Levant, 96
  in driving adits, 95
WATER POWER, economies in use of, 107 et seq.
WATERWHEEL AND BOBS, 98
WESLEY, John, 152, 298
WESTCOTE on conditions, 126
WILLIAM DE WROTHAM, 30, 75, 123
WINDLASS AND BUCKET, 88, 97
"WINZES," 23
WOLFRAM, 314
WRECKING, 147
WRESTLING, 290, 301